Gender, Violence, Refugees

STUDIES IN FORCED MIGRATION
General Editors: Tom Scott-Smith and Kirsten McConnachie

This series, published in association with the Refugees Studies Centre, University of Oxford, reflects the multidisciplinary nature of the field and includes within its scope international law, anthropology, sociology, politics, international relations, geopolitics, social psychology and economics.

For a full volume listing, please see back matter.

Gender, Violence, Refugees

Edited by Susanne Buckley-Zistel and Ulrike Krause

berghahn
NEW YORK · OXFORD
www.berghahnbooks.com

First published in 2017 by
Berghahn Books
www.berghahnbooks.com

Library of Congress Cataloging-in-Publication Data
Names: Buckley-Zistel, Susanne, 1969- editor. | Krause, Ulrike, 1983-
    editor.
Title: Gender, violence, refugees / edited by Susanne Buckley-Zistel and
    Ulrike Krause.
Description: New York : Berghahn Books, 2017. | Series: Studies in forced
    migration ; Volume 37 | Includes bibliographical references and index.
Identifiers: LCCN 2017015092 (print) | LCCN 2017029470 (ebook) | ISBN
    9781785336171 (e-book) | ISBN 9781785336164 (hardback : alk. paper)
Subjects: LCSH: Women refugees--Social conditions. | Women
    refugees--Violence against.
Classification: LCC HV640 (ebook) | LCC HV640 .G45 2017 (print) | DDC
    362.83/981--dc23
LC record available at https://lccn.loc.gov/2017015092

British Library Cataloguing in Publication Data
A catalogue record for this book is available
from the British Library

ISBN 978-1-78533-616-4 hardback
ISBN 978-1-78920-088-1 paperback
ISBN 978-1-78533-617-1 ebook

Contents

Tables

Acknowledgements

Gender, Violence, Refugees resulted out of a research project with the title *Gender Relations in Confined Spaces: Conditions, Scope and Forms of Violence against Women in Conflict-related Refugee Camps* at the Center for Conflict Studies, Philipps University, Marburg. The project was funded from 2013 to 2016 by the German Foundation for Peace Research (*Deutsche Stiftung Friedensforschung*) to which we are very grateful for this support. In the context of the research, we realized that there is a small yet growing body of literature connecting gender, violence and refugees, and we felt that it was important to move the discussion forward by compiling an edited volume on the subject, based on a call for papers. To our delight the call received much attention, and so we were able to work with outstanding academics on fascinating topics – many thanks to all. We are moreover delighted that Berghahn Books, with their series on Forced Migration, were interested in pursuing this project with us. Last but certainly not least, the manuscript owns much to the assistance of Dorothee Fees, Vanessa Köster, Elisabeth Schmidt, Lucia Heisterkamp and Alice Williams, to whom we wish to express our special gratitude.

Gender, Violence, Refugees
An Introduction

Susanne Buckley-Zistel and Ulrike Krause

In February 2015, a report entitled 'Review into recent allegations relating to conditions and circumstances at the Regional Processing Centre in Nauru' was published, which inquired into allegations of rape and sex for favours of so-called 'processees' in one of Australia's off-shore immigration processing centres on the island of Nauru (Moss 2015). Upon reception of the report the then prime minister of Australia, Tony Abbott, remarked: 'Occasionally, I daresay, things happen, because in any institution you get things that occasionally aren't perfect' (see Hurst 2015).

We disagree. That occurrences such as rape and sex for favours in institutions hosting refugees do not 'simply happen' is the subject of this edited volume. Its central contention is that instances of sexual and gender-based violence, as well as other forms of violence, emerge due to the particular conditions in refugee institutions and situations, and that analysing the underlying currents is a first and necessary step towards efforts to prevent them. What makes refugee situations particular is that individuals and communities are taken out of the everyday context in which their social lives follow certain norms and rules sedimented over time. These norms and rules are challenged and put into doubt by the new demands and limitations encountered in displacement, where much of the social, economic and political world is externally formed and restrictively imposed. Often, refugees end up in a situation of dependency on institutions and people in powerful positions, rendering themselves vulnerable to abuse and exploitation – such as in the example of the Nauru processing centre above. While this does not necessarily, in and of itself, lead to violent behaviour, in some cases it might. And although this concerns all refugees, women,

men, girls and boys all experience it – and are affected by it – differently. These aspects will be covered in the present volume.

Gender, Violence, Refugees provides nuanced accounts of how the social identity of men and women, the context of displacement, and the experience or manifestation of violence interact. It offers both conceptual analysis and in-depth case studies to illustrate how gender relations are affected by displacement, encampment and return, and how this leads to various forms of direct, indirect and structural violence.

Gender, Violence, Refugees

Three intertwined notions are central to our volume: gender, violence and refugees. It is important to note that we use them in a wide sense and that while most contributions focus on all three aspects, some zoom in on just one or two. To elaborate in a slightly different order to our title, the term *refugee* broadly refers to a person who has had to leave their home for one or various reasons, even though 'what reasons' and 'where to' are sometimes contested, as apparent in contributions to this volume. In a narrow, legalistic sense the term is defined by the 1951 Convention Relating to the Status of Refugees and its 1967 Protocol where it refers to a person who 'owing to a well-founded fear of being persecuted for reasons of race, religion, nationality, membership of a particular social group or political opinion, is outside the country of his nationality, and is unable to, or owing to such fear is unwilling to, avail himself of the protection of that country'. However, looking at the broad spectrum of people who are on the move involuntarily, refugees as defined by the convention constitute only one of several groups who are more generally called 'forced migrants'. In addition to refugees, forced migration also includes 'internally displaced persons' (IDPs) who seek refuge in their country of origin, victims of trafficking as well as stateless persons. Each of these categories is based on a specific legal definition stipulated in a convention, or in the case of IDPs in the 'Guiding Principles on Internal Displacement'. While these categories may appear to be neutral – including gender neutral as discussed below – they are interpreted in the context of dynamically changing global norms and are thus highly politicized. It is this 'politics of categorization' that enables politicians to artificially separate people by means of imposing these categories (Castles 2007; Foster 2007: 5–21); they divide (forced) migrants from citizens of nation states and contribute to classifying members of categories through distinct legal privileges. Differentiations of (forced) migrants are often based on 'push and pull' factors (Castles 2003; Brubaker 2012), stipulating distinctions between voluntary and forced migration and therefore between 'good' refugees as those deserving protection and 'bad' migrants or 'economic' refugees as those unworthy of aid (Scheel and Squire 2014; Rosenberger and Stöckl 2016: 14). With a focus on refugees, debates about the 'refugee label' reveal economic, political and social exclusion and 'othering' processes of refugees, as well as identity constructions (Zetter 1991, 2007; Ludwig 2013; Krause 2016a).

In order to draw attention to the fact that people also leave their homes for reasons that do not fall into the narrow definition of the 1951 refugee convention, the term 'forced migration' has replaced 'refugee' in discourse and practice. It acknowledges that poverty, ecological degradation, development aid, disasters and crises are also legitimate causes for moving (de Wet 2006; Boano, Zetter and Morris 2008; McAdam 2014). Similar to IDPs, forced migrants who do not fall into the definition of what constitutes a refugee thus do not qualify for assistance from the global refugee regime. Although we chose 'refugees' for the title of this volume to connect to an ongoing debate in refugee studies, some chapters consider wider causes for flight and explicitly situated themselves in the context of forced migration studies, such as Alexander Betts in Chapter 11.

Regarding *gender*, the volume includes the social categories men, women, boys and girls. An unfortunate lacuna are LGBTIs and their particular difficulties, which scholars have increasingly explored in recent years, pointing out their legal neglect yet also developments in refugee status determination processes (Markard 2013; Türk 2013; Berlit, Doerig and Storey 2015) as well as diverse security risks in countries of origin and of asylum (Forced Migration Review 2013; Spijkerboer 2013). Such academic debates and criticism did not remain unnoticed by central institutions such as the United Nations High Commissioner for Refugees (UNHCR) and also by non-governmental organizations (NGOs) who have developed guidelines and handbooks on how to treat cases and how to protect LGBTI people (see UNHCR 2008a, 2011a; ORAM 2012).

One important question to pose in the context of our volume is whether refugees have a gender at all. Legally, the 1951 refugee convention with its 1967 protocol stipulates who qualifies as a refugee and who has access to refugee rights and protection. Yet, its description of refugees not only lacks any reference to gender (Valji 2001: 25; Fiddian-Qasmiyeh 2014: 398–400), losing sight of the fact that men and women experience refuge differently (Crawley 2001: 7), but it is based on a male paradigm with an androcentric framework (Greatbatch 1989: 518; Markard 2007: 377f.; Edwards 2010). The persistent separation of public and private spheres of action for men and women has found its way into international refugee law. It is, inter alia, based on the assumption that men are more active in politics and thus at higher risk of being persecuted, which explains why 'dominant androcentric male-as-norm paradigms' (Edwards 2010: 22) stand in contrast to marginalized women in refugee law. The dichotomies – public/private, political/apolitical, men/women – strongly informed the idea of the refugee figure at the time when legal frameworks were being drafted (Valji 2001: 26; Edwards 2010), yet since the 1980s, feminist scholars have criticized the neglect of women in refugee policies (Indra 1987; Greatbatch 1989), stressing the various yet also different forms of violence that women encounter (Callaway 1985; Ferris 1990). As a result, policies shifted in the early 1990s to include women's protection as a key component of refugee protection and to mainstream 'gender', as further elaborated in by Susan Martin in Chapter 1 to this volume.

In spite of these development, recent studies still criticize the one-sided, legalistic and humanitarian image of refugees, and call for a more differentiated understanding of refugees in general, and men and women in particular (Kebede 2010; Turner 2010: 43–64; Fiddian-Qasmiyeh 2014; Krause 2016b). They argued that flight, expulsion and forced migration should be seen as a gendered process (Hans 2008: 69), leading to an increase in the number of academic contributions with an emphasis on gendered experiences (see Hart 2008; Fiddian-Qasmiyeh 2014; Freedman 2015). It is to this body of scholarship that this volume seeks to contribute.

By aiming to implement a gender-sensitive approach to refugee aid (UNHCR 1990, 1991, 2008b, 2011b), women's needs are increasingly acknowledged in protection and assistance measures. They are often treated as most vulnerable and therefore receive prioritized access to aid and awareness-building projects, and in many cases men are left behind. Elena Fiddian-Qasmiyeh, Chloé Lewis and Georgia Cole illustrate in Chapter 6 how aid agencies frequently equate gender and women, and thus provide aid in manners that favour women to the detriment of men, directly affecting gender relations. Such actions may translate into power imbalances between women and men, challenging the pre-flight relationship in which men were mostly breadwinners and decision makers. In some cases, men react with violence in order to maintain their social status as patriarchs (Lukunka 2011).

The notion of *violence* appears in various forms and with different meanings in this volume. A number of chapters focus explicitly on sexual and gender-based violence. According to UNHCR, this refers to 'violence that is directed against a person on the basis of her or his gender or sex. It includes acts that inflict physical, mental or sexual harm or suffering, threats of such acts, coercion, and other deprivations of liberty, whether occurring in public or in private life' (UNHCR 2008b: 201; see IASC 2015: 5–13). It can take the form of, among others, 'rape, forced impregnation, forced abortion, trafficking, sexual slavery, and the intentional spread of sexually transmitted infections, including HIV/AIDS' (UNHCR 2008b: 7, 10). In refugee camps, in particular, sexual and gender-based violence occurs particularly often in the forms of domestic violence, sexual abuse, structural discrimination and forced recruitment into combatant groups. ✘This is not a new phenomenon but has already been observed and criticized by scholars in the 1980s (Callaway 1985; Harrell-Bond 1986: 155–59; Greatbatch 1989). Studies emphasize that these forms of violence occur repeatedly, perpetrated by fellow refugees as well as by people with an official mandate to protect, such as security forces, government employees, staff of aid agencies and local residents of the home community, often exploiting their power and the dependency of their victims (Ferris 2007; Freedman 2015: 60–68).

Violence also occurs in urban centres. Although refugees may experience fewer restrictions by humanitarian organizations and have more freedom in choosing where to live and work, they can face structural violence in the form of social exclusion and discrimination (Jaji 2009; Crisp, Morris and Refstie 2012). When refugees are not legally allowed to work in host countries, they often have to seek employment in informal sectors. For women, this often means being forced or having to engage in prostitution (Naggujja et al. 2014), exchanging sexual favours for food or shelter (Krause-Vilmar 2011) or facing sexual abuse by colleagues (Crisp, Morris and Refstie 2012).

A number of operational reports have been produced over the past years to shed light on the scope of sexual and gender-based violence against refugees. UN Women (2013), for instance, stresses the danger of early and forced marriage among Syrian refugee girls, while the UN special rapporteur on violence against women (UNGA 2012: 25–29) recently pointed out that female Somali refugees and IDPs, aged from eleven to eighty, face kidnapping, sexual exploitation and abuse, female genital mutilation and forced marriage by al-Shabaab militias, especially in overcrowded camps. 'Women on the Run', UNHCR (2015), emphasizes women's multiple risk factors in South American countries, including threats by criminal armed groups, child recruitment, long-lasting domestic violence, rape and extortion. Moreover, Refugees International (1999) estimates that 25 per cent of female refugees in Tanzania experience sexual violence, and emphasizes the continuity of violence before and after the flight for many Syrian women who seek to escape rape but end up being attacked in camps or suffer from an increase in domestic violence, including marital rape (Refugees International 2012). Similar experiences are reported in the context of the civil wars in Liberia and Sierra Leone, and ensuing refugee and displaced persons' camps in Guinea, Liberia and Sierra Leone (Lindorfer 2009; Women's Refugee Commission 2009: 3; Human Rights Watch 2011). Chapter 2 by Simon Turner critically engages with the normative assumptions of this body of literature.

Although the true scope of sexual and gender-based violence against refugees remains unknown (Freedman 2015: 79), because it is still a taboo and often entails stigmatization and the danger of increased violence after reporting attacks (Martin 2004: 31, 116; Jansen 2011: 87; Krause 2015: 245), most studies continue to focus on violence against women. In this process, binary structures of female victims and male perpetrators are maintained and reproduced, while the scope and impact on male victims is neglected. In contrast, Chris Dolan's (2014: 2) recent study on Congolese refugee men in Uganda shows that 13.4 per cent of male refugees had experienced an incident of sexual violence in the preceding year, and 38.5 per cent reported assaults at some point in their lives.[1] As few studies have focused on male victims of sexual and gender-based violence, there is a distinct need for further research. In this volume, Maria O. Ensor (Chapter 9) and Maja Janmyr (Chapter 10) seek to broaden the discussion by including boys and men, albeit mainly in terms of gender-based violence.

In addition to these direct forms of violence, structural violence is – explicitly and implicitly – central to a number of contributions to this book. Structural conditions during flight, in the place of refuge as well as upon return, may take on forms that harm women and men (often in different ways). In camps, it may be the result of camp structures and hierarchies, gender disparities or negative relations between host and refugee communities. In most cases, refugees are not granted the same opportunities as nationals from the asylum or host countries, and are confronted with wide-scale discriminations in their everyday lives in exile (Jansen 2011; Crisp, Morris and Refstie 2012). This may prevent refugees from meeting basic requirements necessary for a stable and secure life. Even without any direct assault, structural violence may be physically harming when it leads to poor nutrition or limited access to health facilities (for instance for victims of sexual violence). Dale Buscher (Chapter 7) looks at the economic aspects of these types of indirect violence, and Melanie Hartmann (Chapter 5) at the structural.

Violence may also take on a more conceptual form when it refers to what Michel Foucault calls 'biopolitics' (Foucault 2010). This concerns the practice of regulating subjects – in our case, male and female refugees – through numerous techniques that serve to subjugate and ultimately control them. Refugee or displaced persons' camps but also aid institutions assume this role when they determine what is right and wrong behaviour regarding gender roles. Importantly, this type of violence does not operate in the open; it is much more subtle since it is rooted in regulations and regulatory mechanisms. Chapter 4 by Emma Mc Cluskey contributes to this discussion.

In addition to the main themes of *Gender, Violence, Refugees*, chapters in this volume connect empirically. To begin, a number of settings are central to the case studies collected in our volume, including refugee and IDP camps. Temporally, various phases can be delineated – conflict, flight, refuge, return – each of them providing their own particular circumstances, even though it has been argued that there is a continuum of sexual and gender-based violence against women and men (Ferris 1990; Cockburn 2004). While Barbra Lukunka discusses conditions of Burundian returnees in Chapter 12, Ulrike Krause contributes to the continuum discussion in Chapter 8. Many authors moreover focus on the intervention of external agents – humanitarian or aid agencies, development organizations, human rights NGOs, faith-based actors – who might, through their actions, provide services to 'beneficiaries'. In doing so, they have an impact on the living conditions, both materially and socially and on gender relations.

Connecting Gender, Violence, Refugees

How do the experiences of displacement, be it in camps, settlements or in urban settings, have an effect on gender relations? To begin, many refugee situations are long term, thus affecting social relations for years and sometimes decades. Over time, it has transpired that camps exist much longer than anticipated, leading to so-called protracted refugee situations with an average duration of twenty-six years (UNHCR 2016: 20). Structurally, the conditions are very similar all over the world: initially established as short-term, interim solutions, they are confined to a designated space and adhere to organizational and administrative rules and regulations. In addition to UNHCR, national and international aid organizations as well as the national governments of host countries are involved in their administration. This long duration of refugee situations affects the way refugees relate to each other, including along gender lines. Rules and regulations by administrative bodies, such as the command over resources, as well as control and decision-making processes, affect the lives of women and men significantly since they regulate living conditions and opportunities.

Refugee situations may also impact on gender relations since conflict and flight often destroy the fabric of communities and families (Turner 1999; Martin 2004: 15; Carlson 2005), leading to a rearranging of the social relations under new and different conditions. Moreover, the experience of conflict and flight might affect individuals who find it difficult to cope with what they have encountered (Karunakara et al. 2004; Onyut et al. 2009; Lukunka 2011). Some studies point to an increase in drug and alcohol abuse and an associated increase in aggression and violence towards women in particular, including domestic violence (Barker and Ricardo 2005; McCleary 2013). The daily life of refugees is moreover influenced by the labour market, or the lack of perspectives, which again has an impact on gender relations (Carlson 2005: 11; Krause 2015; see also Buscher in this volume). As illustrated by Tania Kaiser (2006), restrictive civil liberties and work permits, coupled with the lack of economic livelihoods, and of access to resources and markets, often led to refugees not being able to perform their former gender roles. For instance, men might be unable to fulfil the role of the family provider, and women might have to take on additional responsibilities (Martin 2004: 15; UNHCR 2008b: 39–40; Buscher 2009: 90).

Many humanitarian agencies and refugee-supporting organizations recognize these changes in general and their impact on sexual and gender-based violence in particular, and become entangled in the renegotiation of relations and the forging of new identities. They often launch specific projects to impact on gender relations, such as the empowerment of women (Martin 2004: 81f.), leading to new hierarchies and power structures (Hyndman 2004: 204; Ferris 2007: 586ff.; Gozdziak 2008: 186ff.). Mulumba's study on Ugandan refugee settlements, for instance, illustrates that for some female refugees empowerment is a liberating process since they gained access to land which traditionally is passed on through the male line of the family (Mulumba 2005: 181). In this process, though, men may lose status, power and influence, rendering them unable to take care of their families. As already argued above, this is a significant shift, since in many cultures the role of the breadwinner is the most important form of recognition and respect a man can receive from his wife and family (Dolan 2002: 60–67; Edward 2007: 140–41) so that the empowerment of women might lead to the disempowerment of men (Krause 2013: 193 ff., and 2014). The perceived loss of status and the related social degradation of men in camps is referred to as emasculation in the literature (Dolan 2009: 204; Grabska 2011; Lukunka 2011).

Importantly, people working for humanitarian aid agencies – both nationals and non-nationals – may themselves engage in sexual abuse. There is an increasing awareness, and increasing data, that people who are mandated with assisting and protecting refugees sometimes misuse their powerful position to exploit them sexually (Ferris 2007; Freedman 2015: 64ff.). This might express itself in the form of direct attacks or sex for favours related to food and relief items, to performance at school or access to medical care. Even though boys and girls are affected, girls aged thirteen to eighteen seem to be most susceptible, in particular if they live in single-parent or child-headed households, are unaccompanied, or work as street traders (Ferris 2007).

What becomes apparent when connecting gender, violence and refugees is that not only the gender or the biological sex of a person is of importance, but also other factors such as age, economic status, origin and education. In short, it highlights what is referred to as intersectionality, pointing to the intersection of different social identities on multiple and often simultaneous levels (Crenshaw 1989). This is discussed in more detail by Melanie Hartmann in Chapter 5 to this volume.

About the Volume

Part I of our edited volume is entitled *Conceptualizing Gender, Violence, Refugees* and provides various perspectives on distinct concepts and their connections. It begins with Susan F. Martin who, in Chapter 1, historically traces the more recent developments of UNHCR concerning a more gender-sensitive approach to refugee assistance. In 1990, almost four decades after UNHCR was founded and acted upon its mandate to protect and assist refugees worldwide, it adopted its first Policy on Refugee Women. While the policy is understood to be a significant milestone in the refugee protection regime – especially for women – Martin questions how effective it has been and highlights various challenges. The chapter is based on her own role in the evolution of the Policy on Refugee Women – including in drafting the UNHCR Guidelines on Protection of Refugee Women of 1991, which were meant to help to implement the policy – as well as on research about the application and impact of the policy.

In Chapter 2, Simon Turner challenges the core assumptions on which many studies and programmes on sexual violence are based. Situated in the analysis of grey literature, he provides a critical reading of current discourses and their dominating narratives. He argues that much of this literature relies on images of refugee societies as being morally in decline, with unbridled young men sexually assaulting women, and a degree of violence that is pathological. These images produce and reproduce orientalist and neocolonial representations of violence and refugees. Without belittling the scope and extent of violence in refugee contexts, Turner calls for an understanding of its occurrences that moves beyond these normative assumptions.

This criticism resonates with the argument of Elisabeth Olivius in Chapter 3, who examines how violence against refugee women is conceptualized in humanitarian policy and practice. She argues that agencies often interpret this form of violence as a sign of underdevelopment and backwardness of refugee communities, and in response seek to engage in processes of social engineering in order to change social, cultural and religious patterns. Drawing on field research in Bangladesh and Thailand, she demonstrates how these practices can lead to conflict and resistance, at times obstructing rather than advancing the empowerment of women.

A somewhat different take on gender, violence and refugees is advanced by Emma Mc Cluskey who, in Chapter 4, explores the notion of violence not in terms of physical harm but as a subtle method through which the lives of refugees are ranked, assessed and criticized by their host community. Based on in-depth field research in a small Swedish town in which a larger group of mainly Syrian refugees found a temporary home, she analyses how the local population evokes a discourse around decency and gender equality as central to what constitutes gender relations in Sweden, in a sense degrading the refugees for having other concepts about the relationship between men and women. In her case study, this turned against and thus further isolated mainly Syrian women, who were criticized for their dress codes, behaviour and poor childcare.

Taking a spatial turn, in Chapter 5 Melanie Hartmann assesses the structural conditions of German reception and accommodation centres where refugees who find their way to Germany first live while they wait for their asylum applications to be processed. She identifies the gendered inequalities enshrined in their structures, and how this affects women in particular. While sexual violence is only an extreme form of their repercussions, their daily lives are affected by insecure situations due to the poor quality and inadequacy of the centres as well as the way they are governed. Importantly, though, (female) refugees have the possibility of appropriating these spaces through their everyday practise.

How to respond to and assess gender relations might be enshrined in a national culture, as the case of Sweden shows, yet it can also be an aspect of religious belief. In Chapter 6, Elena Fiddian-Qasmiyeh, Chloé Lewis and Georgia Cole examine how faith-based images of masculinity and femininity are employed by development and aid organizations with a religious background to affect gender relations in refugee communities in order to reduce the prevalence of sexual and gender-based violence. Based on extensive field research in Sahrawi refugee camps in South West Algeria and displacement contexts in the Democratic Republic of Congo, they argue that in the Sahrawi case, faith is rendered invisible by the dominating discourses in the camp which seek to portray an image to the outside that depicts the camps as secular. In this context, sexual violence is silenced, too. In contrast, in Congo the faith-based programme 'Transforming Masculinities' addresses sexual violence directly and thus has the potential to lead to a transformation of gender relations.

In Chapter 7, Dale Buscher explores the intersectionality of forced migration, gender, violence and livelihoods. He argues that not only does displacement affect men and women differently, but that livelihoods, too, are gendered. Putting the notion of livelihood assets at the centre of his analysis he traces how assets drive conflicts and how, at the same time, their depletion as a consequence of conflict might force people to migrate. In displacement, negative economic copying strategies might lead to gender-based violence, in particular if they further disempower women and adolescent girls. Outside intervention, Buscher concludes, should thus provide equal access and opportunities for all.

Part II of the volume, *Experiencing Gender, Violence, Refuge*, zooms in on conditions and contexts affecting refugees in various settings. It begins in Chapter 8 with Ulrike Krause's focus on the continuum of violence during conflict, flight and encampment. Based on a case study of Congolese refugees in a refugee camp in Uganda, she moves beyond the prevailing context-focused research of either conflict or exile by understanding refugee camps as explicit post-conflict contexts. By means of that, she reveals how women especially are confronted with sexual and gender-based violence during the different phases of their flight, outlining a continuum of violence.

Next, in Chapter 9, Marisa O. Ensor analyses wartime displacement and its opportunities and challenges by zooming in on boys and girls. Drawing on field research amongst South Sudanese refugees in Uganda as well as returnees in South Sudan, she discusses the protracted cycle of war and displacement, and the gender-specific impacts on refugees in camps for both stayees and returnees. In spite of their challenging experiences, she emphasizes that boys and girls reveal a remarkable degree of agency and resourcefulness in their efforts to cope with the situations.

In Chapter 10, Maja Janmyr shifts the perspective towards refugee men and explores the military recruitment of Sudanese refugees by the Sudan People's Liberation Army (SPLA) in refugee camps in Northern Uganda. She argues that the Ugandan government's military and political interests in Sudan exacerbated the protection concerns for many Sudanese refugees, as did the largely negligible approach taken by UNHCR. Based on her field research in Uganda, she discusses how Sudanese refugee men were under persistent pressure to join the SPLA, and that, coupled with the lack of security caused predominantly by the insurgency movement Lord's Resistance Army, the threat of recruitment by the SPLA forced many individuals into a mode of recurrent flight to nearby towns or even to the capital Kampala. As such, these Sudanese refugees became effectively 'displaced' within their country of asylum.

In contrast to the focus on refugees and the challenges to refugee protection, in Chapter 11 Alexander Betts explores how Angolan security forces treated Congolese survival migrants, a social group that falls outside of the refugee protection regime. Between 2003 and 2013, Angola carried out four waves of deportations of these migrants during which women, in particular, were confronted with serious levels of sexual abuse. Yet not only Angola but also the international community failed to establish protective measures for survival migrants, subjecting them to great security risks and leaving them in a state of limbo.

In the final chapter, Chapter 12, Barbra Lukunka analyses the situation of returnees to Burundi who face interpersonal violence over land. After years in exile due to the civil war, returning refugees find themselves in an environment where they encounter land scarcity, or their ancestral land is occupied by neighbours or strangers. Lukunka explores the challenges returnees face and how these affect social relations, leading to violence and killings. She argues that a history and memory of violence, economic needs and structural and contextual issues, in combination with abject poverty, marginalization of the poor and corruption, contribute to the rise in interpersonal violence over land in Burundi.

As we draw this volume to a close in winter 2016, we witness a continuing uprooting of people from African countries such as South Sudan, Central African Republic and Burundi, yet also continued flight from countries such as Syria, Iraq and Yemen, some of whom seek to find their way to Europe. Those who have already arrived are confronted with serious challenges regarding status, shelter and protection, as well as in the longer run regarding employment and economic stability. We are observing this situation with much concern, not least since a number of incidences of violence have occurred, from individuals and groups of the host communities who do not want the refugees to be in their country, from amongst camp populations, as well as sexual attacks against refugees and host country women, the latter most visibly in Cologne on New Year's Eve 2015. Some of the violence in the camps, we assume, may be largely due to conditions of personal insecurity, overcrowded camps, absence of activities, burdening experiences during times of flight, animosities between identity groups, and many other challenges and conditions that are central to refugee institutions and situations. To return to the quote of the former Australian prime minister at the outset of this introduction, in this context violence is not an occasional occurrence that happens by chance. It is very much conditioned by the particular circumstances and living conditions of refugees. This is what we seek to highlight with this book.

Susanne Buckley-Zistel is professor for Peace and Conflict Studies at the Center for Conflict Studies, Philipps-University Marburg, Germany. She holds a PhD in International Relations from the LSE and has held positions at King's College, London, the Peace Research Institute, Frankfurt, and the Free University, Berlin. Her research focuses on issues pertaining to peace and conflict, violence, gender and transitional justice. At present, she directs a research project entitled 'Gender Relations in Confined Spaces: Conditions, Scope and Forms of Violence against Women in Conflict-related Refugee Camps', funded by the German Foundation of Peace Research.

Ulrike Krause is Junior Professor for Forced Migration and Refugee Studies at the Institute for Migration Research and Intercultural Studies (IMIS), Osnabrück University. She was previously a research fellow at the Center for Conflict Studies, Philipps-University Marburg. She is a member of the executive boards of both the German Network Refugee

Research (Netzwerk Flüchtlingsforschung) and the German Association for Peace and Conflict Studies (Arbeitsgemeinschaft für Friedens- und Konfliktforschung e.V.). She received her doctorate in political science from Magdeburg University, and has worked for international organizations in several countries. Her research focus is on conflict-induced displacement, refugee governance, refugee protection and assistance, and gender sensitivity, with a regional focus on sub-Saharan Africa. She has authored a number of articles and working papers as well as the book *Linking Refugee Protection with Development Assistance* (Nomos, 2013).

Note

1. Among others, Johnson et al. (2010) reveal that women carried out conflict-related sexual violence. See also de Brouwer (2015) and Sjoberg (2016).

Bibliography

Barker, G., and C. Ricardo. 2005. 'Young Men and the Construction of Masculinity in Sub-Saharan Africa: Implications for HIV/AIDS, Conflict, and Violence', Social Development Papers, Conflict Prevention and Reconstruction, No. 26. Washington, DC: The World Bank.

Berlit, U., H. Doerig and H. Storey. 2015. 'Credibility Assessment in Claims Based on Persecution for Reasons of Religious Conversion and Homosexuality: A Practitioner's Approach', *International Journal of Refugee Law* 27(4): 649–66.

Boano, C., R. Zetter and T. Morris. 2008. 'Environmentally Displaced People: Understanding the Linkages between Environmental Change, Livelihoods and Forced Migration', *Forced Migration Policy Briefing* No. 1. Oxford: Refugee Studies Centre.

Brubaker, R. 2012. 'Categories of Analysis and Categories of Practice: A Note on the Study of Muslims in European Countries of Immigration', *Ethnic and Racial Studies* 36(1): 1–8.

Buscher, D. 2009. 'Women, Work, and War', in S.F. Martin and J. Tirman (eds), *Women, Migration, and Conflict: Breaking a Deadly Cycle*. Heidelberg, London and New York: Springer, pp. 87–106.

Callaway, H. 1985. *Women Refugees in Developing Countries: Their Specific Needs and Untapped Resources*. Oxford: Refugee Studies Programme.

Carlson, S. 2005. 'Contesting and Reinforcing Patriarchy: Domestic Violence in Dzaleka Refugee Camp', *RSC Working Paper Series* No. 23. Oxford: Refugee Studies Centre.

Castles, S. 2003. 'Towards a Sociology of Forced Migration and Social Transformation', *Sociology* 37(1): 13–34.

———. 2007. 'The Migration–Asylum Nexus and Regional Approaches', in S. Kneebone and F. Rawlings-Sanaei (eds), *New Regionalism and Asylum Seekers: Challenges Ahead*. New York and Oxford: Berghahn Books, pp. 25–42.

Cockburn, C. 2004. 'The Continuum of Violence: A Gender Perspective on Violence and Peace', in W. Giles and J. Hyndmann (eds), *Sites of Violence: Gender and Conflict Zones*. Berkeley and Los Angeles: University of California Press, pp. 24–44.

Crawley, H. 2001. *Refugees and Gender: Law and Process*. Bristol: Jordan Publishing.

Crenshaw, K. 1989. 'Demarginalizing the Intersection of Race and Sex: A Black Feminist Critique of Antidiscrimination Doctrine, Feminist Theory and Antiracist Politics', *University of Chicago Legal Forum* 140: 139–67.

Crisp, J., T. Morris and H. Refstie. 2012. 'Displacement in Urban Areas: New Challenges, New Partnerships', *Disasters* 36, Suppl 1: S23–42.

de Brouwer, A.-M. 2015. 'The Importance of Understanding Sexual Violence in Conflict for Investigation and Prosecution Purposes', *Cornell International Law Journal* 48(3): 639–66.

de Wet, C.J. 2006. *Development-Induced Displacement: Problems, Policies and People*. New York and Oxford: Berghahn Books.

Dolan, C. 2002. 'Collapsing Masculinities and Weak States: A Case Study of Northern Uganda', in C. Dolan and F. Cleaver (eds), *Masculinities Matter! Men, Gender and Development*. London: Zed Books, pp. 57–83.

——. 2009. *Social Torture: The case of Northern Uganda, 1986–2006*. New York and Oxford: Berghahn Books.

——. 2014. 'Into the Mainstream: Addressing Sexual Violence against Men and Boys in Conflict', Workshop, 14 May. London: Overseas Development Institute.

Edward, J.K. 2007. *Sudanese Women Refugees: Transformations and Future Imaginings*. New York and Basingstoke, UK: Palgrave Macmillan.

Edwards, A. 2010. 'Transitioning Gender: Feminist Engagement with International Refugee Law and Policy 1950–2010', *Refugee Survey Quarterly* 29(2): 21–45.

Ferris, E.G. 1990. 'Refugee Women and Violence'. Paper presented at the World Council of Churches, Geneva.

——. 2007. 'Comparative Perspectives Symposium: Women in Refugee Camps. Abuse of Power: Sexual Exploitation of Refugee Women and Girls', *Signs: Journal of Women in Culture and Society* 32(3): 584–91.

Fiddian-Qasmiyeh, E. 2014. 'Gender and Forced Migration', in E. Fiddian-Qasmiyeh et al. (eds), *The Oxford Handbook of Refugee and Forced Migration Studies*. Oxford: Oxford University Press, pp. 195–408.

Forced Migration Review. 2013. 'Sexual Orientation and Gender Identity and the Protection of Forced Migrants', *Forced Migration Review* 42.

Foster, M. 2007. *International Refugee Law and Socio-economic Rights: Refuge from Deprivation*. Cambridge and New York: Cambridge University Press.

Foucault, M. 2010. *The Birth of Biopolitics: Lectures at the Collège de France 1978–1979*. London: Picador.

Freedman, J. 2015. *Gendering the International Asylum and Refugee Debate*, 2nd edition. Basingstoke, UK and New York: Palgrave Macmillan.

Gozdziak, E. 2008. 'Pray God and Keep Walking: Religion, Gender and Identity of Refugee Women', in M. Hajdukowski-Ahmed, N. Khanlou and H. Moussa (eds), *Not Born a Refugee Woman. Reclaiming Identities: Challenges, Implications and Transformations in Research, Education, Policy and Creativity*. New York and Oxford: Berghahn Books, pp. 180–95.

Grabska, K. 2011. 'Constructing "Modern Gendered Civilised" Women and Men: Gender-Mainstreaming in Refugee Camps', *Gender & Development* 19(1): 81–93.

Greatbatch, J. 1989. 'The Gender Difference: Feminist Critiques of Refugee Discourse', *International Journal of Refugee Law* 1(4): 518–27.

Hans, A. 2008. 'Gender, Camps and International Norms', *Refugee Watch* 32: 64–73.

Harrell-Bond, B.E. 1986. *Imposing Aid: Emergency Assistance to Refugees*. Oxford, New York and Nairobi: Oxford University Press.

Hart, J. 2008. 'Dislocated Masculinity: Adolescence and the Palestinian Nation-in-exile', *Journal of Refugee Studies,* 21(1): 64–81.

Human Rights Watch. 2011. 'Liberia: Protect Refugees against Sexual Abuse: Ivorian Women and Girls Compelled to Trade Sex for Food, Shelter'. Retrieved 3 October 2015 from https://www.hrw.org/news/2011/04/20/liberia-protect-refugees-against-sexual-abuse.

Hurst, D. 2015. '"Things Happen": Tony Abbott on Sexual Assault Allegations in Offshore Detention'. *Guardian*, 20 March 2015. Retrieved 3 October 2015 from http://www.theguardian.com/australia-news/2015/mar/20/things-happen-tony-abbott-on-sexual-assault-allegations-in-offshore-detention.

Hyndman, J. 2004. 'Refugee Camps as Conflict Zones: The Politics of Gender', in W. Giles and J. Hyndman (eds), *Sites of Violence: Gender and Conflict Zones*. Berkeley and Los Angeles: University of California Press, pp. 193–212.

IASC (Inter-Agency Standing Committee). 2015. 'Guidelines for Integrating Gender-Based Violence Interventions in Humanitarian Action: Reducing risk, promoting resilience and aiding recovery'. Geneva.

Indra, D.M. 1987. 'Gender: A Key Dimension of the Refugee Experience', *Refuge* 6(3): 3–4.

Jaji, R. 2009. 'Masculinity on Unstable Ground: Young Refugee Men in Nairobi, Kenya', *Journal of Refugee Studies* 22(2): 177–94.

Jansen, B. 2011. 'The Accidental City: Violence, Economy and Humanitarianism in Kakuma Refugee Camp Kenya'. PhD thesis. University of Wageningen, NL.

Johnson, K., et al. 2010. 'Association of Sexual Violence and Human Rights Violations with Physical and Mental Health in Territories of the Eastern Democratic Republic of the Congo', *Journal of the American Medical Association* 304(5): 553–62.

Kaiser, T. 2006. 'Between a Camp and a Hard Place: Rights, Livelihood and Experiences of the Local Settlement System for Long-Term Refugees in Uganda', *The Journal of Modern African Studies* 44(4): 597–621.

Karunakara, U., et al. 2004. 'Traumatic Events and Symptoms of Post-Traumatic Stress Disorder amongst Sudanese Nationals, Refugees and Ugandans in the West Nile', *African Health Sciences* 4(2): 83–93.

Kebede, S.S. 2010. 'The Struggle for Belonging: Forming and Reformig Identities 1.5-Generation Asylum Seekers and Refugees'. *RSC Working Paper Series* No. 70.

Krause, U. 2013. *Linking Refugee Protection with Development Assistance: Analyses with a Case Study in Uganda*. Baden-Baden: Nomos.

___. 2014. 'Analysis of Empowerment of Refugee Women in Camps and Settlements', *Journal of Internal Displacement* 4(1): 29–52.

___. 2015. 'Zwischen Schutz und Scham? Flüchtlingslager, Gewalt und Geschlechterverhältnisse', *Peripherie: Zeitschrift für Politik und Ökonomie in der Dritten Welt* 35(138/139): 235–59.

___. 2016a. '"It seems like you don't have identity, you don't belong". Reflexionen über das Flüchtlingslabel und dessen Implikationen', *Zeitschrift für Internationale Beziehungen* 23(1): 8–37.

___. 2016b. 'Hegemonie von Männern? Flüchtlingslager, Maskulinitäten und Gewalt in Uganda', *Soziale Probleme* 27(1): 119–45.

Krause-Vilmar, J. 2011. *The Living Ain't Easy: Urban Refugees in Kampala.* New York: The Women's Refugee Commission.

Lindorfer, S. 2009. *Verletzlichkeit und Macht: Eine psycho-soziale Studie zur Situation von Frauen und Mädchen im Nachkriegsliberia.* Cologne: medica mondiale.

Ludwig, B. 2013. '"Wiping the Refugee Dust from My Feet": Advantages and Burdens of Refugee Status and the Refugee Label', *International Migration* 54(1): 5–18.

Lukunka, B. 2011. 'New Big Men: Refugee Emasculation as a Human Security Issue', *International Migration* 50(5): 130–41.

Markard, N. 2007. 'Fortschritte im Flüchtlingsrecht? Gender Guidelines und geschlechtsspezifische Verfolgung', *Kritische Justiz: Vierteljahresschrift für Recht und Politik* 4: 373–90.

___. 2013. 'Sexuelle Orientierung als Fluchtgrund – Das Ende der "Diskretion": Aktuelle Entwicklungen beim Flüchtlingsschutz aufgrund der sexuellen Orientierung', *Asylmagazin* (3): 74–84.

Martin, S.F. 2004. *Refugee Women*, 2nd edition. Lanham, MD: Lexington Books.

McAdam, J. 2014. 'The Concept of Crisis Migration', *Forced Migration Review* 45: 10–11.

McCleary, J.S. 2013. 'An Exploration of Alcohol Use in Karen Refugee Communities in the Context of Conflict-related Displacement'. PhD thesis. Minneapolis: University of Minnesota.

Moss, P. 2015. 'Review into Recent Allegations Relating to Conditions and Circumstance at the Regional Processing Centre in Nauru: Final Report'. Retrieved 3 October 2015 from http://apo.org.au/research/review-recent-allegations-relating-conditions-and-circumstance-regional-processing-centre.

Mulumba, D. 2005. 'Gender Relations, Livelihood Security and Reproductive Health among Women Refugees in Uganda: The Case of Sudanese Women in Rhino Camp and Kiryandongo Refugee Settlements'. PhD thesis. University of Wageningen, NL.

Naggujja, Y., et al. 2014. *From The Frying Pan to the Fire: Psychosocial Challenges Faced by Vulnerable Refugee Women and Girls in Kampala.* Kampala: Refugee Law Project.

Onyut, L.P., et al. 2009. 'Trauma, Poverty and Mental Health among Somali and Rwandese Refugees Living in an African Refugee Settlement: An Epidemiological Study', *Conflict and Health* 3(6).

ORAM (Organization for Refuge, Asylum & Migration). 2012. 'Opening Doors: A Global Survey of NGO Attitudes towards LGBTI Refugees & Asylum Seekers' (June). San Francisco.

Refugees International. 1999. 'Hope in the Fight to Reduce Gender Violence in Tanzanian Refugee Camps'. Retrieved 3 October 2015 from http://reliefweb.int/report/united-republic-tanzania/hope-fight-reduce-gender-violence-tanzanian-refugee-camps.

——. 2012. 'Syrian Women & Girls: No Safe Refuge'. Retrieved 3 October 2015 http://refugeesinternational.org/policy/field-report/syrian-women-girls-no-safe-refuge.

Rosenberger, S., and I. Stöckl. 2016. 'The Politics of Categorization – Political Representatives with Immigrant Background between "the Other" and "Standing for"', *Politics, Groups, and Identities* (June): 1–20.

Scheel, S., and V. Squire. 2014. 'Forced Migrants as "Illegal" Migrants', in E. Fiddian-Qasmiyeh et al. (eds), *The Oxford Handbook of Refugee and Forced Migration Studies*. Oxford: Oxford University Press, pp. 188–202.

Sjoberg, L. 2016. *Women as Wartime Rapists: Beyond Sensation and Stereotyping*. New York: New York University Press.

Spijkerboer, T. (ed.). 2013. *Fleeing Homophobia: Sexual Orientation, Gender Identity and Asylum*. Abingdon: Routledge.

Türk, V. 2013. 'Ensuring Protection to LGBTI Persons of Concern', *International Journal of Refugee Law* 25(1): 120–29.

Turner, S. 1999. 'Angry Young Men in Camps: Gender, Age and Class Relations among Burundian Refugees in Tanzania', *New Issues in Refugee Research*, Working Paper No. 9.

——. 2010. *Politics of Innocence: Hutu Identity, Conflict and Camp Life*. New York and Oxford: Berghahn Books.

UNGA (United Nations General Assembly). 2012. 'Report of the Special Rapporteur on Violence against Women, its Causes and Consequences, Rashida Manjoo. Addendum: Mission to Somalia', A/HRC/20/16/Add.3. New York.

UNHCR (United Nations High Commissioner for Refugees). 1990. 'UNHCR Policy on Refugee Women'. Geneva.

——. 1991. 'UNHCR Guidelines on the Protection of Refugee Women'. Geneva.

——. 2008a. 'UNHCR Guidance Note on Refugee Claims Relating to Sexual Orientation and Gender Identity'. Geneva.

——. 2008b. 'UNHCR Handbook for the Protection of Women and Girls'. Geneva.

——. 2011a. 'Working with Lesbian, Gay, Bisexual, Transgender & Intersex Persons in Forced Displacement'. Geneva.

——. 2011b. 'Action against Sexual and Gender-based Violence: An Updated Strategy'. Geneva.

——. 2015. 'Women on the Run: First-Hand Accounts of Refugees Fleeing El Salvador, Guatemala, Honduras and Mexico'. Geneva.

——. 2016. 'Global Trends: Forced Displacement in 2015'. Geneva.

UN Women. 2013. 'Inter Agency Assessment of Gender-based Violence and Child Protection among Syrian Refugees in Jordan, with a Focus on Early Marriage'. Amman, Jordan.

Valji, N. 2001. 'Women and the 1951 Refugee Convention: Fifty Years of Seeking Visibility', *Refuge* 19(5): 25–35.

Women's Refugee Commission. 2009. 'Refugee Girls: The Invisible Faces of War'. Retrieved 3 October 2015 from https://womensrefugeecommission.org/programs/youth/763-girlsstories.

Zetter, R. 1991. 'Labelling Refugees: Forming and Transforming a Bureaucratic Identity', *Journal of Refugee Studies* 4(1): 39–62.

———. 2007. 'More Labels, Fewer Refugees: Remaking the Refugee Label in an Era of Globalization', *Journal of Refugee Studies* 20(2): 172–92.

Part I
Conceptualizing Gender, Violence, Refugees

1

UNHCR Policy on Refugee Women

A 25-Year Retrospective

Susan F. Martin

Introduction

In 1990, the UN High Commissioner for Refugees adopted its first 'Policy on Refugee Women'. The policy aimed to integrate the needs of refugee women and the resources to address them into all aspects of UNHCR's operations. This chapter provides a retrospective assessment of the policy on refugee women and assesses its impact on efforts to improve protection and assistance for this population. It (1) sets out the origins of the policy; (2) discusses the key provisions of the policy and subsequent efforts to update it; (3) discusses actions by UNHCR and its partners to implement the policy in three key areas (legal protection, physical protection and assistance to reduce vulnerability to violence and exploitation), analysing the extent to which the policy has achieved its goals; and (4) draws conclusions regarding the ultimate impact of the policy on the lives of refugee women, making recommendations for the future. The chapter is based on the author's own role in the evolution of the policy (including her role in drafting the UNHCR Guidelines on Protection of Refugee Women [1991], which were meant to help to implement the policy), as well as research into the application and impact of the policy. It focuses specifically on refugee women, although many of the same issues apply to internally displaced women, many of whom are now under the mandate of the UNHCR.

Origins of the Policy on Refugee Women

International attention to the needs and resources of refugee women was given a major boost when the UN General Assembly proclaimed 1976–1985 as the UN Decade for Women: Equality, Development and Peace. The Mexico City conference that ushered in the UN Decade with a World Plan of Action made few references to mobile women, mentioning the needs of rural to urban migrants but nothing explicitly about refugees. By the time of the mid-decade conference in Copenhagen (1980), however, refugee women were a specific focus of attention. The Copenhagen conference emphasized the responsibilities of states to protect and assist refugees, urging governments to take steps to prevent violence against refugee women. It also recommended that UNHCR, in cooperation with other agencies, establish programmes to address the specific needs of refugee women in the areas of health, education and employment. To ensure that programmes were appropriate, UNHCR was encouraged to increase the number of female staff at all levels and establish a high-level position of coordinator of women's programmes. The Copenhagen resolution further requested that family planning information and methods be made available on a voluntary and nationally acceptable basis to both refugee women and men. The 'Forward Looking Strategies' adopted in Nairobi in 1985 gave further impetus to efforts to address the situation of refugee women. In addition to recommending programmes to address the special needs of refugee women, the Forward Looking Strategies also emphasized that the 'potential and capacities of refugee and displaced women should be recognized and enhanced' (UN 1986: paragraph 298).

In October 1985, the Executive Committee of the UNHCR adopted its first resolution on the protection of refugee women. Two years later, the committee called upon the high commissioner to report in detail on the concrete measures to be taken to address the particular protection and assistance problems and needs of refugee women. In February 1988, UNHCR established a Steering Committee on Refugee Women, under the chairmanship of the deputy high commissioner to define, oversee and coordinate a process of assessing, strengthening and reorienting existing policies and programmes. In August of the same year, internal guidelines on the international protection of refugee women were distributed to field offices. A 'Note on Refugee Women' prepared for the 1988 Executive Committee meeting emphasized the need for improved data to ensure that gender-specific needs were systematically considered and addressed.

In 1989, the position of 'Senior Coordinator for Refugee Women' was created (as recommended almost a decade earlier in Copenhagen); a senior Canadian official was seconded to UNHCR to fill this position.

Key Provisions of the Initial Policy and Subsequent Elaborations

Despite the increased attention during the 1980s, it was not until 1990 that UNHCR adopted an official policy on refugee women. The major thrust of the policy was 'to integrate the resources and needs of refugee women in all aspects of programme planning and implementation' (UNHCR 1990: 5). The policy noted that separate women's projects would not necessarily be the best way to address the needs of refugee women; rather, women's issues should be mainstreamed into all of UNHCR's activities. Significantly, the policy recognized that refugee women must themselves participate in the planning and implementation of programmes. Within this framework, women must be considered as more than vulnerable people requiring assistance. They were also to be seen as resources for their own and their communities' development. The policy further noted that planning should include 'more than women's social role as daughter/ wife/mother ... Women's economic role as income-earner for herself and her family, producer and/or manager of food, provider of fuel and water, and ... religious, cultural and political activities' was equally important and too often overlooked (ibid.: 5).

In 1991, in support of implementation of the policy on refugee women, the Executive Committee of the UNHCR adopted Guidelines on the Protection of Refugee Women (UNHCR 1991a). The guidelines were meant to address gaps in protection faced by millions of refugee women and girls who found themselves at risk. These gaps included problems in gaining recognition as refugees when the applicants claimed to be victims of gender-based persecution unrelated to the other grounds contained in the convention; physical security risks that went unattended, particularly those related to sexual and gender-based violence; and problems gaining access to needed assistance and means of economic independence, which in turn undermined economic and social rights.

Also in 1991, UNHCR outlined the importance of taking a gender perspective in developing policies and programmes for refugees. The organization understood gender analysis to encompass four main purposes:

1. Gender analysis highlights both men's and women's capacities, and indicates where opportunities are missed by humanitarian agencies for targeting effective strategies to support and enhance women's skills and capacities.

2. Gender analysis can identify the division of labour within the household and domestic economy as well as identify the burden of reproductive labour that women bear, and highlight the way this intensifies during periods of rapid and violent social change.
3. Gender analysis can reveal the socio-cultural constraints facing women who, as bearers of culture and the social reproduction of norms and values, become subject to new forms of control and victimisation during emergencies.
4. Gender analysis points out that men's experiences and identity in times of emergency are also impacted and that the 'gender' question is not just a woman's issue. The ways in which violence has helped to re-structure 'masculinity' in poverty-affected and marginalised societies is an important factor when considering boys and men's involvement in armed militias and their acts of violence against women. This is particularly important when considering the post-conflict phase where men and boys are re-socialised. (UNHCR 1991b)

The next major step in formulating policies on refugee women occurred in 2001 when UNHCR made five commitments to refugee women that elaborated these points. The commitments relate to:

- Women's and girls' membership and participation in decision making;
- Registration and documentation;
- Tackling SGBV, including domestic violence;
- Participation in food distribution; and
- Providing sanitary materials to women and girls of concern.

The commitments were followed by the promulgation of a new Handbook for the Protection of Women and Girls (UNHCR 2008a), to update the 1991 guidelines and provide further guidance. UNHCR also instituted a dialogue with women to help to ensure greater participation of women in decisions regarding protection and assistance issues. A summary of the findings of these consultations were shared with governments, and published (UNHCR 2013).

Progress in Implementing the Policy, Commitments and Guidelines

This section assesses progress during the past twenty-five years in achieving the aims of the policies, commitments and guidelines described above. One of the most notable areas of progress has been on the research undertaken on refugee women. Twenty-five years ago, the academic literature on refugee women was almost non-existent. Since then, however, the literature has grown into a more comprehensive body of analysis (see Hyndman 1998, 2004; Hajdukowski-Ahmed, Khanlou and Moussa 2008, Fiddian-Qasmiyeh 2010; Edwards 2010; Olivius 2014).

This section focuses on three key areas affecting the protection of refugee women from violence and persecution: legal protection in the context of asylum applications; physical protection from violence; and access to assistance that helps refugee women and girls avoid or recover from violence and exploitation.

Legal Protection

The basic structures and instruments to ensure the legal protection of refugees were established more than sixty years ago. The UN Convention Relating to the Status of Refugees was adopted in July 1951. The essential purpose of the convention was to provide a general definition of who was to be considered a refugee and to define his or her legal status. The 1951 convention was produced in the early days of the Cold War, largely to resolve the situation of the millions of refugees who remained displaced after the Second World War and Fascist/Nazi persecution. At its core, this treaty substitutes the protection of the international community (in the form of a host government) for that of an unable or unwilling sovereign. Defining refugees as people who were unable or unwilling to avail themselves of the protection of their home countries because of a 'well-founded fear of persecution based on their race, religion, nationality, political opinion or membership in a particular social group', the convention included geographic (Europe) and time (displaced before 1951) limitations, which were lifted in the 1967 protocol. Since 1967, the refugee convention has been a universal instrument, applying to refugees worldwide.

In addition, the Organization of African Unity (now African Union) adopted a refugee convention in 1969 (which went into force in 1974) that expanded the definition of a refugee. According to the OAU Convention:

> The term 'refugee' shall also apply to every person who, owing to external aggression, occupation, foreign domination, or events seriously disturbing public order in either part or the whole of his [or her] country of origin or nationality, is compelled to leave his [or her] place of habitual residence in order to seek refuge in another place outside his [or her] country of origin or nationality. (OAU 1974)

The Cartagena Declaration on Refugees, adopted in November 1984 to address the situation of refugees from Central America, includes a similar broader definition that encompassed victims of conflict, not just persecution. Moreover, UNHCR is often asked by the General Assembly or the secretary general to use its good offices to provide assistance and protection to people fleeing conflict and instability.

Gender is not included in the international definition of a refugee as a person with a well-founded fear of persecution on the basis of race, religion, nationality, political opinion or membership in a social group. Yet, women may be fleeing such gender-based persecution as rape, widow burnings, honour killings, domestic violence, forced marriages and female genital cutting,[1] from which their home country governments are unwilling or unable to protect them.

In 2002, UNHCR issued two guidelines to provide guidance for State Parties and national Refugee Status Determination (RSD) authorities on gender-sensitive assessment and processing of asylum claims. The 'Guidelines on Gender-Related Persecution and the Guidelines on Membership of a Particular Social Group within the Context of Article 1A(2) of the of the 1951 Convention and its 1967 Protocol relating to the Status of Refugees' (UNHCR 2002a) complements other UNHCR guidance on aspects of gender-related persecution. These guidelines provide legal interpretive guidance to help to ensure gender-sensitive interpretation of the convention and that RSD procedures do not marginalize or exclude gender-related experiences of persecution.

In its 2002 Guidelines on Gender-Related Persecution, UNHCR noted: 'Though gender is not specifically referenced in the refugee definition, it is widely accepted that it can influence, or dictate, the type of persecution or harm suffered and the reasons for this treatment. The refugee definition, properly interpreted, therefore covers gender-related claims. As such, there is no need to add an additional ground to the 1951 Convention definition' (UNHCR 2002a).

Several governments have issued guidelines or regulations to guide asylum determinations in this area. Examples include Australia, Canada, the United States and the United Kingdom. European Union Directive 2004/83/EC on minimum standards for the qualification and status of third country nationals or stateless persons as refugees and persons otherwise in need of international protection also recognizes gender-based persecution as a basis upon which asylum may be granted. Universities and nongovernmental organizations have supplemented these guidelines. In South Africa, for example, the University of Cape Town Legal Aid Clinic, as a member of the National Consortium on Refugee Affairs, developed gender guidelines on asylum proceedings for the South African government.

Some forms of persecution are in themselves gender-specific: '[G]ender-specific harm may include but is not limited to sexual violence and abuse, female genital mutilation, marriage-related harm, violence within the family, forced sterilisation and forced abortion' (UK Asylum and Immigration Tribunal 2000: 5). The guidelines generally make a distinction as to the perpetrator of the persecution in determining whether the applicant is justified in being unable or unwilling to accept the protection of their home country. In many gender-persecution cases, the harm is carried out by non-State actors – family members, armed elements who are not sanctioned by the government, even community members seeking to hold up social norms. When non-State actors are recognized, as they are in many countries, the asylum applicant must demonstrate a failure of the State to provide protection from the non-State actor.

The most difficult issue to overcome in gender-based cases is the nexus between the harm suffered and one of the grounds for protection. These cases often try to tie the persecution to the applicant's membership in a particular social group. UNHCR guidelines define 'a particular social group' as a 'group of persons who share a common characteristic other than their risk of being persecuted, or who are perceived as a group by society. The characteristic will often be one that is innate, unchangeable, or otherwise fundamental to identity, conscience or the exercise of one's human rights' (UNHCR 2002a: 7).

The forms of persecution that refugees experience are often gendered. For example, a woman may face serious harm because she is unwilling to practise religion as the authorities of her country require. These cases generally involve a refusal by the woman to follow the behaviours that religious leaders say are required of all adherents – for example, wearing the veil or other garments deemed proper for women. In theocracies, opposition to these behaviours may also be, or be seen as, expressions of political opinion. In addition to opposition to social norms upheld by the State, women may be persecuted for their opposition to laws and practices that discriminate against them or make it difficult for them to support themselves and their children.

Women often face special problems in making their case to the authorities, particularly when they have had experiences that are difficult or painful to describe. The female victim of sexual torture may be reluctant to speak about it, particularly to a male interviewer. Rape, even in the context of torture, is seen in some cultures as a failure on the part of the woman to preserve her virginity or marital dignity. She may be shunned by her family and isolated from other members of the community. Discussing her experience becomes a further source of alienation.

The 2008 handbook outlines steps that should be taken to overcome some of these barriers to recognition as refugees. The guidance is aimed at national authorities as well as UNHCR staff who do refugee status determinations in countries in which governments have deferred to UNHCR's expertise. The handbook advises that those making status determinations should ensure that:

- all examiners are familiar with the ways in which gender and age can be relevant to determining whether a particular form of harm or treatment constitutes persecution;

- extensive background information on the situation of women and children in the country of origin is available;
- all adult family members and dependants accompanying a 'principal applicant' have an individual and confidential registration interview to determine if they may have an independent refugee claim;
- women and girls have access to counsellors who are able to explain how the asylum procedure works, including the possibility that gender-related forms of persecution can constitute grounds for refugee status; and
- specially trained female interviewers and interpreters are available to asylum seekers, especially where it becomes evident that sexual or gender-based violence may be an issue.

The guidelines also recognize the need for special procedures for children who are unaccompanied or separated from their parents, particularly in ensuring the child's representation by an adult familiar with the child's background and who can protect her or his best interests (UNHCR 2008a: 140).

Physical Security

Protection goes well beyond legal recognition. The protection of refugee women in conflict situations was recognized in the lead-up to the formulation of the UNHCR policy on refugee women, and remains particularly problematic. UNHCR reported that sexual and gender-based violence (SGBV) was the principal concern expressed by participants in all of its dialogues with refugee women (UNHCR 2013). Civilians are increasingly the targets of attacks in civil conflicts. Articles 7 and 8 of the Rome Statute of the International Criminal Court include rape and sexual violence among the crimes against humanity and war crimes. Rape and sexual assault also occur during flight at the hands of border guards, government and rebel military units, bandits and others. Women's safety may be no more ensured once in refugee camps or reception centres. For example, refugee women have faced serious threats of rape when they pick firewood, often the only source of heating and cooking fuel. Refugee women have been forced to provide sexual favours in exchange for obtaining food rations for themselves and their families. In some cases, only male heads of households have received documentation of their status, leaving their spouses vulnerable to harassment each time they leave their homes.

Many factors contribute to the vulnerability of refugee women and girls to sexual violence and exploitation. UNHCR's report of its dialogue with refugee women concluded that the prevalence of sexual and gender-based violence 'was often linked to lack of income, inadequate shelter and other compounding factors' (UNHCR 2013: 16). Exploitation certainly occurs in the absence of alternatives for refugees. When a group is completely dependent on others for economic survival, members of the group are inherently vulnerable to such exploitation. In many camps, the physical facilities increase the likelihood of protection problems. Camps are often overcrowded. Unrelated families may be required to share a communal living space. A UN team investigating allegations of sexual abuse in West Africa found: 'Bathing facilities in a number of the camps consist of one building with one side for men and another side for women. The isolation and lack of separate and distinctly placed facilities, which would increase the cost, has caused the facilities to occasionally be the site of sexual violence' (UN General Assembly 2002: 12). When refugee women do not have documentation of their status, they are particularly vulnerable to abuse.

Gender-sensitive security mechanisms are often inadequate as well. The responsibility for security generally rests with governments. Yet, government authorities, particularly in poorer countries, usually do not have sufficient resources to fulfil the responsibility. The situation is problematic for both camp and urban refugee populations. Spouse and child abuse and abandonment are problems encountered by women and children in refugee situations. Heightened levels of domestic violence are frequent where refugees have lived for extended periods in the artificial environment of a refugee camp or reception facility, or while waiting for the decision on their asylum application. Psychological strains for husbands and adolescent boys unable to assume normal cultural, social and economic roles can result in aggressive behaviour towards wives, children and sisters (Turner 1999). Recognizing that these problems will not be solved without the engagement of men, UNHCR included meetings with men about sexual violence in its expanded dialogue with refugee women (UNHCR 2013).

Refugee camps in a number of locations house the civilian families of members of armed forces. The camps frequently serve as rest and recuperation sites. The men often bring weapons with them into the camps. A proliferation of weapons can compound the protection problems facing refugee women. Forced recruitment of women into the armed forces of resistance groups is a further problem in some countries. In some cases, military forces recruit them as soldiers. In other cases, they are required to carry ammunition or other supplies, or they are used to clear mines. They may also be forced into sexual slavery by armed forces. Abduction of children remains a particular problem, with girls often experiencing sexual abuse.

A final significant impediment to the protection of refugee women is the general insecurity that places humanitarian operations at risk. In many modern conflicts, civilians have become the targets of armed attack, not just the innocent victims of war. Also targeted are the humanitarian actors who seek to assist and protect civilians. Insecurity is one of the biggest impediments to securing the rights of refugee women, particularly when they remain under the control of military forces in a country of refuge. Insecure conditions impede access to displaced populations for delivery of aid, create protection problems for aid workers as well as their clients, and make it impossible to monitor and evaluate the effectiveness of aid operations.

In 2005, the Inter-Agency Standing Committee (IASC) issued guidelines to prevent and respond to gender-based violence, developed training programmes for staff, raised awareness, and took other steps to prevent sexual exploitation and abuse (IASC 2005). IASC revised the guidance in 2015, with the aim of reducing risk, promoting resilience and aiding recovery (IASC 2015). The guidelines apply to each of the thirteen sectoral areas covered in humanitarian response[2] as well as to each population that is particularly at risk for gender-based violence[3].

More specific to refugees, UNHCR has repeatedly issued guidelines on prevention of sexual and gender-based violence as well as other forms of abuse against women and girls. Specific projects focused on prevention have been implemented in a number of countries, with particular concentration on education for both men and women. UNHCR has also implemented programmes providing assistance to survivors, and engaged in efforts to ensure that perpetrators are not immune from punishment, such as programmes in Zambia and Thailand to facilitate reporting of abuses to the refugee camp justice system or local courts (UNHCR 2013). However, the fundamental problem of dependency on humanitarian aid remains for many refugee women and girls.

Such problems do not necessarily stop when the women return home. The conflict may still be continuing and, even if a peace agreement has been signed, political instability, the continued presence of landmines, and the destruction of the economy and infrastructure make conditions dangerous for returning women and their families. The UNHCR emphasizes that voluntary return must be in safety and dignity. The UNHCR Handbook on Voluntary Repatriation notes that

> among the elements of 'safety and dignity' to be considered are: the refugees' physical safety at all stages during and after their return including en route, at reception points and at the destination; the need for family unity; attention to the needs of vulnerable groups; the waiver or, if not possible, reduction to a minimum of border-crossing formalities; permission for refugees to bring their movable possessions when returning; respect for school and planting seasons in the timing of such movements; and freedom of movement. (UNHCR 1996: section 2.4)

Recognizing that the protection of refugee women and children may require special arrangements, the handbook includes a special box reminding repatriation planners to 'make appropriate arrangements for the physical safety of unaccompanied women and women heads of household in departure, transit or reception centres (such as separate areas close to the relevant infrastructure with adequate security arrangements, lighting)' (ibid.: section 2.5).

International Assistance and Protection against Violence

Many refugee women are dependent on international assistance for all of their material needs including food, shelter, fuel, water and health care. For new arrivals, this situation is not surprising. Refugees fleeing their homes cannot usually bring material resources with them. The clothing on their backs and perhaps a small bundle of belongings are often all that they have been able to bring with them. They may arrive in poor health, malnourished and/or disabled, having experienced famine in their countries of origin and long treks through hazardous terrain.

That large numbers of refugees continue to be dependent on international assistance long after their original flight is more disturbing and presents problems in protecting women against violence. In many host countries, refugees remain in camps or urban areas for years, unable to return to home communities because of continued conflict and instability but denied opportunities to work or access to training or income-producing activities. As of 2010, UNHCR estimated that about 7.2 million refugees were in protracted situations of more than five years (UNHCR 2011: 2). Often, refugees must rely on food rations, clothing and shelter as provided by international donors throughout their time as refugees. The assistance package, being of a bare subsistence nature even at the best of times, is often inadequate during periods of financial strain to meet even the basic nutritional needs of the population. Further, there is too little coordination among the various sections of assistance – health, education, and skills training, for example – to better facilitate independence.

Access to material assistance, employment and health care services has been restricted in a number of developed countries as a way of discouraging new arrivals of refugees. Economic dependency, isolation and lack of integration support may put displaced populations, especially single women, women with children and unaccompanied minors at a risk of SGBV, including sexual exploitation and forced prostitution.

Refugee women are especially affected by the lack of appropriate and adequate international assistance. They and their children suffer from the inadequacies in the assistance package. Unable to obtain employment and often denied participation in training or income-generation programmes,

they are unable to provide for their families without the international assistance. With it, they may still be vulnerable to sexual abuse and exploitation. And, finally, they are not adequately advised about the programmes
in place, nor are they permitted to participate actively in the implementation of projects ostensibly designed to assist and protect them.

Since the promulgation of the policy on refugee women, there has been
increased recognition that women must be involved early in the design
of assistance programmes if the aid is to be provided in a manner that
ensures protection against violence. This has particularly been the case
in food distribution systems as well as in the actual delivery of the food.
As discussed above, one of UNHCR's five major commitments to refugee
women includes ensuring 'that refugee women participate directly and indirectly in the management and distribution of food and non-food items'
(UNHCR 2008a: 316). World Food Programme policies say that women
should control the family food aid entitlement in 80 per cent of WFP food
distributions. The WFP guidelines also state that women should take a lead
role in local decision-making committees on food aid management as well
as the management of assets created through food-for-work programmes.
These policies are aimed at reversing what is often seen when male distribution leads to diversion of food into the black market or military uses, or
food distributed to male heads of households does not reach the wives and
children (Human Rights Watch 2000; Freedman 2012).[4] When adequate
supplies of food do not reach the civilian population, women are more
likely to engage in prostitution and other illicit activities to feed their families, and are more vulnerable to sexual exploitation.

Clean water and fuel are other essential needs. Women in refugee
camps, like many other women in developing countries, spend a great
deal of time in water collection. Containers that are too heavy or pumps
that are inconveniently located can intensify this effort. When clean water
is not available, children, in particular, run the risk of life-threatening diarrhoea diseases. Similarly, collection of fuel for cooking and heating is
also a task for which women are generally responsible. In a refugee or
displaced persons context, however, efforts to find water and firewood can
not only be time-consuming (if located at some distance from the camps)
but dangerous (if located in mine-infested areas, the site of conflict, or
areas with high levels of banditry). As situations become protracted, and
close-by sources of firewood become exhausted, women must go further
and further afield. Persistent violence against women collecting water and
firewood far from camps has been documented in the Dadaab camps in
Kenya for more than two decades (Fitzgerald 1998).[5] A 2006 report assessed the alternatives to firewood collection – including distribution of
firewood, other means of cooking (e.g. charcoal or kerosene), fuel efficient
stoves, use of solar energy – as well as mechanisms to protect women while

they collect firewood and to provide sources of income so they can purchase fuel. Each of these alternatives has a financial cost that the international community has been unwilling to bear in most locations, leaving women and girls to pay the cost in risk to their own lives and well-being (Women's Commission for Refugee Women and Children 2006).

Other gaps in humanitarian assistance also render women and girls more vulnerable to violence, generally by reducing their ability to become self-supporting. One is the distribution of sanitary materials. Since 1996, UNHCR has required all field programmes to include sanitary materials in regular budgets. A survey of fifty-two UNHCR offices found low compliance, however. The unavailability of these materials is not just an inconvenience to refugee women and adolescents but a major impediment to their full participation in the life of the camp society: 'In both Ethiopia and Zambia girls stayed away from school, sometimes remaining in their houses because they had nothing decent to wear during monthly menstruation' (Women's Commission for Refugee Women and Children 2002b: 28). As a result of persistent complaints, UNHCR established as one of its five principal commitments to refugee women to 'provide sanitary materials to all women and girls of concern as standard practice in assistance programmes' (UNHCR 2008a: 273). UNHCR has worked with companies such as Proctor and Gamble, which provided three million sanitary pads in 2008, but shortages remain a problem in many locations (UNHCR 2008b).

When the policy on refugee women was adopted, reproductive health services, including those needed by victims of SGBV, were often scarce in refugee camps. Lack of training of midwives and traditional birth attendants (TBAs), septic abortions, unsanitary conditions during birth, septic instruments, poor lighting during deliveries, and frequency of pregnancies all led to problems for refugee women. In 1999, the Inter-Agency Working Group on Refugee Reproductive Health (IAWG) produced a field manual that outlined a Minimum Initial Service Package (MISP) 'designed to prevent and manage the consequences of sexual violence, reduce HIV transmission, prevent excess neonatal and maternal morbidity and mortality, and plan for the provision of comprehensive reproductive health services' (IAWG 1999: 12). In addition, several NGOs also came together as the Reproductive Health for Refugees Consortium to offer actual services for refugee women and girls.

SGBV programmes generally advocate a multisectoral approach that takes into account prevention of abuse, the physical and psychological ramifications of violence, the potential need of the victim for a safe haven, the longer-term economic needs of vulnerable populations, the legal rights of victims, training of police and security personnel, and other similar issues. Despite the considerable progress made in addressing the reproductive health and needs of refugee women related more specifically to

SGBV, gaps still persist. Urban refugee women often do not have access to appropriate services, particularly if they are not eligible for mainstream services and if refugee-specific services are inadequate to meet their needs. If they are without documentation as refugees in these urban areas, they may have access to no services at all. Adolescent and young women as well as the elderly often require specialized services that are not available (UNHCR 2013).

Other programmes involve the psychosocial needs of refugees. Here, some progress has been made in providing support for refugee women who have experienced trauma, particularly linked to SGBV. Women caught in conflict experience particular stresses that can affect their mental health as well as their ability to cope. Programmes for refugee women and girls tend to range from specialized mental health services to play, sports, and other recreational groups for traumatized children, to income-generation activities for traumatized women. The aims are to prevent, to the degree possible, trauma and stressors that negatively affect mental health, and to strengthen the capacity of refugees to cope with them when prevention fails.

Female education is an area in which minimal progress has been made but much more needs to be done to reduce vulnerability to violence and sexual exploitation. The Executive Committee of the UNHCR has reaffirmed the fundamental right of refugee children to education and, in its 38th Session called upon all States, individually and collectively, to intensify their efforts to ensure that refugee children benefit from primary education. Yet, the right to education continues to be abridged, particularly for girls. A 2002 UNHCR report on education concluded: 'One-third of refugee children (excluding infants) and adolescents in populations categorized as "UNHCR assisted" are in UNHCR-supported schooling, and perhaps 40 per cent are in school altogether' (UNHCR 2002b: 6). By 2009, the overall figures had improved, although on average refugee children were less likely to be enrolled in primary and secondary education than were host country nationals (Dryden-Peterson 2011).

With a majority of refugees now living outside of refugee camps, many in urban areas, access to education is often impeded by a lack of host community capacity. Even when host countries permit refugee children to attend local schools, these may be seriously overcrowded and inhospitable to newcomers. UNHCR recognizes that ensuring quality education in a safe environment is a challenge in many of its operating environments (UNHCR 2008a: 295–306). A 2011 report published by UNHCR found that 'available data indicate that many refugee children are learning very little in schools; among Eritrean refugees in Ethiopia, less than 6% of refugee children had reached benchmark reading fluency by Grade 4' (Dryden-Peterson 2011: 6).

Gender disparities in education persist although there is substantial variation based on where the refugees are located. Dryden-Peterson (2011: 29) concluded:

> Girls have less access to school in urban areas of Asia, the Middle East and North Africa. In Southern and Western Africa, girls have greater access than boys. At secondary levels, the global average suggests near gender parity in access to school. However, this average masks massive disparities between regions. In camp settings in Eastern [Africa] and the Horn of Africa, only five girls are enrolled for every ten boys. On the other hand, in camps in Central Africa and the Great Lakes Region, fourteen girls are enrolled for every ten boys. There are similar regional differences for urban populations.

A number of factors may explain these variations, some resulting from a catch-22. Families in some locations may fear that adolescent girls will be subject to greater sexual harassment if they leave compounds to go to school, even if they understand that education will protect their daughters in the long run by providing greater economic opportunities. Lack of appropriate clothing and sanitary materials may also impede educational attainment. Routine household responsibilities of adolescent girls, such as collecting firewood and water, may make it difficult for them to attend school (Brown 2012). Food shortages also cause students to drop out in order to scavenge for whatever they can pick or find (UNHCR 2014).

Some programmes have tried to address these concerns directly. For example, to address reports of sexual exploitation of girls in schools, 'the International Rescue Committee implemented programs to train women classroom assistants for upper-primary classes. Working alongside male teachers, they serve as role models, monitor risks of exploitation of students by teachers and document cases of abuse' (UNHCR 2008a: 303). Effecting more systemic changes will be difficult, however, without greater commitment of human and financial resources. UNHCR itself describes its education unit as 'shockingly small' (Dryden-Peterson 2011: 35). Improvements are dependent on the more than two hundred implementing partners that provide education, but their expertise varies considerably, with many having had little previous experience with refugee education (Dryden-Peterson 2011). Complicating the situation is the apparent unwillingness of donors to provide full funding for education programmes. In 2011, available funding represented only 39 per cent of what UNHCR requested for education (ibid.). These problems are not exclusive to refugee girls as boys also experience an educational deficit.

Refugee women face many of the same impediments to education and skills training – inadequate resources, teachers and classes. In addition, women face other barriers. The dialogue with refugee women referenced a variety of obstacles to self-sufficiency, including 'difficulty in obtaining work permits or denial of the right to work, non-recognition of qualifications, high unemployment, lack of skills that are in demand, and language barriers' (UNHCR 2013: 26). Traditional views of the role of women sometimes prevent them from accepting work or undertaking training that takes them out of the household. There may also be restrictions on the type of work that is considered to be appropriate for women. Practical problems also constrain enrolment in training programmes, including need for day care and lack of time and energy after household work and/or jobs as a wage earner. Also, many skills training programmes assume some level of prior education, most notably in terms of literacy. Refugee women may not qualify for such programmes, having been discriminated against in their country of origin and not obtaining elementary education.

Other constraints relate to the design and contents of training programmes. In some cases, programmes have been too far removed from the everyday life activities of the refugee women and have therefore appeared to be irrelevant to their needs. Some vocational training programmes have focused on skills that are not marketable in the refugee context, or follow traditional patterns that are not sustainable for income generation. To respond to these criticisms, UNHCR recommends a thorough assessment be undertaken prior to developing skills training and livelihood programmes, to include assessment of markets so that existing skills within the displaced community can be matched to labour needs, including of emerging markets where gender roles are not yet defined; use of participatory assessments to identify the various resources available to women and men of different age groups and backgrounds; consultation with the community, including women and girls, to ensure the design of livelihood programmes reflects their concerns and to ensure that programmes do not automatically reinforce traditional gender roles; and economic mapping exercises to determine what businesses women are engaged in, what skills they have, what obstacles they must overcome and what market opportunities exist for business start-ups and growth. Programmes should be comprehensive, including pre-counselling, apprenticeship, job placement, and technical assistance (UNHCR 2008a: 311).

UNHCR reports successful initiatives in Zambia and Thailand that may be models for other countries:

> In Zambia and Thailand, women also requested a targeted livelihoods programme to prevent women and girls from engaging in survival sex or, in Thailand, in bonded labour, in order to sustain their families. In response, in Zambia, groups of women now receive seeds for growing crops and a newly opened women's centre offers training in tailoring, crafts and poultry production. Training and meetings take into account women's schedules, to accommodate their other tasks. Community farming cooperatives that were

initially supported by UNHCR are now able to secure their own funding. In Thailand, livelihood programmes for refugees include the production and sale of handicrafts as well as micro-finance schemes. A community agriculture and nutrition programme enhances self-reliance and tackles malnutrition. (UNHCR 2013: 27)

Notably, however, UNHCR also recognizes that 'funding constraints keep these projects small in scale' (ibid.).

Theoretically there are a number of ways that refugees can supplement their household income. They include: employment in the local economy or with assistance agencies; agricultural activities; bartering; establishment of trades or small businesses; and participation in skills training programs and formal income-generation projects. Women in developing countries typically find employment in the informal sector of the economy – and refugee women in these countries do the same. In general, refugee women who work in the local economy are within the service sector. For example, it is not uncommon to find a refugee woman supporting her family through her earnings as a domestic. These jobs are often a cornerstone in the household survival strategy for an extended family. Refugee women are often involved in the tending of garden plots surrounding the house, where they can grow vegetables to either supplement their diet or, if they choose, sell to earn some extra cash.

Assistance agencies are an important source of employment for refugees in developing countries. Typically these positions go to younger men who have the language skills to communicate with and relate to the expatriate staff in charge. These positions often offer a higher level of financial compensation than is usually available to refugees in the local market, relatively interesting non-manual labour work (though the employees often feel they are overqualified for the position), more security, higher status, and other benefits such as an increased chance for resettlement to a third country.

The primary area of employment with assistance agencies for refugee women is in the health sector. In a number of cultures, it is more appropriate for women to seek medical advice from and be examined by other women. The employed women work in supplementary feeding programmes, as traditional birth attendants, in mother/child health programmes, as home visitors, particularly in public health education and outreach, as translators, and so on. Following health programmes, the second largest sector for employment is 'women's projects', including income-generation activities.

Livelihoods for urban refugees have received increased attention in the past decades as larger numbers of refugees find shelter in urban areas. Living in cities has both positive and negative consequences for refugee women seeking livelihoods. On the one hand, there are more employment opportunities in cities than in rural areas. On the other hand, refugees often do not have authority to work legally in these areas. Refugee women – and men – often find work in the underground economy rather than in the mainstream labour market. Jobs as domestic workers may be plentiful but may also be highly exploitive. Private homes are the least regulated sector of the economy. Refugees are often vying for limited jobs with other vulnerable populations in urban areas, including locally unemployed groups and recently arrived migrants. Programmes that target both refugees and hosts make sense in this context since, as a recent meeting on urban refugees concluded, 'urban refugees are not that different from (disadvantaged) host populations with regard to their assets, skill sets and vulnerabilities' (International Rescue Committee and Women's Refugee Commission 2013: 15).

Conclusions

Looking back twenty-five years after the promulgation of the UNHCR Policy on Refugee Women, I see much progress to report but have identified fundamental problems that remain and should be addressed in moving forward. In theory, the international community has come down firmly on the side of gender equality in laying out guidelines on the protection of refugee women. As early as 1991, the UNHCR Executive Committee stressed

> that all action taken on behalf of refugee and displaced women and children must be guided by the relevant international instruments relating to the status of refugees, as well as other human rights instruments, in particular, the Convention relating to the Status of Refugees, adopted on 28 July 1951, and its 1967 Protocol, the Convention on the Elimination of All Forms of Discrimination against Women (CEDAW), and the Convention on the Rights of the Child. (UNHCR Executive Committee 1991)

In referencing CEDAW, the Executive Committee, composed of governments (not all of whom signed CEDAW) recognized that UNHCR would be bound by universal human rights principles in its treatment of refugee women, just as it is bound to universal principles contained in the now sixty-year-old Refugee Convention. UNHCR's subsequent Guidelines on the Protection of Refugee Women and more recent Handbook for Protection of Women and Girls reiterated that CEDAW and the other human rights instruments 'provide a framework of international human rights standards for providing protection and assistance to refugee women'.

In practice, achieving protection for refugee women, particularly where gender inequality is a barrier, has been much more difficult. The gap between rhetoric and reality for women and girls is still very large. As

Hyndman (1998), Fiddian-Qasmiyeh (2010) and Olivius (2014) document, efforts purportedly aimed at achieving gender equality too often fail to achieve their goals. There are organizational as well as practical impediments to engaging the participation of women in actual decision making. Refugee women remain the civilian casualties of conflict and, with their dependent children, form a majority of the displaced. They remain the victims of sexual violence and exploitation. They remain without equal access to the types of education and livelihoods that would protect them from sexual exploitation and violence. Women and girls remain the principal target of traffickers; and cultural traditions remain a potent barrier to improving their lives. Nevertheless, it is important to keep in mind that, as UNHCR's dialogue with refugee women concluded: 'Despite these unrelenting challenges, [the consultations] demonstrated the strength, resilience and vision of displaced women and girls' (UNHCR 2013: 36).

Advocacy in support of the following interventions would help women who have been forced to flee their homes to overcome the formidable barriers that still exist: there should be renewed efforts to implement fully the various legal instruments and guidelines that set out norms and standards of protection for refugees generally, and women and girls specifically. These include the 1951 UN Convention Relating to the Status of Refugees and its 1967 Protocol; the IASC Guidelines for Integrating Gender-Based Violence Interventions in Humanitarian Action: Reducing risk, promoting resilience and aiding recovery; the UNHCR Guidelines on the Protection of Refugee Women; the UNHCR Sexual and Gender-Based Violence against Refugees, Returnees and Internally Displaced Persons: Guidelines for Prevention and Response; the Guiding Principles on Internal Displacement; the UNHCR Handbook for Protection of Women and Girls, and other policies and guidance on ways to empower refugee and displaced women and protect their rights and physical safety and security.

Policies and programmes should be adopted to enable refugee women to participate actively in decisions that affect them and their families. The dialogue with refugee women was useful but there needs to be more systemic ways to ensure that women's voices are heard. Improvements are also needed in the socio-economic status of refugee women to enable them to support themselves and their families in dignity and safety. This means improving access to employment, credit, education and skills training, as well as access to adequate and safe housing. Not only are women refugees entitled to the exercise of these rights, but access to them would have strong, positive protection ramifications. In particular, steps should be taken to help refugee women protect themselves from sexual exploitation, trafficking, involuntary prostitution and other exploitable situations. This means lessening dependence on international humanitarian assistance while increasing the potential for self-support.

Policies should ensure access for refugee women to primary and reproductive health care services, including programmes to address sexual and gender-based violence, trauma resulting from conflict and flight, and sexually transmitted diseases and HIV/AIDS. Education programmes should be implemented that inform refugee women of their rights and responsibilities under international and national laws. These programmes should use an array of media techniques to reach the women in a culturally and linguistically appropriate manner.

In order to ensure that reforms continue, improvements are needed in the collection of data on refugees, with particular attention to collecting sex and age disaggregated statistics on all refugees in camps and urban areas alike. A specific focus on those who spontaneously settle, including those with irregular status, would help to ensure that all refugee women find adequate legal and physical protection.

Susan F. Martin is the Donald G. Herzberg professor emerita of international migration at Georgetown University. She was the founder and first director of the Institute for the Study of International Migration at Georgetown. A long-time expert on immigration and refugee policy, she came to Georgetown after serving as the executive director of the US Commission on Immigration Reform. Professor Martin was also the director of research and programs at the Refugee Policy Group, a Washington-based centre for analysis of US and international refugee policy and programs. She is author of *International Migration: Evolving Trends from the Early Twentieth Century to the Present, A Nation of Immigrants* and *Refugee Women* among other publications.

Notes

My thanks to Emily Oehlsen, who provided invaluable research assistance.

1. Female genital cutting refers to the removal of part or all of a girl's external genitalia, and, in a more radical version (infibulation), the stitching up of the vaginal opening.
2. These include camp coordination and management; child protection; education; food security and agriculture; health; housing, land and property; humanitarian mine action; livelihoods; nutrition; protection; shelter, settlement and recovery; water, sanitation and hygiene; and humanitarian operations support sectors.
3. These include adolescent girls; elderly women; woman and child heads of households; girls and women who bear children of rape, and their children born of rape; lesbian, gay, bisexual, transgender and intersex (LGBTI) persons; separated or unaccompanied children; women and men involved in forced and/or coerced prostitution; child victims of sexual exploitation; persons in

detention; persons living with HIV; persons with disabilities; and survivors of violence.

4. This is not to say that involvement of women in food distribution automatically reduces diversion. There have been recurrent complaints, for example, about diversion of food from the Sahrawi refugee camps in Algeria despite the involvement of women leaders in distribution (UNHCR 2005). By contrast, the author evaluated WFP food deliveries to camps along the Thai–Cambodian border in 1986 after the policy had been changed to require distribution to women in response to allegations of diversion to the military; all reports indicated a greatly reduced level of diversion, although women reported that they still had to pay a food 'tax' to the resistance forces that controlled many of the camp operations.

5. As early as 1996, the author interviewed women who had been attacked and raped while collecting firewood in the Dadaab vicinity. When asked why their husbands or older sons did not accompany them, the women responded that their male relatives would be killed if they were to venture so far from camp.

Bibliography

Brown, T. 2012. 'Post-Primary Education Dilemmas in Protracted Refugee Situations', in F.E. McCarthy and M.H. Vickers (eds), *Refugee and Immigrant Students: Achieving Equity in Education*. Charlotte, NC: Information Age Publishing, pp. 189–203.

Dryden-Peterson, S. 2011. *Refugee Education: A Global Review*. Geneva: UNHCR.

Edwards, A. 2010. 'Transitioning Gender: Feminist Engagement with International Refugee Law and Policy 1950–2010', *Refugee Survey Quarterly* 29(2): 21–45.

Fiddian-Qasmiyeh, E. 2010. '"Ideal" Refugee Women and Gender Equality Mainstreaming in the Sahrawi Refugee Camps: "Good Practice" For Whom?', *Refugee Survey Quarterly* 29(2): 64–84.

Fitzgerald, MA. 1998. 'Firewood, Violence Against Women, and Hard Choices in Kenya.' Washington, DC: Refugees International.

Freedman, J. 2012. 'A Gendered Protection for the "Victims" of War: Mainstreaming Gender in Refugee Protection', in A. Kronsell and E. Svedberg (eds), *Making Gender, Making War: Violence, Military and Peacekeeping Practices*. New York: Routledge, pp. 137–53.

Hajdukowski-Ahmed, M., N. Khanlou and H. Moussa (eds). 2008. *Not Born a Refugee Woman: Contesting Identities, Rethinking Practices*. New York and Oxford: Berghahn Books.

HRW (Human Rights Watch). 2000. 'Seeking Protection: Addressing Sexual and Domestic Violence in Tanzania's Refugee Camps'. New York.

Hyndman, J. 1998. 'Managing Difference: Gender and Culture in Humanitarian Emergencies', *Gender, Place & Culture: A Journal of Feminist Geography* 5(3): 241–60.

———. 2004. 'Mind the Gap: Bridging Feminist and Political Geography through Geopolitics', *Political Geography* 23(3): 307–22.

IASC (Inter-Agency Standing Committee). 2005. 'Guidelines for Gender-Based Violence Interventions in Humanitarian Settings: Focusing on Prevention of and Response to Sexual Violence in Emergencies'. New York.

———. 2015. 'Guidelines for Integrating Gender-Based Violence Interventions in Humanitarian Action: Reducing risk, promoting resilience and aiding recovery'. New York.

Inter-Agency Working Group on Reproductive Health in Crises. 1999. 'Reproductive Health in Refugee Situations: An Inter-Agency Field Manual'. Geneva.

International Rescue Committee and Women's Refugee Commission. 2013. 'Urban Refugee Research and Social Capital: A Roundtable Report and Literature Review'. Geneva.

Olivius, E. 2014. '(Un)Governable Subjects: The Limits of Refugee Participation in the Promotion of Gender Equality in Humanitarian Aid', *Journal of Refugee Studies* 27(1): 42–61.

OAU (Organisation of African Unity). 1974. 'Convention Governing the Specific Aspects of Refugee Problems in Africa', adopted by the Assembly of Heads of State and Government at its Sixth Ordinary Session. Entry into Force, 20 June 1974.

Turner, S. 1999. 'Angry Young Men in Camps: Gender, Age and Clas Relations among Burundian Refugees in Tanzania', *New Issues in Refugee Research*, Working Paper No. 9.

UK Asylum and Immigration Tribunal. 2000. 'Immigration Appellate Authority (UK): Asylum Gender Guidelines'. Retrieved 1 November 2000, from http://www.unhcr.org/refworld/docid/3ae6b3414.html.

United Nations. 1986. 'Report of the World Conference to Review and Appraise the Achievements of the United Nations Decade for Women: Equality, Development and Peace', Nairobi, 15–26 July 1985. New York.

UN General Assembly. 2002. 'Investigation into Sexual Exploitation of Refugees by Aid Workers in West Africa', 11 October 2002, UN Document A/57/465.

UNHCR. 1990. 'UNHCR Policy on Refugee Women'. Geneva.

———. 1991a. 'Guidelines on the Protection of Refugee Women'. Geneva.

———. 1991b. 'Mainstreaming Gender in the Humanitarian Response to Emergencies', IASC Working Group XXXVI Meeting, 22–23 April 1991.

———. 1996. 'Handbook on Voluntary Repatriation: International Protection'. Geneva.

———. 2002a. 'Guidelines on International Protection: "Gender-Related Persecution" and "Membership of a Particular Social Group" within the Context of Article 1A(2) of the 1951 Convention and/or its 1967 Protocol Relating to the Status of Refugees'. Geneva.

———. 2002b. 'Learning for a Future: Refugee Education in Developing Countries'. Geneva.

———. 2005. 'Inquiry Report INQ/04/005'. Geneva. Retrieved 14 March 2017 from http://moroccoonthemove.com/wp-content/uploads/2014/02/UNHCR-Inquiry-Report-on-Diversion-of-Food-Aid-in-the-Tindouf-Camps-2005.pdf.

———. 2008a. 'Handbook for the Protection of Women and Girls'. Geneva.

——. 2008b. 'Corporate Gift Highlights Sanitation Problems Faced by Female Refugees'. *News Stories.* Retrieved 28 April 2008 from http://www.unhcr.org/4815db792.html.

——. 2011. 'Global Trends 2010: 60 years and still counting'. Geneva.

——. 2013. 'UNHCR's Dialogues with Refugee Women: Progress Report on Implementation of Recommendations'. Geneva.

——. 2014. 'Food Shortages Trigger Truancy in South Sudan Camps'. *News Stories.* Retrieved 11 June 2014 from http: //www.unhcr.org/539841fd9.html.

UNHCR Executive Committee. 1991. 'Refugee and Displaced Women and Children'. E/RES/1991/23, ECOSOC Resolutions, 30 May 1991.

——. 2002b. 'UNHCR Policy on Refugee Women and Guidelines on Their Protection: An Assessment of Ten Years of Implementation'. New York.

——. 2006. 'Beyond Firewood: Fuel Alternatives and Protection Strategies for Displaced Women and Girls'. New York.

2

Victims of Chaos and Subaltern Sexualities?

Some Reflections on Common Assumptions about Displacement and the Prevalence of Sexual and Gender-Based Violence

Simon Turner

Introduction

According to UNHCR's strategy paper on 'Action against Sexual and Gender-Based Violence' (SGBV),

> [a]ll persons of concern, including refugees, asylum seekers, returnees, stateless persons and internally displaced persons, suffer disproportionally from SGBV, not only as a form of persecution and at the outbreak of a conflict but also during flight and displacement. (UNHCR 2011: 6)

A number of other reports and policy papers similarly stipulate the link between displacement and the enhanced risks of sexual and gender-based violence. A core assumption seems to be that conflict and displacement lead to social disintegration and hence an unleashing of male, sexual violence. It appears as if high levels of violence haunt refugee camps, that men perpetrate this violence and that women and girls are disproportionately the victims of this violence, and that the violence appears to have a sexual form.

This chapter questions the main assumptions behind many of these studies, policy papers and programmes, and argues that we cannot assume refugee societies to be sites of social and moral decay, neither can we assume violence to be pathological or the result of unbridled (black) masculinity. Despite their good intentions to assist refugees and victims of conflict, such assumptions about sexual and gender-based violence tend to be based on, as well as reproduce, orientalist and neocolonial representations of sexualities and violence in the Global South. It is not my intention to trivialize the extent of violence or the pain that the victims of violence must endure for many years after the act of violence. However, if we are to understand the mechanisms of violence in refugee camps and other conflict situations, it is necessary to go beyond normative assumptions. Apart from such assumptions on violence obscuring our understanding of the mechanisms of violence, they may also add harm to damage because they reinforce gender and race stereotypes, constructing the male refugee of colour as a threat to humanitarian care and human rights.

This chapter explores how violence in refugee settings is represented in humanitarian discourse. I argue that assumptions about the nature of social life in camps merge with racial assumptions about masculinities producing certain understandings of violence. These understandings of violence are based on an assumption that conflict and displacement inevitably cause social and moral deterioration, and that without culture and norms to structure society, nature takes over and male violence and sexuality is unleashed. I argue that these assumptions draw on neocolonial and orientalist discourse. Finally, I show how humanitarian discourse on sexual violence differs in contexts of armed conflict and in contexts of displacement and refugee camps. The chapter will rely on a critical reading of publications by refugee scholars, relief agencies, and activists in a broad analysis of how sexual violence is framed in humanitarian discourse.

Understanding Sexual and Gender-Based Violence in Humanitarian Discourse

At present, UNHCR, NGOs and many refugee studies scholars seem to be heavily preoccupied with violence in general and gender-based violence in particular in refugee settings. Numerous reports, studies, special issues, recommendations, documentation systems, policy papers and toolkits address the issue (UNHCR 2003, 2011; UNHCR, UNFPA, UNICEF and IRC 2010). Although they often suggest that gender-based violence is taboo and shameful for the victims, and hence most probably underreported (Stark and Ager 2011; Anani 2013: 76–77), it appears that the issue receives substantial attention in humanitarian circles. Critically, and with reference to the Democratic Republic of Congo, Eriksson Baaz and Stern draw attention to the currency of this form of violence when they argue that 'it is sexual violence that has drawn the lion's share of attention, especially among "outside" observers' (Eriksson Baaz and Stern 2013: 5–6).[1]

Given the amount of attention, one might wonder how prevalent gender-based violence is in situations of displacement. Interestingly, very few studies have been made on the prevalence of the phenomenon, as most of the policy-oriented literature is concerned with finding solutions and with evaluating the policy initiatives that have been put in place so far (Hynes and Cardozo 2000; Annan and Brier 2010; Horn 2010). They take for granted that gender-based violence is particularly rife in situations of displacement, and they take it as a common point of departure rather than something that needs to be explored. To illustrate, in an article on 'Sexual Violence against Refugee Women' in the *Journal of Women's Health & Gender-Based Medicine*, the authors claim:

> Throughout the world, one in every three women has been beaten, coerced into sex, or otherwise abused during her lifetime. Women are particularly vulnerable during times of disintegration of social structures or flight from war-torn countries. Refugees and internally displaced women are especially vulnerable to gender-based violence during armed conflict, during flight from that conflict, and in refugee camps. (Hynes and Cardozo 2000: 819)

Another systematic review of sexual violence among female refugees estimates that 'approximately one in five refugees or displaced women in complex humanitarian settings experienced sexual violence' (Vu et al. 2014: 1). Neither of these reports makes reference to any evidence for these figures. This is, in other words, the starting point and a general assumption of many studies on the topic, as if the figures in themselves make the issue more important. According to a recent study by Stark and Ager, which tried to assess the prevalence of sexual and gender-based violence through a systematic review of all available prevalence studies, very few such studies exist and it is almost impossible to compare them or make any claims at a general level (Stark and Ager 2011). The international community's data consist of what they term 'incidence reports', namely site visits, field investigations and so forth. And while such incidence reports may prove to be useful for legal documentation and criminal investigation, they give no picture of the prevalence of the problem (ibid.: 127).

The data on who commits the violence also appear to be weak. Stark and Ager conclude that there is a greater risk of violence in the home than gender-based violence committed by armed groups (ibid.: 130). There is, in other words, very weak evidence to prove that gender-based violence should be more prevalent in refugee situations. Instead the violence is conjured up through commonsense assumptions about violence in situations of crisis and disorder. To be fair, the studies are not about the prevalence of GBV, but simply need the figures to emphasize the importance and gravity of the issue – the logic being that the more prevalent the issue, the more important it seems to be and hence the more pressing is the need to act on behalf of the victims.

The argument that this chapter is making is not that there is no increase in GBV during conflict or in refugee camps. Rather, it questions the assumptions that there is such an increase. Furthermore, it explores why such assumptions are so widespread and how they relate to other assumptions about gender, race and human nature in crises.

Sexual Violence due to Social Disorganization?

Exploring gender-based violence is of course about more than quantifying and classifying. Explaining why and how gender-based violence takes place is at least as important as estimating its prevalence. Here, too, the literature falls short (with a few marked exceptions such as Annan and Brier 2010; Eriksson Baaz and Stern 2013). Rather than exploring how gender-based violence relates to displacement or why gender-based violence occurs in refugee camps, most publications are concerned with what to do about it. Rather than exploring possible causes, causality is assumed and often this causality is implicitly based on the notion of social disintegration.

Social disintegration serves as a more or less explicit explanatory framework in a number of studies. For instance, in a special issue of the policy-oriented publication *Forced Migration Review* on sexual violence, the fact that sexual violence is somehow more widespread not only in times of conflict but also in situations of displacement, is repeated again and again – although the evidence is rarely put forward. In the words of Manuel Carballo, executive director of the International Centre for Migration, Health and Development (ICMHD), '[i]t is becoming clear that there is something in the chaos and social disorganisation of all types of humanitarian disaster that opens the door to the pathology of sexual violence' (Carballo 2007: 10). Sexual violence is, in other words, perceived as a symptom of a societal pathology, caused by chaos and humanitarian disaster. In a 2013 article on the Syria crisis in *Forced Migration Review*, Ghida Anani, director of ABAAD-Resource Center for Gender Equality, explores '[d]imensions of gender-based violence against Syrian refugees in Lebanon'. The article is indicative of the kind of argument often put forward in such publications. She agrees that 'there is no quantitative data in respect to violence against women' (Anani 2013: 76) but continues suggesting that 'many displaced Syrian women and girls report having experienced violence, in particular rape'. Although she does not claim to explore the reasons behind these (possibly) higher incidences of gender-based violence, she claims that '[m]any newly arrived women and girls are living in unplanned and overcrowded refugee settlements, with minimal privacy and compromised safety' (ibid.). The assumption here is that crowding and 'unplanned' living areas provoke sexual violence.

Another reason for the presumed high incidences of sexual and gender-based violence that is often alluded to in the literature – although never substantiated through empirical evidence – is that traditional social networks in communities and families have been disrupted by conflict and displacement, and that this results in lack of protection for women and girls. Also more scientific publications, such as the above-quoted study on the prevalence of gender-based violence by Stark and Ager, rely on such assumptions. The authors open their article with the following words: 'Many of today's conflicts displace masses of people and result in women's and children's exposure to violence, family separation, and splintering of community solidarity, shattered trust' (Stark and Ager 2011: 127).

A similar view is portrayed in an article on conflict-driven violence against girls in Africa by Florence Tercier Holst-Roness, the Women and War Advisor for the International Committee of the Red Cross (ICRC), who argues:

> Children's vulnerability (and girls' in particular) increases drastically when the traditional protection afforded them by their families and communities is disrupted by displacement or separation. In such circumstances, girls – but also boys – are all too often exposed to threats or acts of violence. (Holst-Roness 2007: 26)

In the above-mentioned Forced Migration Review, Carballo makes similar claims, albeit in more dramatic language: 'Rape, sexual abuse and exploitation prosper wherever there is disorganisation, an absence of structure and lack of hope' (Carballo 2007: 10). He claims that lack of social structure and organization inevitably leads to the evils of sex, violence and exploitation. Intuitively his claim makes sense to the reader; he draws a Hobbesian picture of a world where nature rules if not kept at bay by the sovereignty of the Leviathan. However, there are a number of assumptions in the statement that need to be disclosed. First, we may question the general Hobbesian assumption about human nature. Are humans usually prone to sexual abuse if not under some organizational structure? And can the opposite be claimed; that exploitation and sexual abuse do not take place in organized societies? We have only to mention cases of paedophilia in the Catholic Church and the systematic violence and abuse that takes place in institutions like the army, gangs and prisons to see that such acts also take place in highly organized structures.

Furthermore, Carballo, Stark and Ager, and others assume that conflict and displacement inevitably cause a breakdown of social institutions. During the Cold War, the US federal government invested heavily in disaster research, exploring amongst other things, what might happen to society in the case of a massive disaster. The authorities feared that a disaster might lead to general demoralization and social breakdown. However, by the 1960s research had established that this was not the case and that disaster victims adapt well to the situation (Tierney, Bevc and Kuligowski 2006: 58). Ethnographic research in refugee camps similarly shows that although life is indeed precarious in the camp, and although old social structures may in some cases be challenged, social structures do not collapse, just as new ones emerge (Turner 2004a; Horst 2006; Holzer 2012; Lecadet 2014). Even the violence that does occur in refugee camps is not merely a pathological symptom of the breakdown of social and cultural order. Violence is vested in social meaning; it shapes social and political order (Turner 2010: 107–31; Jansen 2011: 81–121) and may be perceived as a means of resistance (Holzer 2012; Lecadet 2014).

As I will argue below, much of the discourse on sexual and gender-based violence has an orientalist edge to it, as it is the oriental (or rather African) 'other' who is assumed not to be able to live in such situations of presumed chaos. Wartime narratives from the two world wars in Europe are not about rape, disorganization, absence of structure or gender-based violence. They are about strengthened community, family loyalty and individual heroism. The assumed connections between conflict, displacement and (sexual) violence do not apply to Europe or North America, it seems.

Young Men as and at Risk

Dominant discourses on sexual and gender-based violence in conflict and post-conflict situations draw on mainstream perceptions of young men *as* risk and young men *at* risk (Christiansen, Utas and Vigh 2006). In other words, there is a perception that young men are in a transition period where they are *at* risk of falling victim to various temptations such as gang violence, militia engagement, radical Islamism and other violent organizations (Turner 2004b; Honwana 2006). They are perceived to be particularly at risk in vulnerable and precarious situations such as civil war and failed states. Once recruited to these organizations, the young men become a risk to the rest of society, it is assumed, as they act out hypermasculinities (Connell 1995; Large 1997). As Anani explains: 'Lower self-esteem among men because of what being a refugee means, in some cases, leads to a negative expression of masculinity. Violence towards women and children has increased as some men vent their frustration' (Anani 2013: 76). In other words, she argues that the refugee experience challenges local masculinities, resulting in violence towards women.

UNHCR has in the past ten years begun to acknowledge the needs and roles of men and boys in the organization's programming. In its updated strategy on sexual and gender-based violence it argues that conflict and displacement can 'trigger changes in gender roles', exacerbating the incidence of sexual and gender-based violence (UNHCR 2011: 17). In earlier fieldwork, I have also seen that a camp regime can challenge masculinities, with refugees themselves claiming that their women no longer respect them because they can no longer provide for them. 'They think UNHCR is a better husband', the men would say about their wives (Turner 1999: 3). Similarly, in a study on refugee emasculation among Burundian refugees in Tanzania, Barbra Lukunka argues that refugees in camps have little control over their lives and depend on humanitarian agencies. In her words, '[s]uch dependence caused a socio-psychological crisis for refugee men that took the form of a gender identity crisis, specifically, emasculation. In order to reverse the emasculation, refugee men engage in gender-based violence' (Lukunka 2012: 130).

Even though this may be the case in some particular situations, the overall focus on sexual and gender-based violence among humanitarian actors leads to a generalizing assumption about causalities between displacement, masculinity and violence, obscuring other ways in which male refugees react to camp life. Male refugees will often attempt to reverse their perceived emasculation in a number of creative ways (see also Jaji 2009; Kleist 2010). The strategies of recuperating masculinity that I observed in a refugee camp in Tanzania, for instance, rarely blamed women but mostly targeted UNHCR and other men. These strategies could at times be violent, as when competing political parties were fighting for authority over (sections of) the camp – or they could be non-violent, as when men (mis)used the NGOs in the camp to accumulate wealth and power, and hence recognition. Often their struggles to become 'real men' were about proving to other men that they were able to take care of 'their' women.

Stereotypical perceptions of young men as/at risk often have a neo-colonial and orientalist twist; the same aspects that give rise to anxiety and moral panic when it concerns poor, coloured, immigrant youth or youth in the so-called Global South are not perceived as threats when the young men are white, wealthy and from the North. Lack of certainty, lack of place in society and assumed abundant energy/vitality are seen as combining to make a dangerous cocktail when in banlieues of Paris, the streets of Freetown or the rainforests of DRC, while the same aspects are celebrated as virtues of the youth in the West where they are assumed to provide innovation, creativity and change (Turner 2004b). To quote

Eriksson Baaz and Stern, quoting Spivak: '[T]he massive engagement in the plight of Congolese rape survivors offers an illuminating example of the re-enacting of the white wo/man's burden to 'sav(e) brown women from brown men' (Spivak 1988: 297, in Eriksson Baaz and Stern 2013: 11).

A case in point is the reporting of widespread sexual violence in the wake of Hurricane Katrina in New Orleans in 2005, when world media reported incidences not only of general lawlessness and widespread looting but also of violence and numerous rapes – even of a seven-year-old girl – in the Louisiana Superdome, where thousands of the homeless had sought shelter (Younge 2005). These stories of unbridled black sexuality emerged together with stories of man-eating alligators, compounding the Hobbesian dystopia of nature taking over once law and order has been suspended. The arguments are strikingly similar to those put forward by leading humanitarian practitioners when explaining sexual and gender-based violence in situations of forced displacement. Like in the explanations for increased sexual and gender-based violence in the refugee camps, general chaos and lack of order, as well as poor living conditions and overcrowding, were used as reasons for alleged sexual violence in the Louisiana Superdome after the hurricane. The media stories coming out of New Orleans were quickly dismissed as 'disaster myths' (Tierney, Bevc and Kuligowski 2006: 57), reflecting mainstream media representations of 'poor black' sexualities being unleashed in situations of chaos and disorder (Younge 2005).

The narratives about sexual violence in conflict and post-conflict situations in Africa, on the other hand, stand barely unquestioned (with the writings of Eriksson Baaz and Stern as strong exceptions). This may be due to the fact that New Orleans is, after all, 'closer to home', meaning that critical journalism and academia are more prone to question the moral panic in such media representations. A related reason may be that while the media representations of the Superdome were obviously driven by moral panic and racial (and class) prejudice, the representations of chaos in refugee camps in Lebanon and Tanzania are driven by a 'will to help'. The NGOs, activists and scholars working on sexual and gender-based violence in refugee settings are doing so in order to assist those who have been victims of such violence and not in order to strengthen racial prejudice against the 'perpetrators'. However, while the scholars, activists and NGOs engaged in producing these images are neither racist nor prejudiced, their discourse may inadvertently reproduce racial discourse.

Mark Duffield's critique of multiculturalism and its international pendant, developmentalism, may shed light on this apparent paradox (Duffield 1996). He argues that the dominant worldview of development agencies in the 1990s was culturalist-functionalist: 'culturalist' because they, like multiculturalists, believe in difference rather than universal ideas of development; 'functionalist' because they believed that social harmony is the norm in society while conflict and instability are the exception. According to this view, violence is an anomaly and a symptom of cultural disharmony that needs to be resolved. In other words, if conflict is perceived to be an anomaly, rather than linked to structural and political antagonisms, refugees are perceived as symptoms of this pathological situation. In such situations of societies out of equilibrium, social norms are assumed to be out of balance, resulting in moral decay and acts of violence. We may say that according to these interpretations of conflict and displacement a vicious circle occurs where conflict and violence bring imbalance to the social system, which in turn causes more – pathological – violence. In sum, when activists, NGOs and refugee scholars reproduce racial and gender stereotypes, they do so from a point of view of wanting to combat violence and recreate assumed social harmony without having the analytical tools to understand violence in a context of power and politics. The result is that they reproduce racial and gendered stereotypes about the sexual violence of the 'other'.

Sexed and Gendered Stories

In recent studies on the dominant understandings of sexual violence in situations of war, Eriksson Baaz and Stern (2013) argue that there has been a shift from what they call the 'sexed' story to the 'gendered' story; that is a shift from understanding sexual violence as the result of biological sexual drives and violent masculinities to understanding sexual violence as the result of strategic use of rape as a 'weapon of war'. According to Eriksson Baaz and Stern, the present explanation of sexual violence in contexts of armed conflict is that men rape women (and sometimes other men) as a means to humiliate their enemy. They tarnish the women and embarrass the men, who are not able to protect 'their' women. This is a gendered reading of violence, perceiving it as part of a 'strategy', as opposed to a reading of violence as something simply 'natural', resulting from a breakdown of the social (Eriksson Baaz and Stern 2013: 12–42). In my analysis of reports and policy documents on the issue, I found that both 'stories' were being told: namely, that sexual violence is claimed to be a weapon of war while simultaneously arguing that sexual violence is the result of crowding and breakdown of social structures and norms. For instance, in the words of Holst-Roness, '[t]argeting girls, who symbolize the ability to procreate and survive, is a method of demonstrating that they cannot be protected in the absence of their fathers and of bringing "dishonour" upon an entire family or community' (Holst-Roness 2007: 26). In other words, the narrative of 'sexual violence as a weapon of war' is present, but it is, I would argue, overshadowed by a narrative of 'sexual violence as a symptom of social disorganization.'

We may explain this mixing by the fact that conflict and violence are themselves seen as a vicious circle, as mentioned above. While sexual violence may be framed within the 'gendered' story, as Eriksson Baaz and Stern suggest, there is also a widespread perception that conflict and violence – once set in motion and for whatever original reasons – create social disorganization and moral decay, which in turn creates sexual violence, but of the 'sexed' version. In particular when coming to terms with sexual violence in refugee camps, the emphasis is on the latter, as displacement is perceived to be an involuntary forced movement rather than an active choice.[2] The following quotes illustrate how it is assumed that the original, targeted 'gendered' violence morphs into general 'sexed'. 'Many studies have focused on the issue of rape as a weapon of war … Other perpetrators, however, may also include family members, NGOs and humanitarian workers, trusted individuals, or strangers who take advantage of heightened vulnerability' (Vu et al. 2014: 2). 'During both conflict and flight, women are at risk of rape from soldiers, border guards, police and others in authority. Once they arrive in a camp setting, women are at risk from fellow refugees, local residents, and even aid workers' (Hynes and Cardozo 2000: 820). Refugees are, I would argue, perceived to be the passive victims of history rather than the makers of history (see also Nyers 2006; Agier 2008; Turner 2010), and hence the sexual violence that they commit is more likely to be understood within the framework of dysfunctional social networks than as a strategic weapon of war.

Refugees as Victims or Perpetrators?

While Eriksson Baaz and Stern critique common understandings of gun-slinging unemployed young men with bloodshot eyes and high on drugs in Central and West Africa's bloody wars, perceptions of violence and gender are slightly different when the young men become displaced and are recast as innocent victims. If humanitarianism casts refugees as bare, biological life (Agamben 2000), how then does humanitarianism as a universal and universalizing discourse (Agier 2011) account for violence in the refugee camps? Or to put it bluntly: how can victims be perpetrators? I have argued elsewhere that politics and violence disturb the image of the refugee as victim. When, indeed, refugees act violently, the relief agencies pinpoint young men as 'troublemakers' in order to maintain the image of an emasculated, innocent refugee community (Turner 2010: 59–60). In other words, there is a bifurcated construction of refugees in humanitarianism. On the one hand, refugees represent humanity in its purest form as innocent victims with no agency and no responsibility for their fate. This is humanity as feminine, vulnerable and in need of protection. This is also, I have argued, where community as a deep, natural bonding free of personal interests, is assumed to take hold. On the other hand, this picture of bare humanity – stripped of political voice (Malkki 1996) only able to moan in pain (Agier 2010: 33) – also produces the refugees as animal-like (Nyers 2006: 69–97). Having been stripped of any particularities and difference, they no longer have the attributes of men and women; they are more like animals. Being animal-like, they hence also are assumed to be incapable of controlling their animal instincts; reproduction, hunger and violence. Culture is what defines humans as apart from animals, and it controls these instincts and keeps them at bay (Lippit 2008: 1–15), leading to comments such as in the articles quoted above about refugees lacking networks, order and culture to keep sexual violence at bay. In conclusion, the fact that not only are they in situations of war and conflict but also refugees reinforces the image of a population without norms and culture to keep nature's sexual violence under control.

Conclusion

Sexual and gender-based violence appears to be high on the humanitarian agenda. Despite claims that it is overseen and underreported, the number of policy papers, field manuals, reports and articles emerging on the topic is overwhelming. Interestingly, there is very little concrete knowledge on the subject. There are hardly any studies on the prevalence of sexual and gender-based violence in refugee settings, and the difference in methods makes it virtually impossible to gather an overall picture. The qualitative studies that exist on SGBV are more concerned with exploring what has been done and what should be done to tackle it than with exploring how and why it takes place.

I argue that the literature on sexual and gender-based violence does not need evidence in order to 'work', as it rests on assumptions that feed into and reinforce commonsense stereotypes on violence, race, sexuality, gender and displacement. These commonsense assumptions are highly emotional and shape a kind of moral panic, where the audience accepts a number of assumptions without questioning them. One of the central assumptions is that displacement causes social and moral chaos. Secondly, it is assumed that in the lack of social order, male sexualities run amok. Thirdly, there is an orientalist twist to these assumptions, as it is assumed that particularly subalterns cannot deal with this lack of social order. Finally, refugees are assumed to be victims without political subjectivities as violence in refugee settings is perceived to be pathological rather than targeted and instrumental.

On a final note, the lack of evidence-based research is problematic if we are to understand the issue at stake and are to proscribe relevant ways of addressing the problem. More problematic, however, are the ways in which humanitarian discourse on sexual and gender-based violence re-produces racial and gendered stereotypes about displaced persons.

Simon Turner is associate professor at the Centre for Advanced Migration Studies of the University of Copenhagen. His research focuses on gender – in particular masculinities, refugees, refugee camps and humanitarian organizations, ethnic conflict and genocide, diaspora as well as invisibility, secrecy, rumour, and conspiracy theories. He is author of *Politics of Innocence: Hutu Identity, Conflict and Camp.* He is currently engaged in research about, among others, state–diaspora relations, refugee camps and violence.

Notes

1. The danger, they argue, is not only that other types of violence are not recognized or taken account of, but also that it may lead to what they term 'the commercialization of rape'; i.e. when accusations of rape may be made as a means to access services from NGOs or as part of a bargaining strategy (Eriksson Baaz and Stern 2013: 51–55).
2. See Stephen Lubkemann's brilliant analysis of war and displacement in Mozambique for a critique of the assumed victimhood of those who flee violence. He argues that forced immobility may be worse in some cases (Lubkemann 2008).

Bibliography

Agamben, G. 2000. *Means without End: Notes on Politics.* Minnesota: University of Minnesota Press.

Agier, M. 2008. *On the Margins of the World : The Refugee Experience Today.* Cambridge and Malden, MA: Polity Press.

———. 2010. 'Humanity as an Identity and Its Political Effects (A Note on Camps and Humanitarian Government)', *Humanity: An International Journal of Human Rights, Humanitarianism, and Development* 1(1): 29–45.

———. 2011. *Managing the Undesirables: Refugee Camps and Humanitarian Government.* Cambridge and Malden, MA: Polity Press.

Anani, G. 2013. 'Syria Crisis: Dimensions of Gender-Based Violence against Syrian Refugees in Lebanon', *Forced Migration Review* 44: 75–79.

Annan, J., and M. Brier. 2010. 'The Risk of Return: Intimate Partner Violence in Northern Uganda's Armed Conflict', *Social Science & Medicine* 70(1): 152–59.

Carballo, M. 2007. 'An Urgent Issue of Public Health and Human Rights', *Forced Migration Review* 27: 10–11.

Christiansen, C., M. Utas and H.E. Vigh. 2006. *Navigating Youth, Generating Adulthood: Social Becoming in an African Context.* Uppsala: The Nordic Africa Institute.

Connell, R.W. 1995. *Masculinities.* Cambridge: Polity Press.

Duffield, M. 1996. 'The Symphony of the Damned: Racial Discourse, Complex Political Emergencies and Humanitarian Aid', *Disasters* 20(3): 173–93.

Eriksson Baaz, M., and M. Stern. 2013. *Sexual Violence as a Weapon of War? Perceptions, Prescriptions, Problems in the Congo and Beyond.* London and New York: Zed Books.

Holst-Roness, F.T. 2007. 'Conflict-Driven Violence against Girls in Africa', *Forced Migration Review* 27: 26–27.

Holzer, E. 2012. 'A Case Study of Political Failure in a Refugee Camp', *Journal of Refugee Studies* 25(2): 257–81.

Honwana A.M. 2006. *Child Soldiers in Africa.* Philadelphia: University of Pennsylvania Press.

Horn, R. 2010. 'Responses to Intimate Partner Violence in Kakuma Refugee Camp: Refugee Interactions with Agency Systems', *Social Science & Medicine* 70(1): 160–68.

Horst, C. 2006. *Transnational Nomads: How Somalis Cope with Refugee Life in the Dadaab Camps of Kenya.* New York and Oxford: Berghahn Books.

Hynes, M. and B.L. Cardozo. 2000. 'Sexual Violence against Refugee Women', *Journal of Women's Health & Gender-Based Medicine* 9(8): 819–23.

Jaji, R. 2009. 'Masculinity on Unstable Ground: Young Refugee Men in Nairobi, Kenya', *Journal of Refugee Studies* 22(2): 177–94.

Jansen, B. 2011. 'The Accidental City: Violence, Economy and Humanitarianism in Kakuma Refugee Camp, Kenya'. PhD thesis. Wageningen: Wageningen University.

Kleist, N. 2010. 'Negotiating Respectable Masculinity: Gender and Recognition in the Somali Diaspora', *African Diaspora: Transnational Journal of Culture, Economy & Society* 3: 185–206.

Large, J. 1997. 'Disintegration Conflicts and the Restructuring of Masculinity', in C. Sweetman (ed.), *Men and Masculinity.* Oxford: Oxfam, pp. 23–30.

Lecadet, C. 2014. Agamé (Benin): 'Lefeu et la révolte: Le camp comme foyer politique', in M. Agier (ed.), *Un Monde de Camps.* Paris: La Découverte, pp. 129–43.

Lippit, A.M. 2008. *Electric Animal: Toward a Rhetoric of Wildlife.* Minneapolis: University of Minnesota Press.

Lubkemann, S.C. 2008. *Culture in Chaos: An Anthropology of the Social Condition in War.* Chicago: University of Chicago Press.

Lukunka, B. 2012. 'New Big Men: Refugee Emasculation as a Human Security Issue', *International Migration* 50(5): 130–41.

Malkki, L.H. 1996. 'Speechless Emissaries: Refugees, Humanitarianism, and Dehistoricization', *Cultural Anthropology* 11(3): 377–404.

Nyers, P. 2006. *Rethinking Refugees: Beyond States of Emergency.* New York: Routledge.

Stark, L., and A. Ager. 2011. 'A Systematic Review of Prevalence Studies of Gender-Based Violence in Complex Emergencies', *Trauma, Violence, & Abuse* 12(3): 127–34.

Tierney, K., C. Bevc and E. Kuligowski. 2006. 'Metaphors Matter: Disaster Myths, Media Frames, and their Consequences in Hurricane Katrina', *The ANNALS of the American Academy of Political and Social Science* 604: 57–81.

Turner, S. 1999. 'Angry Young Men in Camps: Gender, Age and Class Relations among Burundian Refugees in Tanzania', *New Issues in Refugee Research*, UNHCR Working Paper No. 9. Geneva.

———. 2004a. 'New Opportunities: Angry Young Men in a Tanzanian Refugee Camp', in P. Essed, G. Frerks and J. Schrijvers (eds), *Refugees and the Transformation of Societies: Agency, Policies, Ethics and Politics*. New York and Oxford: Berghahn Books, pp. 94–105.

———. 2004b. *Vrede unge mænd?: globalisering, marginalisering og mobilisering.* Copenhagen: Dansk Institut for Internationale Studier.

———. 2010. *Politics of Innocence: Hutu Identity, Conflict and Camp Life.* New York and Oxford: Berghahn Books.

UNHCR. 2003. 'Sexual and Gender-Based Violence against Refugees, Returnees and Internally Displaced Persons. Guidelines for Prevention and Response'. Geneva.

———. 2011. 'Action against Sexual and Gender-Based Violence: An Updated Strategy'. Geneva.

UNHCR, UNFPA, UNICEF and IRC. 2010. 'Gender-Based Violence Information Management System (GBVIMS)'. http://gbvims.org/.

Vu, A., et al. 2014. 'The Prevalence of Sexual Violence among Female Refugees in Complex Humanitarian Emergencies: A Systematic Review and Meta-analysis', *PLoS Currents* 6.

Younge, G. 2005. 'Murder and Rape – Fact or Fiction?', *Guardian*, 6 September.

3

Refugees, Global Governance and the Local Politics of Violence against Women

Elisabeth Olivius

Introduction

Violence against women has become a priority issue in humanitarian operations, having received immense attention, funding, and programmatic responses in the past decades (Buscher 2010). This chapter explores how violence against women is understood and interpreted in humanitarian policy and practice. How do humanitarian organizations conceptualize the nature of the problem of violence against women; how do they represent its causes and its solutions; and how do they seek to address it in their practical work?[1] The point of departure for this analysis is that it matters what kind of problem violence against women is represented to be, as the understanding of the problem will shape the strategies that are devised to address it and the effects they generate. Therefore, in order to amplify their transformative potential and detect problematic effects, it is important to critically examine current humanitarian representations of, and approaches to, violence against women.[2] In particular, the analysis in this chapter focuses on one representation of violence against women that has gained prominence in humanitarian policy discourse as well as in humanitarian field practices. In this representation, violence against refugee women is interpreted as an expression of the 'underdevelopment' or 'backwardness' of refugee communities and societies. Consequently, the solution to violence against women in refugee situations is seen as lying in efforts by humanitarian organizations to change the social, cultural and religious norms and practices of refugee communities so as to 'develop' them. As the analysis presented in this chapter demonstrates, such approaches have generated conflicts and resistance from refugees, and sometimes obstructed rather than advanced struggles for refugee women's rights. In this chapter, I trace the representation of violence against women as an expression of underdevelopment in four central international humanitarian policy texts, and examine how it has informed humanitarian efforts to address violence against women in refugee camps in Bangladesh and in Thailand. The case studies are based on fifty-eight interviews with humanitarian workers employed by United Nations (UN) agencies, non-governmental organizations (NGOs), and, in the case of Thailand, refugee community-based organizations (CBOs) engaged in the delivery of humanitarian aid and services to the refugee camps. The interviews were conducted by the author in 2010 and 2011.

Next, I situate the representation of violence against women as an expression of underdevelopment in the context of an emerging understanding of humanitarianism as one aspect of a broader project of liberal global governance. Moreover, I review previous literature that has shown how this representation is mobilized in the global governance of refugees. This is followed by the analysis of the humanitarian policy texts and the cases of Bangladesh and Thailand. In conclusion, I discuss some of the local effects that are generated by policies and programmes informed by an understanding of violence against refugee women as an expression of underdevelopment.

Violence against Women in Refugee Communities: An Expression of Underdevelopment?

In the post-Cold War period, a classical humanitarian concern with saving lives without regard to the political categories to which they belong has gradually lost ground to a new conception of the purpose of humanitarian aid. An increasingly powerful strand of contemporary humanitarianism has aligned itself with a broader project of liberal global governance, which aspires to prevent conflicts and emergencies and build stable, effective and legitimate states in the global peripheries (Barnett 2005; Chimni 2009). To this end, humanitarian agencies work to promote development, human rights and democracy as they respond to the needs of displaced and emergency-affected populations. The purpose of humanitarian aid is thus not merely to sustain life and relieve suffering, but to take advantage of emergency situations as strategic opportunities for the development of emergency-affected regions and communities (Reid 2010). In this view, humanitarian aid should lay the foundation for rebuilding better, more developed and more stable societies after conflicts and emergencies.

In this context, discourses of gender and gender equality occupy an increasingly central position in representations of humanitarianism's developmental and peacebuilding responsibilities. The United Nations High Commissioner for Refugees (UNHCR) states that 'gender equality and the empowerment of women and girls are essential preconditions for development, peace, and security' (UNHCR 2008: 22), and the main body for coordination of humanitarian action within the UN, the Inter-Agency Standing Committee (IASC), describes crisis situations as a 'window of opportunity' for reshaping social and cultural structures towards gender equality, and thereby achieve sustainable development (IASC 2006: 6). Conversely, the existence of violence and discrimination against women in refugee communities is taken as evidence of the inability of these communities to govern themselves, and of their need to be reformed and improved through external interventions (Reeves 2012). Violence against women is framed as an expression of underdevelopment, and gender equality is constructed as one aspect of a liberal norm package that prescribes the correct path towards development, stability and security.

This construction of women's roles and status as an indicator of cultural advancement is not new but can be traced in colonial discourses (Narayan 1997: 17) as well as in modernization theories of development (Rostow 1960). A result of this construction is that women from 'traditional' or 'underdeveloped' societies are seen as victims of their culture and thus in need of expertise, protection and salvation from the 'modern' world (Parpart 1993: 451). In the global governance of refugees, notions of gender inequality and violence have frequently been mobilized to construct societies and regions from where refugees originate as dysfunctional, underdeveloped and in need of intervention. In contrast, states that receive or provide aid to refugees can play the part of the morally superior, modern, and gender-equal saviour (Macklin 1995).

In Western media campaigns, refugee women have often been portrayed as 'exotic, vulnerable other', and graphic tales of sexual violence, female genital mutilation and gender discrimination have been deployed to remind donors and decision makers why these 'other' women need aid and protection (Parpart 1993: 36; Macklin 1995; Baines 2004). Moreover, research has demonstrated that when refugee women present themselves as 'particularly vulnerable and helpless' when applying for asylum in Western states, they have a higher rate of acceptance (Razack 1995, 1996). As Oswin argues, in such asylum processes a 'trajectory from backward Third World culture to evolved First World culture is constructed whereby the refugee woman (as universal female subject) wants to become the liberal, rational, autonomous subject by gaining entry to Western countries' (Oswin 2001: 352). The portrayal of refugee women as victims of barbaric underdeveloped cultures sustains a binary between 'refugee-producers' and 'refugee-receivers' that allows Western states to appear as superior and reaffirms global relations of power. In addition, it obscures the fact that violence and discrimination against women goes on within refugee-receiving states as well (Macklin 1995: 264).

In humanitarian aid to refugees at sites such as refugee camps, attempts to promote gender equality are frequently represented as efforts to develop and modernize the refugee population (Olivius 2013, 2014). Gender equality programmes, Grabska argues, are part of an 'accelerated modernity project' that aims to teach refugees how to be 'modern' (Grabska 2011: 88). This project is further linked to the rebuilding of better, more developed societies when refugees return. This is pointedly expressed by an NGO representative in Kakuma refugee camp in Kenya, explaining the role of workshops that provide training on topics such as gender equality, human rights and peacebuilding: 'Through these workshops, we can educate them [refugees] and make them a bit more civilised, modern. They will be ready to go back to their countries and rebuild them' (idem.: 86). In a study of approaches to domestic violence in Dzaleka refugee camp in Malawi, Carlson observes that attempts to address violence against refugee women often take the form of a preoccupation with changing and developing the 'other', based on a view of African societies as flawed (Carlson 2005). However, refugee women do not remain passive in the face of disempowering representations. Just as women seeking asylum, women in refugee camps may portray themselves as 'victims' in accordance with humanitarian expectations in order to facilitate their own survival and improve their situation. While these images of refugee women do perpetuate their marginalization, actively using them to navigate a situation marked by severe constraints is a particular form of agency that is made available to refugee women through humanitarian representations of them as victims of barbaric cultures (Freedman 2010: 600–601).

Gender, Violence and Development in Humanitarian Policy Discourse

In humanitarian policy frameworks on gender and violence, representations of violence against women as a problem rooted in the cultures and traditions of refugee communities are very prevalent. In this section, I make this point by drawing on examples from four key humanitarian policy documents. These texts represent the current normative framework regarding gender and violence in relation to refugee situations, and function as crucial modes for the dissemination of knowledge about gender and violence, and about how it should be addressed. Produced by central humanitarian policy makers within the UN system, these texts inform the work of UN agencies as well as international and national NGOs.

The first two texts are produced by the UNHCR, the central organization of the international refugee regime: 'Guidelines for the Protection of Women and Girls' (UNHCR 2008) and 'Sexual and Gender-Based Violence against Refugees, Returnees and Internally Displaced Persons: Guidelines for Prevention and Response' (UNHCR 2003). The other two texts are produced by the IASC, a forum comprising all major UN humanitarian agencies and many NGOs, which has been a major source of humanitarian policy making on gender. The broad spectrum of actors represented means that policies adopted by the IASC represent widely endorsed principles and positions. The IASC policy texts are the 'IASC Gender Handbook for Humanitarian Action', entitled 'Women, Girls, Boys and Men: Different Needs – Equal Opportunities' (IASC 2006) and the 'Guidelines for Gender-Based Violence Interventions in Humanitarian Settings' (IASC 2005).

In humanitarian policy discourse, violence against women is represented as a problem that is primarily rooted in the social and cultural norms and practices of the society where it occurs, but which may be exacerbated by the upheaval and insecurity of emergency situations. As stated by the IASC, 'gender inequality and discrimination are the root causes of GBV', but because emergencies often result in women and children 'being separated from family and community supports' they become particularly vulnerable to violence in such contexts (IASC 2005: 4; see also UNHCR 2008: 125). According to the UNCHR, '[t]he root causes of sexual and gender-based violence lie in a society's attitudes towards and practices of gender discrimination, which place women in a subordinate position in relation to men' (UNHCR 2003: 21). While this statement is arguably valid for every society, an analysis of humanitarian policy reveals that there are certain types of society that are seen as constituting fertile ground for violence against women. The social, cultural and political structures in which gender inequality is described as rooted are specifically to be found in societies that are traditional, religious, illiterate, and male dominated: 'Cultural and religious practices which violate women's and girls' rights tend also to be underpinned by low literacy levels, limited female presence in public life, lack of information, and a certain cultural fatalism surrounding such practices' (UNHCR 2008: 28). Passing references to subsistence agriculture (IASC 2006: 59) and repeated mentions of 'harmful traditional practices' such as female genital mutilation, honour killings, forced early marriage, and widow inheritance as forms of SGBV (IASC 2005: 1, 8) make it clear that these texts implicitly describe societies located in regions outside of the global North/West on the margins of the global economy.

Further, a representation of the societies or communities that are affected by conflicts and disasters as 'less developed' is intertwined with a representation of refugee women as vulnerable and 'at risk'. The policy texts predominantly describe refugee women as passive subjects in need of humanitarian protection. Assumptions that women in crisis-affected societies are uneducated, unaccustomed to interact with authorities, and 'relegated to the domestic sphere' by husbands who refuse to let them leave the home underline the image of women's passive and subjugated position (UNHCR 2008: 17, 39). This representation of refugee women supports the image of crisis-affected societies as traditional, oppressive and in need of reform.

An understanding of violence against women as a problem of underdevelopment or cultural backwardness consequently points to solutions in the realm of social and cultural change in refugee communities. The UNHCR declares interventions aiming to transform sociocultural norms as being one of the key objectives in an effective prevention strategy (UNHCR 2003: 34), and further states that 'preventing sexual and gender-based violence thus requires changes in gender relations within the community' (UNHCR 2003: 35). In order to achieve such changes, a host of informational and educational interventions are recommended, such as 'printed posters and pamphlets; poster contests; drama, song and dance; radio discussions; public service announcements; video presentations; slogans printed on T-shirts; training workshops; and informal discussions' (UNHCR 2003: 36). In addition, it recommends engaging refugee children and youth in education and awareness campaigns, because 'changing knowledge, attitudes and behaviour is easier when you begin early' (UNHCR 2003: 39). The IASC further emphasizes the importance and developmental potential of educational interventions in emergency situations:

> Education in emergencies provides a channel for conveying health and survival messages, [and] for teaching new skills and values, such as peace, tolerance, conflict resolution, democracy, human rights and environmental conservation. An emergency can be a time to show and teach the value of respecting women, girls, boys and men equally in society. (IASC 2006: 50)

Thus, conflicts and disasters provide opportunities for interventions in presumably less peaceful and less developed societies. The promotion of women's and girls' equality and participation is an important aspect of a project of societal transformation in which humanitarian organizations can play a vital role. Notably, values of peace, tolerance, democracy and human rights are assumed to be absent in societies affected by crisis. The education provided by humanitarian organizations during times of crisis thereby provides the foundation for the improvement of these societies. Violence and discrimination against women are constructed as symptoms of underdevelopment that can be overcome through the transformation of traditional societies into modern, democratic societies with liberal values. The violence and abuse that women in crisis-affected communities suffer thereby legitimizes humanitarian organizations' engagement in a project of development and cultural modernization that reaches far beyond a traditional perspective on what the humanitarian mandate for delivering impartial, non-political and life-saving relief encompasses.

Bangladesh: Educating 'Backward' Refugees

For decades, Bangladesh has hosted large numbers of Rohingya refugees who have fled ethnic discrimination and repeated waves of violent persecution in Western Burma. Today, twenty-eight thousand Rohingya are recognized as refugees and are living in two camps in Eastern Bangladesh, Kutupalong and Nayapara. In addition, however, an estimated two hundred thousand Rohingya who are denied recognition as refugees live in villages and in camp-like settlements in the vicinity of the official camps (UNHCR 2013). Humanitarian aid is provided to refugees in the official camps by UN organizations, such as the UNHCR and the World Food Program (WFP), and a small number of international and national NGOs. The Bangladeshi government does not authorize provision of humanitarian aid to unregistered refugees (Refugees International 2011).

When discussing the situation in the Bangladeshi refugee camps, humanitarian workers generally describe the discrimination and abuse of women as serious and pervasive problems. Rates of violence against women are high; girls drop out of school at puberty to avoid harassment and violence, both in school and on their way to school; and women's participation in decision making and their access to income and services is far from equal to that of male refugees. The causes of gender inequality and problems such as violence against women and unequal outcomes in terms of access to services and resources are overwhelmingly interpreted as being rooted in the culture of the refugees. The Rohingya community is described as a traditional, conservative and religious society, where the norms, beliefs and practices of the refugees are the main obstacles to increased gender equality. Explaining the lack of gender equality to me, an NGO representative remarked:

> The refugee's religious and social background from their ancestral homes across the border is a very backward-looking, orthodox Muslim society.

> The society, social norms, culture and tradition is the root, and they bring this along. It is a very male-dominated society. And an uneducated society in general … The scenario of gender inequality is very clear if you only walk through the camps. Women are less active, women are restricted to the house, the domestic sphere … It is a less progressive society. (Male NGO worker, Cox's Bazar, 12 March 2011)

Gender inequality and violence against women is constructed as inherent in Rohingya culture. By contrast, gender equality is constructed as a characteristic of 'modern' societies, and the low status of Rohingya women is seen as an indicator of the generally 'traditional' and backward nature of Rohingya society. Representations of women as vulnerable and in need of protection from their own cultural context are pervasive in the humanitarian aid operation in Bangladesh. Discussing the risks that refugee women face in the camps, a UN employee concluded, with some despair, that 'it's a dangerous world here for women' (Female UN worker, Cox's Bazar, 7 March 2011). Moreover, descriptions of Rohingya women as subjugated, uneducated and easily manipulated frequently feature in narratives linking violence against women with the underdevelopment and backwardness of Rohingya society:

> Women are controlled by men: traditional leaders, religious leaders. They need permission from husbands, fathers, brothers, to do everything. And they accept it: they are uneducated, illiterate; they believe what they are told. Beliefs in ancestors and spirits are used to motivate rules and constraints on women. They believe it; it is in their religious views. And many think it is normal that husbands beat their wives, and they accept it. (Male NGO worker, Cox's Bazar, 3 March 2011)

When violence against women among the Rohingya refugees in Bangladesh is overwhelmingly understood and represented as a problem of underdevelopment, humanitarian aid interventions seeking to address it are consequently constructed as part of a process of modernization and development of refugee culture and subjectivities. Humanitarian aid is represented as the carrier of modern, progressive norms of gender equality and human rights that should be used to counter inequality and abuse inherent in Rohingya culture.

In order to do so, various forms of awareness-raising and education on gender issues and human rights are the main strategies to address violence against women; constructed as a problem rooted in cultural norms and attitudes, humanitarians seek to combat violence against women through interventions targeting the beliefs and subjectivities of refugees. Workshop sessions on issues such as domestic violence and early marriage target different groups of refugees such as women, men, youth, and religious leaders. Social workers offer individual and family counselling in cases of domestic violence, and billboards throughout the camps display messages promoting women's rights and condemning violence against women. Campaigns and events such as the celebration of International Women's Day and the '16 Days of Activism against Gender Violence' also contribute to the dissemination of messages encouraging changed beliefs and practices in the refugee population with regards to issues of family, marriage, education and decision making.[3]

A representative of an NGO conducting training programmes and counselling on SGBV in the camps argues that to overcome this problem, 'there has to be strong behavioural change advocacy' (Male NGO worker, Cox's Bazar, 14 March 2011). In the narrative of this humanitarian worker, it is clear that to 'raise awareness' means to change the attitudes, beliefs and behaviour of refugees. A government official responding to the question of how SGBV can be stopped answers in similar terms: 'They have to be properly educated! Without education it cannot be done' (Male government official, Cox's Bazar, 10 March 2011). In a long-term process of cultural change, refugees must be re-educated to become gender-equal:

> One of the main reasons for gender inequality is the cultural conservatism, so I think that it does take time to sort of change those ideas, starting especially with the younger boys in school, and even the younger girls to empower them. So, I think it starts with education ... the humanitarian organizations, we usually hold various campaigns, education, seminars ... so those kinds of educational campaigns I think help. (Male UN worker, Cox's Bazar, 7 March 2011)

The opportunity to be educated about gender equality by humanitarian organizations in the camps is constructed as a window of opportunity for the modernization and development of Rohingya society. Explaining why refugees should appreciate and embrace humanitarian gender-equality interventions, a government official exclaimed: 'Why not accept development?' (Male government official, Cox's Bazar, 10 March 2011). Further, a Bangladeshi NGO worker suggested that the reason gender inequality and violence are perpetuated in the camps is that the Rohingyas do not take part in the development of their host country, as they are, in his view, 'not interested in learning anything' (Male NGO worker, Cox's Bazar, 10 March 2011). However, as the refugees' exclusion from the host society is clearly a result of government policies, the suggestion that the Rohingya are choosing to isolate themselves from new social and cultural influences is highly questionable.

While education on women's rights may also have empowering and transformative effects, the suggestion that the solution to violence against women means to 'accept development' and abandon 'backward' Rohingya culture is not well received by all segments of the refugee community.

Humanitarian programmes that seek to address violence against women through awareness-raising practices have generated resistance within the refugee community, sometimes taking violent forms. One notable example in recent years was the aggressive reaction of some refugee leaders towards a drama group put together to raise awareness about sexual and gender-based violence through their performances. The drama group was initiated by an international humanitarian organization, and the cast members were refugees – two of them women. Neither the messages of the drama group nor the choice of drama as a medium of communication were well received by parts of the refugee community, or by its leaders:

> Because there's a lot of conservative members that were against their mes-
> sages of SGBV prevention, and also against dramas ... and certainly against
> females doing that kind of thing, there was actually a big backlash against
> them, and there was a bit of a confrontation; there were death threats, things
> like that ... and pretty open stuff. Even by one, in an open forum of refugee
> leaders, one refugee leader who was, yeah, quite a troublemaker, I guess
> you could say, openly said that if they perform again then ... he made some
> violent threats against them. And this was openly in front of all the refugee
> leaders ... so there was a big backlash against that group. (Female UN
> worker, telephone interview, 31 May 2011)

Fortunately, nothing did happen to the members of the drama group. The country representative of the responsible organization put pressure on the Bangladeshi official in charge of the daily running of the camp, stating that he would be held responsible if anything happened to the members of the controversial drama group. In addition, refugee leaders were told that they too would be held responsible if anything happened. The drama group did continue, but in a less public manner.

Another expression of rejection of humanitarian organizations' programmes has been the tearing down of posters condemning violence against women at a community centre in one of the camps. On this occasion, there was also a sign outside the centre depicting a rapist in chains, being arrested by police. This attempt at communicating that rape is a criminal act was apparently perceived as provocative. A UN employee reported that 'some of the refugee men had been throwing rocks at it [the sign] ... they really don't like the idea of, not all of them, but some of them, really don't like this idea of being thrown into jail for violence against women' (Male UN worker, Cox's Bazar, 7 March 2011).

Some refugees oppose the activities of humanitarian organizations due to fear that they are 'turning our women into Westerners' (Female UN worker, Cox's Bazar, 6 March 2011) – which is perhaps not surprising when humanitarian workers clearly express that, to them, combating violence against women means educating refugees to abandon the 'traditional' beliefs and practices of Rohingya culture. In the context of the Bangladeshi camps, this is deeply unhelpful to any effort to actually improve the situation of Rohingya women. Rohingya refugees have experienced discrimination and persecution on the basis of their claims to ethnic, religious and cultural specificity in Burma and in exile, and many refugees are therefore sensitive to 'attacks' on their culture, and consider it important to preserve what they perceive as traditional features of group identity. When humanitarian organizations represent violence against women as a weapon in a cultural conflict, it effectively eliminates the space for feminist politics from within the refugee community, and makes any proposition for change in women's roles and opportunities deeply sensitive (Narayan 1997: 12–13; 2000: 85). When humanitarian organizations represent gender equality as external to Rohingya culture, there is a risk that refugees who advocate women's rights or challenge existing gender norms are seen as cultural traitors. This situation can actually be quite dangerous for refugee women, as one former UN employee recognized as she reflected on her work in the Bangladeshi camps:

> [B]y trying to protect and promote women's rights, you might inadvertently place them at more risk or make them more vulnerable. I think that was the biggest challenge; there was this constant balancing act between, you know, trying to advance their rights and create more opportunities for them, but at the same time ensuring that there wouldn't be a negative backlash against them. So there was actually one incident where a woman had attended our women's support group meetings, and she ended up going back home and her husband beat her for leaving the home. (Female UN worker, telephone interview, 30 August 2011)

In effect, the strong emphasis on Rohingya culture as the cause of violence against women and on changes in refugee attitudes, norms, behaviours and identities as the way to overcome violence has mobilized issues of gender and violence as weapons in a cultural conflict. The significance of unequal gender relations as cultural boundary markers has increased as gender equality is represented by humanitarian workers as a symbol of 'developed', or Western, culture. Furthermore, the humanitarian preoccupation with developing and educating the Rohingya community draws attention away from what humanitarian organizations could actually do to address violence through their own programming. For example, despite the fact that UNHCR committed to individually registering all refugee women in 2001, this is still not being done in Bangladesh (UNHCR 2001). In the refugee camps in Bangladesh, each family receives a ration book that makes them eligible for food aid (Female UN worker, Cox's Bazar, 7 March 2011). This practice has severe implications for a woman who wishes to leave an abusive husband, as doing so would leave her with no identity documents and with no access to food resources that are essential for her survival. Further, in none of the camps are there any safe houses or other places where women who have been subjected to violence can seek physical safety. Instead, women have to rely on family and friends in acute and potentially life-threatening situations (Male NGO worker, Cox's Bazaar 10 March 2011). Thus, beyond a narrow focus on awareness-raising and cultural change, there is plenty of room for humanitarian organizations to respond more effectively to violence against refugee women in the Bangladeshi camps.

Thailand: Challenges to Humanitarian Approaches to Violence

The first refugee camps on the Thai side of the Thai–Burmese border were established in 1984 when Karen refugees fled across the border following advances in the counterinsurgency campaign of the Burmese military against the Karen National Union (KNU) (Lang 2002). The number of refugees in refugee camps in Thailand has since steadily increased, and currently there are nine camps along the border hosting 130,000 refugees, a majority belonging to the Karen minority (The Border Consortium 2013). Humanitarian aid and services are mainly provided by a network of about fifteen national and international NGOs, and the UNHCR is present in a primarily monitoring role. Further, services are coordinated and partly implemented by the refugees themselves through a system of community-based camp management (Banki and Lang 2008; Thompson 2008).

Evidence collected by humanitarian organizations indicates that rates of violence against women, in particular domestic violence, are rather high in the Thai camps (Female NGO worker, Mae Sot, 1 November 2010). However, several refugee CBOs have long carried out their own work to raise awareness about and prevent violence against women, and to support and assist survivors of such violence. The unique model for refugee self-governance and the strong refugee civil society in the camps have made refugee women's organizations well placed to play a significant role in efforts to combat violence against women in the camps. In particular, the Karen Women Organisation, with a membership exceeding 49,000 women (KWO 2014), is running a large number of programmes ranging from women's rights advocacy and awareness-raising to legal management of cases of violence and support to women survivors (KWO 2013). Thus, in these refugee camps an agenda to address violence against women has by no means only been driven by external humanitarian actors.

However, despite the existence of influential actors such as the KWO who work to stop violence against women from within the refugee community, humanitarian workers recurrently express assumptions that violence is rooted in the particular beliefs and practices of the Karen community. The camps are frequently described as 'traditional societies' where male dominance is upheld because the refugees are 'clinging to their traditions and values' (Male NGO worker, Mae Sot, 19 November 2010), and the causes of gender inequality and violence are represented as originating in 'the cultural mindsets of the refugees themselves' (Group interview, male and female UN workers, Mae Sot, 28 April 2010). Consequently, in order to stop violence against women, humanitarian workers argue that the Karen refugee community needs to move forward and adopt more modern ideas and behaviours. Karen culture is represented as pathological and inherently productive of violence against women, and therefore interventions by humanitarian organizations are perceived as necessary to address it. Whether CBOs can really carry out legitimate and effective work in this area is questioned because they are part of the culture that humanitarian actors perceive as being the root of the problem:

> Some of the women working in these organizations have the same perceptions ... so for someone who is working to promote what we call international standards and guiding principles, from my point of view I see that as problematic. You know, some of them are part of this culture that is accepting of some forms of SGBV against women. (Female UN worker, Mae Sot, 11 November 2011)

As these quotes illustrate, many humanitarian workers describe the refugee camps as 'traditional' societies and cultures that are inherently prone to and accepting of violence against women. Therefore, international humanitarian ownership and control over programmes addressing violence against women is seen as required to ensure that they adhere to international human rights and rule of law standards. Conversely, the work of CBOs is often not recognized as an important and essential contribution to combating violence against women in the camps. In effect, international humanitarian actors are represented as the only legitimate authorities on issues around gender and violence.

From the perspective of CBOs working in the area of violence against women, lack of recognition of their work has resulted in failure to consult and coordinate with CBOs on the part of international humanitarian actors. Instead, international humanitarian actors have been seen as bypassing and duplicating the work of refugee actors, giving rise to considerable anger and frustration, as expressed by this CBO representative:

> NGOs who work in the camps, we don't want them to come and duplicate or overlap our work. They come with a bag of money and we have to work with very scarce resources. Instead of duplicating they should support what's already there, but it's not like that ... we want NGOs to work on women's

issues, gender equality, GBV, but they should consult with us and avoid duplication. For example, on GBV there have been misunderstandings and
conflict, and it creates confusion for the victims. Different NGOs get money
for GBV and then they all work on that issue, but there is, for example, no
one covering gaps in health services. It seems to depend on the donors' interests rather than the needs. (Female CBO worker, quoted in Olivius 2011)

Conflicts over ownership between international humanitarian organizations and refugee community actors have in recent years been especially
manifested in the case of the SGBV committees. The SGBV committees
were established in the early 2000s by the UNHCR as groups composed
of refugees with the purpose of coordinating prevention of, and responses
to, violence against women in the camps. However, by this time refugee
women's organizations had already been running their own programmes
for years, raising awareness and seeking to prevent violence, managing
cases, and assisting survivors. With time, the role of the UNHCR-initiated
SGBV committees expanded, and increasingly overlapped and duplicated
the work of refugee CBOs (Male NGO worker, Mae Sot, 29 October 2010;
Female UN worker, Mae Sot, 11 November 2011). As one humanitarian
worker explained, the UNHCR and other humanitarian organizations involved in the SGBV committees considered this duplication to be legitimate because they did not trust that international standards would be met
if they did not establish and control their own SGBV programmes (Male
UN worker, Bangkok, 26 April 2010). As a result, as an NGO worker critical of this process put it, refugee community actors were 'elbowed out by
these external actors' (Male NGO worker, Mae Sot, 29 October 2010).

As the conflict escalated, the various actors involved in programmes
in the area of violence against women sought to resolve the issue through
clarifying and delineating the responsibilities of different organizations in
a series of meetings during the spring of 2010. However, these meetings
were marked by mutual distrust and uncompromising positions. Refugee
actors argued for the right of the community to govern itself, while international organizations questioned their ability to do so according to their
understanding of international standards (Male NGO worker, Mae Sot, 29
October 2010). Finally, the refugee governing authority, the Karen Refugee
Committee (KRC), declared that the SGBV committees originally initiated
by the UNHCR would be incorporated in the administrative structures of
the KRC (KRC 2010). In response to the perceived lack of recognition for
the role of CBOs and the failure of international organizations to respect
and coordinate with CBOs, this was clearly a move to reassert refugee ownership over efforts to address violence against women in the camps. Still,
the status of the SGBV committees and the roles of different actors in relation to each other remained contested, and relationships remained strained
after this episode (Female UN worker, Mae Sot, 11 November 2011).

Notably, there was no dispute regarding the existence of violence against women in the camps, or the need for efforts to address it. Rather, in the case of the SGBV committees and more generally, refugee representatives have challenged the idea that international humanitarian organizations are the only, or the most legitimate, authorities on defining and promoting gender equality and addressing violence against women in the refugee camps. Humanitarian organizations are described as lacking the necessary contextual knowledge to appreciate what forms of change and what pace of change is possible and desirable:

> We try to upgrade our situation, and some change is happening. But the NGOs and the Western world are not satisfied with our progress. But we try our best ... They think our progress is too slow. But we know our own problems better than outsiders ... NGO expectations are higher than our reality. They need to learn more about our community and our culture, and be more patient. (Male CBO worker, Mae Sot, 5 November 2010)

When humanitarian gender equality interventions are perceived as insensitive to the cultural context, they have frequently sparked anger and resistance in the refugee community. In the context of Karen nationalism and the strong position of refugee organizations in camp management, great value is placed on community ownership and the community's right to define their own needs and priorities. While CBOs frequently emphasize that the presence of international humanitarian actors and the introduction of a discourse of human rights and international standards in the camps have strengthened the role of refugee advocates for gender equality and provided legitimacy to their work of addressing violence against women, they also make clear that many opportunities for cooperation have been missed due to the arrogance of international actors:

> We feel like [name of humanitarian organization] never recognizes our work and our leadership, our long-standing struggle and the results of that struggle. They never consult with us ... they have never been to our office. They do not really trust us. They say we are not neutral. Even though we have not worked together yet and they have not approached us, there are already accusations being made. (Female CBO worker, quoted in Olivius 2014)

In the case of Thailand, a view of violence against women as originating in the 'traditional' culture of the refugees has caused international actors to disregard the potential for fruitful alliances with refugee women's organizations and other CBOs. Instead of recognizing the value of actors pushing for change from within the refugee community, many humanitarians operate with a default assumption that refugee actors represent oppressive and unequal social and cultural systems and thereby constitute obstacles to women's rights. In effect, this understanding of the problem of violence against women in refugee communities delegitimizes the work of CBOs, and denies refugees a role as agents in the transformation of their own communities.

Conclusions

Violence against women is unquestionably a serious problem in many refugee situations. The attention and funding devoted to this issue by humanitarian organizations and donors in recent decades is therefore well needed, and constitutes an important step towards ensuring women's rights more effectively in contexts of emergency and displacement. However, this chapter has argued that it matters how the issue of violence against women is understood, represented and acted upon by humanitarian organizations. In humanitarian policy and practice, violence against women is frequently represented as an expression of the 'underdevelopment' or 'backwardness' that allegedly characterizes refugee communities. As this chapter has demonstrated, this representation of violence against women generates a number of problematic effects when it informs and shapes humanitarian responses.

Firstly, this representation obscures the fact that refugee situations in the Global South are by no means the only context where violence against women constitutes a pervasive and serious form of abuse and oppression. Discursively linking violence against women to 'underdevelopment' renders the fact that violence also occurs in 'developed' societies invisible, and prevents an analysis that connects violence against women, its causes and its possible solutions across different positions in global structures of power and inequality. Instead, violence against women is used to reproduce cultural hierarchies and racist images of non-Western peoples, and legitimates top–down interventions to 'develop' their societies along the lines of liberal global governance. Further, representing gender equality as a step towards Western modernity is seriously counterproductive for efforts to combat violence against refugee women. As the case of Bangladesh shows, mobilizing gender equality as a symbol of Western culture turns it into a weapon of cultural conflict, leading to resistance that makes it even more difficult to challenge or even discuss gender relations and gender violence in a fruitful way. Naturally, if the concept of gender equality is deployed as a tool of cultural domination it is is unlikely to be embraced by the community that is being intervened upon. Moreover, the preoccupation with changing refugee culture draws attention away from other strategies to combat violence against women that could provide effective avenues to address refugee women's needs. While violence against women is not a problem specific to refugee situations, factors such as weak legal protection and access and lack of physical security may increase levels of violence in such circumstances, and could therefore usefully receive more attention in humanitarian responses.

Secondly, assumptions that violence against women is inherent in refugee cultures, and that international humanitarian actors are the only ones who can identify and address such violence, causes humanitarians to neglect the important role of local actors. As the case of Thailand illustrates, even when there are influential refugee actors who actively work to address violence against women, humanitarian organizations fail to recognize their contribution and fail to build mutual and respectful alliances with them. This leads to refugee distrust and resistance to the work of humanitarian organizations, and causes great potential for fruitful partnerships to be wasted. Simplified binaries where refugee communities are seen as the cause of gender discrimination and violence, and humanitarian organizations as its remedy, are not only inaccurate but serve to reify images of a morally superior humanitarian 'self' and a backward refugee 'other' in the humanitarian aid encounter. The consequences of these images are that refugee actors are excluded, delegitimized, and denied a role as agents of social change in their own communities.

To a troubling extent, humanitarian policy and practice represent efforts to address violence against women in refugee communities as a case of 'white men', and women, 'saving brown women from brown men' (Spivak 1994: 93). To better contribute to positive changes that affect the lives of refugee women, humanitarian organizations need to move beyond such stereotypes, be less certain of their own moral advantage, and approach the women they seek to protect and the communities they seek to change in a more respectful manner. As an NGO worker in Thailand aptly points out, successfully promoting gender equality in refugee situations 'requires a lot of listening and a big heart' (Male NGO worker, Mae Sot, 29 October 2010). Acknowledging the legitimacy and importance of local refugee actors as agents of change, rather than 'traditional' peoples to be changed, is critical if the transformative potential of humanitarian efforts to combat discrimination and violence against refugee women is to be realized.

Elisabeth Olivius holds a PhD in political science from Umeå University, Sweden. Her past research has examined how, and with what effects, gender equality norms are constructed, interpreted and applied in the global governance of refugees. Her current research explores the role of diasporic women's organizations in peacebuilding in Myanmar/Burma.

Notes

1. In humanitarian lingo, violence against women is generally termed 'sexual and gender-based violence' (SGBV) or 'gender-based violence' (GBV). These terms theoretically allow for the possibility that men and boys may be victims of violence based on their gender, although in practice forms of violence targeting men and boys – for example, forced military recruitment – largely remain invisible in humanitarian policy and practice. The terms SGBV and GBV are principally used to describe violence against women, as women and girls are also assumed to constitute the majority of victims of SGBV in refugee situations (UNHCR 2003: 10). For clarity, in this chapter I use the term 'violence against women'.
2. As the focus of this chapter is to examine how violence against women is represented and approached in humanitarian policy and practice, it does not assess or discuss the actual prevalence of violence against women in refugee situations per se.
3. The '16 Days of Activism against Gender Violence' is an international campaign originating from the first Women's Global Leadership Institute sponsored by the Center for Women's Global Leadership in 1991. '16 days of Activism against Gender Violence' has been recognized in UNHCR programming since 2007. The 16 days begin on 25 November, International Day against Violence against Women, and end on 10 December, International Human Rights Day, in order to symbolically link violence against women and human rights, and to emphasize that such violence is a violation of human rights (UNHCR 2007).

Bibliography

Baines, E.K. 2004. *Vulnerable Bodies: Gender, the UN, and the Global Refugee Crisis.* Aldershot, Hants and Burlington, VT: Ashgate.

Banki, S., and H. Lang. 2008. 'Protracted Displacement on the Thai–Burmese Border: The Interrelated Search for Durable Solutions', in H. Adelman (ed.), *Protracted Displacement in Asia: No Place to Call Home.* Aldershot: Ashgate, pp. 59–82.

Barnett, M. 2005. 'Humanitarianism Transformed', *Perspectives on Politics* 3(4): 723–40.

Buscher, D. 2010. 'Refugee Women: Twenty Years On', *Refugee Survey Quarterly* 29(2): 4–20.

Carlson, S. 2005. 'Contesting and Reinforcing Patriarchy: Domestic Violence in Dzaleka Refugee Camp', *Refugee Studies Centre Working Paper Series* No. 23.

Chimni, B. 2009. 'The Birth of a "Discipline": From Refugee to Forced Migration Studies', *Journal of Refugee Studies* 22(1): 11–29.

Freedman, J. 2010. 'Mainstreaming Gender in Refugee Protection', *Cambridge Review of International Affairs* 23(4): 589–607.

Grabska, K. 2011. 'Constructing "Modern Gendered Civilised" Women and Men: Gender Mainstreaming in Refugee Camps', *Gender & Development* 19(1): 81–93.

IASC (Inter-Agency Standing Committee). 2005. 'Guidelines for Gender-Based Violence Interventions in Humanitarian Settings'. Geneva.

——. 2006. 'Women, Girls, Boys and Men: Different Needs – Equal Opportunities. IASC Gender Handbook for Humanitarian Action'. Geneva.

KRC (Karen Refugee Committee). 2010. 'Newsletter & Monthly Report June 2010'. Retrieved 2 June 2014 from http://www.burmalibrary.org/docs09/KRCMR-2010-06.pdf.

KWO (Karen Women Organisation). 2013. 'KWO 2011–2012, Two Year Update'. Retrieved 13 May 2014 from http://karenwomen.files.wordpress.com/2013/10/kwo-2011-2012-update.pdf.

——. 2014. 'Karen Women Organisation – Who We Are'. Retrieved 9 May 2014 from http://karenwomen.org/about/.

Lang, H. 2002. *Fear and Sanctuary: Burmese Refugees in Thailand*. New York: Cornell Southeast Asia Program.

Macklin, A. 1995. 'Refugee Women and the Imperative of Categories', *Human Rights Quarterly* 17(2): 213–77.

Narayan, U. 1997. *Dislocating Cultures: Identities, Traditions and Third World Feminism*. London and New York: Routledge.

——. 2000. 'Essence of Culture and a Sense of History: A Feminist Critique of Cultural Essentialism', in U. Narayan and S. Harding (eds), *Decentering the Center: Philosophy for a Multicultural, Postcolonial, and Feminist World*. Bloomington: Indiana University Press, pp. 80–100.

Olivius, E. 2011. 'Humanitarian Assistance and the Politics of Gender Equality: A Study of Refugee Camps on the Thai–Burma Border', in H. Fjelde and K. Höglund (eds), *Building Peace, Creating Conflict? Conflictual Dimensions of Local and International Peacebuilding*. Lund: Nordic Academic Press, pp. 149–68.

——. 2013. 'Gender Equality and Neo-liberal Governmentality in Refugee Camps', *St Antony's International Review* 9(1): 53–69.

——. 2014. '(Un)Governable Subjects: The Limits of Refugee Participation in the Promotion of Gender Equality in Humanitarian Aid', *Journal of Refugee Studies* 27(1): 42–61.

Oswin, N. 2001. 'Rights Spaces: An Exploration of Feminist Approaches to Refugee Law', *International Feminist Journal of Politics* 3(3): 347–64.

Parpart, J.L. 1993. 'Who is the "Other"?: A Postmodern Feminist Critique of Women and Development Theory and Practice', *Development and Change* 24(3): 439–64.

Razack, S. 1995. 'Domestic Violence as Gender Persecution: Policing the Borders of Nation, Race, and Gender', *Canadian Journal of Women and the Law* 8: 45–88.

——. 1996. 'The Perils of Storytelling for Refugee Women', in W.M. Giles and P. van Esterik (eds), *Development and Diaspora: Gender and the Refugee Experience*. Ontario: Artemis Enterprises, pp. 164–75.

Reeves, A. 2012. 'Feminist Knowledge and Emerging Governmentality in UN Peacekeeping', *International Feminist Journal of Politics* 14(3): 348–69.

Refugees International. 2011. 'Bangladesh – The Silent Crisis'. Retrieved 10 June 2014 from http://www.refugeesinternational.org/policy/field-report/bangladesh-silent-crisis.

Reid, J. 2010. 'The Biopoliticization of Humanitarianism: From Saving Bare Life to Securing the Biohuman in Post-interventionary Societies', *Journal of Intervention and Statebuilding* 4(4): 391–411.

Rostow, W. 1960. *The Stages of Economic Growth: A Non-Communist Manifesto.* Cambridge: Cambridge University Press.

Spivak, G.C. 1994. 'Can the Subaltern Speak?', in P. Williams and L. Chrisman (eds), *Colonial Discourse and Post-Colonial Theory: A Reader.* Hemel Hempstead, Herts: Harvester Wheatsheaf.

The Border Consortium. 2013. 'Refugee and IDP Camp Populations: September 2013'. Retrieved 14 November 2013 from http://theborderconsortium.org/camps/2013-09-sep-map-tbc-unhcr.pdf.

Thompson, S. 2008. 'Community-Based Camp Management', *Forced Migration Review* 30: 26–28.

UNHCR. 2001. 'Respect Our Rights: Partnerships for Equality. Report on the Dialogue with Refugee Women'. Geneva.

——. 2003. 'Sexual and Gender-Based Violence against Refugees, Returnees and Internally Displaced Persons: Guidelines for Prevention and Response'. Geneva.

——. 2007. 'Guterres Vows UNHCR to Counter Violence against Women'. Retrieved 10 June 2014 from http://www.unhcr.org/474ae9524.html.

——. 2008. 'Handbook for the Protection of Women and Girls'. Geneva.

——. 2013. 'UNHCR Bangladesh Fact Sheet September 2013'. Retrieved 5 November 2013 from http://www.unhcr.org/50001ae09.html.

4

'Solidarity' and 'Gender Equality' as a Discourse of Violence in Sweden

Exclusion of Refugees by the Decent Citizen

Emma Mc Cluskey

Introduction

The Swedish national myth of 'solidarity' regarding refugee resettlement, as well as exceptionalism regarding gender equality and models of 'good parenting', ignores the way in which such an identity can enable biopolitical categorizations of the population at an anthropological level in day-to-day life. In terms of asylum policy regarding the ongoing civil war in Syria, Sweden's 'generous' position vis-à-vis other European states has enabled the nation to regain its 'moral superpower' image of the 1970s. As the European Union (EU) member state receiving by far the most Syrian refugees[1] and the first European nation to offer automatic permanent residency and a right to family reunification to all Syrians arriving at the border, the Swedish population is managed by what I call a 'governmentality of righteousness'; they are happy in the knowledge that they are most decent, most progressive and 'ahead of the pack' (Towns 2002: 163). Such a governmentality ensures, however, that open criticism to refugee policy goes against what it means to be a 'good citizen' and, aside from the far right, is thus confined to more hidden everyday practices and 'sugar-coated' exclusionary discourses; a 'good taboo' is firmly in place.

This chapter looks at the repertoire of available actions of citizens enabled by this governmentality of righteousness by focusing on a refugee residence facility in Oreby,[2] a village in Southern Sweden in which around one hundred Syrians and twenty refugees of other nationalities are housed. It argues that the culture of righteousness engendered by the national myth of moral exceptionalism, though benevolent, created the conditions of possibility for a more open manifestation of biopolitical violence through the mechanism of a 'moral panic' (Cohen 1980) after the shooting of a Somali refugee by police in the north of the country. Though largely deemed in bad taste to speak openly of the Arab men as violent, lecherous or risky, this chapter argues that the way in which volunteers, as well as the wider village community, individualized and reappropriated discourses of 'decency' and 'gender equality', paradoxically served to enable practices of violence towards those refugees who were considered 'less' gender equal and 'less' decent. This manifested itself in the hierarchical categorization of refugees, with the non-Arabs favoured most by these various actors for living their life the 'proper, Swedish way', and the further segregation and isolation of the Syrian women who were criticized for their modes of dress, modes of behaviour, and for failing to take care of their children properly. The chapter goes on to examine how, although seemingly insignificant, these microscopic biopolitical practices adopted enough uniformity and homogeneity to serve as a base upon which to legitimately reconfigure obligations of 'decency' and to outwardly articulate the Syrian men as a threat to the well-being of the village.

Driven by an unease at the seeming contradiction between official policy towards refugees and asylum seekers in Sweden and the banal, day-to-day practices of exclusion at an anthropological level, I was determined to adopt an anthropological methodology in order to bring these everyday practices to the very forefront of my study. I thus spent around ten months, between February and December 2013, working as a volunteer and translator with a newly formed, ad hoc non-governmental organization working with newly arrived asylum seekers and refugees named 'Friends of Syria', whereby I conducted around fifty interviews of both volunteers and refugees, and undertook around four hours per day of participant observation.[3] In conceiving of violence using Foucault's notion of the biopolitical (c.f. Foucault 2004, 2010), this chapter thus differs from other publications within Refugee Studies discussing violence towards refugees, which focus primarily on physical harm. Instead, the notion of violence describes the more subtle methods through which human life is ranked and hierarchized, and how a refugee never enjoys a full social existence, no matter how caring and benevolent the prevailing regime. By examining my fieldwork through the lens of 'gender', the chapter demonstrates the way in which the concept was used by the villagers to legitimize some of these diffuse and indirect practices of violence towards the refugees.

The chapter thus proceeds in four sections. It first examines the Swedish national myth of 'moral exceptionalism', investigating how notions of solidarity with the vulnerable became intertwined with notions of gender equality and exceptionalism regarding 'good parenting' to form a very specific and much cherished narrative of modernity and progress. The following section examines how this national myth and its reappropriations function as a particular type of governmentality, a code of conduct that nonetheless allows for a fair amount of 'wiggle room' in its manifestations at a day-to-day level. In turning to an anthropological approach, the third section examines how notions of righteousness prohibited any open criticism of the refugees amongst the Oreby dwellers, and confined opposition to a more hidden realm. In an attempt to address this veiled unease, I look at how a group of volunteers took it into their own hands to 'empower the Syrian women', resulting in biopolitical hierarchizations of the refugees. After reports of a violent incident involving a Somali refugee in the north of Sweden, the chapter then goes on to discuss how notions of 'decency' were reconfigured and this hidden unease was able to be publicly articulated to the Syrians in the form of a warning. The chapter concludes by examining the notions of 'violence' brought into being by the story of the refugees in Oreby, arguing that more overt, biopolitical forms of violence are underpinned by the more subtle, seemingly insignificant practices of a 'caring' biopolitics.

Sweden as Morally Exceptional: The Re-emergence of the National Myth

> At a time when refugees are not treated so well … how nice to find people with such a heart! Sweden opens its borders, organizes language classes, gives economic assistance, and offers paths to join society. They do not have anyone in a concentration camp or other such terrifying places. That's an example we can present to the world; because in reality it is the only country that is doing that, and is not filled with misery. It is not thereby suffering. This is the message Sweden presents: Open your heart to your brother, your sister, who has nowhere to live, to work, to sleep peacefully. (Pope Francis, February 2014)[4]

The everyday practices of stigmatization, exclusion and marginalization around the Syrian refugees in the village of Oreby, southern Sweden, need to be understood in the larger context of the Swedish national myth of 'moral exceptionalism'. This somewhat stereotypical Swedish narrative could be seen to be resurrected from the ashes in September 2013, when the Swedish government took the unilateral decision to grant all Syrians arriving at the border refugee status and permanent residency. As national myths go, the moral exemplar standard story is one that is much cherished. The move received cross-party support within Parliament – with the exception of the nationalist party, the Sweden Democrats, who occupy twenty seats – and was greeted largely positively in the mainstream press.[5] Sweden's resettlement programme with the United Nations High Commissioner for Refugees (UNHCR) saw Sweden resettle the second highest absolute number of refugees from camps within third countries, and placed absolutely no 'integration potential criteria' through which to filter seemingly 'undesirable' categories of refugee, which led to the country being held up as exemplar by both the UNHCR and the various NGOs and networks that work on resettlement (for an overview, see for example Perrin and McNamara 2013).

As was the case with Olof Palme's 'Moral Superpower' government during the Cold War, 'solidarity' can thus be seen to be Sweden's raison d'état once more. Certainly, Sweden's exceptional position within the EU has enabled the Swedish political elite to act as spokespersons for a more humane EU asylum policy, whereby it actively encourages the fifteen member states that currently have no resettlement agreement with the UNHCR to adopt one, and presses the remaining member states to take a larger quota.[6]

This 'morally exceptional' national myth extends way beyond ideas of 'openness' towards refugees, and is of course rather multifaceted, embracing more general ideas of 'modernity' and 'progressiveness' as a number of Swedish ethnologists and political scientists have discussed. This 'humanitarian reason' (Fassin 2012) or, in the Swedish case, extending so-called 'solidarity' inside to 'solidarity' outside, sees Sweden as having one of Europe's most generous developmental aid budgets, a historically 'moral' foreign policy in relation to its long-established non-aligned security doctrine and its traditional active stance against foreign interventions (Nilsson 1991; Lawler 1997, 2007; Dahl 2006), as well as having some of the most advanced environmental policies (Lawler 2005).

One of the most important characteristics of this Swedish national myth is the notion of Sweden as the most 'gender equal' state. Indeed, it is now somewhat of a cliché to see Sweden feature at or near the top of various indices that rank gender equality.[7] In her study of how 'immigrant identity' in Sweden is constructed vis-à-vis 'gender equal' Swedes, Ann Towns (2002) points out how it was not until the mid-1990s and its entry to the EU, however, that saw Sweden position itself at the forefront of this issue. The country was ranked as the most gender equal state in two indices that materialized in 1995, the Gender Related Development Index (GDI) and the Gender Empowerment Measure (GEM).

Absorbed into this idea of gender equality are also notions of Sweden as an ideal place to be a parent; aside from the famed generous Swedish parental leave, images of the latte-sipping, metrosexual man about town with a pushchair in tow is a stereotype that is actively propagated by various 'nation-branding' platforms. A core element of Sweden's 'soft' power in the international arena is thus centred around this gender equality in parenting. *Visit Sweden* (2014), an English language website promoting the country, for example, proudly states that 'the modern Swedish man is a feminist', citing the promotion of gender equality or *jämställdhet* from childhood onwards, to the extent that many kindergartens now use gender-neutral pronouns. Ideas of Swedish masculinity within this national myth are thus closely bound up with being 'modern' and 'enlightened'.

Sweden is thus regarded as somewhat peculiar in that regard, in that its particular moral logic is distinct. For Swedish historians Bergrenn and Trägårdh (2009), Swedish gender equality has enabled the most authentic expression of 'love' within relationships. The conjunction of the ideals of independence with economic equality and social solidarity is seen to have been institutionalized by a 'radical alliance' between the Swedish state and the individual, which has served to balance the 'deep existential desire' for personal freedom and, simultaneously, social cohesion, liberating the individual from what they call unequal and patriarchal forms of community, such as the bonds to family, church and charities.[8]

The National Myth as a Governmentality of Righteousness

What is important about the functioning of the Swedish national myth, its reappropriations, re-enactments and reproductions, and what is crucial with regard to the story of the Syrian refugees in the country is not the idea of 'moralism', but rather the notion of 'exceptionality'. This extends from openness to refugees and migrants to, perhaps in a more banal and immediate manner, moral superiority regarding the advancement of gender equality and accompanying notions of a more enlightened masculinity. As a bastion of moral superiority, Sweden positions itself as most progressive and most modern. And indeed, this type of identification engenders a sense of pride. Being certain in one's rightness, especially regarding the rightness of one's group, or indeed one's nation, is a comfortable and secure space. Everyday life, with all its uncertainties, is easier when you are secure in the knowledge that you are one of the 'good guys', or at least 'better' than the others.[9]

In talking about the life of the Swedish national myth, it is important to understand therefore that 'myth' in this context does not mean something false or fictional. Tilly (1994, 1999, 2002) was perhaps the most forceful proponent of the performative element of nationhood; what he saw enacted through the 'standard story', emphasizing the cultural homogeneity and cohesiveness of the nation. The importance of these performances for Tilly was their external audience: 'disciplined, stereotyped public demonstrations of nationness' were crucial for recognition and the granting of statehood (Tilly 1999: 179). In their 'performance', these national myths nonetheless take on a life of their own, enabling certain self-understandings of what it means to be a member of a particular nation. People gain an identification with certain stories as being 'theirs' and hence collude to some extent with the production of these fictions, even to the extent that they are recognized as a sort of background condition of everyday life (Calhoun 1997).

In its permeation throughout society, it is useful to follow the language of the late Foucault and think of this national myth and its reappropriations as functioning therefore as a particular type of 'governmentality', what I have labelled the 'governmentality of righteousness'. This concept allows us to illuminate the art of control by complicating the question of state power, relating state governance to the subjugation and subjectification of individuals. In this respect, such an exercise of power in the form of government can be differentiated from simple coercion or domination. Nikolas Rose best articulated this distinction: 'To dominate is to ignore or to attempt to crush the capacity for action of the dominated. But to govern is to recognize that capacity for action and to adjust oneself to it' (Rose 1993: 4).

To think in these terms enables us to have a better understanding of how the type of power relations engendered within these 'standard stories' are in part salutary; certainly, the productive element of this banal, everyday myth-making sees the generation of self-governing, happy and contented subjects.[10] Foucault labelled 'biopolitical' the type of power concerned with managing not only life, death, health and illness, but also everything to do with what we call 'lifestyle', including the social, cultural and environmental conditions under which we live (Dean, cited in Selby 2007: 333). To think in this way also enables us to envisage how notions of obedience, discipline, obligation and 'taboo' are also in play. To criticize the 'morally exceptional' narrative, with regards to both refugee policy and notions of gender equality, would be to criticize something that everybody has agreed to be unequivocally 'good'; particular debates are therefore 'off limits', at least publicly and within polite company.

To talk of an 'us' and 'them' is a move away from 'solidarity'; the 'good Swedish citizen' is one who sees no barriers to common humanity through either nationality or race, or gender. To be a good citizen is to be a good human. As a value, 'solidarity' can thus be articulated as 'the humanitarian claim *par excellence* ... [the] imperative to act towards vulnerable others without the anticipation of reciprocation' (Chouliaraki 2011: 364, emphasis in original). Solidarity is thus supposed to transcend the hierarchical power relations and moral economy of gift-giving so often talked about in Maussian-inspired studies of hospitality and humanitarianism, and inspires instead to 'a vision of a technocratic Enlightenment Universalism ... [p]opulated by orderly, rational, cooperative, moral individuals. (Tomlinson, cited in Chouliaraki 2011: 368)

These 'moral' individuals, within the discourse of solidarity, are theoretically untroubled by notions of cultural particularity and are ideally able to transcend any cultural differences.

In our turn to the anthropological level, however, it is precisely this move to 'culture' that concerns us, specifically the wide array of practices that may be enabled by actors in this particular governmentality. The particular facets of the national myth and its reappropriations and reproductions allow for a certain amount of 'wiggle room' amongst the 'good citizen'. As just discussed, governmentality is not coercion or domination. Likewise, 'culture' is not something static and immutable. The plane of the quotidian in this respect is not one that is flat and level, but is one in which relations of power are constantly at play, in the form of one-upmanship, denial and saving face, and where social norms are continually negotiated. Within this plane therefore exists a repertoire of available actions for every actor (Somers 1994: 614), which includes modalities of circumvention to these social norms – practices that can simultaneously reinforce, utilize, but also evade these social norms in the most banal of ways. Indeed, governmentality can be seen to subsume such a wide array of scattered and contradictory narratives, the essence and shape of which cannot be defined prior to their enactment, as Michel de Certeau so eloquently asserts: 'The occasion continues to trump definitions, because it cannot be isolated from a conjuncture or an operation' (de Certeau 1990: 127).

Some of available actions, individualizations and reappropriations were, as I witnessed in my fieldwork, naturally often very successful in helping the Syrians to settle into their new lives and relieve some of their suffering. Within the space of eight months, over 120 refugees, most of them Syrian, had been resettled in the village. The type of decency engendered by this national myth ensured that conditions for the refugees were quite comfortable, going way beyond notions of a 'bare life' and generation of a narrow biopolitical subject, as advanced so regularly in ethnographies of refugee camps and the anthropology of hospitality and humanitarianism.[11] The huge bank of donations from the locals ensured that everybody had not only warm clothes for the winter, bicycles for the children to travel to and from school, and basic household utensils, but also provided each family with a television, toys, board games and books in both Swedish and

English. In this way, the governmentality of righteousness could be seen to 'function' effectively.

However, as we have discussed, governmentality is also somewhat precarious. As Neumann (2002) points out, there is always the possibility in a governmentality framework that people will not act precisely according to the established norms and that these norms can be constantly reconfigured and renegotiated. In our case in Oreby, the tiny practices that went slightly against the grain of 'solidarity' nonetheless enabled all the volunteers to retain a righteous identity and a sense of moral superiority by their reinscription of notions of 'gender equality' and 'good parenting'. Within the everyday terrain, a largely 'hidden' and unarticulated resistance to the resettlement of refugees in the village was also able to be voiced without fear of losing one's reputation for 'decency'.

As briefly alluded to, the anthropology of hospitality and humanitarianism, especially ethnographies of refugee 'camps', has gone a long way in conceptualizing how humanitarianism actually produces a hierarchical and unequal ordering of human lives. It has also shown how this is fundamentally intertwined with biopolitics and serves to produce a narrow 'biopolitical subject' (Pandolfi 2003) through various programmes, many of which are based on health or medical care (see for example Fassin 2005, 2010; Ticktin 2006; Redfield 2008; Feldman and Ticktin 2010). This rather restricted focus remains somewhat prisoner to an Arendtian and Agambenian notion of 'bare life' or '*homo sacer*', and the violence of the biopolitical (Agamben 1998); by placing the refugee or migrant in a zone somewhere between merely biological and full social existence, it relegates to lesser importance the more 'pastoral' and compassionate functioning of such technologies of power. Many of these studies also fall short of examining the full social and political consequences of this hierarchization and what wider societal practices are enabled as a result of these moves. As argued by Rozakou (2012), besides investigating the functioning of biopolitical power on the ground, ethnographies would be better to focus more on the *cultural* conceptions with which biopolitical schemata are connected, and the manner in which such conceptions are altered under contemporary circumstances.

When we talk of culture in this sense, a focus on the repertoire of actions available to the 'decent citizen' under this governmentality framework avoids problems of reification or essentialization. Instead, we are able to bring to light exactly which practices are incorporated within this 'wiggle room', and whether these practices can adopt any kind of uniformity. These kinds of practice need not be openly articulated or codified. Instead they point to more or less taken-for-granted actions that embody 'how we have always done things around here' (Neumann 2002: 237). The anthropologists James C. Scott and Michel de Certeau utilize the ancient Greek term 'mētis' to describe these types of practice; a way of behaving in the world that is learnt simply by local knowledge and cunning as opposed to hard and fast rules or principles (de Certeau 1988; Scott 1998; Neumann 2002).

Reflections from the Field: The Village of Oreby and the Performance of Decency

In its manifestations at the anthropological level, engaging with this 'mētis', these everyday practices, was enabled through my role as a volunteer with the Friends of Syria organization itself. After travelling to Sweden with the aim of engaging ethnographically with the day-to-day effects of the productive power brought into being by the labelling of a nation as 'morally exceptional' vis-à-vis migration, as well as looking at how this identity coexists with discourses of unease around the migrant, I began to follow the story in *Sydsvenska* newspaper of the generous donations and support given to one group of around seventy Syrian refugees who had just been placed by the Migration Board in a Skånska village of around sixteen hundred inhabitants. In an area of Sweden with a slightly higher than national-average income, a local municipality whose composition roughly reflected that of the national legislature, and with only two seats on the local council belonging to the far-right *Sverige Demokratarna* party, coupled with the glowing stories in the media of the kindness of this village, I felt it was an interesting site at which to engage with the day-to-day effects of this 'progressive' identity. Over the course of the ten months in which I carried out my fieldwork, the initial group of Syrian families were gradually joined by around fifty more Syrians, as well as around a dozen refugees or asylum seekers from other parts of the world – Georgia, Uganda, Eritrea – until around 130 new arrivals had been resettled there.

As opposed to an abstract notion of 'solidarity' based around the national myth, the particular dynamics between the villagers and the refugees at this site were extremely illustrative of all the taboos, obligations and negotiations of norms in play amongst those who are identified as, and identify themselves as, 'good citizens' in the context of refugees actually being resettled in their neighbourhood. The villagers of Oreby were informed about the arrival of the refugees only three weeks before the first arrivals – but most had already read it in the local newspaper. The Migration Board, *Migrationsverket*, then promptly arranged a meeting in the local school to listen to locals' concerns; a follow-up meeting was promised for the spring, which in fact never materialized.

In terms of performing the role of 'solidarity' with the refugees, however, the meeting in the school saw all notions of 'decency' abandoned, or at least put aside momentarily, in order to counter the imminent threat – in the eyes of the people of Oreby – of the reality of refugees being placed in their village. For this brief moment, it was more important for the villagers to prevent the refugees' resettlement at any cost, rather than maintain the appearance of being 'good citizens'. Resistance to the placement of the refugees was thus articulated along three main lines: that they would cause a fall in house prices; that the children in the village would be in danger from these 'damaged, war-torn' people; and lastly, that the young women and girls would be at increased risk of harassment and sexual advances from the Arab men. The most direct indication of this general unease came from a mother of three teenage daughters, who introduced her family to the *Migrationsverket* representative before stating that, thanks to them, she would no longer feel safe letting her three girls walk around on their own in the village at night. This assertion was met by an enthusiastic round of applause from everybody else at the meeting.

Disappointed at her fellow villagers' reaction to the news of the guests, Bodil, a volunteer with *Svenska Kyrkan*, the Swedish Church, organized a Facebook page and founded the small NGO, Friends of Syria, through which to collect donations of clothes, blankets and kitchen utensils for the refugees. The five women who made up the Friends of Syria were all locals, middle class, and in their forties or fifties. Despite the negative comments at the meeting, Bodil accumulated a huge amount of goods which she then took upon herself to distribute amongst the refugees. As a member of the village community, Bodil was not part of any wider humanitarian organization, and was only loosely affiliated with the church. As opposed to the usual working practices of NGO workers, it was Friends of Syria who initiated contact with the Syrian refugees by knocking on each of their doors a few hours after the officials from *Migrationsverket* had settled them into their new homes, introducing themselves as fellow villagers and neighbours, and volunteering themselves as the first point of contact should the new arrivals be in need of any assistance. A few months after the first refugees arrived, the Friends of Syria campaigned for a nearby house to be rented by *Migrationsverket* to be used as an 'activity centre' for the new arrivals, which became the scene of Swedish lessons, clothing donation and distribution, and general 'hanging out'.

Life in Oreby: A Hidden Transcript of Unease

With the realization that the placement of the refugees in Oreby was something that they would be obliged to live with, rather than something that they were in discussions about, objections to the resettlement of the refugees were no longer voiced or articulated in formal settings, such as the various village events (which took place roughly once or twice a month), such as the Spring Festival or Children's Day. Instead, these fora became a terrain through which the villagers could perform the role of 'decency' to each other, demonstrating 'solidarity' by regaling stories of how terrible the war in Syria is and advertising how much they had personally donated to the new arrivals. The meeting at the school was thus the only occasion of such vocal resistance to the housing of the refugees in Oreby. Indeed, many of those people present at the meeting later denied being present or raising any objections, dismissing the resistance to the resettlement of the refugees as 'ignorant people', or 'people who were simply a bit scared of the unknown'. With the inability to influence *Migrationsverket*'s decision to place refugees in Oreby, power relations reverted to maintaining a certain ideal of respectability, and all the taboos and obligations enabled by the national myth were brought back into play.

Grumbles or complaints I overheard about the perceived deficiencies and flaws of the new arrivals, however, took to the more informal, 'safer' settings of the school gates, the pizzeria and the slimming club. The Arab men were conceived of in familiar orientalized terms, as hypermasculin-ized, lecherous and thus risky; it was only a matter of time before something terrible would happen in the village. Areas of the village in which the refugees congregated were deemed 'no go zones' of sorts, without ever needing to be openly articulated as such; it was simply the way things were. Swedish children and refugee children were 'of course' allowed to play together, but this transpired to be only within the supervised settings of the school (during school time) or the football club every Saturday. During training, Syrian parents congregated along a far end of the football field and Swedish parents separately along the length of the pitch. After the game, most of the local parents left immediately and ensured that their children were quickly shepherded away into cars.

Such a tacit, unspoken understanding between the residents of Oreby as to where the line of 'solidarity' was to be drawn and where it was permitted to falter enabled any outward confrontation to be kept to a minimum, even completely avoided, and for everybody involved to maintain their 'good citizen' reputation. James C. Scott, though talking about domination, talks about this type of shared understanding between members of a group in terms of a 'hidden transcript' – a sort of collective resistance that maintains the illusion of a placid surface, whilst slyly making use of fleeting, seized opportunities that push the limits of what is permitted (Scott 1990: 196). Though far from dominated, the taboos brought into being by obligations of 'decency' within this governmentality framework meant that any resistance against the refugees was pushed into a more 'hidden' realm, able to be voiced behind closed doors amongst the 'in' group and those who were certain to share these views, but unable to be articulated in polite company if one were to maintain a 'decent' image.

Notions of 'solidarity' and the performance of the 'good citizen' were nonetheless permitted to lapse or alter somewhat around the notion of gender equality and the 'children's well-being'. Although the familiar orientalized conception of the Arab man as somewhat dangerous was an accepted truth in the village – unspoken in 'polite company' after the initial meeting, but coming to form a sort of common sense, nobody would now expressly label the men as threatening or undesirable. Instead, open discourse was along the lines of how terrible the suffering of the refugees must have been, how it must be so traumatic to be forced to adapt to such a new culture, and how much help and support they would need. In terms of gender and parenting, however, a great deal more room for manoeuvre was available to still behave decently, from the acceptance of 'no-go' zones for the village children to the adoption of various 'female empowerment' strategies.

Gender (In)Equality: Mending the Deficient Syrians

As an intermediary between the village and the refugees, Bodil and the Friends of Syria were often the target of these grumbles and complaints, and thus took on the role of helping the Syrians to 'integrate' and 'enter society'. Any attempt to directly force the Syrian men to 'mend their ways', however, was deemed taboo. The Friends of Syria volunteers were aware that speaking about the Arab men as fanatical and potentially violent was in bad taste; although acceptable to be articulated behind closed doors, to speak this way publicly would be seen as particularly unsavoury, and something that was relegated in their imagination to the realm of the far right. Eva, for example, the volunteer in charge of running the weekly Swedish classes, would often roll off the platitude that 'sexism and racism are two sides of the same coin'. In this way the 'public transcript' of decency and complete solidarity was able to be upheld. Nonetheless, the Friends of Syria, in accommodating the unease of the wider community, took it upon themselves to 'do something' to help the new arrivals 'adjust' to Swedish life, particularly with regards to the notions of gender equality and the upbringing of children.

One way to avoid more open or direct criticism of the perceived patriarchy or sexism of the Syrian refugees, which would risk being viewed as 'indecent', was to articulate disapproval as though it was not completely serious – simply a 'joke' or light-hearted teasing that could be easily laughed off. This type of interaction was especially prominent between the volunteers in their dealings with the older Syrian men and fathers who had been settled in the village. To every new family who arrived, for example, Bodil would proclaim to the father that 'Sweden is the opposite of your culture; here, women are legally allowed to take four husbands but men are only allowed one wife', before quickly adding that she was 'just joking'. This type of teasing took on the form of anything from trying to shock the Syrian men into dramatically altering their perceived norms of how they expected their wives to dress – 'Don't be surprised come summertime when your wife will be in a bikini! You're not in Aleppo now' – to gently mocking the men for what the volunteers perceived to be a lack of domestic skills – 'A Swedish woman would never let a man get away with that!' This type of advice, though with serious intent behind it, was always given playfully, and as such was easily disowned in the (rare) case of it being challenged or of offence being taken by the Syrian men.

Within the same orientalist episteme, the Syrian women, viewed as more 'passive' and thus a somewhat 'safer' target, were seen as a more receptive group at whom to direct advice. In addition to the Swedish lessons and general drop-in sessions held in the activity centre, the volunteers also devoted every Tuesday to holding cooking classes, whereby two or three of them would show the new arrivals how to make simple Swedish recipes like cinnamon buns and pancakes. The rationality of organizing this event was precisely to attract the women, to facilitate an arena in which they could get to know the 'real' person in the absence of the perceived influence of the husband, and to create a separate form of 'female solidarity'.

The first few cooking lessons were deemed very successful, attended by around twenty or so women, both Syrian and non-Arab. The volunteers spoke to the women in English, but took care to teach them simple, Swedish words as they went along. 'They will never integrate or get a job if they can't even say basic sentences'. Bodil, the chief volunteer, encouraged the women to leave their children at home during these classes, citing the need for the women to have some well-deserved time to themselves, but also promoting the ideal of a more gender-equal style of parenting: 'Besides, now that you're living in Sweden, it's time that your husbands did some childcare for a change'.

After around five or six weeks, however, most of the Syrian women stopped attending the cooking classes, with only a family of two sisters and one of their husbands from Georgia, as well as three Ugandan women, making the weekly visit. This was a source of mild irritation to the Friends of Syria group who saw their time as wasted if the Syrian women would not even make the effort to get to know the Swedish culture and simply 'locked themselves away'. In the absence of any Syrians, conversations at Tuesday's cooking classes often centred on their perceived deficiencies; they were seen to be 'stuck in their ways' and weak willed, unable to 'stand up to their husbands' about the changes needed to integrate in Sweden.

These tiny annoyances at the Syrian women's indifference towards their 'empowerment' strategies were accelerated in Wednesday's Swedish classes, when numbers gradually began to dwindle so that only the family of three from Georgia were regular attendees. The Georgian couple were now expecting their first baby, with the mother-to-be now three months pregnant. Wednesday's casual lessons at the drop-in centre thus became less structured teaching and more general discussions about life in the village, hopes for the future, and challenges being faced 'entering society' in Sweden. Gradually, these conversations again began to be framed in terms of the deficiencies of the Syrians, especially the Syrian women, and a general frustration at their perceived lack of integration. The Georgian woman would often tell us how she too was from a patriarchal culture where women were treated as second-class citizens, however she was willing to fight for her rights to education and equal treatment.

The terrain of the activity centre was thus one in which the 'good' refugee, willing to take on more gender-equal roles, gradually came to be differentiated from the 'bad' refugee, wishing to remain 'traditional' and 'patriarchal', and reluctant to enter Swedish society. The behaviour of the Georgian refugees came to be seen as a benchmark to which all the new arrivals should aspire. The Georgian man, for example, was constantly congratulated by the volunteers for his proactive approach towards parenthood and his involvement with Adriane's pre-natal classes.

Engagement with the Syrian refugees, both male and female, therefore only took place in the more informal 'drop-in sessions' that the volunteers had arranged twice weekly, whereby the new arrivals could stop by to discuss any issues they were having with accommodation, to search through donations and take any clothes they needed, or to come with letters from *Migrationsverket* or *Arbetsförmedlingen*, the Employment Agency, to be translated. The four volunteers thus utilized this opportunity to advise the women on what they should be doing to make 'entering society' easier, on subjects such as how to dress or how to control their children's behaviour. The perceived deficiencies of the Syrians' parenting was amplified during Ramadan when complaints about the refugee children being permitted to stay up late and 'run amok' came to a head, and the group received more and more complaints from fellow villagers.

By focusing on gender equality, albeit mostly aimed at the women, as well as 'good parenting', criticism of the Syrians' way of life, or their imagined way of life, was able to be articulated aloud, and within 'polite company' with an image of decency still kept intact. The national myth of moral exceptionalism and its permeation through society as a 'governmentality of righteousness' ensures that ideas of being a good parent and of 'gender equality' are firmly Swedish qualities, with 'everybody else', though sharing the same idea of 'decency', nonetheless failing to live up to this exemplar. As we have seen, however, this decency also legitimized tiny biopolitical practices of hierarchization and marginalization of the

Syrians. An engineer and mother of two toddlers from Damascus complained of the volunteers 'shoving their ideas of gender equality down her throat', and her husband joked of it being a 'tyranny'. On the whole, however, most of the Syrians regarded the volunteers' work positively and gratefully; the Friends of Syria had been helping them to settle into life in Oreby and it was seen as only natural that they would have negative perceptions of Muslims from what they would have seen on the television and in Hollywood movies.

Indignation and Panic: The Voicing of the Hidden Transcript

Thus far we have examined the multiplicity of ways in which the 'morally exceptional' national myth was reappropriated at an anthropological level by people who saw themselves as 'decent' citizens, claiming to be proud of their country's humanitarian record and stance towards refugees. By never openly criticizing or voicing objection to the resettlement of the refugees, the volunteers and residents of the village reinforced but also utilized the national myth to retain a sense of their own moral superiority. In this respect, a 'public transcript' was firmly in place, giving the appearance of a tranquil, placid surface in which everybody accepts the prevailing norms. Although there was a marked unease in the village over the resettlement of the refugees, any resistance to their resettlement, aside from the initial meeting, was forced into a more hidden realm in order to maintain a decent image. The only realm in which it became acceptable to let this public transcript 'lapse' somewhat was around concerns about the perceived gender inequality and parenting practices of the new arrivals, whereby the 'good citizen' image was still able to be maintained. Any allusion to the Arab men as violent or fanatical, though allowed to be voiced in the initial meeting, was no longer acceptable in public and would now immediately render the speaker a 'dreg' (Gullestad 1992), or at best, un-Swedish. As long as the refugees played by all the rules of being a 'worthy guest' (Rozakou 2012), and accepted the advice of the volunteers on how to be more gender equal and on how to raise their children, then this 'public transcript' of complete acceptance was maintained, and talk of violent, lustful or risky men was kept somewhat hidden.

And indeed, to place oneself in a position of critique regarding Swedish policy and everyday practice towards refugees and asylum seekers is to stand on somewhat shaky ground. To be sure, I am not trying to diminish either the significance of Sweden's role in accepting such a relatively high number of refugees, or the kindness of the Friends of Syria in providing the refugees with not merely a 'bare life' but indeed a 'decent life'. It is important, however, to be able to understand the political as opposed to the ethical implications of such a form of governmentality and to open a space for critique, even in these 'best case' examples: the limits of the functioning of this type of governmentality; the manner in which solidarity is reappropriated as generosity; and the very fragile relationship between a seeming acceptance of the refugees and the complete disbanding of social relations.

To see the tiny, almost insignificant micro-biopolitical practices of exclusion and hierarchization around 'gender equality' and 'good parenting' as the 'whole story' and as having only minimal implications or a limited reach would be an extreme error. Indeed, as analysts of social action, we are interested in how these tiny biopolitical practices go on to inform a more far-reaching phenomenon, 'adding up' to a type of social change (Neumann 2002). The unease that was markedly present within the village regarding the issue of the refugees did not disappear because of the projects of the Friends of Syria or because it was acceptable to be voiced in open after the initial meeting.

Indeed, one could conceptualize this 'hidden transcript' of unease within the village and the micro-biopolitical practices of hierarchization, marginalization and stigmatization of the Syrian refugees by the volunteers as the 'concealed base of the iceberg' (Veyne 1997: 154), which, through the mechanism of a 'moral panic' (Cohen 1980), enabled the more 'public' articulation of the Syrian men as a threat, and the controversy over the perception of Arab hypermasculinity and their tendency towards violence to be openly voiced, as we will discuss below. In articulating the shared unease of the Arab men as dangerous, we also see how moves towards an 'us and them' become more acceptable within the public domain.

The Shooting of the Man in Jämtland

Whilst driving to Oreby on the morning of 13 November 2013, I heard on the news about a young Somali man who had been shot dead by police the previous night in a small village further north, in the county of Jämtland. The news reported that the man had been brandishing a knife and waving it around the small block of apartments where a few refugee families were housed. The report was very brief, with the newsreader stating only that the man was said to have been drinking alcohol and running towards the police when he was shot.

When I arrived at the activity centre, it was much busier than usual, with around thirty people milling around in the lounge and kitchen. All four members of the Friends of Syria were present, with Bodil explaining that she had called a meeting to discuss what had happened the previous night and what implications this may have. The atmosphere was a little tense and Bodil seemed tired, a little irritated and short tempered.

She explained to the Syrians that, throughout the course of the morning, 'dozens' of people had phoned her or approached her at the school gate to talk about the incident up in Jämtland. People were worried that something similar could happen in Oreby, reasoning that damaged people, straight out of a war zone, were capable of anything. Despite refugees having lived in Oreby for around eight or nine months by this point, with no 'incidents', the actions of one refugee hundreds of miles north had legitimized, for the first time since the school meeting, speaking openly of the Arab men as potentially very dangerous, with some sort of 'action' needing to be taken to ensure that Oreby would remain free from this sort of trouble. This was the first time that Bodil had conveyed this general unease to the refugees themselves, positioning herself as one of the villagers, instead of taking the usual role as an intermediary: 'I just want to tell you men that you have to behave yourselves. This is what happens in Sweden if you don't behave yourself. It is a good country but if you come here, you have to respect our rules'. Bodil's speech to the thirty or so people who had gathered was short and to the point, directed at every Syrian man there.

The protests of an articulate, twenty-two-year-old male medical student from Aleppo that this man was 'Somali' and thus, in his reasoning, was completely uncivilized and backward, as opposed to Syrians who were cultured and peaceful people, was quickly dismissed by Bodil. True, he may be from another country, but he was also a 'guest' in Sweden, who the good people of Jämtland had been so kind as to protect. When the meeting was finished and most people had left, only Ahmed and the young Georgian couple remained, along with Bodil and myself, and talk around the kitchen table once again reverted back to the police shooting. Ahmed was astounded at the shoot-to-kill policy of the Swedish police, stating plainly to Bodil that the exact details around this incident were unclear, and admonishing her for being so quick to tell everybody to 'behave' themselves, when in actual fact it could be the Swedish police that needed to 'behave'.

This was the first time that there was a firmly demarcated line between the people of Oreby and the refugees. The incident legitimized, in the eyes of the Oreby dwellers, the move away from 'solidarity' – even the thin veneer of solidarity that was being performed thus far – to an open articulation of an 'us and them'. Cohen (1980) famously articulates such an event as a 'moral panic', recognizing the way in which a person, or group of people, can emerge and come to be framed by the media as a threat to societal values and interests through exaggerated and somewhat distorted reporting. The resulting frenzy thus engenders a largely disproportionate response to the perceived 'deviancy'. Crucial to the success of a moral panic, however, is its capacity to tap into somewhat pre-existing societal orientations, perhaps not previously publicly voiced, but which become more crystallized and organized as the result of the panic, and hence more legitimate (Cohen 1980: 47).

Indeed, this vignette of the police shooting and the subsequent reaction in Oreby is extremely telling. The Somali man in Jämtland had most spectacularly broken the rules of being a 'worthy guest' (Rozakou 2012) by wielding a knife. The media articulation of the refugee as threatening and dangerous thus altered the power dynamics in Oreby and rendered sayable what had been taboo only a day previously. The repertoire of available actions for the 'decent' citizen became far more wide ranging. Although the episode did not take place in Oreby, or indeed anywhere near it, a subsequent moral panic ensued allowing Bodil to publicly voice what people had being saying more or less privately in phone calls and in conversations at the school gate.

Concluding Thoughts: Conceptualizing the Everyday Practices of Violence in Oreby

In telling the story of the resettlement of refugees in a small Swedish village we have brought to light some of the number of ways in which the national myth of solidarity, of moral exceptionalism, and gender equality can enable and create the possibility for practices of violence. But how can we conceptualize violence in such an instance? As we have discussed, the standard of living of the refugees in Sweden was high; the villagers were generally all kind and well-meaning people (at least within polite company). 'Solidarity' as a national myth enabled an outwardly tranquil, cordial relation between the villagers and the new arrivals, at least for most of the time.

The 'moral panic' created by the media report of the shooting of the man in Jämtland, however, created the conditions for a seemingly 'exceptional' moment. Here, the Syrian men were told, in no uncertain terms, that they were deemed deviant, risky and abnormal, and would have to 'behave' if they did not want to be shot dead by the police. This notion of violence as explicit and crude mirrors a wide array of governmentality- and biopolitics-inspired scholarship which illuminates the fundamental interweaving of humanitarian practices and biopolitical hierarchization of human life into that which is desirable and that which is undesirable (most notably Fassin 2005; Agier 2008, 2011). Drawing on Agamben's (1998) re-inscription of biopolitical governance as producing 'bare life', the refugee in these instances is one who does not enjoy the benefits of inclusion in the political realm, residing instead in a 'zone of indistinction' (Ojakangas 2005). For Agamben, the *homo sacer* of the camp is defined therefore, as with the panic around the perceived passionate, angry, unhinged Somali man in Jämtland, only by his capacity to be killed. Through this very spectacular framing, it is possible to see the 'governmentality of righteousness' working like any other racist discourse, creating the conditions of possibility to control, correct and ultimately exterminate 'the other' (Foucault and Ewald 2003).

This conceptualization, however, would be a hugely reductionist reading of the biopolitical practices at play in Oreby, the more pastoral functions of such a type of power and their own particular relation to violence. By turning our attention to mētis – to culture as a dynamic interplay between discourse and practice and the wide repertoire of available actions of the 'good citizen' as an actor within this governmentality of righteousness – the complexities of this relationship are brought to light. Indeed, the national myth and its reappropriations produced certain taboos whereby any criticism of the refugees was deemed in bad taste – not completely unsayable, but only able to be articulated behind closed doors. The villagers of Oreby had a shared understanding of what it was to be 'decent' in polite company. In the same vein, 'correction' took the more gentle form of 'female empowerment' talks at cooking classes and Swedish classes, giving advice about what to wear to make 'entering society' easier, and on how to prevent children from 'running amok' – advice that was only deemed offensive by one or two people, but was generally laughed off or even appreciated for the good intentions behind it.

The moral panic around the shooting of the man in Jämtland could therefore be seen as only the 'tip of the iceberg' of wider, more subtle practices of hierarchization and categorization, as well as the public voicing of the general, more hidden unease that had been present in the village since the school meeting. Indeed, we have seen how it was within the realm of 'gender equality' and 'good parenting' that taboos regarding solidarity and decency could be seen to be redrawn. As 'morally exceptional' in these regards, one could retain an image of decency whilst acting slightly against the grain of complete 'solidarity' and unity. It was within this domain that some requirements of reciprocation and rules of hospitality were brought into being. As Sweden has been labelled morally exceptional vis-à-vis gender equality in addition to, or perhaps even prior to, showing 'solidarity' towards refugees, there was some compulsion for the refugees to 'mend their ways' in this regard.

Far from a biopolitics of 'bare life', we must also therefore examine how this 'benevolent' biopolitics (Vrasti 2014: 74) enables more subtle and invisibilized conditions for violence. The national myth of 'moral exceptionalism', by its very definition, thus enables a move away from solidarity to one of humanitarianism, complete with notions of generosity, gift giving and hierarchization. The labelling of Sweden as 'best' regarding gender equality and parenting enables an asymmetric power relation between those who have been labelled 'exceptional' and those who have just arrived and are obliged to 'mend their ways' to meet this 'morally exceptional' standard. To speak of the refugees as 'deficient' in these regards is commonsensical, benign and indeed objective.

It is within the Swedish national myth and the governmentality of righteousness that we can see the relation between subtle, invisibilized biopolitical practices and more overt, seemingly spectacular public violence. Though somewhat benign, caring and commonsensical, these practices can instead be seen to form the base of an iceberg of exclusion, stigmatization and marginalization, in which it takes only a story in the media to legitimize, in the eyes of the Oreby dwellers, the open articulation of the Syrian men as a threat; coercion as crude and explicit. The Syrians moved quickly from being objects of care and assistance, to being undesirable and able to be 'sacrificed in the name of protection' (Balzacq et al. 2010: 10). What is interesting, however, is that all this can occur with notions of 'decency' and even 'solidarity' remaining firmly intact.

Emma Mc Cluskey is a postdoctoral research associate at the Department of War Studies, King's College London. Her research interests include refugees and migrants in the European Union, ethnographic approaches to Critical Security Studies and International Political Sociology. She is currently working on a European Union-funded multidisciplinary and multi-institutional project examining the effect of Schengen borders on third country nationals.

Notes

1. According to Eurostat, Sweden received 34 per cent of all Syrian asylum seekers granted protection in the EU, followed by Germany, which received 25 per cent (European Commission 2014).
2. All names within this chapter have been changed for reasons of confidentiality.
3. In terms of research ethics, my fieldwork complied with all requirements of the Ethical Approval Committee at King's College, London. All participants were provided with an information sheet detailing the nature of my project. In addition, participants who are quoted or referred to were required to sign a consent form (translated into Swedish when required) permitting me to use this data. The consent form made clear that any names of participants would be anonymized and that withdrawal of their approval could be granted at any time.
4. On meeting Carlos and Rodolfo Luna, two Argentinian brothers who were given refugee status in Sweden in the 1970s.
5. Main editorials in *Aftonbladet*, for example, called it a 'good decision' and stated that more needs to be done, especially at the European level, in order to

accommodate more Syrian refugees (Lindberg 2013). *Dagens Nyheters* editorial page on the day following the decision stressed the position of the UNHCR regarding the war in Syria, likening it to the genocide in Rwanda. The piece pointed out Sweden's generous attitude, quoting a study by the SOM (Society, Opinion, Media) institute at Gothenburg University which showed that 85 per cent of Swedes regarded war as an acceptable reason to be granted asylum in Sweden (Helmerson 2013).

6. In an interview for *Know Reset*, for example, the Swedish justice minister stated that '[o]ften, at the EU-level, Sweden stands out as the odd country proposing to improve asylum policy, to receive more refugees' (Perrin and McNamara 2013).

7. Sweden is ranked in 4th place in the 'Global Gender Gap' (World Economic Forum 2013), ranked in 4th place in the 'Gender Empowerment Measure' (UNDP 2013) and has the 4th highest proportion of parliamentary seats being occupied by females, according to the Inter-Parliamentary Union (IPU 2014).

8. These authors draw on a cartography produced by Inglehart and Welzel, based on cultural values from the World Values Survey, which positions Sweden as having the world's most 'secular-rational' and most 'self-expressive' values (WVS 2014).

9. Indeed, there has been a great deal of scholarship that argues that, since the neoliberalization of the 1980s and moves towards a Europeanization of asylum policy, Sweden is no longer 'exceptional' in this regard (Pred 2000; Hansen 2009; Ålund and Schierup 2011). I argue, however, that the notion of 'exceptionality' is relational, and as long as Sweden is 'the best', even 'the best of a bad bunch', then the national myth is able to be reproduced.

10. Sweden is currently ranked in the top five of the United Nation's 'World Happiness Report' (Helliwell, Layard and Sachs 2013).

11. I will go on to discuss this notion of 'bare life' with regards to the ethnographies of humanitarian practices later.

Bibliography

Agamben, G. 1998. *Homo Sacer: Sovereign Power and Bare Life*. Stanford, CA: Stanford University Press.

Agier, M. 2008. *On the Margins of the World: The Refugee Experience Today*. Cambridge and Malden, MA: Polity Press.

———. 2011. *Managing the Undesirables: Refugee Camps and Humanitarian Government*. Cambridge and Malden, MA: Polity Press.

Ålund, A., and C.U. Schierup. 2011. 'The End of Swedish Exceptionalism? Citizenship, Neoliberalism and the Politics of Exclusion', *Race & Class* 53(1): 45–64.

Balzacq, T., et al. 2010. 'Security Practices', in R.A. Denemark (ed.), *International Studies Encyclopedia Online*. Blackwell Reference Online: Blackwell Publishing.

Bergrenn, H., and L. Trägårdh. 2009. *Är svensken människa?: Gemenskap och oberoende i det moderna Sverige* [Is the Swede human? Togetherness and independence in modern Sweden]. Stockholm: Nordstedt.

Calhoun, C.J. 1997. *Nationalism*. Minneapolis: University of Minnesota Press.

Certeau, M. de. 1988. *The Practice of Everyday Life* (Translated by S. Rendell). Berkeley and Los Angeles: University of California Press.

——. 1990. *L'Invention du quotidien. 1. Arts de faire*, 2nd edn. Paris: Gallimard.

Chouliaraki, L. 2011. '"Improper Distance": Towards a Critical Account of Solidarity as Irony', *International Journal of Cultural Studies* 14(4): 363–81.

Cohen, S. 1980. *Folk Devils and Moral Panics: The Creation of the Mods and Rockers*, 2nd edn. London: Routledge.

Dahl, A.-S. 2006. 'Sweden: Once a Moral Superpower, Always a Moral Superpower?', *International Journal* 61(4): 895–908.

European Commission. 2014. 'Asylum Decisions in the EU28', *Eurostat News Release STAT/14/98*, 19 June. Retrieved 15 April 2015 from europa.eu/rapid/press-release_STAT-14-98_en.pdf

Fassin, D. 2005. 'Compassion and Repression: The Moral Economy of Immigration Policies in France', *Cultural Anthropology* 20(3): 362–87.

——. 2010. 'Inequality of Lives, Hierarchies of Humanity: Moral Commitments and Ethical Dilemmas of Humanitarianism', in I. Feldman and M.I. Ticktin (eds), *In the Name of Humanity: The Government of Threat and Care*. Durham, NC: Duke University Press, pp. 238–55.

——. 2012. *Humanitarian Reason: A Moral History of the Present*. Berkeley and Los Angeles: University of California Press.

Feldman, I., and M. Ticktin. 2010. *In the Name of Humanity: The Government of Threat and Care*. Durham, NC: Duke University Press.

Foucault, M. 2004. *Security, Territory, Population: Lectures at the Collège de France 1977–1978*. London: Picador.

——. 2010. *The Birth of Biopolitics: Lectures at the Collège de France 1978–1979*. London: Picador.

Foucault, M., and F. Ewald. 2003. *'Society Must Be Defended': Lectures at the Collège de France 1975–1976*. London: Macmillan.

Gullestad, M. 1992. *The Art of Social Relations: Essays on Culture, Social Action and Everyday Life in Modern Norway*. Oslo: Scandinavian University Press.

Hansen, P. 2009. 'Post-national Europe – Without Cosmopolitan Guarantees', *Race & Class* 50(4): 20–37.

Helliwell, J.F., R. Layard and J. Sachs (eds). 2013. 'World Happiness Report 2013'. New York: UN Sustainable Development Solutions Network.

Helmerson, E. 2013. 'Syriska Flyktingar: Rätt att öppna dörren' [Syrian Refugees: Right to open the door], *Dagens Nyheter*, 4 September. Retrieved 30 July 2014 from http://www.dn.se/ledare/signerat/syriska-flyktingar-ratt-att-oppna-dorren/

IPU (Inter-Parliamentary Union). 2014. 'Women in National Parliaments: World Classification'. Retrieved 29 July 2014 from http://www.ipu.org/wmn-e/classif.htm

Lawler, P. 1997. 'Scandinavian Exceptionalism and European Union', *JCMS: Journal of Common Market Studies* 35(4): 565–94.

——. 2005. 'The Good State: In Praise of "Classical" Internationalism', *Review of International Studies* 31(3): 427–49.

——. 2007. 'Janus-Faced Solidarity: Danish Internationalism Reconsidered', *Cooperation and Conflict* 42(1): 101–26.

Lindberg, A. 2013. 'Ge fler flyktingar en väg till Sverige' [Give more Syrians a way into Sweden], *Aftonbladet*, 3 September. Retrieved 6 June 2014 from http://www.aftonbladet.se/ledare/ledarkronika/anderslindberg/article17398931.ab

Neumann, I.B. 2002. 'Returning Practice to the Linguistic Turn: The Case of Diplomacy', *Millennium: Journal of International Studies* 31(3): 627–51.

Nilsson, A.-S. 1991. *Den moraliska stormakten* [The moral superpower]. Stockholm: Timbro.

Ojakangas, M. 2005. 'Impossible Dialogue on Bio-power: Agamben and Foucault', *Foucault Studies* 2: 5–28.

Pandolfi, M. 2003. 'Contract of Mutual (In)Difference: Governance and the Humanitarian Apparatus in Contemporary Albania and Kosovo', *Indiana Journal of Global Legal Studies* 10(1): 369–81.

Perrin, D., and F. McNamara. 2013. 'Refugee Resettlement in the EU: Between Shared Standards and Diversity in Legal and Policy Frames', *KNOW RESET RR 2013/03*. Florence: Robert Schuman Centre for Advanced Studies, European University Institute.

Pred, A.R. 2000. *Even in Sweden: Racisms, Racialized Spaces, and the Popular Geographical Imagination*. Berkeley: University of California Press.

Redfield, P. 2008. 'Vital Mobility and the Humanitarian Kit', in A. Lakoff and S.J. Collier (eds), *Biosecurity Interventions: Global Health and Security in Question*. New York: Columbia University Press, pp. 147–71.

Rose, N. 1993. 'Government, Authority and Expertise in Advanced Liberalism', *Economy and Society* 22(3): 283–99.

Rozakou, K. 2012. 'The Biopolitics of Hospitality in Greece: Humanitarianism and the Management of Refugees', *American Ethnologist* 39(3): 562–77.

Scott, J.C. 1990. *Domination and the Arts of Resistance: Hidden Transcripts*. New Haven, CT and London: Yale University Press.

——. 1998. *Seeing Like a State: How Certain Schemes to Improve the Human Condition Have Failed*. New Haven, CT and London: Yale University Press.

Selby, J. 2007. 'Engaging Foucault: Discourse, Liberal Governance and the Limits of Foucauldian IR', *International Relations* 21(3): 324–45.

Somers, M.R. 1994. 'The Narrative Constitution of Identity: A Relational and Network Approach', *Theory and Society* 23(5): 605–49.

Ticktin, M. 2006. 'Where Ethics and Politics Meet', *American Ethnologist* 33(1): 33–49.

Tilly, C. 1994. 'A Bridge Halfway: Responding to Brubaker', *Contention: Debates in Society, Culture, and Science* 4: 15–19.

——. 1999. *Durable Inequality*. Berkeley and Los Angeles: University of California Press.

——. 2002. *Stories, Identities, and Political Change*. Oxford: Rowman & Littlefield.

Towns, A. 2002. 'Paradoxes of (In)Equality: Something is Rotten in the Gender Equal State of Sweden', *Cooperation and Conflict* 37(2): 157–79.

UNDP (United Nations Development Programme). 2013. 'Gender Empowerment Measure Report 2013'. New York.

Veyne, P. 1997. 'Foucault Revolutionizes History', in A. Davidson (ed.), *Foucault and his Interlocutors*. Chicago: University of Chicago Press, pp. 146–82.

Vrasti, W. 2014. *Volunteer Tourism in the Global South: Giving Back in Neoliberal Times.* London: Routledge.

World Economic Forum. 2013. 'Global Gender Gap Report 2013'. Geneva.

WVS (World Values Survey). 2014. 'Findings and Insights: Inglehart–Welzel Cultural Map'. Retrieved 17 May 2014 from http://www.worldvaluessurvey.org/WVSContents.jsp?CMSID=Findings

5

Spatializing Inequalities

The Situation of Women in Refugee Centres in Germany

Melanie Hartmann

Introduction

The rapidly rising number of asylum seekers in Germany in 2015[1] led to a severe shortage of suitable accommodation, a situation that had already been a focus of criticism from several refugee and advocacy organizations even before their arrival (Die Landesflüchtlingsräte and Pro Asyl 2011). Being rather unprepared to appropriately assist and accommodate the high number of refugees, government authorities put in place spontaneously erected emergency housing during the peak of the so-called 'crisis' in the summer of 2015. Numbers continued to increase and reception facilities were soon overcrowded, which was partly also a result of the immense backlog in the processing of asylum applications. The resultant conditions in the reception facilities made life there challenging at best. However, challenges not only arose due to density but especially also because of poor overall conditions that in many places existed prior to the crisis and continue today: for example, bathroom facilities without adequate locks, and a complete lack of private space, with people sharing their dormitories, tents and old warehouses with complete strangers. People with special needs, some traumatized and physically/psychologically injured, women, children and the elderly all suffer particularly from the structural situation at these centres. Sexual and gender-based violence (SGBV),[2] especially against women who are not accompanied by male family members, has been reported as posing a major problem in the facilities (Rabe 2015; Hersh and Obser 2016).

This chapter takes a closer look at the structural conditions of German reception centres (*Erstaufnahmeeinrichtungen*) and accommodation centres (*Gemeinschaftsunterkünfte*) from a spatial perspective to identify forms of inequality that female refugees face inside them.[3] To this end, I draw on French philosopher Henry Lefebvre's writing on *The Production of Space* (Lefebvre [1974] 1991). In this work, Lefebvre identifies the three dimensions of *spatial practice*, *representations of space*, and *representational spaces* as being relevant for the social production of space. I will use these dimensions as a theoretical framework and structure for my analysis.

Importantly, inequalities and vulnerabilities to violence primarily result from the fact that refugees find themselves in these spaces in the first place. However, by focusing on the situation of female refugees, this chapter reveals that intersecting categories of inequality or discrimination may still increase a person's likelihood of being exposed to violence. Violence is here understood according to Johan Galtung's broad definition of direct, structural and cultural violence (Galtung 1969, 1990), stressing its various forms, facets and origins. While direct violence refers to the (threat of) physical or psychological violence, acted out by one person against another, structural violence, in contrast, points to forms of injustice built into a social system or institution that privileges some while preventing others from fulfilling their basic human needs. This form of violence 'shows up as unequal power and consequently unequal life chances' (Galtung 1969: 171). Cultural violence, lastly, is defined 'as any aspect of a culture to legitimize violence in its direct or structural form' (Galtung 1990: 291). As illustrated in this chapter, all of these three forms are relevant for my analysis of the living conditions for female refugees in reception and accommodation centres.

Moreover, I approach the concept of violence not only via its actual occurrence but also as a potentiality, a possibility that is more likely to affect some than others. Somewhat analogous to Erving Goffman's discussion of stigma, where he delineates between the actual discredited and those potentially discreditable (Goffman 1963: 41), my aim is to provide a better understanding not merely of the violations that occur in these spaces but also to identify what makes an individual more violable in general. This is to highlight that while not all women become victims of violence in refugee centres, they generally face specific challenges and discrimination due to their gendered identities that men do not, or do to a lesser extent. I argue that looking at the centres through a spatial lens provides valuable insights into identifying what these challenges are.

This chapter is structured in three sections: first, a brief overview of the German asylum procedure and the reception of refugees will be given. Secondly, there is the discussion of two concepts – space and intersectionality – which are first explored separately and then brought together in the third section of the chapter, in which an analysis of intersecting inequalities experienced by refugee women in reception and accommodation centres along Lefebvre's three-dimensional approach to space will be provided. In order to illustrate my argument, I draw on participatory observation at a reception centre (October 2013 – February 2014), an accommodation centre for women (Spring 2016), and a mixed-sex accommodation centre (August/September 2016). I include three formal interviews with social workers (Spring 2016) and various informal 'ero-epic' conversations (Girtler 2001: 147) with social workers, (former) refugees, volunteers and activists. The empirical research was conducted in Hesse, Germany.

Reception and Accommodation of Refugees in Germany

Anyone seeking protection in Germany has to file an application for asylum, and so they first have to register as an asylum seeker at a state organization, like a border or police station or directly at a reception centre.[4] Depending on their countries of origin, asylum seekers are grouped into four different 'clusters', each undergoing somewhat different procedures during the asylum processes. This cannot be the place to elaborate on any of these in much detail but one of the most significant differences is the time people spend in the initial reception facilities. Some (e.g. from countries with high acceptance quotas) are sometimes fast-tracked in so-called arrival centres, while others are allocated to the regular reception facilities of the federal states. This chapter takes as a basis the 'normal procedure' (Frings und Domke 2016:25) where people are required to stay in a reception facility for a maximum of six months before being transferred on to the municipalities, usually to a shared accommodation centre.[5]

The reception facilities are mandated by the federal states (*Bundesländer*) with the distribution of refugees to these centres following various reception quotas (BAMF 2016a: 5). Here, basic equipment of clothing, bedding and toiletries is provided and the refugees are assigned a dormitory, usually single-sex. Typically, the reception centres host a social workers' office, and sometimes an additional counselling service for advising on the legal requirements of the asylum procedures, or for psychological counselling. The latter is usually either funded by external sponsors such as faith-based organizations, or is staffed by volunteering professionals. Volunteers often also organize and coordinate activities inside or close to the facilities, such as German language classes or events for children. Some reception centres provide additional on-site infrastructure like day care for children, kitchen-ettes, and communal spaces. Outside the business hours of social services, the security personnel, who are on site 24 hours a day, turn into the primary point of contact in case of medical emergencies or basic subsistence needs.

Asylum seekers undergoing the 'normal procedure', are usually re-quired to live in the reception centres for up to six months before being transferred to a municipality within the same federal state. During their application procedure, asylum seekers are liable to residence obligations – that is to say they are required to stay within their assigned cities or mu-nicipalities of residence.

Since refugee accommodations are the responsibility of the various federal states and local authorities, accommodation facilities vary across Germany, which is why general statements on living conditions should be avoided. There is no national regulation regarding size, equipment or facility standards, and while some of the federal states have implement-ed binding rules on minimum standards, others have not (Wendel 2014). Moreover, it is for state and local authorities to decide whether to place people primarily in collective accommodation centres on the municipal level or to support decentralized living arrangements such as private apart-ments (BAMF 2014). Some of the collective accommodation centres host only half a dozen people, or two or three families, while others accom-modate several hundreds. Due to this large variance in accommodation situations, it is not possible to speak of 'the' German refugee centre per se.

As stated above, in this chapter my empirical insights are based on the situation at facilities in the federal state of Hesse. For the purpose of my argument, though, local differences assume a minor role since I seek to draw out the prevalence and effect of more general or generalizable spatial structures and inequalities. To this end, my overall concern is less with small housing units and private apartments but more with the accom-modation situations in the larger reception and collective accommodation centres.

A Spatial Approach to Inequalities in Refugee Centres: Preliminary Reflections

This chapter begins from the premise that, like all spaces, refugee centres are socially constructed. Numerous scholars have contributed to debates around the topic of 'space' in the past decades (Augé 1995; Gupta and Ferguson 1997; Crang and Thrift 2000; Löw 2001; Low and Lawrence-Zúniga 2003; Massey 2005; Soja [1989] 2011), arguing that space must not be perceived merely as the background of social action – an empty container that exists 'prior to whatever ends up filling it' (Lefebvre [1974]

1991). Rather, they argue that space is a product in and of itself, and at the same time provides a condition in which social action takes place. Both sides – the social construction of space and the spatial construction of society – are relevant for the endeavour here, as both imply that 'space' is not a neutral concept.

Constructing and Appropriating Spaces

Although spaces may appear as objective or natural entities, they are products and resources of power-driven social relations, reflecting the broader social reality that they are bound up with (Elden 2004). Not all social agents hold the same relational or distributive capabilities to constitute spaces. Their ability to position and situate themselves, other persons and goods in and as spaces reflects their access to material resources, knowledge and power (Löw 2001, 2008). Consequently, the production of space by social agents can be seen as being permeated by power relations and processes of domination and subordination, mediated inter alia by class, race and gender.

Spaces themselves may be highly fluid, such as a group of people who perceive themselves to form a space, like a circle. Other spaces, such as refugee encampments, are institutionalized spaces as 'their ordering remains effective beyond the action of the agents' (Löw 2008: 37). They are, for example, grounded on normative regulations or are materially consolidated. However, despite their structural affirmation, even institutionalized spaces are not static, not fixed once and for all. Authors writing in the postmodern, constructionist or poststructuralist tradition point to the preliminary character of spaces (Massey 1992; Howarth 2006; Murdoch 2006; Soja [1989] 2011; Glasze 2012, 2013) and argue that spaces are contingent results of societal processes – temporary fixations resting upon hegemonic acts and thus prone to constant negotiation and renegotiation.

It is crucial to note that spaces as social constructions are not simply there to be found, holding a universally valid meaning for their users or inhabitants. Their material and ideal aspects can be subject to processes of individual appropriation and modification. Importantly, if spaces are social constructs and not pre-given, they can be appropriated and, in the process, changed by various agents. Among others, Roberta Feldman and Susan Stall deduce what they call space appropriation:

> individuals' and groups' creation, choice, possession, modification, enhancement of, care for, and/or simply intentional use of a space to make it [their] own ... Space appropriation is conceptualized as an interactive process through which individuals purposefully transform the physical environment into a meaningful place, while in turn transforming themselves. (Feldman and Stall 1994: 172)

This understanding of space appropriation, that is the intentional turning of spaces into one's own in an interactive process with one's (built) environment, is very useful for discussing how refugees engage with their sites of residence. Below, I will show that despite the regulations, restrictions and constraints they are facing, they also act to make intentional and creative use of their environment – for example, transforming the centres, if only temporarily, into places of exchange and solidarity.

Along similar lines and following the writing of bell hooks, Feldmann and Stall point to the importance of the appropriation of homeplaces for creating a feeling of 'at-homeness', of safety and belonging, especially for subordinated groups of society (Feldman and Stall 1994: 174). This is seen not as an end in itself, but essentially as a political act, an act of creating a place of nurturance that allows oneself to recover, to resist and heal from the 'brutal reality of racial apartheid, of domination' (hooks 1990: 42; cited in Feldman and Stall 1994: 189).

Large refugee facilities with their barbed-wired fences, bald linoleum floors and shared dormitories – in addition to continuous uncertainties about one's own or the family's future – often undermine exactly this basic human need for creating safe spaces, and places of at-homeness. Given the multiple facets of oppression and domination that refugees often experienced in their home-countries, during and after flight, the denial of this need, conveyed in and through these spaces, is particularly bitter and, hence, represents a form of structural violence in the above-introduced meaning.

But how can these constraining aspects of space be brought together with forms of agency or even empowerment, as suggested above? The writing of Henri Lefebvre is quite revealing for pursuing this question. In his seminal work *The Production of Space*, he laid out a relational conception of space that includes material as well as ideal processes, essentially entailing three, dialectically interconnected dimensions of the production of space(s): *spatial practice, representations of space,* and *representational spaces.*[6] The first dimension, *spatial practice,* refers to material and physical social practices in (the production of) space, including everyday routines, performatively evoked routes and networks that link up places to individual spaces (Lefebvre [1974] 1991: 38). The second dimension, *representation of space,* is the realm of knowledge and concrete power, the conceptualized spaces of scientists, planners, technocratic subdividers and social engineers (ibid.). In line with his Marxist social critique, Lefebvre argues that in modern capitalist societies, this dimension essentially colonizes the spatial practices of its members. As a consequence, people experience alienation and monotonous repetition while at the same time reproducing the dominant, homogenized, capitalistic space through their everyday spatial routines. However, Lefebvre does not halt at this rather pessimistic evaluation of the social constitution of space but introduces a third dimension of thought (and practice): the level of *representational spaces*. It is through this dimension that he pictures the dominated spaces to be changed and appropriated via material as well as ideal processes, where he sees the promise that alternative spaces may be imagined but also lived and sensorially encountered. He remains hopeful that spaces may come into being that fundamentally serve the needs of their inhabitants. In line with the argument above, for Lefebvre, the more a space is dominated and functionalized, the less amenable it is to tactics of appropriation (Lefebvre [1974] 1991: 356). Nevertheless, this third dimension suggests that even under such highly restrictive conditions, acts of social and/or material (re-)negotiation and (re-)appropriation of spaces by disempowered groups may confront power relationships, and may work towards empowerment or emancipation.

Despite the promise that lies in this third dimension, Lefebvre's dialectics is essentially non-teleological as he does not prioritize one dimension over the others, nor is he looking for some form of synthesis, negation or culmination.[7] Rather, he points at the constant movement between the three dimensions (Elden 2004: 36). This is also one reason why Lefebvre's three-dimensional conception of space is particularly useful as a starting point for the analysis of refugee accommodations: even in light of locally confined processes of appropriation of these spaces, like a selective turning of these spaces into places of exchange or solidarity, one may at the same time pay tribute to contemporaneously existing constraining aspects of space. It is thus possible to look at practices of appropriation and (re-)negotiation, and to acknowledge their creativity and promise, without at the same time romanticizing them or losing sight of the inequalities and vulnerabilities that are (re-)produced in and through spatial relations.

In this chapter Lefebvre's work provides the theoretical background but also the structure for my analysis of the situation of women in refugee centres, which, as explained below, follows his general assumptions and is also structured along his three dimensions of space. However, by also looking at Galtung's forms of direct, structural and cultural violence on the level of spatial practice, I aim to circumvent the fact that in Lefebvre's post-Marxist reading of space(s) the primary focus of his power analysis is on the dimension of representations of space. In his view, this is the decisive dimension for the domination of social space and the colonization of the everyday. My argument here is that in the everyday spatial practice, factors of subordination, domination or inequality that come into play cannot necessarily or immediately be traced back to the level of representations of space or the capitalist mode of production.

Before turning to a closer examination of the concrete forms of inequalities that exist in refugee spaces, let me briefly introduce a framework that facilitates the reasoning of the complexity of social inequality more generally.

Intersections of Social Inequality

In the 1970s, US-American black feminist movements pointed to the fact that, while all women may be united in their struggle against patriarchy and androcentrism, in the cases of women of colour, gender is not necessarily the predominant, let alone a sufficient category to describe the systems of hierarchical oppression they are confronted with (Anthias and Yuval-Davis 1983; hooks [1984] 2015: xiii). The American legal scholar Kimberlé Crenshaw eventually coined the term 'intersectionality' to highlight that:

> many of the experiences Black women face are not subsumed within the traditional boundaries of race or gender discrimination as these boundaries are currently understood, and that the intersection of racism and sexism factors into Black women's lives in ways that cannot be captured wholly by looking at the race or gender dimensions of those experiences separately. (Crenshaw 1991, S. 1244)

What is specifically intriguing about the so-called 'intersectional theories' that developed out of this consciousness of intersecting forms of discrimination is their ability to go beyond an analysis of hierarchical social positions on the basis of only one facet of a person's identity. The binary division of men vs. women is rejected in favour of a more nuanced, dynamic and integrated analysis of the multiple forms of subordination and interlocking systems of oppression that women face within society (Collins [1990] 2000).

Moreover, these factors are not merely added up but they are co-constituting, often interacting sources, arranged in a 'matrix of domination' (Collins [1990] 2000: 227) that determines a woman's position within the social hierarchy and define the choices she has in shaping her life. Over the following decades, the debate on the original triad of race, class and gender was supplemented by an acknowledgement of other forms of difference and discrimination, such as age, (dis-)ability, sexual orientation, and nationality, with the emphases changing over time and in accordance with broader societal developments (Lutz, Herrera Vivar and Supik 2011: xi; see also McCall 2005; Nash 2008; Bastia 2014). An approach that acknowledges a variety of forms of discrimination and power differentials, and looks at how these intersect and co-constitute themselves, appears to be particularly relevant regarding the multidimensionality of the refugee experience that is central to this chapter.[8]

When transferring intersectionality from one academic context to another, a certain degree of adaption is required (Bal 2002; Neumann and Nünning 2012: 2). For the examination of reception and accommodation centres, I use irregularity and gender as primary, interlinking categories of discrimination. The reason for this is that at the centre of this inquiry are women who are identified (or ascribed the identification) as 'irregular migrants', or, its legal implications set aside, as 'refugees'. I chose irregularity over other possible social categories, like displacement, in order to highlight that the focus is on the person's classification in the host country – in this case, Germany. People are irregular only when viewed from what they are differentiated against: The European Union's (EU) border regime neither generally prevents migration nor are its external borders closed lines per se. The European border regime 'decides what and especially who is to be included and excluded ... The EU regulates who is considered legal input and who is considered unwanted input – a threat to the system, hence redundant and deportable people' (van Houtum 2010: 964). From this perspective, the border becomes a 'difference-producing machine' (ibid.: 958) that among other things determines who may trespass it more or less freely or who needs individual permission to do so. For example, anyone whose country of nationality is listed on the 'positive' Schengen list does not need a visa for visits to the EU. In contrast, people who are nationals of countries on the 'negative' Schengen list *do* need a visa. Since most of today's refugees stem from a country listed on the latter and are generally not granted legal permission to enter the EU, they are subjected to this 'inequality of difference' (ibid.: 964) and turn into irregular or undocumented migrants the very moment they set foot on EU territory. The ordering logic of the border regime still goes on, as it furthermore determines under what conditions and endowed with what rights those who managed the crossing continue to find themselves on the other side (Ralser 2013: 281).

When analysing the situations and everyday lives of people in the reception and accommodation centres, other markers of identity, such as language, (dis-)ability, age, and sexual orientation are also relevant as they may cause additional disadvantages for some. The centres may not be properly adapted for the needs of the disabled, staff may transmit information in certain languages but not others, structural racism or heteronormativity may hamper the daily lives of people of color or homosexual refugees. However, a structured examination of all of these additional intersecting categories of inequality would go beyond the scope of this chapter and must be suspended for future research.

Gender Inequalities in the Social Constitution of Refugee Spaces in Germany

This section now examines, from a spatial perspective, vulnerabilities and inequalities that female refugees may come to be confronted with in refugee centres. The structure of the analysis corresponds to Henry Lefebvre's above-introduced spatial dimensions of *Spatial Practice, Representations of*

Space, and *Representational Spaces*. For reasons of accessibility, I will begin with the second dimension, *representations of space*.

Representations of Space: Governance and Planning

Although refugee centres are located at specific places, their concrete and abstract, material, ideal and symbolic productions are grounded in discourses, rules and legislation on a multiplicity of scales. International, European, national, state and local decision making (or the lack thereof) not only have different impacts on the concrete materiality of the centres – for example, how and where they are erected – but they also affect their relational aspects, especially determined by questions of who is made (or allowed) to stay there and for how long. People from so-called safe countries of origin, often pejoratively labelled 'economic migrants', receive significantly different treatment from those who are considered to be 'real' refugees. The determination of who *deserves* to receive the label refugee (Zetter 1991, 2007) alongside the related rights and obligations is substantiated in international, European and national law (e.g. the Refugee Convention or the German Basic Law). There are various spatial implications of these processes. Especially people who do not receive a protection status in Germany are not usually allowed to move to private apartments but are obligated to stay in accommodation centres for extended periods of time, sometimes several years, until their deportation is executed or other decisions on their protection status are made (Wendel 2014: 61). Likewise, under the latest changes of legislation, people from so-called 'safe countries of origin' are usually not transferred from arrival or reception centres to the generally somewhat more comfortable accommodation centres on a municipal level but are made to stay in the former until their departure or deportation is executed (see above).

On a more fundamental level, it is also this conceived dimension of the production of space(s) that fuels the original exclusion logic – the distinction between the ones inside and outside the centres, between the so-called refugees and the citizens. The coming into being of the category of 'refugee' is essentially also the result of the global ordering of the world into nation states and political entities, as well as their continuous affirmation through institutions, discourses and practices of their border regimes, rendering (forced) migration an anomaly in the nationalistic order of the world (Turner 2015: 2; see also Wimmer and Glick Schiller 2002; Walters 2006; Hess and Kasparek 2010; van Houtum 2010). Consequently, there is no denying the fact that the most striking logic of inequality concerning refugee centres is the exclusion logic that differentiates between those inside these spaces and those outside, between the ones who were forced to flee, the uprooted, the ones then labelled 'irregular migrants' on the one hand, and the regular citizens on the other. The implicit and explicit justification of this order as the natural order of things, with all the implications of global and local inequalities, is an example par excellence for the above-introduced understandings of structural as well as cultural violence.

Moreover, this fundamental difference, materialized in and through these spaces, is also the starting point of spatial analyses that engage with refugee spaces as 'camps' and, in following Giorgio Agamben, as spaces subjected to a 'state of exception' (Agamben [2003] 2005; see also Agamben [1994] 1998; Ek 2006; Minca 2006).[9] However, one of the main points of critique of these approaches is that they are hardly able to address what constitutes the social situation inside these spaces (Ramadan 2013; Turner 2015). Taking a closer look at the challenges that individuals face in these spaces also involves looking at those inside not only as the victimized, as 'bare lives' (Agamben [1994] 1998). Rather, it requires also an acknowledgment of their struggle, their activities, tactics and strategies to confront these challenges on an everyday basis – an issue I will address more closely below.

It is sometimes not only the regulation and planning that pre-structure life in refugee centres and that is challenging, but also the lack of it. For instance, on the level of the German federal states, only about half have implemented binding minimum standards for accommodation centres (Wendel 2014: 37), a fact that has long been criticized by various advocacy organizations who on their part demand the strict implementation of social and architectonical minimum standards for all centres throughout the country (Flüchtlingsrat Baden-Württemberg 2012; Liga der Freien Wohlfahrtspflege Hessen 2014; Cremer 2014).[10]

But how is this also an issue for further examination from a gender-sensitive perspective? Refugee centres often have poor housing conditions, with non-lockable bathrooms, dormitories or marquees, and so on. These have proven to have a particularly severe effect on women and children, for instance by facilitating the occurrence of SGBV (Papst 2015; Rabe 2015; Bonewit 2016). Without anticipating the following section, it also becomes clear how the governance procedures and the (lack) of planning activities have an immediate effect on the everyday lives of its inhabitants. For instance, even if cases of SGBV are reported – and it is very likely that most cases are not (Rabe 2015: 11) – women who have encountered SGBV may face situations where there are no standard operating procedures or intervention concepts in place. On the contrary, there is often a complete lack of procedural regulations concerning what measures and steps are to be taken from the moment of receiving a report of an SGBV incident. Moreover, legal restrictions, such as residence obligations, often impede timely relocation of either perpetrator or victim, or the moving in of SGBV survivors with family or friends elsewhere (ibid.: 14).

Most of the cases [of SGBV] are not reported. Last year, however, we also saw what happens if someone does report something – that is: nothing. ... He [the father] has reported the day after that his daughter, aged thirteen, had been abused. She had had to sleep with 140 men in a tent, nobody knows why. And then, everyone was completely clueless[11] and nobody knew what to do. The youth welfare office (*Jugendamt*) said that she did not fall under their jurisdiction because the reception centre was not based in the city [*name*], and the state authorities said that the others should look after it. The centre management said: 'Well, we will have to see; we also do not know what to do in such a situation'. And three days later, she was still sleeping with those same men in the tent ... What is missing is a concept for protection against violence. (Female social worker, April 2016, my translation from German)

The combination of poor accommodation conditions and the lack of firm violence protection contributed to the occurrence of SGBV; there was also inadequate handling of the case after it was reported. Undoubtedly, intersecting categories of inequality or discrimination, such as language skills, health condition and skin colour, further influence the potential and actual vulnerability of a person in cases such as the one just described, as these may further undermine a person's ability to make themselves heard. A lack of language proficiency in English or German, and psychic conditions such as Post Traumatic Stress Disorder (PTSD), further hamper communication with potentially helpful people like security personnel and social workers in the centres. Subtle and overt forms of racism within the chain of complaint management may intersect with the gender dimension to increase 'testimonial injustice', as both interact in causing the hearer to give 'a deflated level of credibility to a speaker's word' (Fricker 2007: 1).

This is not to say, however, that there are no alternative ways for conceiving these spaces on the governance and planning level. In some locales, like the area where I am conducting my research, local actors have been quite successful in raising societal and political awareness of the situation of women. Also, beginning in the autumn of 2015, national and local news outlets started to report more extensively on the situation of women in the centres. In light of this, several cities and communes have opened special accommodation centres for women and children, and for other particularly vulnerable groups such as LGBTIQ refugees. These measures have in some cases led to a certain improvement of the situation for those affected, at least as far as direct violence related to sexual orientation or gender identity is concerned. Preferable to a gradual improvement or upgrading of standards, however, would be to limit more effectively its structural dimensions by significantly reducing the time that people have to spend in these spaces, such as by putting more effort into decentralizing accommodation.

Spatial Practice: Interactive Spaces of the Everyday

The dimension of spatial practice refers to the daily performance of space, routes and routines that produce and reproduce space (Lefebvre [1974] 1991: 33). While societal members are trying to grant cohesion and continuity to space, they enact, materialize and appropriate the ideal and material facets that are laid out in the conceived dimension of space. In order to do so, they build up a certain competence and knowledge about these facets, while at the same time always being predetermined, prearranged and controlled by them. Spatial practice includes relations and interaction of people with the concrete spatial materiality as well as with others in these spaces. It also entails a temporal dimension, as it points to the very way people experience and perceive space, which, of course, may change over time (Elden 2004: 185).

Refugee centres are a case in point. While refugees may have initially had feelings of relief or even gratitude with the spatial arrangements of reception and accommodation centres, over time this often devolves into feelings of frustration, insecurity and desperation. After months or years in such centres, people increasingly lose faith in the liminality of their experience, no longer perceiving them as only transit zones but as places where they are stranded for good (see also Thorshaug 2016). This is also due to the fact that the occupants often have only very limited control over their passages in and out of these spaces.

For the women in the women's housing I visited, for instance, being allowed to move out of the *Heim*, as they usually refer to the accommodation centre, and into a private apartment was highly important, but at the same time constituted a matter of vagueness and a guessing game. They repeatedly debated who had already been assigned permanent housing and what the reason for this might have been, as the decision-making procedures were very obscure to them. Although the accommodation centres are viewed by these women as spaces of liminality, they themselves do not possess much control over when this liminality will end. This situation is further aggravated for those who face additional risks of vulnerability, like traumatic experiences or forms of mental illnesses. Against this backdrop, psychologists working with refugees repeatedly point to the limits of their therapeutic attempts to stabilize traumatized people as long as the living conditions and residence perspectives remain in limbo. As one psychiatrist continuously emphasized, 'there is no inner security without outer security' (Male psychiatrist, June 2016).[12]

As mentioned above, and despite the lack of reliable statistical data, SGBV as a form of violence against women in refugee centres in Germany was reported by several agents to be an alarming problem. In addition to studies commissioned by the European Parliament (Bonewit 2016), the Women's Refugee Commission (Hersh and Obser 2016) and the German

Institute for Human Rights (Rabe 2015), local actors such as social workers, counselling services and local physicians continued to raise the issue. They describe the spatial conditions in the facilities as a major exacerbating factor for the occurrence of harassments and assaults.[13] Despite the fact that women and men are usually housed in single-sex dormitories, assaults against women are facilitated due to the fact that these dormitories are within the same buildings. Hence, men and women still share their routes to the bathrooms and use common kitchen areas. Moreover, dormitory doors are often barely lockable due to the fact that there is usually only one key given to a group of people sharing one bedroom. Main entrance doors in accommodation centres are often left unlocked due to the high number of people having to frequent them. With this practice, people from outside the centres also have free access to the buildings. As a result, women may become victims of harassment not only from people inside but also from those living elsewhere, as was the case in one of the facilities I researched (participant observation, shared accommodation centre, August 2016).

Beyond occasions of violence that are classified as SGBV, women, especially those unaccompanied by male partners or friends, seem to be easier targets for various forms of petty crime than their male counterparts. Like incidents of SGBV, these may result in feelings of insecurity or threat, turning the allegedly safe spaces into spaces of anxiety. A social worker reported:

> We had several women who felt very vulnerable because they could not lock their doors. There were, for example, three Somali women who shared a room. They did not even sleep in a tent, but they reported that they woke up at night because of a loud noise and their door was open and all their handbags were gone ... Obviously, someone had been in their room, which was highly threatening for them ... There was this awareness that someone was in their room. (Female social worker, April 2016, my translation from German)

It is worth noting that the context of this interview was also a situation where petty criminals from the surrounding area were repeatedly caught climbing the centre's fences at night and breaking into the overcrowded buildings, and where it was difficult to determine later on whether the crimes had been committed by people inside or outside the camp. Confronted with these conditions, many women develop tactics and strategies to be able to better handle them. The social worker described how many women started to take night shifts in order to watch over each other, and that they used the bathroom at night only in groups to protect themselves and one another from sexual harassment.

A former refugee woman furthermore described in an interview how women step in for one another:

Women protect each other, also children. I do admire this. Again and again, there are very brave women in the camps. For example, they help each other when a woman is being beaten, or go and get help. Often, in the reception centre, women do not turn to the security personnel themselves when something happens – other women do this for them. (Female, former refugee, April 2016, my translation from German)

In general, social support networks and solidarities between groups of refugees are highly important to prevent the occurrence of violence, especially against more vulnerable members of the group. Women fleeing without male partners frequently join with families or receive protection and help from other refugees, male and female alike.[14] In the case mentioned above, where a woman was stalked by someone living outside the centre, she had male friends patrolling the premises at night to protect her against this person until the issue had been resolved with the support of police and social workers (participant observation, shared accommodation centre, August 2016). This speaks against the general suspicion, often connected to neocolonial and racist arguments, that refugee men, by nature, are more likely to become perpetrators of SGBV (see Turner, Chapter 2 in this volume).[15] Hence, the question pursued here is not why perpetrators conduct violence, but rather how spatial conditions facilitate the occurrence of violence and the violation of refugee women. With regards to the importance of the just mentioned solidarities, for example, it is all the more damaging for women (and, of course, to everyone else), when newly established social networks are again ripped apart as refugees are repeatedly transferred (e.g. from reception to accommodation centres or from one accommodation centre to another).[16]

Beyond these direct forms of violence, women face additional forms of structural and cultural violence. Daily routes and routines are often characterized by either 'hanging out' (i.e. tediousness, waiting and pointless killing of time) or by predetermined obligations, such as participation in integration seminars or collecting documents from different public authorities. When asked how the day is spent at the reception centre, a juvenile refugee answered: 'In the morning we are queuing up for breakfast, and at midday we are queuing up for lunch. That's all' (Male, underage refugee, reception centre, July 2015). Again, the dimension of the everyday spatial practice in the centres has a gender dimension because gender relations as well as gender inequalities predetermine interactions among refugees, between refugees and other actors, as well as with the materiality of these spaces. Especially common areas where refugees can socialize – if these exist – are mostly occupied by men, while women generally feel (or are made to feel) less comfortable lingering there. Programmes installed by volunteers, such as German classes that often bridge the time until asylum seekers are permitted to take official language courses, are often less accessible for women as they bear the primary responsibility for taking care of the children. Generally speaking, access to and exchange of knowledge and information is therefore much more readily available for men. From my experience as a volunteer German teacher, I know that German classes are also a platform for the exchange of relevant information, like where to find second-hand shops, or how to get discount cards for public amenities. But the number of men in the classes is disproportionately high, and as a consequence, women may not receive such information, or only via their male partners.

Another aspect is related to self-conception and understanding of one's role as a woman and the interrelation of individual conceptions of gender identity with the material conditions of the refugee centres. The following quote by a refugee woman elucidates this:

> There are a lot of spatial problems. Women are caring for the whole family, and in the camps they have no opportunity to do so. They suffer because they cannot sufficiently provide for their children. When the children have to go to school, they sometimes have to go without breakfast because the kitchen is crowded. Women then suffer that they have to send their children without breakfast.[17]

Looking at these everyday experiences of women mentioned in the quote, including a sensitivity to diffusion of power(s) in and through space, allows one to grasp their (in)security and vulnerability in general, and not only in light of their victimization through sexual or gender-based violence. It shows how their self-understanding as a woman, mother, or caregiver may be seriously compromised in refugee centres. Again, this point is not made in order to essentialize the role of women, family or gender relations, and nor does it aim to suggest what these roles should look like (Smith 1987). The argument is to call for increased attention to the individuality of refugees' experiences and specificities of suffering, violations and violence that exist in refugee centres due to the lack of choices that exist in defining one's own (gendered) identity. These sufferings also have their origins in the interactive dimension of the everyday, for example in the interaction of refugee women with spatial materiality, with refugee men, security and other personnel at the facilities, or even with other refugee women. To briefly illustrate the latter: one woman, who had fled her home country after breaking up with her abusive husband, told me how she was repeatedly bullied and disciplined by another woman in the accommodation centre for her allegedly inappropriate behaviour, such as not wearing a headscarf or inviting over (female) friends from her language classes (Participant observation, women's accommodation centre, July 2017). In the everyday of the refugee centre, where large numbers of people from numerous backgrounds, cultures, classes and biographic experiences are living together in congested spaces, spaces where the private and the public spheres often completely amalgamate simply because there are no private spheres,[18] there is also a much less solid basis of what usually informs and lends structure to the social life of the everyday – the things taken for granted, the things that are immediately comprehensible in a social encounter, the practices considered 'normal' (Newman 2009: 44). Hence the particular and burdening imperative of an ongoing (re)negotiation of one's own gendered identity and the conception of what it means to be a woman.

Representational Space: (Re-)Appropriated Spaces

Due to their very characteristics, refugee centres severely contradict the individual's ability to appropriate them, to turn these spaces into places of 'at-homeness' or empowerment. When asked whether, after his fourteen months of stay in Germany, he had started to begin to feel at home, an interlocutor of mine responded resolutely: 'Here? This is not a home. This is a *Heim!*' (Male refugee, September 2016). However, it would be a misconception to perceive the people in these spaces as passive victims or even 'bare lives', as Agamben and others would have it. By drawing on examples, the following illustrates how lived spaces in a Lefebvrian sense are carved out by refugees, despite the overall restrictions. Similar examples can certainly be observed at many other refugee centres.

A Syrian interlocutor pointed to the fact that Syrian refugees who were deeply engaged in the opposition movement in their home country immediately took charge in the reception centres by looking after others, helping those in need, and bringing to the table their own biographic experiences and sets of knowledge (Female, former refugee, online conversation, March 2016). Moreover, there are several refugee self-organizations and movements in Germany that do not take these spaces as a given, and that call for a radical improvement of the living situations, if not the abolishment of the camps altogether: Women in Exile, Lampedusa in Hamburg, and Refugees for Change are just some of these. Ad hoc protest, demonstrations organized by refugees,[19] hunger strikes and other activities complement the picture.

The following is an example from a women's shelter where I was invited by one of the women for a dinner during Ramadan (Participant observation, women's accommodation centre, June 2016).[20] The centre hosts about twenty women, some of whom have one or more children. Since many of the women are Muslim, groups of women gathered in the bedrooms in the evening to have the fast-breaking meal together. As a single mother, I had brought my three-year-old son, and when he fell asleep later that evening my host and I joined the other women in the corridor, where they had begun to gather after finishing their meals. They moved chairs and an old sofa together and a lively conversation – a mixture of German, English and Arabic, complemented by mime and gestures – got underway. There was a lot of joking and collective laughter; a recurrent topic was the alleged uselessness of men, on which all agreed, with winking eyes and expressed by a pantomime kicking out of ex-husbands. All of the six women present, including myself and the two teenage daughters of one of the women sitting together in the circle, had either deliberately left their husbands in their home country, or left them after their arrival, or had not been married yet. There was a collective reassertion that women are strong and could also make it on their own, especially in a country like Germany. The atmosphere temporarily got more serious when one of the women briefly went to her room and the others shared that physical violence had caused her to leave her husband. Later on, music on a mobile phone was turned on and one woman performed an Arabic dance. She then continued by acting a pantomime joke, causing everyone to burst out in laughter. When suddenly crying was heard from one of the bedrooms, three of the women immediately got up, obviously very concerned, and went to the room to comfort the sobbing woman. As soon as they learned that only lovesickness was behind the sobbing and that the woman was on the phone with a lost love, they returned to the circle, visibly relieved.

The evening evidently revealed moments of mutual nurturance, solidarity and also a (temporary) reappropriation of the space, including its materiality as well as its atmospheric-sensorial aspects. The moving of chairs, the gathering, the playing of music, the serving of tea, and the watching of dance and pantomime transformed the otherwise rather glum corridor into a lived and lively social space. At the same time, the women's reaction to the crying woman pointed out to me that this gathering was more than simply 'having a good time'. Many of the women had lost close relatives in the war, especially in Syria, and had relatives who continue to live in their war-torn home country. Besides the spatial restrictions of the centres, it is also this reality that is always on the brink of interrupting such spaces. It is all the more important to support the refugees' efforts to create safe spaces, spaces of 'at-homeness', in all of the spatial dimensions described above.

Conclusion

The focus of this chapter has been on examining reception and accommodation centres for refugees in Germany and looking more closely at the situation of women in these spaces. It was argued that gender intersects with other categories of inequality and discrimination, and increases the likelihood of female refugees being exposed to different forms of direct, structural and cultural violence. To this end, spatial theory, especially Henry Lefebvre's three-dimensional understanding of the social production of space, was consulted. It proved to offer a valuable framework of analysis to examine discrimination and subordination of female refugees, but also creative actions of appropriation and renegotiation in refugee spaces in Germany.

When conducting a sociological analysis of reception and accommodation centres, one should discern the restrictions and limitations that these spaces impose on refugees and be sensitive to the facilitating effect they may have on the occurrence of various forms of violence. At the same time, reducing their inmates to victims or even 'bare life' is a shortened characterization as it neglects the variety of everyday experiences and the peoples' perseverance and creativity in shaping it. Taking the spatiality of reception and accommodation centres seriously by looking at them through the lenses of spatial theory, as suggested in this chapter, offers just that: the ability to grasp the multidimensionality of these centres as conceived, perceived and lived spaces, as well as the agency of refugees themselves, without belittling or romanticizing their struggle.

Although only briefly mentioned in this chapter, it would be interesting for future research to examine more closely the interlinking of space and time in refugee centres. How, for example, does the length of one's stay in a centre affect the individual attitude towards it, one's everyday spatial practice as well as the (re-)appropriation of the spaces? Here, a stronger differentiation between reception and accommodation centre would also be required. A recurring topic in almost all of my conversations with people in the accommodation centres was their wish to move on to private housing and to end the condition of liminality that they feel to be in. Also, a systematic comparative analysis of mixed-sex and female-only accommodation centres could reveal more explicitly if and how women could profit from being accommodated in the latter, or else what accommodation situations ideally should look like. In my research, I have come across various women who, despite the somewhat better conditions in female-only accommodations, preferred to stay in mixed-sex facilities because they did not want to lose contact with their (partly male) solidarity networks. This raises more questions, for instance, of how spaces must look to be considered as safe spaces, especially by vulnerable groups, while at the same time not undermining their own active engagement in building their material and social environments like homeplaces or solidarity networks. Overall, one can deduce that any prolonged stay in a large reception or accommodation centre is significantly contradicting these very efforts. Hence, practical activities as well as academic approaches towards the matter should be sensitive to the individuality of experiences, and, most of all, listen carefully to the affected people themselves about their needs.

Melanie Hartmann is a PhD candidate at the International Graduate Centre for the Study of Culture at the Justus-Liebig University Giessen in Germany. She is a lecturer and affiliated researcher at the Center for Conflict Studies at Philipps University Marburg in Germany. She holds an MA in Political Science, Cultural Anthropology and Communication Science from Ludwig-Maximilians University in Munich. She was a Fulbright Scholar at the School for Conflict Analysis and Resolution at George Mason University in Fairfax. Her current research focuses on refugee accommodation in Germany from a spatial theoretical perspective.

Notes

1. In 2015, the German Federal Office for Migration and Refugees (Bundesamt für Migration und Flüchtlinge, BAMF) recorded a total of 476,649 asylum claims (BAMF 2016a). Due to the backlog in the processing of the asylum applications, the actual estimated number of people who arrived in Germany during 2015 is likely to exceed one million (BAMF 2016b).
2. Sexual and gender-based violence is understood as defined in the Introduction of this book.
3. Although the focus here is on female refugees, it goes without saying that gender identity goes far beyond this and that it is a dynamic rather than an essential category of human identity. Sexual orientation and gender identity may have various impacts on the refugee experience. Especially lesbian, gay, bisexual, transgender, intersex and queer (LGBTIQ) refugees often become victims of various forms of violence (Refugee Studies Centre, University of Oxford 2013).
4. While the wording chosen in this paragraph mostly follows the official language, it is important to bear in mind that this language is not seen to be neutral, or innocent (see Barthes 1968). A case in point is the phrase 'reception centre', which more critical voices usually prefer to replace with the word 'camp' – obviously evoking quite different associations.
5. In other cases, however (e.g. for those coming from so-called 'safe countries of origin'), people are not transferred to the municipalities at all and must stay in arrival or reception facilities until their deportation is carried out. Special procedures also apply for other groups such as unaccompanied minors, but are not considered in this chapter.
6. This summary cannot do justice to the content of each of these or their levels of interconnectedness. To avoid an abridged account of these dimensions, one would have to approach Lefebvre's spatial theory through his broader theoretical work – more specifically, alongside his indebtedness to Hegelian dialectics, Marxian materialism and Nietzschean theory of language. For more detailed introductions to Lefebvre's work, refer to Elden (2004) and Schmid (2008, 2010).
7. The discussion about whether Lefebvre's dialectic reasoning is in fact the replacement of dialectics with 'trialectics', as Christian Schmid (2008) infers, or

rather its complementation by a third term, respectively a three-way process, as Stuart Elden (2004) suggests, must be suspended in this chapter.

8. For a similar attempt in the neighbouring discipline of migration studies, where 'intersectionality' has been taken up to explain the various forms of oppression that (female) migrants experience as they are pushing and crossing boundaries of race, nation, ethnicity, class and gender, see Nash (2008), Gutiérrez Rodriguez (2010) and Bastia (2014).

9. In his magnum opus, the 'Homo Sacer' trilogy, Giorgio Agamben (1998) describes the camp as the nomos of modernity, a place where the state of exception, determined by the sovereign, has its rule, and general law is suspended. Its inmate is the *homo sacer*, a person who may be killed by anyone but not sacrificed, who is essentially stripped of his humanness, his legal rights, and reduced to the passivity and brutality of the 'bare life'.

10. Other examples on the national level would be the delay in the implementation of the EU Recast Reception Conditions Directive 2013/33/EU into German law, or the delay in the ratification of the Istanbul Convention, both of which also make specific reference to the accommodation conditions of refugee women.

11. The German interview here reads: 'Alle standen wie der Ochs vor'm Berg' ('everyone stood like the ox in front of a mountain'), a German idiom that translates roughly into everyone being completely clueless, maybe even paralysed.

12. The psychiatrist is a representative of a local network of experts aiming at improving the psychological coverage for refugees, e.g. those suffering from PTSD. Memorandum of conversation (memcon) during public hearing.

13. A range of other aspects, such as the psychological condition of the perpetrators and cultural constructions of gender relations are also seen to factor into the occurrence of SGBV.

14. The former refugee woman in the interview stated that, based on her experience, fellow countrymen often protect women during and after the flight. Besides refugees, other actors such as security personnel and smugglers have been reported to commit SGBV against refugee women.

15. A highly unfortunate intermingling of anti-violence argumentation with racist and neocolonial discourses, for example, followed the incidents that occurred on New Year's Eve in Cologne, where several women were severely harassed by men with migration backgrounds.

16. In determining the accommodation after the initial reception centre, German law only requires unity in the case of core family members.

17. Memcon: Answer of a refugee women, representative of *Women in Exile e.V.*, on my question as to how the experience of women differs from that of men in the centres (public Q&A session at Marburg University, July 2016). The importance of being able to care for one's family was also mentioned in various other conversations with refugee women.

18. One could maybe argue that the private realm is strengthened as people are moved on in the asylum process from reception centres to accommodation centres, and eventually maybe even private housing. For instance,

accommodation centres are usually smaller than reception centres; food is not distributed but self-made; the fluctuation of people is lower, etc.

19. In one of my cities of research, for instance, refugees accommodated in the reception centre organized a protest march to the town hall in December 2014 to demonstrate for better living conditions at the centre.

20. I assume that this evening would not have happened in a similar manner in a mixed-sex accommodation, and the particular familial background of the women who contributed to it was certainly a reason why they stated that they preferred to live without male refugees. This is not to say, however, that networks of solidarity as well as reappropriations and renegotiations of space do not happen in mixed-sex accommodation as well. The point here is to argue for a greater sensitivity, and to cater for the refugees' needs while not victimizing them.

Bibliography

Agamben, G. (1994) 1998. *Homo Sacer: Sovereign Power and Bare Life.* Stanford, CA: Stanford University Press.

——. (2003) 2005. *State of Exception.* Chicago and London: University of Chicago Press.

Anthias, F., and N. Yuval-Davis. 1983. 'Contextualizing Feminism: Gender, Ethnic and Class Divisions', *Feminist Review* 15: 62–75.

Augé, M. 1995. *Non-Places: Introduction to an Anthropology of Supermodernity.* London and New York: Verso.

Bal, M. 2002. *Travelling Concepts in the Humanities. A Rough Guide.* Toronto, Buffalo and London: University of Toronto Press.

BAMF. 2014. 'Germany's Asylum Procedure – in Detail: Responsibilities, Procedures, Statistics, Legal Consequences'. Nuremberg: Abteilung Grundlagen des Asylverfahrens, Sicherheit. Retrieved 24 May 2016 from http://www.bamf.de/SharedDocs/Anlagen/EN/Publikationen/Broschueren/das-deutsche-asylverfahren.pdf;jsessionid=EC3EEFD69323B96729B9403F-23284CB2.1_cid294?__blob=publicationFile.

——. 2016a. 'Das Bundesamt in Zahlen 2015'. Nuremberg. Retrieved 9 August 2016 from http://www.bamf.de/SharedDocs/Anlagen/DE/Publikationen/Broschueren/bundesamt-in-zahlen-2015-asyl.pdf?__blob=publicationFile.

——. 2016b. '476.649 Asylanträge im Jahr 2015'. Nuremberg. Retrieved 9 August 2016 from https://www.bamf.de/SharedDocs/Meldungen/DE/2016/201610106-asylgeschaeftsstatistik-dezember.html.

Barthes, R. 1968. *Writing Degree Zero.* New York: Hill & Wang.

Bastia, T. 2014. 'Intersectionality, Migration and Development', *Progress in Development Studies* 14(3): 237–48.

Bonewit, A. 2016. 'Reception of Female Refugees and Asylum Seekers in the EU – Case Study Germany'. European Parliament. Retrieved 9 August 2016 from http://www.europarl.europa.eu/RegData/etudes/STUD/2016/536497/IPOL_STU(2016)536497_EN.pdf.

Collins, P.H. (1990) 2000. *Black Feminist Thought: Knowledge, Consciousness, and the Politics of Empowerment*, 2nd edn. New York and London: Routledge.

Crang, M., and N. Thrift (eds). 2000. *Thinking Space*. London and New York: Routledge.

Cremer, H. 2014. 'Menschenrechtliche Verpflichtungen bei der Unterbringung von Flüchtlingen: Empfehlungen an die Länder, Kommunen und den Bund'. Retrieved 10 July 2016 from http://www.institut-fuer-menschenrechte.de/fileadmin/_migrated/tx_commerce/Policy_Paper_26_Menschenrechtliche_Verpflichtungen_bei_der_Unterbringung_von_Fluechtlingen_01.pdf.

Crenshaw, K. 1991. 'Mapping the Margins: Intersectionality, Identity Politics and Violence against Women of Color', *Stanford Law Review* 43: 1241–99.

Die Landesflüchtlingsräte and Pro Asyl. 2011. 'AusgeLAGERt: Zur Unterbringung von Flüchtlingen in Deutschland'. Hildesheim.

Ek, R. 2006. 'Giorgio Agamben and the Spatialities of the Camp: An Introduction', *Geografiska Annaler: Series B, Human Geography* 88(4): 363–86.

Elden, S. 2004. *Understanding Henri Lefebvre: Theory and the Possible*. London and New York: Continuum.

Feldman, R.M., and S. Stall. 1994. 'The Politics of Space Appropriation', in I. Altman and A. Churchman (eds), *Women and the Environment*. New York: Springer Science and Business Media, pp. 167–200.

Flüchtlingsrat Baden-Württemberg. 2012. 'Human und dezentral – für eine bessere Unterbringung von Flüchtlingen in Baden-Württemberg! Positionspapier für die "AG FlüAG"'. Retrieved 10 July 2016 from http://fluechtlingsrat-bw.de/files/Dateien/Dokumente/INFOS%20-%20Unterbringung/2012-07-24%20FRBW%20FlueAG%20Unterbringung%20-%20human%20und%20dezentral.pdf.

Fricker, M. 2007. *Epistemic Injustice: Power and the Ethics of Knowing*. Oxford and New York: Oxford University Press.

Frings, D., and M. Domke. 2016. *Asylarbeit: Der Rechtsratgeber für die soziale Praxis*. Roßdorf: Fachhochschulverlag.

Galtung, J. 1969. 'Violence, Peace, and Peace Research', *Journal of Peace Research* 6(3): 167–91.

——. 1990. 'Cultural Violence', *Journal of Peace Research* 27(3): 291–305.

Girtler, R. 2001. *Methoden der Feldforschung: 4., völlig neu bearbeitete Auflage*. Vienna, Cologne and Weimar: Böhlau Verlag.

Glasze, G. 2012. 'Eine politische Konzeption von Räumen', in I. Dzudzek, C. Kunze and J. Wullweber (eds), *Diskurs und Hegemonie: Gesellschaftskritische Persektive*. Bielefeld: Transcript, pp. 151–72.

——. 2013. *Politische Räume: Die diskursive Konstitution eines "geokulturellen Raums" – die Frankophonie*. Bielefeld: Transcript.

Goffman, E. 1963. *Stigma: Notes on the Management of a Spoiled Identity*. Englewood Cliffs, NJ: Prentice Hall.

Gupta, A., and J. Ferguson (eds). 1997. *Culture, Power, Place: Exploration in Critical Anthropology*. Durham, NC and London: Duke University Press.

Gutiérrez Rodriguez, E. 2010. *Migration, Domestic Work and Affect: A Decolonial Approach on Value and the Feminization of Labor*. New York: Routledge.

Hersh, M., and K. Obser. 2016. 'Falling Through the Cracks: Refugee Women and Girls in Germany and Sweden'. New York: Women's Refugee Commission. Retrieved 10 July 2016 from https://www.womensrefugeecommission.org/gbv/resources/1308-protection-germany-sweden.

Hess, S., and B. Kasparek (eds). 2010. *Grenzregime: Diskurse, Praktiken, Institutionen in Europa*. Berlin: Assoziation A.

hooks, bell (1984) 2015. *Feminist Theory: From Margin to Center*, 3rd edn. New York and Abingdon: Routledge.

Howarth, D. 2006. 'Space, Subjectivity, and Politics', *Alternatives: Global, Local, Political* 31(2): 105–34.

Lefebvre, H. (1974) 1991. *The Production of Space*. Malden, MA, Oxford, Carlton, VIC: Blackwell Publishing.

Liga der Freien Wohlfahrtspflege Hessen. 2014. 'Positionspapier zu den Mindestanforderungen an die Unterbringung von Asylsuchenden und Flüchtlingen in Gemeinschaftsunterkünften'. Retrieved 10 July 2016 from http://www.liga-hessen.de/material/folder_listing_aktuelles.

Low, S.M., and D. Lawrence-Zúniga (eds). 2003. *The Anthropology of Space and Place: Locating Culture*. Malden, MA, Oxford, Carlton, VIC: Blackwell Publishing.

Löw, M. 2001. *Raumsoziologie*. Frankfurt am Main: Suhrkamp.

———. 2008. 'The Constitution of Space: The Structuration of Spaces through the Simultaneity of Effect and Perception', *European Journal of Social Theory* 11(1): 25–49.

Lutz, H., M.T. Herrera Vivar and L. Supik (eds). 2011. *Framing Intersectionality: Debates on a Multi-Faceted Concept in Gender Studies*. Farnham, UK, Burlington, VT: Ashgate.

Massey, D. 1992. 'Politics and Space/Time', *New Left Review* (196): 65–84.

———. 2005. *For Space*. London, Thousand Oaks, CA and New Delhi: SAGE Publications.

McCall, L. 2005. 'The Complexity of Intersectionality', *Signs: Journal of Women in Culture and Society* 30(3): 1771–1800.

Minca, C. 2006. 'Giorgio Agamben and the New Biopolitical Nomos', *Geografiska Annaler: Series B, Human Geography* 88(4): 387–403.

Murdoch, J. 2006. *Post-Structuralist Geography: A Guide to Relational Space*. London, Thousand Oaks, CA and New Delhi: SAGE Publications.

Nash, J.C. 2008. 'Re-Thinking Intersectionality', *Feminist Review* 89: 1–15.

Neumann, B., and A. Nünning (eds). 2012. *Travelling Concepts for the Study of Culture*. Berlin: De Gruyter.

Newman, D.M. 2009. *Sociology: Exploring the Architecture of Everyday Life, Brief Edition*. Thousand Oaks, CA, London, New Delhi and Singapore: Pine Forge Press.

Papst, F. 2015. 'Empfehlungen an ein Gewaltschutzkonzept zum Schutz von Frauen und Kindern vor geschlechtsspezifischer Gewalt in Gemeinschaftsunterkünften'. Berlin. Retrieved 3 May 2016 from http://infothek.paritaet.org/pid/fachinfos.nsf/0/251f9481d1383accc1257e8100560c6e/$FILE/parit_empf_gewaltschutz-konzept_gemeinschaftsunterkuenfte_web.pdf.

Rabe, H. 2015. 'Effektiver Schutz vor geschlechtsspezifischer Gewalt – auch in Flüchtlingsunterkünften'. Berlin. Retrieved 10 July 2016 from http://www.

institut-fuer-menschenrechte.de/fileadmin/user_upload/Publikationen/ Policy_Paper/Policy_Paper_32_Effektiver_Schutz_vor_geschlechtsspezifis- cher_Gewalt.pdf.

Ralser, M. 2013. 'Die Bio-Politik der Migrationsregime und die Normalität des Rassismus', in P. Mecheril et al. (eds), *Migrationsforschung als Kritik? Konturen einer Forschungsperspektive.* Wiesbaden: Springer VS, pp. 277–87.

Ramadan, A. 2013. 'Spatialising the Refugee Camp', *Transactions of the Institute of British Geographers* 38(1): 65–77.

Refugee Studies Centre, University of Oxford. 2013. 'Sexual Orientation and Gender Identity and the Protection of Forced Migrants', *Forced Migration Review* 42.

Schmid, C. 2008. 'Henri Lefebvre's Theory of the Production of Space: Towards a Three-Dimensional Dialectic', in K. Goonewardena et al. (eds), *Space, Difference, Everyday Life: Reading Henri Lefebvre.* New York and Abingdon: Routledge, pp. 27–45.

———. 2010. *Stadt, Raum und Gesellschaft: Henri Lefebvre und die Theorie der Produktion des Raumes.* Stuttgart: Franz Steiner Verlag.

Smith, D.E. 1987. *The Everyday World as Problematic: A Feminist Sociology.* Boston: Northeastern University Press.

Soja, E.W. (1989) 2011. *Postmodern Geographies: The Reassertion of Space in Critical Social Theory.* London and New York: Verso.

Thorshaug, R.Ø. 2016. 'Reception Centres for Asylum Seekers as Architectures of Mobility?'. Paper presented at the 16th Conference of the International Association for the Study of Forced Migration, trans. IASFM. Poznan, Poland.

Turner, S. 2015. 'What Is a Refugee Camp? Explorations of the Limits and Effects of the Camp', *Journal of Refugee Studies* 29(2), 139–48.

van Houtum, H. 2010. 'Human Blacklisting: The Global Apartheid of the EU's External Border Regime', *Environment and Planning D: Society and Space* 28(6): 957–76.

Walters, W. 2006. 'Border/Control', *European Journal of Social Theory* 9(2): 187–203.

Wendel, K. 2014. 'Unterbringung von Flüchtlingen in Deutschland: Regelungen und Praxis der Bundesländer im Vergleich'. Frankfurt am Main.

Wimmer, A., and N. Glick Schiller. 2002. 'Methodological Nationalism and Beyond: Nation-State Building, Migration and the Social Sciences', *Global Networks* 2(4): 301–34.

Zetter, R. 1991. 'Labelling Refugees: Forming and Transforming a Bureaucratic Identity', *Journal of Refugee Studies* 4(1): 39–62.

———. 2007. 'More Labels, Fewer Refugees: Remaking the Refugee Label in an Era of Globalization', *Journal of Refugee Studies* 20(2): 172–92.

6

'Faithing' Gender and Responses to Violence in Refugee Communities

Insights from the Sahrawi Refugee Camps and the Democratic Republic of Congo

Elena Fiddian-Qasmiyeh, Chloé Lewis and Georgia Cole

Introduction

Since the 1990s, many studies have examined the gendered nature and impacts of religion and faith-based actors, in development processes. It is only recently, however, that academics, practitioners and policy makers have concretely taken an interest in the roles played by religion and spirituality on the one hand and by faith-based actors, on the other, in humanitarian responses to forced migration (Fiddian-Qasmiyeh 2011, 2015). In particular, academic enquiry into why, how and to what effect faith-based organizations (FBOs) and local faith communities (LFCs) have responded to displacement situations has expanded in the 2010s (ibid.). This has both resulted in, and reacted to, statements made by major international agencies, including the United Nations High Commissioner for Refugees (UNHCR), that increasingly aim to partner with faith-based actors in order to support forced migrants. UNHCR, for instance, coordinated the high profile High Commissioner's Dialogue on Faith and Protection in December 2012, launched a 'Welcoming the Stranger' initiative with key faith leaders in 2013, and published 'Partnership Note on Faith-based Organizations, Local Faith Communities and Faith Leaders' 2014. This increasing academic and policy interest is in part due to challenges faced by external actors in accessing conflict and disaster-affected areas (Fiddian-Qasmiyeh and Ager 2013: 27), as well as the fact that state service providers are often weakened or destroyed as a result of conflict and disasters, 'leaving religious institutions as the main providers of essential services, support and solace for society' (RfP 2004: 11).

However, with major agencies such as UNHCR having recently 'discovered' the potential roles that FBOs and LFCs[1] may play in supporting refugees, it is particularly notable that religion (as identity, belief and practice) is often perceived as being likely to maintain or reinforce the gendered status quo by reproducing patriarchal structures, including in refugee contexts (Fiddian-Qasmiyeh 2015). In essence, it is commonly argued that '[r]eligion is [often] used to legitimize patriarchal hierarchies' (Tadros 2010: 14), and that hegemonic religious attitudes to sexuality and marriage, for instance, may endorse 'gender inequality in relationships', and reinforce 'practices that increase women's vulnerability to domestic and sexual violence' (Smith and Kaybryn 2013: 36). Such assertions therefore raise questions with regards to the potential roles of religion, and of organizations and communities motivated by faith principles, with regard to gender roles and relations, as well as sexual and gender-based violence (SGBV) in refugee situations.

As noted by Tomalin, '*little evidence* is available about the gender-related implications of current *development* policies and practical initiatives that actively engage with religion' (Tomalin 2013: 193; emphasis added). Even less evidence exists regarding current humanitarian policies and programmes. In effect, a recent Joint Learning Initiative (JLI)[2] scoping survey (Fiddian-Qasmiyeh and Ager 2013) has demonstrated that there has been limited academic or policy engagement with respect to the intersections between religion, refugees and gender, including vis-à-vis SGBV (also see Fiddian-Qasmiyeh 2016). This gap can partly be explained by the wariness of secular organizations 'about being openly critical of religious organizations for their attitudes towards gender, or indeed probing very far at all into their values and policies on gender equality' (Tomalin 2011: 6). Beyond this wariness, in one of the twelve preliminary interviews we conducted with academics and practitioners between December 2014 and March 2015 to examine the intersections between gender, faith and humanitarian responses to forced migration,[3] Michael J. Sharp, the former Eastern DRC coordinator at the Mennonite Central Committee, said: 'If I'm honest, I had not thought of those three concepts [faith, gender and humanitarianism] together in the same sentence until you mentioned this project to me' (Skype interview, 31 December 2014).

Indeed, several of the individuals from 'secular' and faith-based organizations we interviewed in 2014–15 spoke of the need for empirically informed research, guidance and advice to assist them in dispelling preconceived ideas about the intersections of faith, gender and violence in contexts of forced migration (interviews with technical advisor at Tearfund, Skype, 20 February 2015; and Oxfam GB humanitarian representative, 6 February 2015). Interviewees did not seek such research to strengthen relationships in field contexts, where several of them suggested that a natural affinity between the approaches of FBOs and secular organizations had long resulted in productive partnerships (interview with MENA representative for Terre des Hommes, 9 February 2015). Rather, it was requested to present to colleagues within these organizations' headquarters, who maintain a steadfast opposition to engaging with LFCs and FBOs due to an inherent suspicion about the 'place' of faith-inspired ideologies in the humanitarian sphere, and a set of assumptions about the primordial nature of religious approaches (Fiddian-Qasmiyeh 2015).

Recognizing this evidence gap, this chapter aims to contribute to these emerging debates by examining the relationship between religion/secularism, gender and violence in refugee situations from a variety of perspectives. The first section offers a brief historical introduction to the shifting roles of religion and secularism in development and humanitarian discourse, policies and programmes. It focuses in particular on the nature and impacts of the widely held assumption that secularism offers the most appropriate means to empower women and reduce women's risks to violence, including in contexts of forced migration. The chapter then turns to two case studies that respectively explore the roles of secularism and religion – firstly, in a North African protracted refugee camp, and secondly, in a major context of conflict-induced internal and international displacement in the Great Lakes. The first case study revolves around the Sahrawi refugee camps in South West Algeria, home to UNHCR's second-longest protracted caseload. It examines how, and to what effect, members of the Sahrawi refugee elite strategically mobilize the intersecting discourses of secularism, gender empowerment and the eradication of violence against refugee women, to position themselves as 'the ideal refugees'. The case study highlights the paradoxical impacts of the secular discourse of global good governance, and the ways gender-based conditionalities can lead to the *repress-entation* both of a refugee's religious belief and identity, and of gender-based violence in refugee situations. Subsequently, the second case study focuses on the current and emerging work of Tearfund in the Democratic Republic of Congo (DRC), where the scale of displacement inside and outside of the country 'remains serious' as a result of ongoing violence and conflict in the region (UNHCR 2015). This case study explores the potential for FBOs to promote gender equality and develop a preventative framework against SGBV by engaging men and boys through theologically inspired programming.

Through these two geographically distinct case studies, and drawing on the trope of (in)visibility, this chapter brings faith to the foreground in discussions of gender and violence in refugee communities and displacement contexts. In the Sahrawi case study, we show that Islamic religious identity and practice are rendered invisible by the Polisario, as is violence against women, to prove the community's 'secular' and therefore 'ideal' nature to international funders and observers. In effect, this section of the chapter points to some of the possible consequences of making faith invisible in displacement contexts. In converse, the DRC case study discusses an emerging response to sexual and gender-based violence centred on and driven by religion, in this case Christianity, in Tearfund's 'Transforming Masculinities' intervention. This second case study makes both religion and masculinity visible in humanitarian contexts in a way that might challenge patriarchal gender norms as a means for enhancing the protection of displaced women.

Historical Context: A Return to Faith in Humanitarianism?

The lack of critical inquiry into the significance of religion in experiences of and responses to contemporary refugee contexts, including with particular reference to gender and different forms of violence, is particularly notable when we place contemporary debates in historical context. What we currently refer to as 'humanitarianism' – including humanitarian responses to forced migration – is largely informed by the West's colonial projects and their 'civilizing mission'. As is extensively documented, both of these endeavours were actively supported by Christian missionary societies. Furthermore, these intersecting missionary and colonial discourses were intrinsically gendered in nature, with such faith-based interventions including missionaries' roles in implementing paternalistic and orientalist colonial policies that aimed to 'save brown women from brown men' (Spivak 1993: 93). In effect, feminist studies have long revealed that colonial discourses and policies have historically been based upon a 'discursive strategy that constructs gender subordination as integral only to certain [non-Western] cultures', for highly political purposes (Volpp 2001: 1181).

Although Christian discourses, doctrines and actors were pervasive in colonial-cum-development programmes throughout the eighteenth and nineteenth centuries, the birth of the 'professionalized' aid industry in the post-Second World War era through to the early 2000s prioritized secular approaches. The latter has generally been conceptualized as the most effective means to secure democratic political structures, good governance, and women's rights. With particular reference to faith-based responses to refugees, Ferris notes that religion 'is often perceived to be conservative, steeped in tradition, and invariably resisting change ... [W]hile modern secular values are invariably presented as espousing gender equality, religion is assumed to confine women to traditional roles' (Ferris 2011: 623). The official promotion of secularism in the international aid industry prior to the 2000s was thus effectively justified through a continuation of colonial assumptions that 'traditional' religious and cultural frameworks were barriers to sociocultural 'change' (read: 'modernization') in general, but also to women's empowerment and women's rights more specifically, including the right for refugee women to be free from violence (see Fiddian-Qasmiyeh 2015).

Refugee Situations and the Promotion of Gender Equality, Female Empowerment, and Freedom from SGBV

The nexus between sexual violence and displacement is a complex and multifaceted one. The prevalence of SGBV in refugee camps around the world has long been widely documented (Callamard 1999; El-Bushra 2000), and clear guidelines and operational standards have been developed by UNHCR to protect refugee women and girls (including UNHCR 1991, 1995, 2002). These aim to identify risk factors that can be addressed to maximize the prevention of SGBV in displacement camps (UNHCR EXCOM 2004; UNHCR 2008), rather than merely responding to SGBV post facto. Simultaneously, displacement has been identified as providing a space for 'positive' change and gender empowerment due to the resulting disruption of traditional social systems and the reconfiguration of the gendered division of labour. Indeed, as part of its international protection mandate, UNHCR has the responsibility to promote gender equality (UNHCR 2008: 23), including by facilitating the 'empowerment and enhancement of productive capacities and self-reliance of refugees, particularly of women, pending durable solutions' (UNHCR 2003: 5). Despite the rationale underpinning UNHCR's gender equality and empowerment policies (where 'gender' generally continues to be synonymous with 'women'), studies have increasingly examined their paradoxical impacts, including the extent to which such policies can lead to the increased marginalization of certain social groups in refugee situations (see Turner 2000; Fiddian-Qasmiyeh 2014a, 2014b). One key question that thus emerges is whether secular frameworks and institutions are necessarily the best means of addressing SGBV in displacement settings, or if there is a place for religious identity, belief and practice in such processes and contexts?

In much of the existing literature, FBOs' relationship with patriarchy is implicitly (and often explicitly) contrasted with a firmly held *assumption* that secular organizations have overcome these oppressive frameworks, practices and dynamics, and are therefore ideally positioned to promote the empowerment of women. This assumption in many ways reproduced in a 2006 Special Issue of *Gender & Development*, which explored 'how faiths and institutions [that] have a history of repression of, and discrimination against women, and [that] continue to be dominated by patriarchy in many areas of belief and practice, can act as catalysts for and supporters of positive social change for women' (Greany 2006: 346). Framed in this manner, it could appear that secular organizations, unlike FBOs, *are* already well positioned to 'act as catalysts for and supporters of positive social change for women' since they do *not* have a 'history of repression' or 'discrimination', and are *not* 'dominated by patriarchy' (ibid).

Such assumptions are highly problematic on multiple levels, and are contradicted by numerous examples of patriarchal dynamics pervading secular organizations, agencies and agendas. It is precisely *because* of the prevalence of gender bias across the development industry that proponents of gender and development have advanced sophisticated critiques of the androcentric foundations and implications of mainstream development and humanitarian theory, policy and practice for beneficiaries (Fiddian-Qasmiyeh 2015). Moreover, the uncritical acceptance of such assumptions obscures the fact that programmes guided by secular frameworks to 'empower' and 'protect' women often have paradoxical impacts, and can ultimately reproduce systems of oppression and violence. Such a paradox forms the crux of the first case study of this chapter centring on the 'ideal' Sahrawi refugee camps. These are represented by the Sahrawis' refugee leadership (Polisario) as secular spaces characterized by a total absence of violence against women, at least in part to fulfil the gender-based conditionalities of the (secular) discourse on global good governance.

Furthermore, it is increasingly recognized that secular frameworks and organizations do not always succeed in promoting gender equality, female empowerment, or a reduction of gender-based violence. They are, moreover, increasingly recognized as 'no better or worse' than FBOs in their attitudes, for instance towards lesbian, gay, bisexual, transgender and intersex (LGBTI) asylum seekers (ORAM survey, cited by UNHCR in Fiddian-Qasmiyeh and Ager 2013). Conversely, it is increasingly posited that local faith leaders and LFCs are often well positioned to engage with issues within their communities that are considered too sensitive, taboo or stigmatized to openly share with external actors (Fiddian-Qasmiyeh and Ager 2013). For instance, Parsitau's study of female internally displaced Kikuyu victims of sexual and gender-based violence in Kenya highlights that faith communities were the only actors able to provide trauma counselling in that context (Parsitau 2011). Concurrently, it is asserted that certain FBOs officially promote the empowerment of women and the transformation of both female and male subjectivities. Indeed, emerging literature maintains that FBOs are 'positive agents for the advancement of gender equality ... highlighting the positive role faith and faith-based initiatives can play in eliciting social change' (Tadros 2010: 1). This is explored in the second case study below through an analysis of Tearfund's initiative to reduce SGBV by promoting the development of a positive, 'Christ-like' masculinity in the DRC. With the above in mind, we now turn to the first case study.

Case Study 1: The 'Ideal' Sahrawi Refugee Camps: Secular = Gender Equal = Free from Violence against Women

The Sahrawi refugee camps were established in South West Algeria in 1975, and are estimated to be home to between 125,000 and 150,000 refugees from the Western Sahara (for a detailed history of the conflict over the Western Sahara, see Fiddian-Qasmiyeh 2014a). This territory was formerly known as the Spanish Sahara, is still pending self-determination and is now commonly known as 'Africa's last colony'. Whilst almost entirely dependent upon externally provided support, the Sahrawi refugee camps have, since their establishment, been managed by the Polisario Front and its camp-based 'state-in-exile', the Sahrawi Arab Democratic Republic (SADR). Recognized as a state by over seventy non-Western countries and as a full member of the African Union (formerly the Organization of African Unity), the SADR has developed its own constitution, camp-based ministries, police force (and prisons), army and parallel 'state' and religious legal systems, the latter implementing a Maliki interpretation of Islam. The Sahrawi 'state', law and religion are thus intimately interconnected in the camps, with Islam explicitly identified in the Sahrawi Constitution as the fundamental source of the Sahrawi legal system (SADR 2003: Art. 2), and the Ministry of Justice and Religious Affairs has joint functions.

Despite these interconnections, and despite the significance of Islamic belief and practice to refugees' everyday life in the camps (Fiddian-Qasmiyeh 2014a), the Sahrawi refugee camps have habitually been heralded by European and North American observers as 'ideal' spaces and locales of 'best practice' through explicit reference to the 'secular' and 'gender equal' nature of the camps (Fiddian-Qasmiyeh 2010a, 2010b, 2014a, 2014b). Indeed, of particular pertinence to this chapter are the official accounts made by SADR representatives that directly relate the absence of violence against women to the self-proclaimed 'secular' nature of the Sahrawi refugee camps. One example is embodied in a selection of interviews given by Maima Mahmud Nayem, the director of the Dakhla refugee camp's Women's School and Dakhla camp's representative of the SADR Secretary of State for Social Affairs and Emancipation of Sahrawi Women. She has re/created a constant connection between the 'empowered' position of women in the camps and the Sahrawi's 'secularism', both of which are re/produced as unique and exceptional:

> You must remember that the Sahara is *a secular country* and the position of Sahrawi women is *very privileged* when compared with other women of the Arab world and Europe. Just to give you an idea, *we are the only women who do not suffer physical abuse*, and our society has imposed a Law [*sic*] to reject any man who raises his hand to a woman. (Quoted in Barrera 2008; EFQ's translation and emphasis)

In this series of accounts, Nayem claims that Sahrawi women are free in 'the Sahara' (i.e. the camp-based SADR) specifically because it is a 'secular country', a space where the Sahrawi 'have' what she labels 'secular Islam': 'Here we speak of the rights of women, of the secular Islam we have' (quoted in Portinari 2007, EFQ's translation; see also Zin 2007).

This is therefore not to claim that the Polisario/SADR unequivocally represent the Sahrawi as non-Muslims in their interactions with Western audiences, despite the reality of Sahrawi refugees' commitment to their faith. Rather, during encounters with European secular and Christian audiences, the Polisario/SADR mobilizes two intersecting strategies: first, it has a tendency to 'silence' and render invisible the multiple, and at times contested, roles of Islam in the camps; second, on those occasions when religion is mentioned, the Polisario systematically projects an image of 'secular Sahrawi Islam' that is resolutely different from any other Islam (Fiddian-Qasmiyeh 2014a). The Sahrawi refugee camps can thus be conceptualized as stages from which particular discourses and political campaigns are projected internationally to convince non-Sahrawi audiences of the justifiability and necessity of their support for the Sahrawi 'struggle' for self-determination (ibid.). The Polisario and its supporters explicitly present the Sahrawi as fulfilling all the non-economic priorities associated with contemporary notions of 'good governance', and therefore as a proto-typical example to be followed by other actors in the international arena: 'peaceful', 'secular', 'democratic', and 'gender equal' (ibid.). With reference to the latter, the success of this strategic representation is clearly reflected in UNHCR's statements vis-à-vis the refugee camps: in 2001, UNHCR's Refugee Women and Gender Equality Unit not only declared that the case of Sahrawi refugee women's empowerment is 'unique' but explicitly presented the camp-based National Union of Sahrawi Women, which has been active since the mid-1970s, as an example of 'good practice on gender mainstreaming' in its publication 'A Practical Guide to Empowerment' (UNHCR Refugee Women and Gender Equality Unit 2001).

In effect, immediately opposing the more frequently reproduced image of women as helpless victims of war and forced displacement (Malkki 1995a, 1995b), academic, NGO and journalistic accounts constitute Sahrawi refugee women as omnipresent (Vidal 1986), empowered, liberated and active agents, who, to a large extent, appear to overshadow their male compatriots (see Fiddian-Qasmiyeh 2014a). Such accounts reflect Sahrawi women's political, managerial and professional roles in the camps, with the World Food Programme stressing that Sahrawi women 'are known to be assertive and to participate in all aspects of camp life' (WFP 2002). They go as far as to (incorrectly) claim that 'Saharan society is primarily *matriarchal* and the women are *totally empowered*' (WFP 2004: 8, emphasis added). Such a resolute representation of Sahrawi women's participation and agency is simultaneously reminiscent of an OXFAM representative's declaration almost twenty years earlier that Sahrawi society 'is the most fundamentally balanced society I have ever come across in terms of the relationships between men and women' (Mowles 1986: 9).

Indeed, a male Polisario/SADR representative to Syria explicitly constructed the uniqueness of 'Sahrawi society' by equating the Sahrawi refugee camps with the absence of violence against women whilst reproducing the Middle East as a space characterized by their abuse:

> There are many differences between Sahrawi and Syrian societies ... Sahrawi women have more freedom ... Unlike in Jordan, where honour killings and sexual abuse prevail ... [Sahrawi] women do not suffer from domestic violence in the camps – she would be able to divorce him [her husband] immediately if he did, and a Sahrawi man would be unable to re-marry if he hit his wife or abused her in any way; his reputation would be destroyed. (EFQ interview with the male SADR representative to the Middle East, Damascus, July 2006)

Images of active and empowered Sahrawi refugee women are thus particularly powerful precisely because they are 'unexpected' when compared with the 'standardized' and 'generic images' that have become the norm when discussing refugee camps (following Fisk 1995: 15 in Shami 1996: 9). The Sahrawi refugee camps, as portrayed by Polisario/SADR and Western observers alike, are in essence the antithesis of what refugee camps 'are meant to look like':[4] they are democratic, secular empowering spaces that are free from violence against refugee women. The assertion that Sahrawi women are free from violence in the camps is therefore intimately related to the representation of other refugee women, and Muslim Arab women more broadly, as eternal victims of violence against women.

Denials of the existence of violence against women are not specific to the Sahrawi refugee camps. This is a particularly sensitive topic to discuss in any context, and its prevalence is frequently denied in both refugee and non-refugee situations (Gill 2004; Rees and Pease 2007). However, by not only claiming that violence against women does not exist in the Sahrawi refugee context, but also creating this as a significant part of the 'national' Sahrawi identity projected to an international audience, it becomes increasingly difficult for violence against women to be dealt with effectively and holistically in the camps (as documented in Fiddian-Qasmiyeh 2010a). Instead, violence against women (VAW) is systematically silenced, erased or concealed from international view to protect this idealized vision of the camps, a problem that is also recognized by a female Sahrawi blogger known as Wurud Asahra:

> The topic of physical violence is another issue which our leaders [the Polisario and NUSW] congratulate themselves for every day. It's true that it's not at all normal for a man to hit a woman in our culture. However, no -one intervenes when he does. Our society is not exempt from other manifestations of violence against women .... These are situations which seriously affect the lives of many women, and which, nonetheless, are neither stopped nor addressed from a legal point of view. (Asahra 2008)

In effect, if we agree with Farmer (2004: 305) that 'oppression is a result of many conditions', including processes of 'erasure', in this case we would suggest that the discursive processes that make VAW invisible in the camps can themselves be understood as a mode of structural violence. This compounds the physical and sexual abuse experienced by an unknown number of ('real' rather than 'idealized') women in the camps (see Fiddian-Qasmiyeh 2010a).

This case study has therefore shown that although agencies including UNHCR embrace and promote 'the mantras of gender mainstreaming and gender equality' (Kandiyoti quoted in Hammami 2005: 1352), discourses surrounding gender equality and, indeed, secularism may have paradoxical effects on aid recipients. Refugees and their political representatives frequently strategically adopt and reproduce discourses of gender equality and secularism when interacting with non-Sahrawi audiences to secure the support of relevant state and non-state actors. Indeed, as stressed by Harrell-Bond (1999: 151), 'most refugees are able to infer' that in order to be 'successful in obtaining aid' and gaining 'the approval of the helper', one of 'the most effective survival strategies' is to 'ingratiate themselves' with aid providers. Such strategies may result in donors celebrating the successes of their 'ideal' aid recipients and partners, reproducing the assumption that the 'secular' outlook embraced by their refugee interlocutors has facilitated the establishment of 'unique' camps which are characterized by gender equality and the absence of violence against women. Beyond rendering invisible the role that Islam plays in everyday life in the camps on the one hand, and the institutional structures of the camps on the other, this further obscures the ways in which Islamic teachings can intersect with wider sociocultural determinants to influence the prevalence of, and indeed potential responses to, SGBV within the camps. As the next case study will show, endogenous models of change developed from within religious paradigms provide an alternative and potentially more effective way of redefining gender roles in ways that are relevant to, and sustainable for, displaced populations.

Case Study 2: Transforming Masculinities to Reduce and Prevent SGBV in DRC

As noted above, thinking about the intersections of faith and gender in displacement contexts habitually conjures up a host of assumptions centring on women, and violence against women in particular. As also shown above, this has its reasons. Moreover, in a multi-religious training manual for transforming conflict, the coalition Religions for Peace observed that 'the combination of religion, women and conflict often invokes the images of oppression, brutality and misogyny' (RfP 2004: 14). Faith-based interventions aimed at redressing SGBV in conflict, displacement and humanitarian settings are thus, like their secular counterparts, conventionally female-centred (e.g. RfP 2013; WVI Zambia 2014).

The past decade has, however, seen a rapid shift in humanitarian programming towards engaging men and boys in efforts to prevent and respond to SGBV and to promote gender equality more generally. While such initiatives have been implemented in diverse ways and settings since the early 2000s (e.g. UNFPA 2000; Connell 2003), their value was recognized at the policy level in UN Security Council Resolution 2106 (adopted in 2013), which affirmed that 'the enlistment of men and boys in the effort to combat all forms of violence against women are central to long-term efforts to prevent sexual violence in armed conflict and post-conflict situations' (UNSC 2013, Preamble, paragraph 5).[5] This second case study explores a recent example of such an emerging initiative conducted in the eastern provinces of the Democratic Republic of Congo by the Christian development and relief organization, Tearfund. With Tearfund's collaborative work funded by the UK's Foreign and Commonwealth Office (FCO),[6] this analysis, therefore, sits at the heart of two parallel trends in humanitarian response efforts: the shift towards 'official' engagement with faith-based or faith-inspired humanitarian programming on the one hand, and engaging men and boys in addressing SGBV on the other. As such, critical reflection on the early stages of programmes and interventions such as this one is important; this applies not only to this specific faith-based initiative in DRC, but also to others like it being developed and implemented elsewhere.

By means of preliminary background, DRC has in many ways become defined by its protracted armed conflicts and resulting humanitarian crises, including large-scale displacement and widespread sexual and gender-based violence. With reference to displacement, in March 2015, over 2.8 million people had been internally displaced as a result of ongoing conflicts.[7] In turn, the high levels of sexual violence recorded in DRC have in particular captured international attention, contributing to DRC becoming the largest country-level recipient of funds for SGBV-related projects by a significant margin at US$ 24 million in 2012 (Development Initiatives 2014: 3). In terms of religious affiliation, ninety six per cent of the population identifies as Christian (Tearfund 2014a: 28). As such, according to Tearfund, 'the Christian faith is extremely influential in the lives of [Congolese] people, locally and nationally' (ibid.) and is identified as a potentially important 'catalyst for change' in preventing SGBV (ibid.: 9).[8]

Originally founded in 1968 out of the Evangelical Alliance fund created to 'distribute cash to evangelical agencies caring for the needs of refugees around the world', Tearfund is currently active in fifty countries (Tearfund 2016a, 2016b) and has worked in DRC, then Zaire, since 1986 (Tearfund 2016c). Since then, Tearfund has worked with local partners to, inter alia, provide healthcare to displaced persons and their host communities, reduce HIV/AIDS, and support women survivors of sexual violence. The organization's evolving work on masculinities in DRC began in 2013 with a series of formative baseline studies in Rwanda, Burundi and DRC, and grew out of its existing project 'Silent No More', which 'aim[ed] to empower the church and other faith communities to reduce [sexual violence] in conflict-affected areas in DRC' (Tearfund 2014a: 4; Deepan, personal communication, 14 July 2016). The particular component of Tearfund's work explored in this case study is still, then, in its preliminary stages. As a result, the discussion that follows is primarily based on a discourse analysis of Tearfund's baseline assessment conducted in North and South Kivu to lay the foundations for the implementation of theologically inspired SGBV prevention interventions. As such, the case study does not centre on a displaced community in eastern DRC per se. It is, however, estimated that 65 per cent of DRC's 2.8 million IDPs are located in North and South Kivu,[9] and it therefore appears likely that Tearfund's work in rural communities in those areas will directly engage with individuals who have been affected by changes in their communities due to the region's broader dynamics of displacement and/or with individuals who currently are, or have been in the past, displaced by conflict.

With this in mind, the remainder of this section proceeds by presenting a brief overview of the rationale behind the shift towards engaging men and boys in efforts to respond to and prevent SGBV in conflict and displacement settings, and highlights the general omission of a faith perspective in existing programming. It subsequently critically discusses Tearfund's 'Transforming Masculinities' initiative in the context of DRC, identifying potential gaps and challenges of rendering 'visible' the role of men and boys, and faith in this context.

The rationale behind male-inclusive gender programming is twofold. First, UNHCR states that such strategies can help to overcome the perception held by displaced and conflict-affected men that the goal of gender equality and SGBV responses is to 'empower women to dominate men and to discriminate against men' (UNHCR, cited in Lewis 2014: 214). Secondly, as the primary perpetrators of SGBV and the 'gatekeepers of the current gender order', efforts to address these issues may be 'thwarted or ignored' without the active participation of men (WRC 2005: 15; Guedes 2012: 4). In effect, the theoretical premise underlying engaging men and boys is the understanding that 'gender inequalities are fundamental to the prevalence of gender-based violence, and that these inequalities are embedded in complex and multidimensional relationships between men and women ... then it is clear that we must engage both men and women in changing unequal gender relations' (Freedman 2012: 9).

Recognizing the complex and constructed nature of gender therefore provides the opportunity to 'rewrite the dominant constructions and norms of masculinity' (Freedman 2012: 10). Ultimately, in the words of the Women's Refugee Commission, it provides an opportunity to 'redefine manhood' (WRC 2007) and promote so-called 'positive masculinities' (Tearfund 2014a: 29; see also, e.g., COMEN n.d.). This is especially pertinent to contexts of conflict and forced migration, which have long been known to disrupt gendered roles and relations, and are continuously negotiated and renegotiated as a consequence (e.g. El-Bushra 2000: 4; Tearfund 2014a: 40–41; Barker, Levtov and Slegh 2014). Yet, the acknowledgment of the complex and intersecting nature of gender notwithstanding, interventions and indeed research on gender and displacement rarely consider the role of religious belief, identity and practice in influencing day-to-day understandings and practices of masculinities and femininities. As shown by Tearfund's Transforming Masculinities work in the Great Lakes region, however, this general neglect of faith omits an important lens through which gender roles and relations are understood and navigated by beneficiary communities. This gap can perhaps partly be explained by the discomfort on the part of 'secular' humanitarian organizations to engage with faith and faith-based actors (interview with Prof. Alastair Ager, Columbia University, New York, 16 February 2015) and also by the commonly held assumption that many FBOs are reluctant to address SGBV (interview with Shatha Khaled El Nakib, Columbia University Research Assistant, New York, 16 February 2015). Cognisant of this gap, Tearfund conducted a baseline study on 'Men, Faith, and Masculinities' in DRC,[10] which is especially instructive for our purposes.

In the baseline assessment, Tearfund aimed to generate a deeper understanding of 'gender dynamics driving sexual and gender-based violence' from a 'faith perspective' so as to promote 'positive masculinities' that are based on a 'Christlike' model of manhood (Tearfund 2014b: 2). Tearfund defines the traits of positive masculinities as 'non-violent, dominant [*sic*], equitable, and promoting the equality of women and men' (Tearfund 2014a: 9). The research was commissioned by the FCO's Prevention of Sexual Violence Initiative (PSVI) to provide an evidence base to constitute the foundation for work 'engaging men and boys to end SGBV' (Tearfund 2014a: 13; Tearfund 2014c: 4).

Reaching 346 respondents (159 men and 187 women) through seventeen group surveys and ten focus group discussions (Tearfund 2014a: 15; Tearfund 2014c: 1), the findings go some way to illuminating the extent to which perceptions of gender, and male superiority over women in particular, are grounded in 'misinterpreted views of biblical scripture' (Tearfund 2014b: 6, 41). According to the report, religious teachings influence expectations of 'manhood', and by extension 'womanhood', in areas such as violence against women and sexual and reproductive health more broadly (Tearfund 2014a: 7, 45–52). Construing such understandings as 'misinterpretations' or 'misunderstandings', as Tearfund does, creates an opportunity to 'engender change in [male] behaviour within theological parameters' by 'work[ing] with the church to shatter these misinterpretations and promote instead biblical truth' (interview with Tearfund representative, 20 February 2015; Tearfund 2014a: 6). To achieve this, Tearfund seeks to 'retrain' pastors in a 'correct biblical understanding of Christlike equity between men and women, which is depicted in the Bible' (Tearfund 2014a: 53).

Overall, this model differs from similar initiatives implemented by 'mainstream'[11] organizations due to its explicitly faith-based approach. An important question nonetheless remains unanswered: how, if at all, do community perceptions of FBOs differ from perceptions of 'mainstream' organizations, and with what effect? This question is worth consideration in light of the roles of Western religious institutions historically in the region, including in embedding the 'conservative' gender roles and relations described in the report (Daley 2008: 29). The apparent contradiction and ensuing confusion was expressed by one of the respondents in Tearfund's study: 'When missionaries brought the gospel to our countries, it seemed to resonate with our existing cultures, which make men superior to women, and reduces the responsibilities. But now, when we want to help women, we are confused, as our faith and culture tell us the opposite' (Tearfund 2014a: 41).

As a final point, while such efforts to broaden understandings of gender beyond the all too pervasive equation that 'gender = women' are promising, male engagement remains limited in scope. In DRC, existing studies suggest that between 9.6 and 23.6 per cent of men have directly experienced sexual violence (Barker, Levtov and Slegh 2014: 27; Johnson et al. 2010: 553). These figures are not insignificant, and yet male inclusivity in mainstream sexual violence discourse and practice is generally restricted to three male personas: the 'Perpetrator', the 'Strategic Ally', and the (elusive) 'Male Victim Subject' (Lewis 2014: 203–20). As a whole, these tropes also underlie Tearfund's Transforming Masculinities. In effect, although reference to male victims of sexual violence are now relatively frequent in institutional documentation, recognition is 'subsequently absented from the main text, rendering the "Male Victim Subject" something of a disappearing or elusive "Other"' (ibid. 216).

Tearfund's various materials (2014a, 2014b, 2014c, 2014d, 2014e) do, however, make reference to male victimization. In fact, the DRC report acknowledges that:

> [m]en and boys are also victims of SGBV, but the development sector does not focus on this issue due to its complexity in the programmatic theme of gender. The discussion on SGBV in the DRC needs to include men's experiences of violence, and the frustrations caused by the gendered expectations of men and boys in society. (Tearfund 2014a: 27)

Beyond recommending 'safer spaces' for men and boys to 'share frustrations, challenges and traumatic experiences' (Tearfund 2014a: 54), more comprehensive responses to male victims of sexual violence are not discussed. In our interview, a Tearfund representative stated that they 'definitely create a space for that [male victims], but the programme isn't geared towards responding to that [sexual violence against men and boys]' (Skype, 20 February 2015). Indeed, this reflects a wider trend identified by Sivakumaran. Referring to UN Security Council resolutions specifically, Sivakumaran (2010: 267) notes that the texts might appear inclusive in their descriptive sections but when it comes to measures of implementation or enforcement, 'the language becomes exclusory', or female-specific. This observation is applicable beyond Security Council resolutions (e.g. Lewis 2014: 217) and is to a large extent reflected in the 'Men, Faith and Masculinities' report, as cited above. As with mainstream, secular approaches, Tearfund's emerging efforts to engage men and boys is similarly limited to 'men's "instrumentalist capacity" as agents of change' in reducing sexual violence (ibid.: 213). This 'serve[s] to reinforce the assumption that men are inevitably the perpetrators [of sexual violence], and rarely, if at all, the victims' (ibid.: 216).

To conclude, this second case study explored the role of FBOs in engaging men and boys to end sexual violence in conflict and displacement contexts. Specifically, through the example of Tearfund's emerging work on Men, Faith and Masculinities in DRC, this section highlighted, on the one hand, the potential added leverage of a 'faithed' approach over a 'secular' one, once the influence of religious scriptures in shaping understandings of gender roles and relations is made visible. On the other hand, it also pointed to some of the boundaries of both faith and 'mainstream' approaches, and the limited engagement with sexual violence against men and boys beyond mere acknowledgement of the issue.

Concluding Remarks

Faith-inspired programmes, and partnerships with faith-based organizations, are increasingly prevalent in institutionalized responses to forced displacement and refugees. An underlying assumption has nonetheless remained that religion and religious approaches constitute a necessarily 'regressive' force for change in terms of gendered roles and relationships, with implications for SGBV and other forms of gendered violence. This plays off the juxtaposition of 'secular' approaches to forced displacement – and their ostensibly gender 'progressive' impacts – with 'faith-based' approaches, which are presented as perpetuating 'traditional' (read 'oppressive') gender roles. This ignores the historical roots of contemporary 'secular' humanitarianism in paternalistic and orientalist policies pursued by amalgams of Christian and colonial organizations throughout the nineteenth century. More pertinently for the evolving humanitarian landscape, however, is that the drawing of this false binary has resulted in very little empirical engagement by organizations and scholars into the impacts and roles that FBOs, LFCs and 'secular' organizations play in responses to gender-based violence in refugee communities. Whilst our conceptualizations of how the camp environment itself impacts upon gendered roles and gender-based violence remain inadequate, how we understand the intersections of faith with gender and violence in this setting has proven even more deficient. Archaic *doxa* concerning the immutable patriarchal foundations of contemporary religion has at times been uncritically carried over and rehashed, thus obscuring from view the more nuanced relationship that faith plays in the lives of forcibly displaced people, and ignoring the broader environment in which the role of faith and religion is articulated.

As the discussions above demonstrate, a more complex understanding of the particularization of religious approaches must be superseded by a research agenda equally attentive to the heterogeneous ideologies and principles underpinning the 'secular' humanitarian gender agenda (interview with Alastair Ager, Columbia University, New York, 16 February 2015). As the example of the Sahrawi refugee camps in South West Algeria shows, 'secular' agendas promoted by Western, 'liberal' humanitarian organizations have no straightforward relationship to desired endpoints vis-à-vis gender-based violence in the camps. The presentation of the camps as 'ideal spaces' of 'secular Islam' has stigmatized other articulations of Islam in the Middle East and North Africa, and reproduced strategic allusions to the technocratic 'norms' of good governance that are considered to be essential prerequisites for a modern society. Whilst donors have celebrated this façade of conformity to their universalizing prescriptions, these strategic essentialisms have simultaneously served to 'erase' (Farmer 2004), or render invisible, continuing incidences of SGBV within the camps.

In turn, the Tearfund example has served to highlight the chronology of thinking on this point. Through acknowledging, firstly, that faith is often highly significant in the lives of beneficiaries, and, secondly, that faith-inspired gender roles have both constructive and constrictive potentialities for preventing and better responding to gender-based violence in displacement contexts, the organization has sought to engage explicitly with faith-based structures and teachings in their work. They have articulated alternative models of 'masculinity' based on theological teachings. These have served to illustrate the openness for change within religious institutions, and the ways in which this may be endogenously derived and driven. Their work – and the case of the Sahrawi camps above – has nonetheless highlighted that the catalyst for promoting changes around gendered roles, and the reception that they receive, is not reducible to a simple understanding of the intersections of gender, violence and faith. The history of previous interventions, the political environment, the nature of the displacement and time spent within the camps, in addition to the broader array of conditionalities imposed within refugee environments, all serve to incentivize strategic, and at times paradoxical, behaviours in recipient communities and the organizations working with them.

Further evidence is therefore needed to critically establish what distinguishes explicitly faith-based approaches to gender, and what role these differences play, if any, in addressing SGBV within contexts of displacement. A critical question to interrogate is why different actors believe that change vis-à-vis gender should occur in displacement contexts, and what the implications are of these differing ideological approaches for how change is envisaged and operationalized in terms of reducing gender-based violence. Relatedly, those factors that uniquely distinguish the activities of faith-based actors must be further explored and, when appropriate, built on. These include enhanced access in situations where religious status engenders greater trust, and the theologically informed frames of reference that, as shown in the case of Tearfund's work outlined above, can be drawn upon in their activities to explain 'how' and 'why' gender roles can change to mitigate against gendered forms of violence.

Expanding our understanding of the roles that FBOs may play in addressing SGBV in displacement settings will, however, require a more nuanced exploration of the different ways that individuals and groups choose to relate to religion and faith, including as a potential source of psycho-social support, theological teachings, financial assistance and/or cultural guidance. This may assist in recognizing when, where and why FBOs and LFCs constitute critical actors in responding to SGBV in displaced communities (interview with Benjamin Schewel, Catholic University of Leuven, 2015). Concurrently, dispelling the notion of faith as a monolithic entity remains important for taking seriously the internal inconsistencies within faith-based and secular organizations' interpretations of 'gendered approaches' to violence in camp-contexts (interview with Oxfam GB representative, Oxford, 6 February 2015). Standardizing these throughout any organization is clearly complicated, and highlights the 'difficulty in sometimes determining the nature of an FBO's gender agenda, because a single organisation often takes different standpoints on various gender issues' (Tadros 2010: 1), including different forms of SGBV. At the Jesuit Refugee Service (JRS), for example, the organization's reputation in the United States and certain parts of Europe and Latin America as a more 'liberal' Catholic organization has attracted employees motivated by a commitment to more 'liberal' strands of theological interpretation. When individuals have then transferred to other regional centres, where discussions on SGBV or LGBTIQ rights may not be met with the same degree of openness, the conflicting interpretations of social justice and faith-based identities have manifested in a lack of institutional cohesion and an inability to prevent certain staff discriminating based on religiously motivated criteria, which in itself constitutes a form of gender-based structural violence (interview with former JRS advocacy officer, 4 February 2015).

Finally, the vocabularies used and representations invoked to describe the relationships between 'secular' and faith-based organizations, and both of their approaches towards SGBV in displacement contexts, must be consistently nuanced. Although the case of Tearfund's work above suggests the increasing recognition of faith as an essential element of any strategy designed to address gender-based violence in refugee communities, it risks a totalizing conceptualization of religion that paints theological reform as the panacea for SGBV, much like 'secularism' was in the example of the Sahrawi refugee camps. Countering concerns about the role of faith-based approaches to SGBV through assertions such as 'people who are religious are good people, they are not there to exclude' (anonymous, interview, 2015) does little to reassure organizations considering partnerships with faith-inspired actors that the latter will embrace self-critique and reflection. Conversely, a less denunciatory approach to religious approaches must not result in the essentializing of other traits – such as culture, gender, politics, tradition, ethnicity and class – as the source of 'oppressive' and violent gender relations. Several key stakeholders countered religion as being the main impediment to discussing contentious topics such as gender minorities and sexual violence towards men and boys, by instead citing culture and tradition as community 'silencers'. Embracing other traits as monolithic entities clearly does little to advance the understanding of the specific dynamics driving gendered forms of violence experienced by refugees.

Overall, this chapter has thus offered a preliminary exploration of the multiple, and at times unanticipated, ways in which faith intersects with gender and violence in refugee communities. In doing so, it has demonstrated that following a blind secular approach risks leaving invisible an important component of lived experiences and understandings of gender roles and relations in displacement contexts. Looking forward, it has also sought to trace a path to enable researchers and practitioners alike to move beyond the strict binaries that have dominated gender-based interventions to date, namely: secular versus faith-inspired; traditional versus progressive; and female victims versus male perpetrators.

Acknowledgements

This chapter is based on research generously funded through a Special Grant awarded to Fiddian-Qasmiyeh by The Henry Luce Foundation in 2014.

Elena Fiddian-Qasmiyeh is reader (associate professor) in Human Geography and co-director of the Migration Research Unit at University College London (UCL), where she is also the coordinator of the UCL-wide 'Refuge in a Moving World' interdisciplinary research network. Elena's research focuses on the intersections between gender and religion in experiences of and responses to conflict-induced displacement, with a particular regional focus on the Middle East. Between 2016 and 2022 she is leading two major projects involving multi-sited ethnographic research across Lebanon, Jordan and Turkey: 'Local Community Experiences of Displacement from Syria' (jointly funded by the UK's AHRC and the ESRC – see www.refugeehosts.org) and 'Analysing South–South Humanitarian Responses to Displacement from Syria' (funded by the European Research Council). Her recent books include *The Ideal Refugees: Gender, Islam and the Sahrawi Politics of Survival* (Syracuse University Press, 2014), *The Oxford Handbook of Refugee and Forced Migration Studies* (co-editor, Oxford University

Press, 2014), *South–South Educational Migration, Humanitarianism and Development: Views from Cuba, North Africa and the Middle East* (Routledge, 2015), and *Intersections of Religion and Migration: Issues at the Global Crossroads* (co-editor, Palgrave Macmillan, 2016).

Chloé Lewis is a DPhil candidate in International Development at the University of Oxford where she is exploring responses to sexual violence in the Democratic Republic of the Congo. In particular, her work explores the different ways in which institutions represent, engage, and work with men and women and the implications thereof. Her research has taken her to the United Nations Headquarters in New York where completed a Policy Research Fellowship with the NGO Working Group on Women, Peace and Security, as well as to the North and South Kivu provinces in eastern DRC. Alongside her doctorate, Chloé has also worked an independent researcher for the Human Rights Center Sexual Violence Program at the University of California, Berkeley, School of Law researching accountability for sexual violence in DRC, and with Dr Elena Fiddian-Qasmiyeh and Georgia Cole examining the role of faith-based responses to sexual and gender-based violence in humanitarian and displacement settings. She is currently working with The World Bank Gender Innovation Lab following the implementation of the International Rescue Committee's programme Engaging Men through Accountable Practices (EMAP) seeking to better understand the opportunities and limits for promoting gender equitable norms through such an approach across North and South Kivu.

Georgia Cole is the Joyce Pearce Junior Research Fellow at the Refugee Studies Centre at the University of Oxford. She recently completed her doctorate there, examining the politics, implementation and impacts of the 'ceased circumstances' Cessation Clause of the 1951 Convention, with particular reference to Eritrean and Rwandan refugees. Its theoretical focus was on rethinking assumptions around the politics of labelling within the refugee regime. Her postdoctoral research project explores the 'value' of refugee status, given the forms of restriction imposed on those in exile, and the paucity of durable solutions accessible to them. She has held a Visiting Research and Teaching Fellowship at the College of Arts and Social Sciences in Eritrea, interned with UNHCR in Ghana during the Cessation Clause for Liberian refugees, and continues to teach on durable solutions and the end of refugee status at the Refugee Studies Centre.

Notes

It is with the most profound regret and sadness that we pay our respects to Michael J. Sharp. We express their deepest thanks and gratitude to Michael for his utmost support for this project and for sharing his insights on the intersections of faith, gender, and humanitarianism in eastern DRC. Since our interview, Michael went on to work for, and then coordinate, the Group of Experts on DRC. On 12 March 2017, Michael and his colleague, Zaida Catalan, were abducted and executed while on a mission in Central Kasai. Their legacy of working with Congolese people in the search for truth and justice in DRC will not be forgotten.

1. Used here for ease of reference, the label 'faith-based organization' may not be used by members of a given organization or network, since faith principles are often conceptualized as a foundational part of 'a community's heritage, culture and broader way of life', rather than as a 'religious' framework per se (Ives, cited in Fiddian-Qasmiyeh and Ager 2013). 'Faith' may thus be indistinguishable from the community's broader social, cultural and political life.

2. For further information, see the Joint Learning Initiative (JLI) Resilience Hub webpage: http://jliflc.com/resilience-hub-2/ (last accessed 8 March 2017), in addition to the JLI Refugees and Forced Migration hub website: https://refugee.jliflc.com (last accessed 8 March 2017).

3. This forms part of a project generously funded through a Special Grant awarded to Fiddian-Qasmiyeh by The Henry Luce Foundation in 2014.

4. This was an exclamation of surprise made by a visitor to a Tanzanian refugee camp (quoted in Malkki 1995a: 40), and indicates the extent to which observers have come to accept the 'generic' representations of refugee camps and themselves.

5. Albeit a preambular one, this represents the first explicit reference to men and boys in the Security Council's seven resolutions on Women, Peace and Security (Lewis 2014: 203).

6. Tearfund's work in this area has also been in support of USAID and IMA World Health (USAID, US Government Programs: Sexual and Gender-Based Violence in the Democratic Republic of the Congo, p. 1).

7. Available online: http://www.unhcr.org/pages/49e45c366.html (last accessed 28 June 2015).

8. This echoes Religions for Peace, which stated that '[r]eligion, more than any other collective value, has been used throughout history to spur collective action' (RfP 2004: 11).

9. These figures relate to the provinces of: North and South Kivu, Maniema, Province Oriental and Katanga Available online: http://reliefweb.int/sites/reliefweb.int/files/resources/DRC%20Factsheet%20Population%20Movement%20_english_2%20eme%20trimestre%202013.pdf [Last accessed 28 June 2015].

10. Tearfund conducted baseline surveys in Rwanda, Burundi and DRC (Tearfund 2014c, 2014d, 2014e).

11. The term 'mainstream' is used by Tearfund to refer to 'secular' or 'non-faith-based' approaches (e.g. Tearfund 2014a: 1).

Bibliography

Asahra, W. 2008. Collection of Blogs. Retrieved 10 November 2008 from wuruda-sahrablogspotcom-wurud.blogspot.com/.

Barker, G., R. Levtov and H. Slegh. 2014. *Gender Relations, Sexual and Gender-Based Violence and the Effects of Conflict on Women and Men in North Kivu, Eastern Democratic Republic of Congo: Results from the International Men and Gender Equality Survey (IMAGES)*. Washington and Cape Town: Promundo-US and Sonke Gender Justice.

Barrera, M. 2008. 'Están esperando que vayamos a la guerra para incluirnos en su lista de organizaciones terroristas. Entrevista a Maima Mahamud Nayem. Secretaria de Estado de Asuntos Sociales y Promoción de la Mujer del Frente Polisario'. Retrieved 24 September 2008 from http://www.bottup.com/index.php?option=com_contentandtask=viewandid=2904andItemid=114.

Callamard, A. 1999. 'Refugee Women: A Gendered and Political Analysis of the Refugee Experience', in A. Ager (eds), *Refugees: Perspectives on the Experience of Forced Migration*. London: Continuum, pp. 194–214.

COMEN (Congo Men's Network). 'MenEngage – DR Congo'. Retrieved 6 April 2015 from http://menengage.org/regions/africa/dr-congo/.

Connell, R.W. 2003. 'The Role of Men and Boys in Achieving Gender Equality', Expert Group Meeting No. EGM/Men-Boys-GE/2003/BP. Brasilia: United Nations Division for the Advancement of Women (DAW). Retrieved 6 April 2015 from http://www.un.org/womenwatch/daw/egm/men-boys2003/Connell-bp.pdf.

Daley, O.P. 2008. *Gender and Genocide in Burundi: The Search for Spaces of Peace in the Great Lakes Region*. Oxford: James Currey.

Deepan, P. 2016. Tearfund Transforming Masculinities. Personal communication: email, 14 July 2016.

Development Initiatives. 2014. 'Trends in Donor Spending on Sexual and Gender-Based Violence'. Retrieved 2 April 2015 from http://devinit.org/wp-content/uploads/2014/06/SGBV-Briefing-June-2014-FINAL.pdf.

El-Bushra, J. 2000. 'Gender and Forced Migration: Editorial', *Forced Migration Review* 9: 4–7.

Farmer, P. 2004. 'An Anthropology of Structural Violence', *Current Anthropology* 45(3): 305–18.

Ferris, R. 2011. 'Faith and Humanitarianism: It's Complicated', *Journal of Refugee Studies* 24(3): 606–25.

Fiddian-Qasmiyeh, E. 2010a. 'Concealing Violence against Women in the Sahrawi Refugee Camps: The Politicisation of Victimhood', in H. Bradby and G. Lewando-Hunt (eds), *Global Perspectives on War, Gender and Health: The Sociology and Anthropology of Suffering*. Farnham: Ashgate, pp. 91–110.

_____. 2010b. '"Ideal" Refugee Women and Gender Equality Mainstreaming: "Good Practice" for Whom?' *Refugee Survey Quarterly* 29(2): 64–84.

_____. 2011. 'The Pragmatics of Performance: Putting "Faith" in Aid in the Sahrawi Refugee Camps', *Journal of Refugee Studies* 24(3): 533–47.

_____. 2014a. *The Ideal Refugees: Gender, Islam and the Sahrawi Politics of Survival*. Syracuse: Syracuse University Press.

——. 2014b. 'Gender and Forced Migration', in E. Fiddian-Qasmiyeh, G. Loescher, K. Long and N. Sigona (eds), *The Oxford Handbook of Refugee and Forced Migration Studies*. Oxford: Oxford University Press, pp. 395–408.

——. 2015. 'Engendering Understandings of Faith-Based Organisations: Intersections between Religion and Gender in Development and Humanitarian Interventions', in A. Cole, L. Gray and J. Momsen (eds), *Routledge Handbook of Gender and Development*. London: Routledge, pp. 560–70.

Fiddian-Qasmiyeh, E. (ed.) 2016. *Gender, Religion and Humanitarian Responses to Refugees*, MRU Policy Brief. Retrieved 8 March 2017 from http://www.geog. ucl.ac.uk/people/research/research-centres/migration-research-unit/pdfs/ Low Res.Gender Religion and Refugees.MRU PB.pdf.

Fiddian-Qasmiyeh, E., and A. Ager. 2013. 'Local Faith Communities and the Promotion of Resilience in Humanitarian Situations: A Scoping Study', *RSC Working Paper Series* No. 90.

Freedman, J. (ed.). 2012. *Engaging Men and Boys in the Fight against Gender-Based Violence: Case Studies from Africa*. New York: Palgrave Macmillan.

Gill, A. 2004. 'Voicing the Silent Fear: South Asian Women's Experiences of Domestic Violence', *The Howard Journal of Criminal Justice* 43(5): 465–83.

Greany, K. 2006. 'Editorial', *Gender & Development* 14(3): 341–50.

Guedes, A. 2012. 'Men and Boys', *Virtual Knowledge Centre to End Violence against Women and Girls: Programming Modules*, Ch. 9. UN Women and MenEngage.

Harrell-Bond, B.E. 1999. 'The Experience of Refugees as Recipients of Aid', in A. Ager (ed.), *Refugees: Perspectives on the Experience of Forced Migration*. London: Pinter, pp. 136–68.

Hammami, R. 2005. 'Deniz Kandiyoti', *Development and Change* 37(6): 1347–54.

Johnson, K., et al. 2010. 'Association of Sexual Violence and Human Rights Violations with Physical and Mental Health in Territories of the Eastern Democratic Republic of the Congo', *Journal of the American Medical Association* 304(5): 553–62.

Lewis, C. 2014. 'Systematic Silencing: Addressing Sexual Violence against Men and Boys in Conflict and Post-conflict Settings', in D. Otto and G. Heathcote (eds), *Rethinking Peacekeeping, Gender Equality and Collective Security*. New York and Basingstoke: Palgrave Macmillan, pp. 203–23.

Malkki, L. 1995a. *Purity and Exile: Violence, Memory and National Cosmology among Hutu Refugees in Tanzania*. London: University of Chicago Press.

——. 1995b. 'Refugees and Exile: From "Refugee Studies" to the National Order of Things', *Annual Review of Anthropology* 24: 495–523.

Mowles, C. 1986. 'Desk Officer's Report on Trip to the Sahrawi Refugee Camps near Tindouf, Southern Algeria, June 16–21, 1986'. Oxfam.

Parsitau, D. 2011. 'The Role of Faith and Faith-Based Organizations among Internally Displaced Persons in Kenya', *Journal of Refugee Studies* 24(3): 473–92.

Portinari, B. 2007. 'Quiero que cuando una mujer abra las piernas sepa por qué lo hace', *El País*, 12 May 2007. Retrieved 12 May 2007 from http://elpais.com/.

Rees, S., and B. Pease. 2007. 'Domestic Violence in Refugee Families in Australia: Rethinking Settlement Policy and Practice', *Journal of Immigrant and Refugee Studies* 5(2): 1–19.

Religions for Peace (RfP). 2004. 'Women of Faith Transforming Conflict: A Multi-Religious Training Manual'. New York: World Conference of Religions for Peace.

———. 2013. 'Restoring Dignity: A Toolkit for Religious Communities to End Violence against Women', 2nd Edn. New York: Religions for Peace.

SADR (Sahrawi Arab Democratic Republic). 2003. *Constitution de la RASD, 2003*. Rabouni.

Shami, S. 1996. 'Transnationalism and Refugee Studies: Rethinking Forced Migration and Identity in the Middle East', *Journal of Refugee Studies* 9(1): 3–26.

Sivakumaran, S. 2010. 'Lost in Translation: UN Responses to Sexual Violence against Men and Boys in Situations of Armed Conflict', *International Review of the Red Cross* 92(877): 259–77.

Smith, A., and J. Kaybryn. 2013. 'HIV and Maternal Health: Faith Groups' Activities, Contributions and Impact'. Joint Learning Initiative on Faith and Local Communities. Retrieved 28 May 2015 from http://jliflc.com/.

Spivak, G.C. 1993. 'Can the Subaltern Speak?', in P. Williams and L. Chrisman (eds), *Colonial Discourse and Post-colonial Theory*. New York: Harvester Wheatsheaf, pp. 66–111.

Tadros, M. 2010. *Faith-based Organizations and Service Delivery: Some Gender Conundrums*. Geneva: UNRISD.

Tearfund. 2014a. 'Men, Masculinities and Faith: DRC: A Baseline Assessment on the Social Attitudes, Relations, and Practices of Men in Relation to Gender, and Sexual and Gender-based Violence in the Democratic Republic of Congo'. Belfast and Glasgow.

———. 2014b. 'Transforming Masculinities: Great Lakes Region Summary Report: Social Attitudes and Practices of Men in Relation to Gender'. Belfast and Glasgow.

———. 2014c. 'Masculinities, Faith and Ending Sexual Violence and Gender-Based Violence: DRC Summary Report'. Belfast and Glasgow.

———. 2014d. 'Masculinities, Faith and Ending Sexual Violence and Gender-Based Violence: Rwanda Summary Report'. Belfast and Glasgow.

———. 2014e. 'Masculinities, Faith and Ending Sexual Violence and Gender-Based Violence: Burundi Summary Report'. Belfast and Glasgow.

———. 2016a. 'About Us: History'. Retrieved 13 July 2016 from http://www.tearfund.org/en/about_us/history/.

———. 2016b. 'About Us: Where We're Working'. Retrieved 13 July 2016 from http://www.tearfund.org/en/about_us#whereweworkmap

———. 2016c. 'About Us: Where We're Working – Democratic Republic of the Congo'. Retrieved 13 July 2016 from http://www.tearfund.org/en/about_us/what_we_do_and_where/countries/east_and_central_africa/democratic_republic_of_congo/

Tomalin, E. 2011. 'Introduction', in E. Tomalin (ed.), *Gender, Faith and Development*. Oxford: Oxfam, pp. 1–12.

———. 2013. 'Gender, Religion and Development', in M. Clarke (ed.), *Handbook of Research on Development and Religion*. Northampton: Edward Elgar Publishing, pp. 183–200.

Turner, S. 2000. 'Vindicating Masculinity: The Fate of Promoting Gender Equality', *Forced Migration Review* 9: 8–9.

UNHCR. 1991. 'Guidelines on the Protection of Refugee Women'. Geneva.

——. 1995. 'Guidelines on the Protection of Refugee Women (1995)'. Geneva.

——. 2002. 'UNHCR Remedial Actions and Preventive Measures against Sexual Exploitation and Abuse of Refugees'. UNHCR Press Releases.

——. 2003. 'Framework for Durable Solutions for Refugees and Persons of Concern'. Core Group on Durable Solutions, Geneva.

——. 2008. 'Handbook for the Protection of Women and Girls'. Geneva.

——. 2015. 'UNHCR Country Operations Profile – Democratic Republic of the Congo'. Retrieved 28 June 2015 from http://www.unhcr.org/pages/49e45c366. html.

UNHCR EXCOM. 2004. 'Protracted Refugee Situations'. Executive Committee of the High Commissioner's Programme, Standing Committee, 30th Meeting.

UNHCR Refugee Women and Gender Equality Unit. 2001. 'A Practical Guide to Empowerment: UNHCR Good Practices on Gender Equality Mainstreaming'. Geneva.

UNFPA (United Nations Population Fund). 2000. 'Partnering: A New Approach to Sexual and Reproductive Health'. *UNFPA Technical Paper* No. 3.

UNSC (United Nations Security Council). 2013. 'Security Council Resolution 2106 on Women, Peace and Security'. Adopted by the Security Council at its 6984th meeting, on 24 June 2013. S/RES/2106.

Vidal, D. 1986. 'Apre, doux, suave', *Révolution*, 22 March.

Volpp, L. 2001. 'Feminism versus Multiculturalism', *Columbia Law Review* 101(5): 1181–1218.

WFP (World Food Programme). 2002. 'Protracted Relief and Recovery Operation – Algeria 10172.0. Assistance to Western Sahara Refugees'. Rome.

——. 2004. 'Protracted Relief and Recovery Operation – Algeria 10172.1. Assistance to Western Saharan Refugees'. Rome.

WRC (Women's Refugee Commission). 2005. 'Masculinities: Male Roles and Male Involvement in the Promotion of Gender Equality. A Resource Packet'. New York.

——. 2007. 'Redefining Manhood, Rebuilding Nations: How Men Can Empower Women to Lift Post-Conflict Communities'. New York.

WVI (World Vision International) Zambia. 2014. 'WV Zambia Opens a GBV One-Stop Center in Keembe ADP'. Retrieved 6 April 2015 from http://www. wvi.org/zambia/article/wv-zambia-opens-gbv-one-stop-center-keembe-adp.

Zin, H. 2007. 'Mujeres saharauis, lucha y ejemplo', *Viaje a la Guerra*, 16 April. Retrieved 16 May 2008 from http://blogs.20minutos.es/enguerra/ post/2007/04/16/mujeres-saharauis-lucha-y-ejemplo.

7

Formidable Intersections
Forced Migration, Gender and Livelihoods

Dale Buscher

Introduction

Forced migration, gender and livelihoods are interlinked phenomena – each influencing and impacting the other. Movement, displacement and settlement in new and foreign locations impact gender roles and responsibilities, which, in turn, are impacted by market barriers, market access and livelihood opportunities. A 'livelihood', as commonly understood, refers to the capacities, assets and strategies that people use to make a living. A livelihood is sustainable when it can cope with and recover from stresses and shocks, and maintain or enhance its capabilities and assets both now and in the future without undermining the natural resource base (DFID 1999). Conflict is a devastating 'shock' to livelihoods that impacts individual, household and market capabilities as well as the full range of assets – human, social, financial, physical and natural – that people use and require for their livelihoods. Markets collapse, resources become scarce, mobility is restricted due to insecurity, and purchasing power diminishes. Access to fields, grazing lands, markets and other resources vital for one's livelihood may become dangerous or impossible.

Over the past several decades, as the nature of conflict has changed, so too, have its consequences; more often being internal conflicts about access to and control over resources rather than about ideology, civilians are often uprooted and in harm's way, leading to large waves of forced migration. As a result, household and community livelihoods are severely disrupted, with assets stripped, discarded or depleted. Formal economies constrict and so parallel, unregulated shadow economies – or even more harmful, war economies that benefit from and further fuel the conflict – emerge (Buchanan-Smith and Fadul 2008: 12).

This chapter looks at the intersectionality of violence, forced migration, gender and livelihoods. While accepting the commonly understood notion that displacement impacts women, men, girls and boys differently, it notes that the impacts on livelihoods are also gendered. The chapter examines how livelihood assets are drivers of conflict while being simultaneously depleted by conflict, as well as how the need to reacquire livelihood assets provides impetus for forced migration. The links between livelihoods and gender-based violence are also explored both from the angle of how the lack of opportunities leads to the adoption of negative economic coping strategies and, contrarily, how economic opportunities themselves create new risks. The means to economically empowering women are delineated as is the notion that it requires starting with adolescent girls. The chapter concludes with thoughts on effective practice, and posits that safe, market-driven livelihoods are both possible and increasingly necessary.

Competition over Livelihood Resources drives Violence

Conflict plays a dual role vis-à-vis livelihoods. It is often driven by the desire for livelihood assets – land, water, minerals and oil, for example – while simultaneously destroying livelihood assets at the individual, household, community and national levels. The resources that groups compete and fight over are seldom in the hands of women, yet women often suffer most from the resulting conflict and subsequent displacement (Buscher 2009: 88). In the eastern Democratic Republic of the Congo (DRC), for example, exploitation of the rich natural resources has fuelled and funded the ever-simmering conflict (Meger 2011: 111), which has led to an epidemically high incidence of sexual violence against women. War entrepreneurs in the region have a vested interest in prolonging the conflict, as they continue to profit from the spoils of war, and the havoc and lack of governance allow them to plunder resources for personal gain (ibid.). Access to and control over vital assets, referred to as the 'resource curse' (Autesserre 2012: 211) have been drivers of conflicts from Liberia and Sierra Leone to Angola, where natural resources such as timber, diamonds and minerals have helped to fund armies and militias who murder, rape and commit other human rights abuses against civilians (Heath, n.d.; Bassey, 2012: 16).

Natural resources thus often lie at the heart of wars and civil strife (Global Policy Forum 2014). In fact, research conducted on behalf of the

European Union into the political economy of armed conflict over the past twenty years suggests that the ability of non-state combatants to mobilize economic resources depends either on external support or, more likely, on gaining control of locally available economic resources (Garret and Piccinni 2012: 4). Internal conflicts in natural resource-rich countries have become progressively understood as 'resource wars', and the local economic systems from which combatants mobilize their resources defined as 'war economies' (Ballentine and Nitzschke 2005: 2). Ross has analysed conflicts across the globe and identified the following resources as drivers or contributors to those conflicts: Afghanistan – gems, opium; Angola – oil; Burma – gems, timber, opium; Cambodia – timber, gems; Colombia – opium, coca; Democratic Republic of Congo – coltan, diamonds, coffee; Liberia – timber, diamonds, cocoa, coffee, rubber, gold; Indonesia (Aceh) – natural gas; Peru – coca; Sierra Leone – diamonds; and Sudan – oil (Ross 2003: 6). As this competition over resources demonstrates, economic life does not cease to exist during war, it rather adapts and takes on new forms (Ballentine and Nitschke 2005: 7) – forms that seldom benefit women.

Destroyed Livelihoods and Forced Migration

Violence often leads to humanitarian crises while also having significant developmental impacts – short- and longer-term, negative and positive – affecting human and social capital, economic growth, poverty reduction, the environment and societal fragility (World Bank et al. 2012: 5). The effects of conflict on livelihoods are felt at both the individual household level and at the national economic level. The Syrian economy, for example, when almost five years into the civil conflict, had already shrunk rapidly as industrial and agricultural output fell, leaving almost two-thirds of the population in extreme poverty. The International Monetary Fund (IMF) estimates that the gross domestic product (GDP) in Syria has contracted 40 per cent since the start of the conflict in 2011, with losses estimated at $143.8 billion (Al-Khalidi 2014). Similarly, Liberia's per capita GDP was at a high of $727.76 in 1972 and shrunk to a low of $50.04 at the height of the country's civil conflict (1989–2003) (Trading Economies 2014); GDP per capita fell more than 85 per cent between 1980 and 2003 (Konneh 2009). Since the end of the war, it has only rebounded to $299.45 – less than half of the country's pre-war high (Trading Economies 2014). The situation is much the same in conflict-ridden countries throughout the world: markets shrink, trade networks break down, land lies barren, and vital infrastructure is destroyed, impacting livelihoods in the near and much longer term, including in the post-conflict recovery phase.

Conflict destroys and simultaneously transforms societies, causing people to adapt and modify their activities and livelihoods in order to survive or to minimize risk, or to capitalize on the opportunities that conflict presents (Ballentine and Nitzschke 2005: 9). The threats to people's livelihoods and their protection are closely linked. Populations affected by conflict often have to make difficult choices between their safety and their livelihood. Continuing to pursue their livelihoods can put people at extreme risk, while prioritizing safety can lead to neglect of livelihoods and the resultant poverty and desperation, and little choice but to flee (Jaspers and O'Callaghan 2010). People flee for both physical safety and to access the livelihoods and resources they require to survive. The decision to flee may be related to one or more trigger factors that may compound pre-existing underlying factors, such as poverty, war (Haysom 2013), disenfranchisement, the lack of opportunities and resource scarcity. In other words, displacement may be triggered by events related to or caused by the conflict, rather than direct exposure to military operations.

If their assets were not stripped from them while fleeing, displaced populations often quickly deplete any assets they have managed to bring with them. This is especially true for those displaced in urban and non-camp areas – some 58 per cent of the total refugee population (UNHCR 2014b: 36–37) – where expenses are higher and refugees are less likely to receive food, shelter and other basic assistance. In the Syrian crisis, for example, it was found that refugees deploy a variety of highly risky coping strategies, including the sale of personal assets (Ruaudel and Zetter 2014: 6), the depletion of savings, increasing levels of indebtedness and the adoption of negative economic coping strategies (Seferis and Sood 2014: 14). In a vulnerability assessment of fourteen hundred Syrian refugees in Lebanon, it was found that 75 per cent of households had debts, that the average debt was $600 and that households registered longer ago were significantly more likely to have higher amounts of debt (WFP, UNICEF and UNHCR 2013: 7). Nearly all Syrian refugees living in camp settings in the Kurdistan Region of Iraq (KRI) reported having exhausted their savings: while 66 per cent reported having had savings at the time of arrival in the KRI, as of April 2014, only 4 per cent of the Syrian refugees in the camps still had savings (UNHCR and REACH 2014: 18).

Not only are the forcibly displaced depleting their assets – assets vital to their longer-term economic recovery; they are also fleeing to countries and regions least able to assist and provide for them. While often fleeing from impoverished nations, refugees are also largely fleeing 'into' poverty. More than 80 per cent of refugees are hosted by less-developed nations (UNHCR 2014b). Even in the lower-middle-income context of the Syrian refugee crisis, 60 per cent of registered Syrian refugees in Lebanon are in the North and Beka'a Valley regions – the poorest regions in the country

(Dahi 2014: 12). Further, many people flee weak states because they are affected by conflict, only to find themselves in similarly unstable environments – Afghans in Pakistan and Somalis in Yemen, for example (ibid.).

Just as women and men are affected differently by conflict and displacement, so, too, are their livelihoods. Women often leave land-based, agrarian work for work in the unregulated informal sector in jobs that offer little security, safety or dignity – as maids, servants or commercial sex workers (Buscher 2009: 90). Men often lose their ability to fulfil their traditional roles of protector and provider, and find themselves ill equipped for new urban or camp-based market opportunities. Men's livelihoods are often less adaptive to new environments than are women's, whose childcare and household experiences can easily translate into domestic and service industry work.

Forced displacement leads, often by necessity, to the adoption of new economic coping strategies, some of which can have detrimental short- and longer-term consequences for the health and safety of those displaced, as well as having negative consequences for their children and their children's future. Women and adolescent girls may engage in transactional sex – bartering their bodies for food or other basic needs. Children may be pulled from school to engage in child labour. Females may risk rape and abuse when venturing out to collect firewood and other vital resources, and families may reduce meal and nutritional consumption to stretch the few financial assets they have.

Challenges to Livelihood Programming of the Forcibly Displaced

In spite of the increasing need for effective livelihood interventions, the humanitarian community is often ill-equipped to address the challenge of promoting early self-reliance for the forcibly displaced. The challenge ranges from mindset to skill set. Irrespective of the increasing length of displacement, humanitarian actors continue to treat every new crisis as a short-term emergency. Life-saving, Band-Aid approaches are applied with little forward planning for the long term. Instead, those responding should start with the assumption that the displacement is likely to be for a decade or a generation, thereby necessitating a dramatic shift in planning and programming from the start. Few humanitarian practitioners, however, come from an economic background. Macroeconomics, business and finance, and emerging markets are not part of the general humanitarian repertoire of skills. As mindsets have historically thought and planned only for the immediate or near term, this skill set has not been deemed necessary. As a result, emergency response often starts on the wrong foot – the wrong people, the wrong skill sets and the wrong responses – which undermines the longer-term self-sufficiency of the forcibly uprooted population.

Further, when livelihood programmes are implemented, they seldom build on the existing skill sets of the target population. Crossing a border and arriving in a new country is treated as 'day zero', with little recognition of the wealth of education, knowledge and work experience that uprooted populations bring with them. Livelihood programmes are designed with little attention to the diversity of the target population and their differing needs and abilities. Markets are also little understood by humanitarian practitioners. Understanding the demand for goods and services, the intricate link between supply and demand, and how the market is evolving and changing in response to the crisis, and how that impacts opportunity, is seldom part of a humanitarian's training. As a result, practitioners tend to focus on a small piece of the labour or goods market with little regard for how it 'fits' within the larger socio-economic environment. The quality of the labour supply is improved through vocational and skills training programmes without the complementary expansion of market demand for such labour. Women are given access to credit without inclusion of vital business development skills and mentorship to enhance their likelihood of success in undertaking new ventures that may be well outside their previous experience. Cash transfers may be disbursed with little planning for transitioning families off assistance to ensure that they do not end up equally vulnerable when the transfers stop.

Cash Transfers: Unrealized Potential

While the future of livelihoods work in the context of displacement is evolving and expanding, the implications of such for the promotion of gender equality are less clear. Even though the United Nations High Commissioner for Refugees (UNHCR) is increasingly emphasizing refugee self-reliance, especially for those displaced in urban contexts, humanitarian agencies are increasingly forgoing direct economic programme implementation, and instead implementing cash transfers and other cash-based interventions as a 'livelihood' support. While these programmes can be a cost-effective tool that allows the displaced to meet their own needs and increase their dignity, choice and protection (UNHCR 2012: 5), they do not meet the definition of a sustainable livelihood as presented at the beginning of this chapter; and while they help households to recover from shocks, they do not build longer-term capacity. Additionally, while they are effective social protection interventions, cash transfer programmes are often gender-neutral, as unconditional cash transfers are generally disbursed to households to address basic consumption needs – food, shelter, winterization, and perhaps education and health care – rather than as a tool for women's economic empowerment or as a means to transform gender norms.

While cash transfer programmes can increase access to school and reduce child labour as well as contribute to the local economy (International Rescue Committee 2014: 6), much remains to be learned about how to ensure that these programmes are as effective as possible. Desired programme length, and the frequency and ideal size of cash disbursements, have yet to be determined and contextualized. Many of the cash transfer programmes currently implemented are not complemented, for example, with financial literacy training, nor are they used as building blocks to promote more sustainable livelihoods. While a non-conflict setting, the VISA corporation, which supported cash transfers via preloaded debit cards during the Pakistan floods of 2012, reported that nearly 100 per cent of beneficiaries withdrew the full amount of the cash soon after receipt of the debit cards, and that many female beneficiaries sold their card for a fraction of its worth, neither understanding its value nor how to use it.[1] On a more positive note, the International Rescue Committee's study of cash transfers in Lebanon concluded that every dollar that beneficiaries spent generated 2.13 dollars of GDP for the Lebanese economy (ibid.). The gendered impacts of the cash transfers on both the beneficiary population and the host population, however, have not been fully studied, and hence their utility as a tool to enhance gender equality remains unrealized.

Improving Programming: Requisite Components

Improving the design and implementation of livelihood programming and getting it right from the start requires more upfront work and more thoughtful, context-specific approaches. At a minimum, three interrelated assessments should be undertaken, and while conducting these may delay the response, using the findings of the assessments will lead to more informed, strategic and sustainable programming. The three requisite assessments are: a participatory needs assessment; a gender analysis; and a market analysis. The three are linked and complementary.

The participatory needs assessment with the target population, generally conducted through sex- and age-disaggregated focus group discussions, in-depth structured interviews and key informant interviews, facilitates the capture of existing skill sets, current economic coping strategies, and available resources and assets, as well as plans and ambitions. The participatory needs assessment engages the community in the identification of solutions, and empowers community members by making them part of the learning process (WRC 2009: xiii). The displaced bring skills, education and assets with them when they flee, and these vary by socio-economic class, age and gender. Their ability to earn an income and secure employment in their new host communities will be influenced by the intersectionality of those characteristics – all of which need to inform programme choice and programme design.

A gender analysis, which delineates roles, responsibilities, time use, and access to and control over resources, can be conducted as part of the participatory assessment. Without an understanding of the gender dynamics of the population and how it is or is not changing and evolving as a result of the crisis and displacement, it is impossible to design effective livelihood interventions. Humanitarians, for example, often target women in their livelihood programmes, with little recognition of the myriad responsibilities women assume and take on. Already overburdened caring for children, cooking and managing households, women often have the least time to participate in training and work programmes; but unless practitioners have undertaken a gender analysis, this may not be obvious. For poor women, time is often their most valuable resource; the care work done by women and girls in the poorest households tends to be extremely time and labour intensive (Sen 2008: 6–7), and this care burden generally increases during displacement. And yet, contrarily, the disruption of social norms resulting from crisis and displacement can lead to changes in gender norms and provide new openings for women's participation in programmes and services, and opportunities for creating a more gender-equitable society (WRC 2014c: 14).

A gendered assessment of cash transfer programmes carried out by Concern Worldwide and Oxfam found that the cash transfers tended to reinforce rather than challenge women's traditional household and social roles, and that despite clear organizational commitments to gender equality, this was badly translated into practice (Concern Worldwide and Oxfam GB 2011: 6). Rhetoric and policy commitments to address gender equality are usually strong, but are often operationally weak. Programmes that target women often reflect an assumption that by giving women cash, 'empowerment' or gender benefits will follow (ibid.: 20). Unless a gender analysis is undertaken to understand the way money is divided, controlled and used within households, it will be unclear as to whether giving money to women actually improves the lives of household members and promotes better gender relations and improvements to women's status, or if such instead contributes to harm (ibid.).

While the two aforementioned assessments are relatively straightforward and not particularly complicated, a market analysis is more challenging and demanding to both understand and undertake. The market refers to the full range of goods and services produced and exchanged, and all the support structures that facilitate the transfer of such goods and services – everything from transportation to banking services to the internet. The market is increasingly global and increasingly virtual. For a humanitarian practitioner, more often than not an outsider to the country if not the region, understanding the complexity of the existing market as well as how it is evolving requires knowledge, practice and tools that seldom coexist in these contexts. While there are some tools at practitioners' disposal, such as the Emergency Market Mapping and Analysis Toolkit (EMMA) (Albu 2010), Market Research for Value Chain Initiatives (Jones and Miehlbradt 2007), the Market Assessment Toolkit for Vocational Training Providers and Youth (WRC and Columbia University 2008) and the Oxfam 48-hour Assessment Tool (Oxfam GB 2012), one could argue that the tools are both overly complicated for the majority of non-specialized humanitarian responders, and simultaneously, that they lack comprehensiveness. Each focuses on a particular type of intervention, such as value chains; or a time period, such as the first forty-eight hours; or a specific market, such as the labour market. There remains a lack of tools for conducting a relatively quick and yet comprehensive market analysis that would provide at least a snapshot of the market barriers, gaps and opportunities that exist within a given time period and within a given context.

In order, however, to design effective livelihood programmes that work for women as well as men, and for youth as well as adults, practitioners need to marry the three types of assessments, carry them out in concert and then design interventions that take into account existing skills, that build on current economic coping strategies (if not harmful), that recognize workloads and assets as differentiated by gender, and that match those with market opportunities. While this may seem a tall order, putting these pieces even minimally in place would improve the effectiveness and impact of current livelihood programming in the majority of humanitarian contexts. Humanitarians may never be equipped to fully get it right, but practitioners can certainly do it better.

At present, because programmers are not doing it well, the nearly twenty years of average displacement represent, at best, a waste of potential and, at worst, an erosion of existing skills, leaving those displaced dependent on humanitarian assistance for years on end, unprepared for any of the three durable solutions – return, local integration or third-country resettlement. Humanitarian and development actors and their donors must use these years of displacement to build their capacity and prepare forced migrants for economic futures, as they will need to participate in and contribute to longer-term recovery and rebuilding efforts.

Women's Economic Empowerment and Gender Equality

In addition to designing effective livelihood interventions, humanitarian practitioners have both an opportunity and a responsibility to capitalize on the shifts in gender roles and gender relations that conflict and displacement deliver. Moments of major political transformations, including wars and conflicts, provide opportunities for a transgression from stereotypical gender roles and expectations, even if only temporarily (WRC 2014c: 14). The vast majority of internally displaced Syrians, for example, have reportedly undergone an almost complete shift in traditional roles within their families and community structures, with women from poorer communities, who before had generally been confined to roles within the household, now being the only adults in the home left to support themselves, their children and elderly family members. Out of sheer necessity, Syrian women have become economically active, transforming themselves and traditional social norms (Haddad 2014: 46). Similarly, Afghan refugee women in Pakistan have had access to reproductive health services; for many of them it was for the first time. Some of their daughters also had access to primary and secondary education that was lacking or even unavailable back home. Donors and practitioners need to exploit these opportunities to promote women's economic empowerment, and ensure equal access and equal opportunity for all among the affected population.

Many economic programmes targeting displaced women, however, while often the 'right thing to do', have not necessarily led to the right results. There are myriad reasons for this. Women are already shouldering too many of the household responsibilities to take full advantage of the opportunities on offer. Social norms may limit their mobility as well as their access to well-paid employment. And, critically, because of historical and inherent gender discrimination, they may have had fewer opportunities for education, skills development and work experience, rendering them ill-prepared for the humanitarian interventions targeting them. Women without previous entrepreneurial experience, for example, cannot be expected to start a small business with a loan unless they receive proper business planning, financial literacy, coaching and follow-on support.

Women's work still tends to be of lower status in the labour market, concentrated in the informal economy in jobs that are poorly paid, offer less security, are less valued, and are often performed under poorer working conditions. The jobs also generally offer fewer opportunities for advancement (Heintz 2008: 12–13). Gender segmentation is endemic in labour markets, with women largely concentrated in unstable and poor-quality employment (ibid.). Focus, therefore, cannot just be on securing employment or self-employment for women but rather on dignified work with decent pay, and with the goal of economic empowerment for women. Women's economic empowerment, however, is closely linked with and dependent on women's political and social empowerment. Income alone does not equate with empowerment. Empowerment is a multifaceted, long-term goal that relies on individual, social, institutional and infrastructural change (Concern Worldwide and Oxfam GB 2011: 12).

The United Nations Population Fund (UNFPA) defines women's empowerment through five major components: women's sense of self-worth; their right to have and determine choices; their right to have access to opportunities and resources; their right to have the power to control their own lives, both within and outside the home; and their ability to influence the direction of social change to create a more just social and economic order, nationally and internationally (United Nations Population Information Network 1995). These five components are challenging to achieve in stable, developed countries; how much more so when women are displaced in situations where they have largely lost control of their lives, their access to and control over resources, and their ability to influence change. Women's empowerment programmes implemented during displacement are, therefore, fraught with obstacles. Too often, economic programmes are implemented as stand-alone interventions focusing on building financial assets without the corresponding attention to building or strengthening social and human assets. The mix and balance of assets is increasingly deemed vital for successful economic engagement.

As with pre-displacement, so too during displacement, women face a trade-off between their livelihood and their protection (Buscher 2012: 46). Many of the economic opportunities that displaced women have access to and that humanitarian practitioners support, expose them to heightened risks: few practitioners put an emphasis on protection and the prevention of gender-based violence within their programmes. These risks can include frequent movement in the public sphere, use of public transportation, travelling after dark, the lack of safe places to save income, abusive employers, and exploitative work in the unregulated, informal economy. When humanitarian actors design and implement livelihood programmes without considering the beneficiaries' risk of harm, interventions are less likely to achieve their stated objectives and more likely to compromise personal safety (WRC 2014a: 3). Without proper analysis, livelihood programmes can reinforce women's traditional gender roles, add burden by increasing workloads, upend power relations within the household, introduce women to new activities or places that heighten their risk of experiencing violence, and attract attacks by outside groups due to coveted assets (ibid.: 6). When the economic programmes implemented are neither safe nor market driven, they can actually undermine progress towards women's economic empowerment.

In spite of well-intentioned efforts to promote gender equality, providing access and opportunities for adult women when they have had fewer educational, skills development and employment opportunities than their male counterparts, is often a set-up for failure. This is not, however, to imply that empowerment programmes should not be attempted, but rather that programme designers and implementers should recognize the barriers and challenges, and the need to link economic opportunity with political and social participation, as well as with access to and control over resources.

In order to level the playing field so that women can have the same opportunities for success in business and employment, programmers must start with adolescent girls, building their social, human and financial assets early so that they have the building blocks for later economic participation. This requires building girls' self-esteem and self-efficacy, strengthening their social networks with both peers and adult or older-girl role models, providing financial literacy and entrepreneurial skills, and ensuring access to both formal and informal educational and vocational training opportunities.

In displacement contexts, however, adolescent girls are often overlooked, lumped in with children or with adults. There are few programmes that target their specific needs and that mitigate the myriad of risks they face. And yet, starting with girls allows for later success with women. Displaced adolescent girls are at heightened risks of gender-based violence, forced and early marriage, pregnancy and school-leaving, and are more likely to have their access to services restricted (WRC 2014b: 2–3). Identifying, reaching and prioritizing them with both mainstream and targeted programming has been challenging. Improving the socio-economic outcomes for girls and young women is not only beneficial to them but also to their communities, and indeed to the next generation. Even marginal investments in girls can have a substantial impact on GDP growth and well-being (Chaaban and Cunningham 2011: 21). Policy and practice, however, seldom explicitly target development opportunities for girls (ibid.: 2). Until practitioners manage to do so, they will have limited success promoting women's economic empowerment and a broader gender-equality agenda.

Female labour force participation plays a critical role in cushioning households from the impact of economic shocks and keeping them out of poverty (Morrison, Raju and Sina 2008: 16). This thinking has huge implications for how and why humanitarians must engage displaced women in livelihood programmes. Displaced women often respond to situations of deprivation in amazing ways: what emerges is a picture of resilience, resourcefulness, ingenuity and flexibility of response (Golooba-Mutebi 2004: 7). The women can drive economic development in their countries or communities of displacement, as well as in their countries of origin when they are able to return safely. The experience of a decade or generation of displacement populations provides a window and an opportunity to change women, their societies and, in the process, to promote a more equitable world. Robert Zoellick, former President of the World Bank Group, has stated: 'Gender and women's empowerment are at the core of what we need to do in development. It's not just a women's issue. Improved economic opportunities for women lead to better outcomes for families, societies and countries' (International Finance Cooperation and the World Bank 2014). *The Economist* added, 'Forget China, India and the internet: economic growth is driven by women' (*The Economist* 2006). The millions of women uprooted and displaced by violence and conflict must be included in the process and provided with opportunities to contribute and to drive economic development – for their sake, for the sake of their families, and for the sake of the future of their countries of displacement, and of origin and eventual return.

Reflections on Making it Work for Refugees and Host Countries

Despite the fact that many countries do not allow refugees to work or relegate them to the informal economy, refugees do contribute to the local economy, both directly and indirectly. Refugees rent from host country nationals, shop at the local markets, purchase services and goods, and often do the dirty, degrading, low-earning jobs that many locals are unwilling to do. As an example of the indirect contributions, the World Food Programme estimates that its food voucher programme has injected $800 million into the economies of refugee-hosting countries that border Syria (UNHCR 2014a). A study on refugee economies in Uganda by the Refugee Studies Centre at the University of Oxford, on the more direct measures, concluded that refugees often make a positive contribution to the host-state economy as exemplified by the significant volume of exchange between refugees and host-country nationals, as well as by refugees' creation of employment opportunities for Ugandans (Betts et al. 2014: 5). The Oxford research found that refugees are economic actors, with 60 per cent of those studied self-employed and 39 per cent employed by others. Further, it found that some 21 per cent of urban refugees employ others and that 40 per cent of these employees are Ugandan nationals (ibid.: 42). The challenge for humanitarian actors is to ensure that these employment and self-employment opportunities are available to women as well as men, that female and male youth can also benefit, that the jobs do not perpetuate gender inequality, and that they are safe, dignified, market-based and sustainable.

Perhaps the most effective way of achieving this is through use of the graduation approach – a model conceptualized by CGAP (Consultative Group to Assist the Poor) and the Ford Foundation (de Montesquiou et al. 2014: 8), which was inspired by BRAC's[2] work in Bangladesh working with the poorest of the poor and moving them out of extreme poverty (BRAC 2012). The approach includes social protection to provide basic consumption support for those living in extreme poverty while providing inputs and services to build their skills (human assets) and providing access to financial assets (savings, financial literacy, in-kind transfers, grants) until the targeted individuals 'graduate' into microfinance interventions, self-employment or job-placement programmes. The objective is to lift people out of poverty through a stepped approach and off the need for direct humanitarian or development assistance. While the approach has often focused on those living in extreme poverty, the model can be used for all those assisted as it allows targeted individuals to start in different places on the continuum and have access to different interventions based on their specific needs and capacities (WRC 2011). The model is perhaps particularly relevant for trying to make programmes gender inclusive and gender sensitive as it allows for interventions to be tailored to individual needs and capacities, and focuses on building assets that may be weak or non-existent. It can, therefore, help to compensate for the differential starting points that women and men may have with respect to livelihoods, because of differing experiences and opportunities. The model has been adopted by UNHCR and is being piloted in partnership with BRAC and Trickle Up in Cairo and Costa Rica (UNHCR 2014c). The model can address the gap previously identified with cash transfers, as the approach uses interventions like cash transfers as a building block to address consumption needs while helping targeted populations to move upwards towards more sustainable economic interventions and onwards towards eventual self-reliance.

The most effective economic interventions start with the existing skills of those displaced, build on current economic coping strategies, if constructive, focus on further capacitating and diversifying assets (human, social, financial, natural and physical) and marry new and existing skills with market opportunities. The interventions should provide equal access and opportunities for all – women and men, female and male youth – recognizing that women's and youths' contributions to household economies are often primary and must, therefore, be substantive. Men, especially men affected by conflict and displacement, are no longer the sole or even the most significant breadwinners. Giving preference to women in assistance programmes, though, may contribute to further eroding men's roles. Gender implies the complex web of relationships between men and women, young and old, powerful and powerless (El-Bushra 2000). As such, economic programmes must target and include women, not because they are deemed vulnerable or needy or deemed 'victims', but because targeting them can bring about change in gender roles and contribute substantively to economic development. And these programmes must target and include men to support their roles as fathers, co-contributors and providers as male marginalization is a serious obstacle to programmes seeking to take steps towards gender equality and sustainable social change (Concern Worldwide and Oxfam GB 2011: 18). Only in the aggregate can gender be dealt with more than superficially and indeed transformatively.

The growing numbers of the forcibly displaced – now over 65 million (UNHCR 2016) – and the increasing length of their displacement – approaching twenty years, on average, for refugees (Loescher 2011) – coupled with the growing number of crises and over-stretched humanitarian resources, when viewed collectively, make it ever more critical that self-reliance be promoted early and systematically. The complexity and frequency of crises and the expanding urban nature of displacement result in populations that are more dispersed, and harder to reach and service. As their seemingly ever-growing needs now far outstrip the parallel growth in humanitarian resources, it is unlikely that donor governments' political will and resultant financial contributions will keep pace. Consequently, the forcibly displaced must be enabled to address their own needs as quickly and sustainably as possible. This means assisting them to preserve the assets they do have and to build the assets they require, which means providing safe, dignified opportunities for all – women and men, youth and adults – and using the upheaval of displacement to promote a more gender equitable world.

Dale Buscher is adjunct associate professor at the School of International and Public Affairs at Columbia University, and the senior director for programs at the Women's Refugee Commission where he oversees the commission's research and programmatic work on refugee livelihoods, disabilities, adolescents and youth, urban refugees, and sexual and reproductive health. Prior to joining the Women's Refugee Commission in 2005, Buscher consulted with the United Nations High Commissioner for Refugees and wrote their handbook, *Operational Protection in Camps and Settlements*. He has been working in the refugee assistance field since 1988 in a variety of capacities, including with Vietnamese boat people in the Philippines, with Haitian refugees interned at Guantanamo Bay, with displaced Kurds in Northern Iraq, with Bosnian refugees in Croatia, and with Kosovars in Albania and in Kosovo.

Notes

1. Phone interview with two senior staff at VISA, April 2014.
2. BRAC is an international development organization based in Bangladesh and the largest non-governmental development organization in the world in terms of number of employees (as of September 2016). Sir Fazle Hasan Abed established the organization in 1972 after Bangladesh's independence; today BRAC is present in all 64 districts of Bangladesh as well as 13 other countries in Asia, Africa and the Americas.

Bibliography

Albu, M. 2010. *Emergency Market Mapping and Analysis Toolkit.* Warwickshire: Practical Action Publishing, Oxfam GB.

Al-Khalidi, S. 2014. 'Syria's Economy Heads into Ruin: U.N. Sponsored Report', *Reuters.* Retrieved 18 November 2014 from http://www.reuters.com/article/2014/05/28/syria-economy-idUSL6N0OE3JG20140528.

Autesserre, S. 2012. 'Dangerous Tales: Dominant Narratives on the Congo and their Unintended Consequences', *African Affairs* 111(443): 202–22.

Ballentine, K., and H. Nitzschke. 2005. 'The Political Economy of Civil War and Conflict Transformation', *Berghof Handbook.* Berghof Research Center for Constructive Conflict Management. Retrieved 3 December 2014 from http://www.berghof-foundation.org/fileadmin/redaktion/Publications/Handbook/Dialogue_Chapters/dialogue3_ballentine_nitzschke.pdf.

Bassey, N. 2012. *Destructive Extraction and the Climate Chaos in Africa.* Cape Town: Pampazuka Press.

Betts, A., et al. 2014. *Refugee Economies: Rethinking Popular Assumptions.* Oxford: University of Oxford, Refugee Studies Centre, Humanitarian Innovation Project.

BRAC. 2012. *Moving Out of Extreme Poverty: Graduation Program Improves Lives of the Poorest.* Retrieved 9 December 2014 from http://www.brac.net/content/moving-out-extreme-poverty-graduation-program-improves-lives-poorest.

Buchanan-Smith, M., and A. Fadul. 2008. *Adaptation and Devastation: The Impact of the Conflict on Trade and Markets in Darfur.* Boston: Feinstein International Center, Tufts University.

Buscher, D. 2009 'Women, Work and War', in S.F. Martin and J. Tirman (eds), *Women, Migration, and Conflict: Breaking a Deadly Cycle.* New York: Springer Publishing, pp. 87–106.

———. 2012. 'Making Work Safe for Displaced Women', *Forced Migration Review* 41: 46.

Chaaban, J., and W. Cunningham. 2011. 'Measuring the Economic Gains of Investing in Girls: The Girl Effect Dividend', World Bank Policy Research Working Paper 5753.

Concern Worldwide and Oxfam GB. 2011. 'Walking the Talk: Cash Transfers and Gender Dynamics'. Retrieved 12 December 2014 from https://www.concern.

net/sites/default/files/resource/2011/05/cash_transfers_in_gender_relations. pdf.

Dahi, O. 2014. 'The Refugee Crisis in Lebanon and Jordan: The Need for Economic Development Spending', *Forced Migration Review* 47: 11–13.

de Montesquiou, A., et al. 2014. *From Extreme Poverty to Sustainable Livelihoods.* Consultative Group to Assist the Poor (CGAP) and the Ford Foundation.

DFID. 1999. 'The Sustainable Livelihoods Distance Learning Guide', DFID Sustainable Livelihoods Guidance Sheets, DFID-adaptation of Chambers and Conway, London.

Economist, The. 2006. 'Women in the Workforce: The Importance of Sex'. Retrieved 8 December 2014 from http://www.economist.com/node/6800723.

El-Bushra, J. 2000. 'Gender and Forced Migration: Editorial', *Forced Migration Review* 9: 4–7.

Foulkes, I. 2014. 'Global Refugee Figures Highest since WW2, UN says', *BBC News.* Retrieved 23 November 2014 from http://www.bbc.com/news/world-27921938.

Garret, N., and A. Piccinni. 2012. 'Natural Resources and Conflict: A New Security Challenge for the European Union'. Retrieved 2 December 2014 from http://www.sipri.org/research/conflict/pko/PKO_archive/resources/RCSfull1206.pdf.

Global Policy Forum. 2014. 'The Dark Side of Natural Resources'. Retrieved 24 December 2014 from https://www.globalpolicy.org/dark-side-of-natural-re-sources.html.

Golooba-Mutebi, F. 2004. 'Refugee Livelihoods, Confronting Uncertainty and Responding to Adversity: Mozambican War Refugees in Limpopo Province, South Africa', *New Issues in Refugee Research* 105.

Haddad, Z. 2014. 'How the Crisis is Altering Women's Roles in Syria', *Forced Migration Review* 47: 46–47.

Haysom, S. 2013. 'Sanctuary in the City? Urban Displacement and Vulnerability: Final Report', *HPG Report* No. 33.

Heath, N. n.d. 'How Conflict Minerals Funded a War that Killed Millions, and Why Tech Giants are Finally Cleaning up Their Act', TechRepublic. Retrieved 10 April 2015 from http://www.techrepublic.com/article/how-conflict-minerals-funded-a-war-that-killed-millions/.

Heintz, J. 2008. 'Poverty, Employment and Globalisation: A Gender Perspective', *Poverty in Focus: Gender Equality* 13: 12–13.

International Finance Cooperation and the World Bank. 2014 'Promoting Women's Economic Empowerment', Global Private Sector Leaders Forum. Retrieved 8 December 2014 from http://www.un.org/en/ecosoc/phlntrpy/notes/world_brochure.pdf.

International Rescue Committee. 2014. *Emergency Economies: The Impact of Cash Assistance in Lebanon.* Beirut.

Jaspers, S., and S. O'Callaghan. 2010. 'Challenging Choices: Protection and Livelihoods in Conflict', *HPG Policy Brief* No. 40.

Jones, L., and A. Miehlbradt. 2007. *Market Research for Value Chain Initiatives. Information to Action: A Toolkit Series for Market Development Practitioners*, MEDA.

Konneh, A. 2009. Global Economic Symposium. Retrieved 20 November 2014 from http://www.global-economic-symposium.org/knowledgebase/the-global-polity/repairing-failed-states/proposals/liberia-rebuilding-for-growth-and-development.

Loescher, G. 2011. 'The Global Crisis of Protracted Displacement', *World Politics Review*. Retrieved 23 November 2014 from http://www.worldpoliticsreview.com/articles/7804/the-global-crisis-of-protracted-displacement.

Meger, S. 2011. 'The Role of Globalization in Wartime Sexual Violence', *African Conflict and Peacebuilding Review* 1(1): 100–132.

Morrison, A., D. Raju and N. Sina. 2008. 'Gender Equality is Good for the Poor', *Poverty in Focus: Gender Equality* 13: 16–17.

Oxfam GB. 2012. 'Emergency Food Security & Livelihoods 48 hours Evaluation Toolkit'. London.

Ross, M. 2003. 'Oil, Drugs, and Diamonds: The Varying Roles of Natural Resources in Civil War', in K. Ballentine and J. Sherman (eds), *The Political Economy of Armed Conflict: Beyond Greed and Grievance*. Boulder, CO: Lynne Rienner Publishers, pp. 47–70.

Ruaudel, H., and R. Zetter. 2014. 'Development and Protection Challenges of the Syrian Refugee Crisis', *Forced Migration Review* 47: 6–10.

Seferis, L., and A. Sood. 2014. 'Syrians Contributing to Kurdish Economic Growth', *Forced Migration Review* 47: 14–16.

Sen, G. 2008. 'Poverty as a Gendered Experience: The Policy Implications', *Poverty in Focus: Gender Equality* 13: 6–7.

Trading Economies. 2014. 'Country Indicators: Liberia'. Retrieved 20 November 2014 from http://www.tradingeconomics.com/liberia/gdp-per-capita.

UNHCR. 2012. 'An Introduction to Cash-based Interventions in UNHCR Operations'. Geneva.

——. 2014a. 'Syrian Refugees: Inter-Agency Regional Update, 1 December 2014'. Retrieved 9 December 2014 from http://reliefweb.int/report/lebanon/syrian-refugees-inter-agency-regional-update-1-december-2014.

——. 2014b. 'Global Trends 2013: War's Human Cost'. Geneva.

——. 2014c. 'The Graduation Approach Newsletter'. Retrieved 10 April 2015 from http://www.trickleup.org/media/publications/upload/UNHCR-Graduation-Pilots-Newsletter-1-1-FINAL_US.pdf.

——. 2016. Global Trends 2016: Forced Displacement in 2015. Geneva.

UNHCR and REACH. 2014. 'Economic Survey of Syrian Refugees: Refugee Camps, Kurdistan Region of Iraq, Thematic Assessment Report', ACTED and UNOSAT.

United Nations Population Information Network. 1995. 'Guidelines on Women's Empowerment'. UN Population Division, Department of Economic and Social Affairs, with the support of the United Nations Population Fund (UNFPA). Retrieved 7 December 2014 from http://www.un.org/popin/unfpa/taskforce/guide/iatfwemp.gdl.html.

WFP, UNICEF and UNHCR. 2013. 'Vulnerability Assessment of Syrian Refugees in Lebanon: 2013 Report'. New York.

WRC (Women's Refugee Commission). 2009. 'Building Livelihoods: A Field Manual for Practitioners in Humanitarian Settings'. New York.

___. 2011. 'Dawn in the City: Guidance for Achieving Self-Reliance for Urban Refugees'. New York.

___. 2014a. 'A Double-Edged Sword: Livelihoods in Emergencies. Guidance and Tools for Improved Programming'. New York.

___. 2014b. 'Strong Girls, Powerful Women: Program Planning and Design for Adolescent Girls in Humanitarian Settings'. New York.

___. 2014c. 'Unpacking Gender: The Humanitarian Response to the Syrian Refugee Crisis in Jordan'. New York.

Women's Refugee Commission and Columbia University School of International and Public Affairs. 2008. 'Market Assessment Toolkit for Vocational Training Providers and Youth: Linking Vocational Training Programs to Market Opportunities'. New York.

World Bank et al. 2012. 'Assessing the Impacts and Costs of Forced Displacement: Volume 1, A Mixed Methods Approach'. Retrieved 6 December 2014 from https://openknowledge.worldbank.org/bitstream/handle/10986/16096/7826 50WP0Box0377336B00PUBLIC00.txt?sequence=2.

Part II
Experiencing Gender, Violence, Refuge

8

Escaping Conflicts and Being Safe?

Post-conflict Refugee Camps and the Continuum of Violence

Ulrike Krause

Introduction

The majority of refugees worldwide are forced to flee their homes because of violent conflicts, in which women especially are often targets of sexual and gender-based violence. Over the past years, Peace and Conflict scholars have increasingly focused on wartime violence, revealing that rape and other forms of sexual and gender-based violence (SGBV) are not (only) caused by male sexual urges as was argued in the 1990s (Seifert 1996: 35, 36); such violence rather constitutes socially and politically constructed acts (Buckley-Zistel 2013: 91–92). Those who can escape conflicts seek safety and protection in a country of asylum, but a growing body of literature of Forced Migration and Refugee Studies emphasizes that refugees are also confronted with diverse challenges including SGBV in camps and settlements, despite protection measures by humanitarian organizations. Since most studies focus on either the setting of conflict or of encampment, the possible connection between violence during conflict and during displacement has been widely neglected.

In this chapter I want to challenge the notion of violence during conflict and displacement as being separate cases. Research conducted in a refugee settlement in Uganda has revealed that especially female but also male refugees were not only confronted with violence during conflict but also during flight, and they continued to face various structural restrictions, and forms of cultural, social and economic discrimination, as well as physical assault, during displacement. This indicates a continuity of violence from conflict to camps. By focusing on SGBV during conflict, flight and encampment, I seek to find out whether its prevalence and continuity suggest a continuum of violence. The approach of conflict-induced displacement is employed to underline the conflict–exile nexus by means of which refugee contexts are understood as post-conflict settings,[1] as they are either geographically outside or chronologically after conflicts.

This chapter will explore the scope, structures and conditions of SGBV during conflict in the Democratic Republic of Congo (DRC), flight to Uganda and encampment in a settlement in Uganda. To do so, it first outlines the theoretical framework and research approach, and then describes the experiences of refugees during the different phases. This constitutes the main part of this study and is based on the findings of the ethnographic field research but also reconnects with academic debates. The strings of arguments are brought together and analysed in the third section, which explores whether the continuity reveals a continuum of sexual and gender-based violence. To conclude this chapter, a summary is provided and remaining questions noted.

Beyond the Mainstream: Broadening Research Approaches

Traditionally, the international refugee regime along with the research about it is reactive, exile-oriented and refugee-centred as the protection focus is on the displaced rather than the causes of displacement (Loescher, Betts and Milner 2008: 18). This is why conflict and displacement have mainly been observed as separate phases, although it is acknowledged that violent conflicts can force people to leave their homes. Theoretical approaches such as survival migration, climate change-related displacement, crises migration or conflict-induced forced migration go beyond the exile-orientation in current scholarship, and generally relate to specific triggers for displacement or motivation of forced migration. However, they only recently received more attention (Boano, Zetter and Morris 2008; Betts 2013; McAdam 2014). Buckley-Zistel, Krause and Loeper (2014: 56–57) emphasize the need for a holistic approach to linking conflict and displacement, and grasping refugee contexts as post-conflict settings, but scholars have yet to agree on a coherent definition of the concept of conflict-induced displacement. While Lischer defines it as 'situations in which people leave their homes to escape political violence' (Lischer 2007: 143), Lindley explains that a 'conflict-induced migrant [is] characterised by the absence of original positive intent to move ... and flight in response to ongoing violent conflict which threatens the migrant's life and livelihood' (Lindley 2008: 8). In the context of this research, conflict-induced displacement is understood as a situation in which people are forced to flee due to the explicit or implicit effects of violent conflicts, including social, political, economic and ecological aspects, as well as direct or indirect psychological and physical impacts on individual levels.

Sexual and gender-based violence has received increasing attention in the context of Peace and Conflict Studies as well as Forced Migration and Refugee Studies in recent years.[2] While recent studies highlight that such acts constitute socially and politically constructed acts rather than ways to gain physical pleasure (Buckley-Zistel 2013: 91–92), the different discourses have thus far existed separately. Nevertheless, refugee contexts can be understood as post-conflict settings, and it has been emphasized that the end of conflict does not constitute the end of SGBV (Turshen, Meintjes and Pillay 2001; Pankhurst 2008). The aim of this chapter is to bring the discourses together and understand if and how SGBV during conflict and in refugee camps – as post-conflict settings – are connected. In accordance with the internationally recognized definition of the Inter-Agency Standing Committee, SGBV is understood as 'an umbrella term for any harmful act that is perpetrated against a person's will and that is based on socially ascribed (i.e. gender) differences between males and females. It includes acts that inflict physical, sexual or mental harm or suffering, threats of such acts, coercion, and other deprivations of liberty. These acts can occur in public or in private' (IASC 2015: 5), and include physical, emotional, sexual and psychological acts, attempts or threats (UNHCR 2003: 10; 2008: 7, 10).

While scholars have increasingly looked into issues of SGBV during conflict and displacement, the linkage of the different phases remains widely neglected. Only singular studies consider the continued violence; while Ferris (1990) stresses how women face different forms of SGBV during conflict, flight and protected encampment, Cockburn (2004) discusses how violent events are linked in 'uneasy' peace, conflict and post-conflict situations, stressing the power imbalance between women and men. Also Alden (2010), Freedman (2015: 45–68) and Nagai et al. (2008) touch on the issue of continued violence from specific academic perspectives. My chapter is embedded in this debate, and contributes to it with an empirical case study, in-depth insights of scope, forms and conditions of violence, and by informing about additional impacting factors.

The ethnographic field research that this chapter is based on was conducted with a case study of Kyaka II Refugee Settlement in Uganda. It constitutes a local rural refugee settlement and therefore differs from refugee camps.[3] Since the 1980s, refugee camps and settlements constitute the main form of shelter for refugees in countries of first asylum (Loescher, Betts and Milner 2008: 3) where assistance and protection is provided to refugees; they are generally understood to be short-term or interim solutions used until one of the three durable solutions – voluntary repatriation, local integration or resettlement to a third country – can be applied. Jacobsen defines local rural settlement structures as

> organized settlements, ... planned, segregated agricultural enclaves or villages created specifically for refugees, but which differ from camps in that refugees are expected to become self-sufficient pending their repatriation. ... There is limited freedom of movement (refugees are usually not permitted to leave the areas of residence defined for them by the authorities), more permanent housing construction, and refugees have access to land provided by the government. (Jacobsen 2001: 7)

The definition suits Kyaka II Refugee Settlement; a confined space of 84 km² with an estimated carrying capacity of seventeen thousand refugees, purposely set up for their protection and assistance. It is located in Kyegegwa District in central Uganda, a remote and rural region. The settlement was established in 1983 and is therefore a protracted refugee situation. It is under the overall supervision of the Office of the Prime Minister (OPM), Government of Uganda, and the United Nations High Commissioner for Refugees (UNHCR). The measures in the different sectors are implemented by a number of operational and implementing partners of UNHCR, mainly non-governmental organizations. In ten zones and twenty-eight clusters, which are set up as villages, refugees live side by side with nationals; refugees receive two plots, one for residence and one for agriculture, to become self-sufficient and thus be relatively independent from aid delivery. Diverse representative committees exist among the refugees, such as the refugee welfare committee, to solve conflict in the community and channel information to organizations. The settlement therefore encompasses social units, organizational rules, administrative procedures and institutionally developed norms and values. This entails the creation of structural and formal hierarchies among the aid agencies, as well as relatively informal structures among the refugees, which Inhetveen describes as poly-hierarchical (Inhetveen 2010: 16–18, 165ff.). Although the settlement structures are discussed as having advantages when compared to camps (Jacobsen 2001; Krause 2013), scholars stress a variety of security challenges such as armed robbery, ethnic-based assaults, as well as SGBV in different settlements worldwide (see Buckley-Zistel, Krause and Loeper 2014: 49–51).[4]

Conducting research in such an environment about a subject that is likely to involve traumatized individuals requires a suitable research design and ethical considerations. The ethnographic field research was carried out in 2014 by employing a mixed-method approach consisting of participatory observation as well as structured and semi-structured expert interviews with twenty-eight employees of aid agencies and other institutions in the settlement. Refugees were engaged in the research by means of sixty-five ero-epic dialogues (EEDs), which constitute an unstructured interview form that takes place in a surrounding that is comforting for the interviewees, seven focus group discussions (FGDs) with thirty-five participants, and a survey reaching 351 refugees. The survey was conducted by means of anonymous, written, multiple-choice questionnaires. Thirty-seven adolescents were engaged through journal writing as a child-friendly method with open-ended questions. Medical statistics and programme reports were furthermore accessed. Ethical considerations include the awareness of the scholar of the potential impact on the research object, the 'balance of risks and benefits, unbiased selection of research samples, and assurance of the rights of individual participants' (Seedat et al. 2004: 202), which were adhered to by the research team at all times. The team consisted of two political scientists and a clinical psychologist who designed the research approach as a team, and continuously re-evaluated it during data collection. All participants took part in the research voluntarily after being informed about the research and their rights.

From Conflict to Camp

Most refugees worldwide escape violent and armed conflicts. UNHCR estimates that in 2015, thirty-four thousand people per day were displaced due to conflict and persecution, while it was twenty-three thousand in 2012 (UNHCR 2013: 2; 2016: 2). In 2015, 86 per cent of all refugees were in developing countries in the Global South, and more than 41 per cent had to endure protracted situations with an estimated average duration of twenty-six years but some situations last for more than thirty years (UNHCR 2016: 2, 20). Conflicts not only drive people from their homes and countries of origin, they also prolong the duration of displacement as refugees are unable to repatriate. In spite of that, voluntary repatriation remains the preferred durable solution for national and international actors.

Violence during Conflict

Conflicts impact on all members of society – social structures erupt, infrastructures break down, livelihoods become inaccessible, and widespread violence causes harm and traumatization. In the case of the Democratic Republic of Congo (DRC), in particular the eastern region of North Kivu and South Kivu, three conflicts have caused widespread chaos and reached extreme scales of violence. The first one, between Banyamulenge and the military, started in 1996 and lasted for about one year. In 1998, the second conflict began, which is understood to be a continuation of the first one, and ended in 2003 when the transitional government took over. In spite of that, the Kivu regions continued to experience violence, resulting, in April 2012, in the third resurgence of the conflict between the rebel group 'Mouvement du 23 Mars' and the military Forces Armées de la République Démocratique du Congo (Breytenbach et al. 1999; Reyntjens 2009: 144–52; Human Rights Watch 2014: 103–7).

The scope of violence in DRC has been vast, and despite a UN peacekeeping mission (MONUC), and later a UN stabilizing mission (MONUSCO), it was not possible to calm conditions, provide security and build peace. In addition to murder, kidnapping and displacement, sexual violence especially was used as a weapon of war. The body of operational and research literature on the scale and forms of SGBV has grown over the past decade and has identified, among others, widespread rape, gang rape, sex slavery, defilement and genital manipulation (see OHCHR 2011). Based on hospital reports, Pratt and Werchick found that from 1996 to 2003 'a *minimum* tens of thousands' of women were raped and/or sexually mutilated (Pratt and Werchick 2004: 11). Meger looks at the broader timeframe of ten years, and notes that 'hundreds of thousands of women and girls in the DRC have been raped' (Meger 2010: 126). More detailed figures are provided, among others, by Malteser International, indicating that 20,517 women were raped in South Kivu from 2005 to 2007 (Elbert et al. 2013: 17). According to UN Women, the UN entity for gender equality and empowerment of women, '[t]he UN registered 7,703 new cases of sexual violence in the Kivus in 2008; and between January and June 2009, 5,387 rapes were reported in South Kivu alone – a 30 per cent increase compared to the same period the previous year. In total, 15,275 rape cases were registered in DRC over the course of 2009' (Anderson 2012: 11). These statistics reveal reported cases, and it can be assumed that a number of cases remain unreported, thus increasing the actual scope. Although victims report cases of violence, impunity of perpetrators remains a great challenge (Eriksson Baaz and Stern 2009: 503; Meger 2010: 127–28; OHCHR 2011).

In addition to sexual violence, refugees also noted that domestic violence took place in DRC. One man stressed that 'the ones who beat their wives, most of them, they were also beating their wives back home' (male refugee, EED, 5 March 2014, Base Camp). While the intensity of domestic violence was explained as dependent on the 'tribes' and their customs (FGD with male refugees, 19 March 2014, Base Camp), refugee women said it increased in the refugee settlement (FGD with female refugees, 12 March 2014, Base Camp).

Perpetrators of SGBV in DRC were among unidentified armed groups, common criminals and members of the Congolese armed forces or the police (Pratt and Werchick 2004: 9; Pacéré 2007; Maedl 2010: 44). In accordance with that, some refugees were unable to identify the perpetrators of sexual violence. In the words of one refugee woman:

> [U]niformed men raped me and took clothes and money ..., they hit the door with a big stone, it fell in and they came. They held me at gun point and I gave them the money. Some were stealing while others were raping me. That morning I went to the chairman but nothing could be done. (Female refugee, EED, 5 March 2014, Kaborogota Zone)

Based on a household study, Johnson et al. reveal that the range of attackers is wider than just male perpetrators. The authors note that both women and men performed similar roles in armed groups, despite sexual slavery (Johnson et al. 2010: 558) and stress a relatively wide scope of female perpetrators[5] of violence, as '[w]omen [were] reported to have perpetrated conflict-related sexual violence in 41.1 per cent ... of female cases and 10.0 per cent ... of male cases' (ibid.: 553).

Personal reasons for wartime sexual violence in DRC can be mainly excluded as the victims are mostly unacquainted with their attackers, which is in line with other studies (Ohambe, Muhigwa and Mamba 2005: 36–38; Pacéré 2007: para. 67–91). Although the majority of victims of sexual violence are women and girls, sexual violence also takes place against men, which often brings stigmatization and social exclusion for the victims (OHCHR 2011: 6, 13). A recently published study by Dolan highlights that, 'a population-based survey conducted in eastern DRC in March 2010 showed rates of reported sexual violence were 39.7% among women and 23.6% among men' (Dolan 2014: 2). Johnson et al. found that 74.3 per cent of the women and 64.5 per cent of the men had been exposed to sexual violence; of these, 51.1 per cent of the women and 20.8 per cent of the men reported having been raped (Johnson et al. 2010: 557). In a qualitative study, Christian et al. (2011: 234) stress that men were often raped alongside family members, which is revealed by information provided by male survivors: 'I was raped along with my wife and daughter. There were many men and I had lost sense. I was not able to count [how many men raped me or my wife and daughter] as my face was towards the ground'. Hence, although female victims constitute the main group of victims, many men also faced attacks.

During conflict, sexual violence constituted a widespread threat and interviewed refugees in Uganda explained that perpetrators attacked villages and community members, often without specific targets, and assaulted people during daily work such as collecting firewood and farming. Other studies support the diversity of the locations, including spontaneous and planned assault and rape incidences. Ohambe, Muhigwa and Mamba (2005: 36) note that, especially in the context of planned sexual violence, the victims were often raped by several men in the presence of witnesses, which indicates the intended public character of the scenes. However, the authors stress that although 38.2 per cent of the interviewed women were raped in such public circumstances, the majority (61.8 per cent) were raped away from villages and without any witnesses. Despite the remote locations, these spaces are still understood as 'public' because the intimate character of homes within social circles is missing. Hence, most crimes take place in public spaces.

The systematic and widespread use of different forms of sexual violence during the conflicts in DRC reveals that it is used as a strategic weapon of war (Eriksson Baaz and Stern 2013: 46–49). In line with that, findings of the survey highlight that most refugees believe it was used to create fear and hurt, or to banish the community. A man in Uganda also explained the separation from is inner family circle: 'My father was captured by some wrong people who came during the night, beat up my Mum, raped her, broke her leg and infected her with HIV. My wife and two children were also taken by soldiers during the war; until today I am not sure whether they are alive' (male refugee, EED, 18 March 2014, Bukere Zone). In addition to family separation, this statement indicates abduction and forced military recruitment by armed forces, which was particularly directed against men and is therefore seen as a form of gender-based violence. Some refugees also indicated in the survey that sexual violence was committed for pleasure and relief, which is in line with findings of Eriksson Baaz and Stern who highlight the classification of rape in their study about soldiers in DRC: 'the normalized "rape" that stems from lust and want … and the rape which is evil, inhuman, and connected to brutality and violence', which is 'not acceptable – but still "understandable"' (Eriksson Baaz and Stern 2009: 508, 497). Meanwhile Schäfer explains that women are often seen 'as icons of national or ethnic unity and symbolical "purity as the guardians" of culture and tradition' (translated Schäfer 2009: 4), and therewith stresses that violence against women translates into violence against the opponent. At the same time, Christian et al. (2011: 235–36) note that violence against men aims to emasculate and humiliate them, their family and community. Considering that sexual violence occurs against female and male victims, the violence is to be seen as acts of degradation, power and dominance against conflict opponents, with individuals representing the opposing party.

Violence during Flight

The conflicts in eastern DRC destroyed livelihood conditions and pro-tecting social structures, caused insecurity and therefore forced people to leave their homes. Congolese refugees in Uganda explained that they fled the country due to the conflict, and noted that they left either because of personal threats or attacks by armed groups, or because of killings or kidnappings of family and/or community members. Conflict-related vio-lence subsequently affected the interviewed refugees in Uganda directly or indirectly, revealing that the flight from DRC is to be understood as 'conflict-induced displacement', as defined above.

The process of the flight as a part of conflict-induced displacement has received relatively little attention in research thus far because scholars have mainly focused on one of the two confined spaces: either the conflict in the country of origin triggering displacement, or the refugee situations often in camps or settlements in the country of asylum. Although scholars acknowledge that while fleeing people face numerous challenges includ-ing SGBV, which often lasts for weeks or even months (see, among others, Carlson 2005: 11; Edward 2007: 6; Martin 2011: 79), few studies and op-erational documents go beyond noting threats and challenges.[6] Among others, Ferris distinguishes between violence against women during conflict, flight and protected encampment (Ferris 1990), and Bariagaber focuses on political violence during flight but excludes SGBV (Bariagaber 2006: 41–77). In its prevention and response guidelines on SGBV, as well as in the protection handbook, UNHCR acknowledges the different phases of conflict, flight and protection in camps, and notes that protecting social systems disrupt, which makes those fleeing more vulnerable to violence (UNHCR 2003: 20; 2008: 49; 2011).

The scope of SGBV during flight from DRC appears to be wide, as the interviewed refugees repeatedly mentioned the hardships they faced while fleeing and seeking safety elsewhere. One man explained why he had had to leave DRC:

> I flew when there was a war between the Hindu and Hema in 2002. It was at night on March 2002 when people were raising an alarm. There were gunshots everywhere. I left the village with my family. We crossed with my family even other people, and we camped in Paida and later settled in Kiryandongo districts of Uganda. (Male refugee, EED, 27 March 2014, Base Camp)

A refugee woman said that when they reached the border of DRC and Uganda, they were approached by Congolese armed men whom she des-ignated as soldiers. They attacked them and killed her sister in front of them, which she described as 'cutting with a panga in several pieces; then we ran away and we arrived in Uganda, just the three of us – me, my mother and my niece', whose mother had been murdered. After passing through Kanungu in Western Uganda, they reached a UNHCR vehicle that brought them to Kyaka II Refugee Settlement (female refugee, EED, 18 March 2014, Swe Swe Zone). Another woman said she was raped twice by different men (female refugee, EED, 25 February 2014, Base Camp).

A man who fled by himself explained that it took him nine months to reach Uganda, as he continuously had to hide in the bushes (male refugee, EED, 27 March 2014, Base Camp), while another man who fled with his wife stated that close to the border they were approached by 'rebels who took our properties like clothes, bags among others, and also were beating my wife' (male refugee, EED, 27 March 2014, Base Camp). A 15-year-old boy explained: 'I was kidnapped and landed in the bush. They killed my mother and father. We ran and we got a place where we met people. Now I stay with my aunt. They killed my sister, my mom. My mom was carrying my young sister on her back' (refugee boy, journal writing, 4 April 2014, Bujubuli Primary School). Experiences like these were explained by several interviewed refugees, revealing how prevalent violence in general, and SGBV in particular, was during flight. Violence therefore not only triggered the flight but also continued to constitute a challenge and security risk while fleeing.

Refugees frequently spoke about a number of forms of physical violence, including murder and abduction of both men and women. However, there were forms that were gender-specific; while men often faced dangers of forced military or rebel recruitment, which is understood as a form of gender-based violence, women were mainly targets of sexual assault and abuse, including rape and gang rape. Although the political developments during field research prevented us from collecting data about sexual violence against men, staff of aid organizations indicated during expert interviews that men and boys were also raped and sexually abused but they rarely reported such cases after reaching the country of first asylum due to stigmatization and fear (female employee, UNHCR, expert interview, 10 April 2014; male employee, aid agency [anon.], expert interview, 10 April 2014). Moreover, refugees of both sexes regularly explained that they feared attacks during their flight, which not only reveals widespread threats but also indicates how violence impacted on them collectively, and caused psychological and emotional pressure.

Perpetrators of SGBV during flight are mainly members of armed forces but can also be other fleeing persons. A refugee woman noted that she was raped by different men who were also fleeing the conflict (female refugee, EED, 25 February 2014, Base Camp). The fact that attackers can come from among other fleeing persons complicates conditions and increases risks, especially for those who travel alone such as women with their children.

Since the attacks were committed against people fleeing, the violence took place in public spaces. A refugee woman who was raped before fleeing noted that 'people were being raped, and I saw them' (female refugee, EED, 5 March 2014, Kaborogota Zone), which not only stresses the great extent of visibility of such acts but also provokes the assumption that the violence conducted by members of armed groups was intended to be seen and committed in order to create fear among the displaced. However, fleeing persons were also named as perpetrators of sexual violence, which is assumed to be related to traumatization, disrupted social structures and cultural-related masculine dominance.

Violence in Camps

Reaching the country of first asylum and receiving protection and assistance from UNHCR and its implementing partners is the hope of the refugees who escaped the conflict in DRC. However, interviewed refugees and staff of aid agencies indicated that SGBV constitutes a challenge in Kyaka II Refugee Settlement. The official statistics of 2013 from the police, health, psychosocial, and SGBV focal points reveal the scope of reported case per type.

Refugees and aid workers explained that victims often do not report cases because they fear increased violence by the perpetrator, and stigmatization, prefer to handle cases at a community level, or cannot pay reporting fees to the police or the Refugee Welfare Council and therefore would not receive treatment (female refugee, EED, 17 March 2014, Bugibuli Zone;

Table 8.1 *Official statistics of sexual and gender-based violence cases reported in Kyaka II Refugee Settlement in 2013*

Classification /Type	Sub-Total		Total
	Female	Male	
Rape	35	0	35
Sexual Assault	1	1	2
Physical Assault	89	1	90
Denial of Resources	26	4	30
Psychological/Emotional Abuse	13	7	20
Forced Marriage	1	0	1
Total	**165**	**13**	**178**

Notes: 'Physical assault' was explained to include domestic violence. 'Denial of resources' was explained to be the rejection or denial of resources such as food or the financial means of one person towards their partner (intimate couple or marriage).

Religious Leaders, 19 March 2014, Base Camp; female employee, Africa Humanitarian Action, expert interview, 22 April 2014). Especially male victims would not report cases due to fear and stigmatization (female local employee, UNHCR, expert interview, 10 April 2014). Considering these challenges, the scope of SGBV is assumed to be broader than the statistics reveal, which is in line with findings of the survey. It reveals that 64.67 per cent of the interviewed refugees believe that sexual violence takes place 'regularly', 14.81 per cent 'daily', 18.50 per cent 'rarely' and 1.7 per cent 'never'. Moreover, all interviewed refugees noted that domestic violence exists; among them, 55.71 per cent believe that it occurs 'regularly', 36.86 per cent 'daily' and 7.43 per cent 'rarely'. Although this only reflects the perception of the refugees instead of the actual number of cases, it highlights that the scope of SGBV is wide.

Diverse forms of SGBV were referred to during interviews with aid staff and dialogues with refugees, including acts, attempts and threats of physical, psychological and sexual harm. During one expert interview, an employee listed the main forms: 'rape (both in country of origin and country of asylum), domestic violence, early/forced marriages, denial of resources and physical assault' (female employee, UNHCR, expert interview, 10 April 2014). Refugees mentioned domestic violence, sexual violence and structural discrimination particularly often.

Domestic violence takes place between the intimate partners or spouses and within private spheres of homes. A woman explained that

> domestic violence is common in Kyaka and is especially done by Congolese men who never consider women to be people. ... Their wives are to be their workers and even only sex object. Women are not involved in family issues. They are always under the men and there is a church that promotes that violence. Women are beaten and forced to have sex in their own homes. They are made to work for nothing by their husbands. Not even the food is enough. They are harassed and seen as helpless people in the society. (Female refugee, EED, 11 March 2014, Bukere Zone)

Although it was stated that women and girls were the main group of victims, refugees explained that men and boys were also confronted with physical abuse in domestic spheres. For example, a female refugee said that 'men also are being violated, and when they report [it] they are not helped because everyone knows it is mainly women who are always beaten' (female refugee, EED, 18 March 2014, Swe Swe Zone). Sexual violence cases included rape, attempts of rape, and sexual harassment, with varying groups of victims and locations. Several women spoke about acts or attempts of rape during daily work by strangers and acquaintances, including husbands and neighbours. Refugee girls and boys faced danger on their way to school, mainly by unknown persons, and while at school by teachers (refugee boy, age 15, journal writing, 4 April 2014, Bujubuli Primary School; refugee girl, age 16, journal writing, 5 March 2014, Bujubuli Secondary School).

Structural violence, which is understood to be part of psychological harm, was especially referred to regarding early and forced marriage of girls and denial of resources. Adolescents highlighted that girls often face early and forced marriage, which appears to be related to cultural traditions of some ethnic groups among the refugees. Denial of resources encompasses the rejection of access to certain resources from one intimate or marital partner towards another, or towards other members of the family. Although primary education is supposed to be free and accessible for girls and boys in refugee settlements, in several contexts it was noted that girls often lack access to primary or secondary education either because care-takers are unable to pay the school fees or due to the cultural beliefs about traditional gender relations of some ethnic groups, which included that girls do not need education since women are only responsible for domestic spheres. Denial of resources was also explained to be the cause in most domestic violence cases. In an expert interview, it was explained that it can include 'denying shelter to a person, denial of right to economic benefits, denial of support, school fees to the children etc. The women are always denied these things by their spouse or even their family relatives and in-laws' (female employee, Danish Refugee Council, expert interview, 20 May 2014). In focus group discussions, participants explained that husbands would often sell the harvest and use the money for alcohol without sharing food or money with their wives. When women asked for their share, men would use physical force, especially when drunk (FGD, Refugee Welfare Council leaders, 19 March 2014, Base Camp; FGD, female refugees 12 March 2014, Base Camp). This was supported by numerous refugees.

The main group of victims in the refugee settlement appears to be refugee women and girls. Survey-based findings reveal that 88.6 per cent of the participating refugees believe that it is mainly refugee women and girls (55.27 per cent women and 33.33 per cent girls) who face SGBV, while 9.97 per cent believe it is refugee men and boys (3.42 per cent men and 6.55 per cent boys) and 1.42 per cent Ugandan women and girls. On the other hand, 78.35 per cent believe it is refugee men committing such cases, 13.11 per cent Ugandan men, 4.56 per cent aid workers, 3.42 per cent refugee women and 0.57 per cent Ugandan women. While the data does not present the actual scope of groups of victims and perpetrators, it does reflect the sentiments that are likely to be influenced by personal experiences. Medical records of the health centre in Kyaka II Refugee Settlement covering the period from January to March 2014 reveal that out of sixty-one reported cases, thirty-eight were sexual or gender-based violence: twenty-one cases were perpetrated by acquaintances (14 husbands, 2 wives, 4 neighbours, 1 teacher), six cases by more than one male offender (up to 5 men) and eleven cases were acts or attempts of child rape and defilement against victims aged 10 to 18.[7] Hence, groups of victims and perpetrators are more diverse and include men and women of different age categories – this opposes the widely acknowledged binary categories of female victims and male perpetrators. Moreover, the relationships of victims and perpetrators vary, and include intimate or marital partners, acquaintances such as teachers or neighbours, and strangers who appear to have attacked victims randomly.

The data also sheds light on locations of violence, which include domestic spheres, neighbourhoods, meeting points such as markets and water boreholes – familiar yet remote areas – while, among others, collecting firewood, schools, as well as random areas such as public roads. Similar to victims and perpetrators structures, the locations are also diverse and encompass private and public spaces; this leads to the assumption that a culture of SGBV exists in the refugee settlement. The question could be raised of whether the refugee settlement, which is under the protection of agencies, actually provides sufficient security. Are there safe places? Aid agencies established protection areas – so-called safe houses – in the base camp in which victims of proven and immediate threats received short-term shelter. However, these facilities can only provide protection for a few people or households for a short period, which is why they are understood to be an interim solution until cases are settled. Despite that, it was found that incidences of SGBV can occur anywhere and at any time in the refugee settlement.

SGBV appear to occur due to limitations in the settlement, cultural and traditional beliefs about gender relations, drug consumption and a lack of law enforcement. Early and forced marriages and denial of access to education for girls are related to cultural traditions and practices, as women are traditionally seen as being responsible for the household while men are the decision makers and therefore obtain a higher hierarchical status. Sexual violence, including acts and threats, are affected by traditional beliefs as well as livelihood factors. While it appears that views are maintained that women are supposed to satisfy their partners sexually although forced intercourse against a person's will is (marital) rape, sexual abuse and harassment by unknown male perpetrators seems to be used to punish women and gain power over them. In addition, the limited livelihood conditions, lack of employment and therefore deficit access to economic resources in the refugee settlement not only lead to theft, which is at times connected with violent acts or threats, but also impact on the personal wellbeing and appear to increase the level of aggression. During a focus group discussion, it was explained that

> In the settlement a man has no power, has no property, and therefore this has caused problems and separation in the family because some women have taken over; for example, some women want to get food ration cards [for] themselves and their children, and the man is left out. (FGD, refugee religious leaders, 19 March 2014, Base Camp)

Men's loss of the traditional masculine status, which can be described as emasculation (Lukunka 2011), appears to cause challenges for men that translate into increased aggression. While domestic violence in particular is reasoned to happen in relation to resources (and the denial of access to them) as well as the consumption of alcohol, men also noted that women are punished for disobeying men's demands when trying to regain or maintain their patriarchal or hegemonic positions.[8] A man explained during a focus group discussion:

> We beat women because some women disobey. They don't understand. They want to talk and talk and do everything. … For example, a Congolese man in Swe Swe [a region in the settlement] who was tortured by his wife decided to save his money and then decided they [should] move back to Congo. He now beats his wife like a drum, and she cannot do anything because the law is not effective in Kyaka. (FGD, male refugees, 13 March 2014, Base Camp)

The limited treatment of cases, ineffective punishments of perpetrators and thus a lack of law enforcement seems to impact on the continued use of violence, which has been largely neglected in research. A refugee man explained that they 'feel that there is no safety here in Kyaka [II Refugee Settlement] and there is no justice for us', which further underlines the lack of law enforcement (male refugee, EED, 27 March 2014, Base Camp).

A Continuum of Violence

Findings of this study show that SGBV continues not only during conflict and displacement but particularly also during flight. People are therefore confronted with continuous threats of SGBV while trying to escape conflicts and insecurity to seek safety, and thus while possibly already being outside the conflict zones. Research findings therefore support both the argument that the end of conflict does not constitute the end of violence, as well as existing studies stating the connectedness of violence during conflict, flight and displacement and thus the need to employ a broader scope of analyses instead of merely looking at one phase (Ferris 1990; Cockburn 2004).

When reconnecting my research findings with other studies, it is possible to move away from the single case study and generalize features of the continued existence of SGBV, including perpetrator–victim structures as well as forms, conditions and scenes of violence.

During conflict, most cases of sexual violence are perpetrated by members of armed groups against mainly unacquainted and randomly chosen female but also male civilians, which seems to be used as a (strategic) weapon of war in public spaces. During flight, most cases are also sexual violence committed by members of armed groups and other fleeing individuals mainly against unacquainted randomly chosen female civilians in public spaces in order to spread fear and to steal. In the refugee camps and settlements, diverse forms of acts, attempts and threats of SGBV is conducted by unacquainted and acquainted male refugees, nationals and aid staff against mainly female but also male refugees in public and private spaces due to limitations, cultural and traditional beliefs about gender relations, drug consumption and an ineffective legal justice system. This is all summarized in Table 8.2.

Table 8.2 *Linking violence during conflict, flight and encampment*

	Conflict	Flight	Camp
Forms	Mainly sexual violence (different forms of sexual assault and abuse) but also gender-based violence (e.g. forced military recruitment)	Mainly sexual violence (different forms of sexual assault and abuse) but also gender-based violence (e.g. forced military recruitment)	Mainly gender-based violence (physical, emotional and psychological, socio-economic violence; harmful traditional or cultural practices) but also sexual violence (different forms of rape)
Group of victim	More female than male	Mainly female but also male	Mainly female but also male
Group of perpetrator	Mainly male (unacquainted members of armed groups) but also female	Mainly male (unacquainted members of armed groups and fleeing persons)	Mainly male (refugees and Ugandans) but also female
Relations	Mainly unacquainted	Mainly unacquainted	Unacquainted and acquainted
Spaces	Mainly public	Mainly public	Public and private
Main Conditions	(Systematic) weapon of war	To spread fear or steal	Livelihood limitations, cultural and traditional beliefs, drugs, lack of law-enforcement

The linearity of the prevalence and continuity of sexual and gender violence in the phases of conflict, flight and displacement provokes a description of the phenomenon as a continuum of violence. The continuum is distinguished by transformative character due to changing structures, forms, spaces and conditions, and reveals a diachronic increase of complexity. The forms of violence do not occur isolated from each other and the different phases but appear to be dynamically connected though social, political and economic aspects within the surrounding context. It reveals that violence moves from public spaces in conflict to more and more private space in refugee camps and settlements, and along with this quasi-privatization of violence, victims, perpetrators and forms alter. Moreover, considering the findings of violence in refugee camps and settlements, the continuum applies to both, although refugee settlements are believed to have structural advantages to camps. However, why does the continuum of sexual and gender violence exist although contexts change?

The existence of SGBV against women in conflicts and refugee camps has been explained by means of different approaches. In the past, wartime SGBV was reasoned to be committed due to the 'sexual urge' of warriors, which is why violence became a 'regrettable side effect' of conflicts (Seifert 1996: 35, 36), and male nature legitimated such acts (Eriksson Baaz and Stern 2009: 498; Eifler and Seifert 1999: 13). More recent studies emphasize that SGBV is a socially and politically constructed act perpetrated to impact on the opposing conflict party (Turshen, Alidou and De Marcellus 2000: 83; Buckley-Zistel 2013: 92–93), which, however, is not limited to conflict zones but is likely to continue in post-conflict settings (Handrahan 2004; Haynes, Aolain and Cahn 2011). Neuropsychological analyses explain the continuity of violence through the exposure to traumatic occurrences of violence and learned violent patterns. Integrated in fighting structures, combatants receive rewarding incentives through the release of hormones that prevent posttraumatic stress disorder symptoms, as well as social incentive in forms of power and dominant statuses in the collective (Elbert, Weierstall and Schauer 2010; Weierstall et al. 2011). Feminist political science studies reveal that gender relations change and have to be renegotiated in post-conflict settings (Schäfer 2010: 33), which is why displacement is a gendered process (Hans 2008: 69). In refugee situations, these changing gender relations[9] reveal that women often gain responsibilities while men lose the traditional hegemonic status due to economic, social and political limitations and legal restrictions in camps and settlements, which, it is argued, translate into violent acts against women (Turner 1999; Carlson 2005; Lukunka 2011; Buckley-Zistel, Krause and Loeper 2014: 55–58; Krause 2016). However, these explanations refer to particular phases of conflict, flight and displacement, and do not capture the continuum.

Despite the transformation and plurality of conditions as well as hetero-geneity of victims and perpetrators with their relations in the continuum of violence, the findings of the field research stress two significant factors that appear to dominate the explanation of the continuum and that correspond with other studies: power and impunity. On the one hand, during conflict, flight and displacement, former familiar and protecting social structures erupt, women often have additional responsibilities (which can be overwhelming) and men lose traditional masculine roles as decision makers (Turner 1999; Buscher 2009: 90; Lukunka 2011), which relates to an unfamiliar imbalance of power and an increasing privatization of violence. The privatization regards the perpetrator structures during flight and displacement as well as the scenes of violence, which increasingly shift from public to private spaces, such as homes – the symbol of peace, safety and privacy (Sideris 2001). Hence, as social, economic and political factors impact on homo-socially and hetero-socially changing gender relations, SGBV appears to become a tool of power against both men and women. On the other hand, each of the phases of conflict, flight and displacement is distinguished by a lack of legal regulations, governance and law enforcement (Marsh, Purdin and Navani 2006: 138). Although the national law is supposed to protect refugees, and although refugees face a poly-hierarchical system in camps, in the case of Kyaka II Refugee Settlement the law was not or hardly accessible for refugees, as well as not or ineffectively implemented by agencies (Holzer 2013). Since other studies have similar findings (Crisp 1999: 20–23; Human Rights Watch 2000: 27; Meger 2010: 127–28), it can be assumed that the continuum of SGBV exists due to a lack of access to or enforcement of legal systems.

Conclusions

This chapter has analysed the continuum of SGBV during the different phases of conflict, flight and displacement based on a case study in Uganda, and has thereby linked discourses in Peace and Conflict Studies and Forced Migration and Refugee Studies through a gender-sensitive analysis of the prevalence and continuity of SGBV during times of conflict, as well as in post-conflict refugee contexts.

While adopting the concept of conflict-induced displacement, it was possible to connect refugees' experiences gained during conflict, flight and displacement in Uganda and trace the persistent existence of SGBV, thus revealing a transformative character. The transformations comprised the groups of victims and perpetrators, and forms and conditions of attacks, as well as scenes or spaces of violence, while SGBV per se remained to be a security challenge during the different phases for the conflict-affected, fleeing and displaced individuals.

With the aim to identify conditions of violence during the different phases and eventually for the transformative continuum, field research results and academic debates of different disciplines revealed that although women were mainly victims and men mainly perpetrators, both were to some extent revealed to be both victims and perpetrators, which presents greater heterogeneity than was projected in most studies. This also stresses that the binary category of 'male attacker vs. female victim' should be questioned. Although the structures and forms of violence alter, the crimes remain strongly related to and interdependent with power and dominance, which take place homosocially and heterosocially and are therefore to be seen as gendered processes. A thus far widely neglected factor, which nevertheless should be acknowledged, is legal justice and law enforcement. In each of the timeframes and surroundings of conflict, flight, and displacement in camps, crimes are noted to occur because they are not or only rarely legally avenged and punished. The impunity of perpetrators may increase the likelihood of continued or even increased use of such acts, but definitely will not limit or stop them.

This chapter has offered an exploration of the continuum of violence from conflict to camps by employing conflict-induced displacement. Ample studies based on empirical data reveal the existence of SGBV within the different phases; however, due to the lack of a theoretical concept of the continuity in transformation or transformative continuum, the explanations remain suggestive. Hence, an avenue for further research is the identification or development of a suitable theory that comprises the complex conditions, violence prevalence and transformations. In addition, it remains to be analysed if the continuum of violence also includes members of communities after one of the three durable solutions is found and applied. Does SGBV continue even after a solution has been identified and implemented?

Ulrike Krause is Junior Professor for Forced Migration and Refugee Studies at the Institute for Migration Research and Intercultural Studies (IMIS), Osnabrück University. She was previously a research fellow at the Center for Conflict Studies, Philipps-University Marburg. She is a member of the executive boards of both the German Network Refugee Research (Netzwerk Flüchtlingsforschung) and the German Association for Peace and Conflict Studies (Arbeitsgemeinschaft für Friedens- und Konfliktforschung e.V.). She received her doctorate in political science from Magdeburg University, and has worked for international organizations in several countries. Her research focus is on conflict-induced displacement, refugee governance, refugee protection and assistance, and gender sensitivity, with a regional focus on sub-Saharan Africa. She has authored a number of articles and working papers as well as the book *Linking Refugee Protection with Development Assistance* (Nomos, 2013).

Notes

This chapter was written in the context of the research project 'Gender Relations in Confined Spaces. Conditions, Scope and Forms of Violence against Women in Conflict-related Refugee Camps' at the Center for Conflict Studies, Philipps University of Marburg, which was funded by the German Foundation for Peace Research (DSF). A previous version of this chapter was published in the *Refugee Survey Quarterly* (Krause 2015a). I would like to thank the DSF for the generous funding, as well as Susanne Buckley-Zistel and the anonymous reviewers for their valuable comments. Moreover, I thank all aid workers and especially the refugees in Kyaka II Refugee Settlement very much for taking the time and trusting us to share their stories.

1. Refugee camps can be understood as post-conflict settings, when they arise due to violence conflicts and those displaced are settled there. However, this is not always the case, considering that people may be displaced for a variety of reasons, including development projects (see Muggah 2003).
2. The body of literature has been growing during the past years and so cannot be listed exhaustively. For debates in Peace and Conflict Studies, see, among others, Handrahan (2004), Engels (2008), Schäfer (2010) Haynes, Aolain and Cahn (2011) and Buckley-Zistel (2013). For debates in Forced Migration and Refugee Studies, see, among others, Lukunka (2011); Buckley-Zistel, Krause and Loeper (2014), Fiddian-Qasmiyeh (2014) and Freedman (2015: 45ff).
3. See, among others, Jacobsen (2001) for a discussion on camps and settlements.
4. Several scholars have analysed security challenges. See, among others, Crisp (1999), Kaiser (2005), Carlson (2005) and Horn (2010).
5. Based on the article, it is not possible to discern which exact forms of violence women committed. However, the authors list a number of forms, including molestation, rape and gang rape, forced marriage, abduction, sexual slavery and forced performance of sexual acts with other civilians (Johnson et al. 2010: 557).
6. The Executive Committee merely notes in two conclusions that women and children face threats and acts of sexual and gender-based violence during flight (UNHCR 2009: No. 98 (LIV), No. 105 (LVII)), and some operational documents refer to the challenges of sexual and gender-based violence with a focus on displaced women and girls (Human Rights Watch 2000: 92; Arrault and Miquel 2007: 23–24).
7. Among them, 3 unknown men, 3 unknown women, 3 male neighbours, 1 teacher and 1 case of 2 unknown men.
8. In a recent article I question the argument of refugee men always using violence to protect their hegemonic status, but analyse how encampment impacts on men employing Jeff Hearn's theory of Hegemony of Men (Krause 2016).
9. In another article I analyse how gender relations change during encampment, revealing three patterns: a patriarchal violent pattern characterized by male dominance; a more 'liberal' pattern with tendencies towards gender equality; and a single-focused pattern in which single mothers decide to remain without a partner (Krause 2015b).

Bibliography

Alden, A. 2010. 'A Continuum of Violence: A Gendered Analysis of Post-conflict Transformation', *POLIS Journal* 3: 1–37.

Anderson, L. 2012. *Addressing Conflict-Related Sexual Violence: An Analytical Inventory of Peacekeeping Practice.* 2nd edition. New York: UN Women.

Arrault, M., and J. Miquel. 2007. 'UNFPA GBV Assessment Report, Ethiopia'. New York: United Nations Population Fund.

Bariagaber, A. 2006. *Conflict and the Refugee Experience: Flight, Exile and Repatriation in the Horn of Africa.* Burlington, VT: Ashgate.

Betts, A. 2013. *Survival Migration: Failed Governance and the Crisis of Displacement.* New York: Cornell University Press.

Boano, C., R. Zetter and T. Morris. 2008. 'Environmentally Displaced People: Understanding the Linkages between Environmental Change, Livelihoods and Forced Migration', *RSC Forced Migration Policy Briefing* No. 1.

Breytenbach, W., et al. 1999. 'Conflicts in the Congo: From Kivu to Kabila', *African Security Review* 8(5): 33–42.

Buckley-Zistel, S. 2013. 'Redressing Sexual Violence in Transitional Justice and the Labelling of Women as "Victims"', in C. Safferling and T. Bonacker (eds), *Victims of International Crimes: An Interdisciplinary Discourse.* The Hague: T.M.C. Asser Press, pp. 91–100.

Buckley-Zistel, S., U. Krause and L. Loeper. 2014. 'Sexuelle und geschlechterbasierte Gewalt an Frauen in kriegsbedingten Flüchtlingslagern: Ein Literaturüberblick', *Peripherie: Zeitschrift für Politik und Ökonomie in der Dritten Welt* 34(133): 45–63.

Buscher, D. 2009. 'Women, Work, and War', in S.F. Martin and J. Tirman (eds), *Women, Migration, and Conflict: Breaking a Deadly Cycle.* Heidelberg, London and New York: Springer.

Carlson, S. 2005. 'Contesting and Reinforcing Patriarchy: Domestic Violence in Dzaleka Refugee Camp', *RSC Working Paper Series* No. 23.

Christian, M., et al. 2011. 'Sexual and Gender-Based Violence against Men in the Democratic Republic of Congo: Effects on Survivors, their Families and the Community', *Medicine, Conflict and Survival* 27(4): 227–46.

Cockburn, C. 2004. 'The Continuum of Violence: A Gender Perspective on Violence and Peace', in W. Giles and J. Hyndmann (eds), *Sites of Violence: Gender and Conflict Zones.* Berkeley and Los Angeles: University of California Press, pp. 24–44.

Crisp, J. 1999. 'A State of Insecurity: The Political Economy of Violence in Refugee-Populated Areas of Kenya', *UNHCR New Issues in Refugee Research* No. 16.

Dolan, C. 2014. 'Into the Mainstream: Addressing Sexual Violence against Men and Boys in Conflict'. Workshop, 14 May 2014. London: ODI.

Edward, J.K. 2007. *Sudanese Women Refugees: Transforming and Future Imaginings.* New York and Basingstoke: Palgrave Macmillan.

Eifler, C., and R. Seifert (eds). 1999. *Soziale Konstruktionen – Militär und Geschlechterverhältnis.* Münster: Verlag Westfälisches Dampfboot.

Elbert, T., R. Weierstall and E. Schauer. 2010. 'Fascination Violence: On Mind and Brain of Man Hunters', *European Archives of Psychiatry and Clinical Neuroscience* 260(2): 100–105.

Elbert, T., et al. 2013. 'Sexual and Gender-Based Violence in the Kivu Provinces of the Democratic Republic of Congo: Insights from Former Combatants', *LOGiCA Study Series* No.1.

Engels, B. 2008. *Gender und Konflikt: Die Kategorie Geschlecht in der Friedens- und Konfliktforschung.* Saarbrücken: Vdm Verlag Dr Müller.

Eriksson Baaz, M., and M. Stern. 2009. 'Why Do Soldiers Rape? Masculinity, Violence, and Sexuality in the Armed Forces in the Congo (DRC)', *International Studies Quarterly* 53: 495–518.

———. 2013. *Sexual Violence as a Weapon of War? Perceptions, Prescriptions, Problems in the Congo and Beyond.* London and New York: Zed Books.

Ferris, E.G. 1990. 'Refugee Women and Violence'. Geneva: World Council of Churches.

Fiddian-Qasmiyeh, E. 2014. 'Gender and Forced Migration', in E. Fiddian-Qasmiyeh et al. (eds), *The Oxford Handbook of Refugee and Forced Migration Studies.* Oxford: Oxford University Press, pp. 395–408.

Freedman, J. 2015. *Gendering the International Asylum and Refugee Debate*, 2nd edition. Basingstoke and New York: Palgrave Macmillan.

Handrahan, L. 2004. 'Conflict, Gender, Ethnicity and Post-Conflict Reconstruction', *Security Dialogue* 35: 429–45.

Hans, A. 2008. 'Gender, Camps and International Norms', *Refugee Watch* 32: 64–73.

Haynes, D., F. Aolain and N. Cahn. 2011. *On the Frontlines: Gender, War, and the Post-conflict Process.* Oxford: Oxford University Press.

Holzer, E. 2013. 'What Happens to Law in a Refugee Camp?', *Law & Society Review* 47(4): 837–72.

Horn, R. 2010. 'Exploring the Impact of Displacement and Encampment on Domestic Violence in Kakuma Refugee Camp', *Journal of Refugee Studies* 23: 356–76.

Human Rights Watch. 2000. 'Seeking Protection: Addressing Sexual and Domestic Violence in Tanzania's Refugee Camps'. New York.

———. 2014. 'World Report 2014: Events of 2013'. New York.

IASC (Inter-Agency Standing Committee). 2015. 'Guidelines for Integrating Gender-Based Violence Interventions in Humanitarian Action: Reducing Risk, Promoting Resilience and Aiding Recovery'. Geneva.

Inhetveen, K. 2010. *Die Politische Ordnung des Flüchtlingslagers: Akteure – Macht – Organisation. Eine Ethnographie im Südlichen Afrika.* Bielefeld: transcript Verlag.

Jacobsen, K. 2001. 'The Forgotten Solution: Local Integration for Refugees in Developing Countries', *UNHCR New Issues in Refugee Research* No. 45.

Johnson, K., et al. 2010. 'Association of Sexual Violence and Human Rights Violations with Physical and Mental Health in Territories of the Eastern Democratic Republic of the Congo', *Journal of the American Medical Association* 304(5): 553–62.

Kaiser, T. 2005. 'Participating in Development? Refugee Protection, Politics and Developmental Approaches to Refugee Management in Uganda', *Third World Quarterly* 26(2): 351–67.

Krause, U. 2013. *Linking Refugee Protection with Development Assistance: Analyses with a Case Study in Uganda*. Baden-Baden: Nomos.

———. 2015a. 'A Continuum of Violence? Linking Sexual and Gender-Based Violence during Conflict, Flight, and Encampment', *Refugee Survey Quarterly* 34(4): 1–19.

———. 2015b. 'Zwischen Schutz und Scham? Flüchtlingslager, Gewalt und Geschlechterverhältnisse', *Peripherie: Zeitschrift für Politik und Ökonomie in der Dritten Welt* 35(138/139): 235–59.

———. 2016. 'Hegemonie von Männern? Flüchtlingslager, Maskulinitäten und Gewalt in Uganda', *Soziale Probleme* 27(1): 119–45.

Lindley, A. 2008. 'Conflict-Induced Migration and Remittances: Exploring Conceptual Frameworks', *RSC Working Paper Series* No. 47.

Lischer, S.K. 2007. 'Causes and Consequences of Conflict-Induced Displacement', *Civil Wars* 9(2): 142–55.

Loescher, G., A. Betts and J.H.S. Milner. 2008. *The United Nations High Commissioner for Refugees (UNHCR): The Politics and Practice of Refugee Protection into the 21st Century*. London and New York: Routledge Global Institutions.

Lukunka, B. 2011. 'New Big Men: Refugee Emasculation as a Human Security Issue', *International Migration* 50(5): 130–41.

Maedl, A. 2010. 'Towards Evidence-Based Post-War Reconstruction'. PhD thesis. Konstanz: Universität Konstanz.

Marsh, M., S. Purdin and S. Navani. 2006. 'Addressing Sexual Violence in Humanitarian Emergencies', *Global Public Health* 1: 133–46.

Martin, S.F. 2011. 'Refugee and Displaced Women: 60 Years of Progress and Setbacks', *Amsterdam Law Forum* 3(2): 72–91.

McAdam, J. 2014. 'The Concept of Crisis Migration', *Forced Migration Review* 45: 10–11.

Meger, S. 2010. 'Rape of the Congo: Understanding Sexual Violence in the Conflict in the Democratic Republic of Congo', *Journal of Contemporary African Studies* 28(2): 119–35.

Muggah, Robert. 2003. 'A Tale of Two Solitudes: Comparing Conflict and Development-Induced Internal Displacement and Involuntary Resettlement', *International Migration* 41(5): 5–31.

Nagai, M., et al. 2008. 'Violence against Refugees, Non-Refugees and Host Populations in Southern Sudan and Northern Uganda', *Global Public Health* 3(3): 249–70.

Ohambe, M.C.O., J.B.B. Muhigwa and B.M.W. Mamba. 2005. *Women's Bodies as a Battleground: Sexual Violence against Women and Girls during the War in the Democratic Republic of Congo South Kivu (1996–2003)*. London: International Alert.

OHCHR (Office of the High Commissioner for Human Rights). 2011. 'Report of the Panel on Remedies and Reparations for Victims of Sexual Violence in the Democratic Republic of Congo to the High Commissioner for Human Rights'. Geneva.

Pacéré, T.F. 2007. 'Progress Report Submitted by the Independent Expert on the Situation of Human Rights in the Democratic Republic of the Congo. Promotion and Protection of Human Rights: Human Rights Situations and Reports of Special Rapporteurs and Representatives'. New York: United Nations.

Pankhurst, D. 2008. *Gendered Peace: Women's Struggles for Post-War Justice and Reconciliation.* London: Routledge.

Pratt, M., and L. Werchick. 2004. *Sexual Terrorism: Rape as a Weapon of War in Eastern Democratic Republic of Congo – An Assessment of Programmatic Responses to Sexual Violence in North Kivu, South Kivu, Maniema, and Orientale Provinces.* Washington: USAID/DCHA.

Reyntjens, F. 2009. *The Great African War: Congo and Regional Geopolitics, 1996–2006.* New York: Cambridge University Press.

Schäfer, R. 2009. 'Männlichkeit und Bürgerkriege in Afrika – Neue Ansätze zur Überwindung sexueller Kriegsgewalt'. Eschborn: GTZ.

_____. 2010. 'Kriegerische Maskulinitätskonstrukte und sexualisierte Gewalt in Sierra Leone und Uganda', *Sicherheit und Frieden (S+F). Themenschwerpunkt: Gender und Sicherheit* 1: 29–34.

Seedat, S., et al. 2004. 'Ethics of Research on Survivors of Trauma', *Current Psychiatry Reports* 6(4): 262–67.

Seifert, R. 1996. 'The Second Front: The Logic of Sexual Violence in Wars', *Women's Studies International Forum* 19(1–2): 35–43.

Sideris, T. 2001. 'Rape in War and Peace: Social Context, Gender, Power and Identity', in M. Turshen, S. Meintjes and A. Pillay (eds), *The Aftermath: Women in Postconflict Transformation.* London: Zed Books, pp. 142–58.

Turner, S. 1999. 'Angry Young Men in Camps: Gender, Age, and Class Relations among Burundian Refugees in Tanzania', *New Issues in Refugee Research* No. 9.

Turshen, M., O. Alidou and O. De Marcellus. 2000. 'Commentary', *Race & Class* 41(4): 81–99.

Turshen, M., S. Meintjes and A. Pillay (eds). 2001. *The Aftermath: Women in Postconflict Transformation.* London: Zed Books.

UNHCR. 2003. 'Sexual and Gender-Based Violence against Refugees, Returnees and Internally Displaced Persons. Guidelines for Prevention and Response'. Geneva.

_____. 2008. 'UNHCR Handbook for the Protection of Women and Girls'. Geneva.

_____. 2009. 'Conclusions Adopted by the Executive Committee on the International Protection of Refugees', Conclusion No.1-109. Geneva.

_____. 2011. 'Action against Sexual and Gender-based Violence: An Updated Strategy'. Geneva.

_____. 2013. 'Global Trends 2012. Displacement: The 21st Century Challenge'. Geneva.

_____. 2016. 'Global Trends. Forced Displacement in 2015'. Geneva.

Weierstall, R., et al. 2011. 'The Thrill of Being Violent as an Antidote to Posttraumatic Stress Disorder in Rwandese Genocide Perpetrators', *European Journal of Psychotraumatology* 2.

9

Lost Boys, Invisible Girls
Children, Gendered Violence and Wartime Displacement in South Sudan

Marisa O. Ensor

Introduction

In South Sudan, a newly independent African nation mired in unresolved conflict, young boys and girls must navigate the multiple and complex difficulties inherent in growing up in a context of adverse humanitarian conditions and recurrent forced displacement. The pronounced age- and gender-based inequalities that characterize traditional South Sudanese society constitute additional constraints that continue to differentially shape young people's experiences both throughout the various phases of the war and during the short-lived peace.

For the large numbers of boys and girls who, alone or with their families, sought refuge within or across their country's borders, wartime displacement brought about its own set of unique challenges and opportunities. Local normative understandings of age and gender dynamics combined with global imperatives to greatly influence the options available to the members of the youngest generations. As I have discussed elsewhere, '[t]he position occupied by most South Sudanese girls, in particular, is not an easy one given not only the renewed conflict and adverse humanitarian conditions, but also the pronounced gender inequalities that characterise their ethnically diverse but consistently patriarchal society'[1] (Ensor 2014: 16).

During the Second Sudanese Civil War (1983–2005), special pro- grammes and interventions were established in an effort to ease the plight of those categorized as unaccompanied minors but excluded other young- sters at risk, often using criteria unreflective of local perceptions. Moreover, gendered views of children's role in society resulted in unaccompanied girls' preferential access to foster families (which often caused them to become invisible to international humanitarian agencies), while boys were primarily targeted for resettlement opportunities by refugee-supporting organizations (as was the case with the close to four thousand famous Lost Boys of Sudan who arrived in the United States in 2001). Violence, dep- rivation and uprootedness constituted common denominators in the lives of most of these youngsters. In other respects, however, their experiences have been quite diverse, depending, among other factors, on their migra- tory trajectories and exilic life conditions (Ensor 2013a, 2013c).

Drawing on fieldwork conducted primarily among South Sudanese ref- ugees in Uganda and returnees in South Sudan, this chapter presents some of the findings of a larger study of young people's experiences in processes of post-conflict reconstruction and peace- and nation-building in Africa. More specifically, I examine the multiple ways in which gender shapes local realities of conflict, displacement and survival, focusing on the often overlooked experiences of children and youth. My approach emphasizes the significance of adopting an age- and gender-sensitive approach to both scholarly analyses of displaced populations and humanitarian program- ming of their behalf. This perspective, I argue, allows for a more fruitful elucidation of the mechanisms of growing up in violent contexts, and the broader refugee experience in South Sudan, other African nations, and elsewhere.

Following the introduction, I present a brief discussion of the methods and conceptual frameworks that guided the research on which this chapter is based. I situate my analysis of children, gendered violence and wartime displacement in South Sudan within the new paradigm of childhood studies as well as the broader feminist approaches to the study of gender asymmetries in times of crisis and rapid change. I then examine the his- torical and recent determinants underlying the protracted cycle of war and displacement that has framed the living conditions of South Sudanese children for generations. The link between geopolitical conditions and so- ciocultural change allows me to contextualize girls' and boys' gender-dif- ferentiated experiences in refugee camps, those of the children who stayed behind, and the resurgence of violence and new waves of displacement. In the concluding section, I suggest that despite their troubled present and un- certain futures, South Sudanese children display remarkable agency and ingenuity in their efforts to navigate multiple social *loci* and adapt to challenging geopolitical and local conditions. As their experiences illustrate, understanding the gendered and generational dimensions of wartime violence and displacement is critical for a reconceptualization of war-affected diaspora children as simultaneously vulnerable and resilient – victims at times, but also survivors and innovators.

Studying Children and Wartime Violence: Frameworks, Concepts and Methods

Displaced children have become the focus of a growing body of scholarly work from a variety of perspectives and disciplines (Rutter 2006; Watters 2008; Ensor and Goździak 2010). Most of this focus on uprooted youngsters has been directed to the Global South, which hosts roughly 85 per cent of the world's youth population (Abbink 2005; Jeffrey, Jeffery and Jeffery 2008; Ensor 2013b).

Africa remains the world's youngest continent, with 70 per cent of its people under the age of thirty, and approximately 147 million children under the age of five (UNICEF 2008: 49). As I have discussed elsewhere, '[t]he limited corpus of reliable research on Africa's youngest citizens has tended to adopt a negative outlook' (Ensor 2012a: 1), a viewpoint not entirely unwarranted given Africa's turbulent realities. Gender differentials among crisis-affected children are also quite pronounced. It is, for instance, widely recognized that girls and young women are not only more likely to be exposed to gender-based and sexual abuse and exploitation than boys and male youth, but are often also discriminated against in the provision of assistance during humanitarian emergencies and situations of protracted displacement.

Acknowledging these realities, a number of studies from Africa and elsewhere illustrate the premise that wartime violence and displacement are deeply gendered and generational processes (Kibreab 2003; Grabska 2014), affecting girls and boys differently from each other and from their adult counterparts (Schrijvers 1999; Newhouse 2012; Ensor 2014). It is also important to bear in mind that conflict and displacement do not, on their own, generate heightened levels of sexual and gender-based violence (SGBV) in a vacuum; rather, generalized violence and dislocation often expose and exacerbate underlying prejudice and gender discrimination. It is thus crucial to consider gender and inter-generational relationships in order to fully understand the various manifestations of violence that often characterize the processes of rapid societal change experienced by refugees and other displaced groups.

A further issue crosscutting current approaches to the study of children in crises pertains to the very definition of childhood. The fixed chronological parameters that mark the boundary between childhood and adulthood in international law and humanitarian practice are seen as alien and confusing by many South Sudanese, for whom social criteria and individual behaviour are more reasonable predictors of one's generational position. Among some of the largest ethnic groups in South Sudan (i.e. the Nuer and the Dinka) the initiation of boys into adulthood is traditionally marked by facial scarification, with initiated young men expected to take on adult responsibilities. Although far less common, young females may have their faces scarified as well, but in their case scarification tends to be more a sign of high status than of initiation into adulthood.

Understandings of childhood for South Sudanese boys, however, go beyond being non-initiated and include being single, not steadily employed, and still dependent on one's family (Jok 2005: 144–45). The category 'male youth' is equality flexible, with the transition to social maturity being assessed on an individual basis. For South Sudanese girls, on the other hand, the primary route to womanhood is marriage, which often takes place around, or soon after, reaching puberty.[2] As a result, the category 'female youth' scarcely exists in South Sudan, further illustrating the premise that local understanding of 'childhood', 'youth' and 'adulthood' are gender-differentiated and 'socially, politically, economically and culturally constructed' (Ensor and Goździak 2010: 19–20).

Acknowledging the importance of considering local constructions and culturally situated definitions, my study of children affected by gendered violence and wartime displacement in South Sudan is inspired by the new paradigm of childhood studies. Adopting insights from sociology and cultural anthropology, this perspective argues for the social construction of childhood, a respect for children and childhood in the present rather than as 'adults in the making', and recognition of children as social actors and rights holders (James, Jenks and Prout 1998). I also draw on gender-sensitive approaches that facilitate the analysis of gender asymmetries and the gender-differentiated impact of wartime violence, including feminist perspectives (Indra 1999; Martin 2004; Cornwall, Harrison and Whitehead 2007), and those that focus attention to changing notions of masculinity (McSpadden 1999; Lindsay and Miescher 2003; Sommers 2012). Anthropological understandings of war and displacement as 'social conditions' rather than 'states of exception' (Lubkemann 2008) provide a contextual lens for my study of conflict-affected girls and boys. The premise that, as sites of both social reproduction and prolific social production (Hoffman and Lubkemann 2005), 'warscapes may provide privileged sites within which to theorize processes of social change and innovation' (Lubkemann 2008: 24), exemplifies this framework. The combination of these related standpoints inspired my field research, and undergirds this discussion of South Sudanese children's life under extraordinary circumstances.

I draw on data obtained though field-based interviews and focus group conversations conducted in Juba, Yei, Magwi and Nimule (South Sudan), and Kampala and Adjumani (Uganda) in June to August 2011, August 2012, and December 2012 to January 2013, combined with a review of the literature and official documents. Approximately twenty-five open-ended interviews were conducted at each location (fifty in Juba), with some participants being interviewed more than once. Since, as already discussed, the terms 'child' and 'youth' are not defined within fixed chronological parameters in South Sudan (or in northern Uganda), I relied on self-identification to determine each participant's age group. Additionally, I interviewed representatives from UN agencies, international and national non-governmental organizations (NGOs), community-based organizations, donors, and national, state and local government officials in both Uganda and South Sudan. Conversations explored the ways in which wartime violence and conflict-induced displacement affected boys and girls, causing shifts in power relations along gender and generational lines.

Violence and Wartime Displacement: Historical and Contemporary Determinants

The Second Sudanese Civil War triggered one of the worst humanitarian disasters of the twentieth century, reportedly resulting in over 2 million casualties, most of them civilians including hundreds of thousands of children – the world's highest death toll since the Second World War (United States Department of State 2006). Numerous youngsters – mainly boys, but also some girls – were targeted for recruitment by armed forces and rebel groups. In May 2002, nineteen years into the Second Civil War, interagency assessments identified at least seventeen thousand children associated with armed groups, with many of them directly involved in fighting at the height of the conflict (Save the Children et al. 2002). In 2004, the year before the Comprehensive Peace Agreement (CPA) was signed, less than 30 per cent of those living in the south had access to clean drinking water, and every fourth child died of malnutrition and/or preventable and waterborne diseases by the age of five (NSCSE/UNICEF 2004).

For the large majority of displaced South Sudanese, children and adults alike, the 2005 CPA marked the official ceasefire – a welcome cessation of hostilities between the North and the South – but did not represent the end of political, structural or inter-personal violence. Many of the child protection concerns that dominated the war period – i.e. the double need to safeguard children from widespread violence and deprivation while also protecting civilians from violent militarized youth – remained prevalent after peace was declared. The process of disarmament was never fully completed. Neither were efforts to demobilize the thousands of minors associated with the armed forces during earlier phases of the war. Reintegration was hindered by the dearth of educational, livelihood and other social and economic opportunities. Widespread small arms, mines and unexploded ordnances were additional concerns (UNICEF 2011).

From a geopolitical perspective, the CPA established a shared system of governance between the Government of National Unity (GoNU) in the North and the semiautonomous Government of Southern Sudan (GoSS). In accordance with the terms of this peace accord, the GoSS conducted a referendum on self-determination in January 2011, which resulted in an overwhelming turnout, almost universally voting in favour of secession (Save the Children 2011: 3). The Republic of South Sudan formally seceded from Sudan on 9 July 2011 as a result of an internationally monitored referendum held in the January, and was admitted as a new member state by the United Nations General Assembly on 14 July 2011.

Since 2013, less than three years after their hard-won independence, the young country has once again been engulfed in violent conflict which, at the time of writing in the spring of 2015, shows few signs of abating. On 15 December 2013, gunfire erupted again in the South Sudanese capital of Juba. Within hours, the violence had spread within and beyond this city following what some have categorized as an attempted coup. What started as a political confrontation between power contenders within the Sudan People's Liberation Movement (SPLM) soon escalated, giving way to a deadly pattern of revenge and counter-revenge attacks along Dinka–Nuer ethnic lines. Ethnic divisions have, however, been largely acknowledged as a consequence rather than a cause of the conflict, as ethnic identity has become an easily manipulated structure for exploiting inter-tribal differences and maintaining or gaining power.

The modest improvements made since independence are being once again negated by the resurgence of violence that has engulfed the country since 15 December 2013. In May 2014, UNICEF reported that an estimated nine thousand children had been recruited into armed forces and groups by both sides in the conflict (Tidey 2014), in spite of official pronouncements[3] to the contrary (UNICEF 2014). Sexual and gender-based violence[4] against women and girls is reportedly common in all the main conflict-affected zones including Juba, the country's capital, and areas in Unity, Jonglei and Upper Nile states (Amnesty International 2014a), as well as in refugee and internally displaced persons (IDP) camps. The UN Mission in South Sudan (UNMISS) similarly noted in its 8 May 2014 report that the 'conflict has exacerbated the vulnerability of women and children in South Sudan to sexual violence' (UNMISS 2014: 49). The impact of the massive displacement within and across South Sudan and its neighbours Ethiopia, Sudan and Uganda, which has been caused by the current conflict and worsening humanitarian conditions (Hovil 2014) are clearly age- and gender-differentiated, and likely to have a profound impact on social dynamics in South Sudan now and in years to come.

More than a year of conflict has devastated the lives of millions of South Sudanese, uprooting nearly 2 million children, women and men. Nearly 1.5 million people have been displaced internally, and another 480,000 have sought refuge in neighbouring countries (OCHA 2014). A plethora of initiatives – peace negotiations mediated by the Inter-Governmental Authority on Development (IGAD, a regional political and economic development block for Eastern Africa), plus international sanctions, arms embargoes and intraparty dialogues – have culminated in a range of peace agreements, all of which have to date been almost immediately dishonoured by the warring parties. The unrelenting violence has further ravaged the population, leading to a worsening of the already dire humanitarian conditions and the additional displacement of children and their families (Wissing 2014; OCHA 2014).

Lost Boys and Invisible Girls

As previously discussed, there is now a growing body of work concerned with gender asymmetries in conflict, although most studies have tended to focus on the experiences of adult women and men. Prevalent constructions of childhood and youth as they intersect with notions of protection, deservedness, acceptable survival choices, and changing social roles during humanitarian crises and displacement have, on the other hand, remained largely 'de-gendered' (Ensor 2014). The general inattention to gender issues among war-affected and displaced children has been attributed to the prejudicial attitudes prevalent in international development and humanitarian arenas, which privilege the perspectives and agendas of boys. As Nordstrom argues, '[t]he lack of political, economic and educational development for girls is a symptom of many societies' failure ... to see women as political, economic or educated actors' (Nordstrom 1999: 44–45).

In South Sudan, few groups faced greater risks and dislocation during the protracted civil war than the country's children. Girls were even more adversely affected as a result of patriarchal attitudes that conferred on females of all ages a lower status in society, legitimized sexual and gender-based violence, and undervalued young women's contributions to the war effort. Regardless of age, females are typically ascribed lower status in South Sudanese society than boys and men. Females in South Sudan carry the burdens of heavy workloads, early marriages, and bride prices, while gender roles and negative stereotypes contribute to the unequal distribution of resources. At the same time, women's and girls' involvement in wartime survival activities – as combatants, army support personnel, or female heads-of-household – necessitated a considerable rethinking of traditional gender roles. As illustrated in the following subsections of this chapter, the experiences of South Sudanese girls and boys in refugee camps, those of the children who stayed behind, and those impacted by the renewed violent conflict in their country, are clearly gendered.

South Sudanese Children's Life in Exile

For the large numbers of girls and boys who, alone or with their families, sought refuge within or across their country's borders, displacement brought about its own set of unique challenges and opportunities. Their experiences were quite diverse, depending, among other factors, on their migratory trajectories and exilic life conditions, with gender factors greatly influencing the options available to them. Wartime violence and dislocation had markedly dissimilar consequences for different members of society. So did mobility as a survival strategy, 'with those in privileged positions having greater access to more secure places, and boys and men being more mobile [than girls and women] as they searched for protection, livelihood and education' (Grabska 2014: 38).

During the protracted conflict, large numbers of boys lived segregated from their adult counterparts – often in large camps – following pre-war traditional customs. These include the expectation that boys would spend much of their time living alone in cattle camps, or else leave their family's rural homes to complete their education in boarding schools (Johnson 1989, 1992). As the conflict intensified, a significant number of boys found their way to Kakuma, a vast refugee camp in the north-western region of Kenya administered by the United Nations High Commissioner for Refugees (UNHCR). Many had undertaken a long journey on foot from Ethiopia to Kenya during which many had died or become ill or severely malnourished. Many travelled with relatives and clan members but some had been separated from their families, while others had been orphaned by the war. The majority of unaccompanied and separated boys were placed in large groups or homesteads, following the South Sudanese tradition. Regardless of their original trajectories, these male youths came to be known as the 'Lost Boys'. The term 'Lost Boys', derived from the story of Peter Pan, was given to this group in the 1990s when international aid workers in the humanitarian agencies learned about their harrowing journeys and conditions. The name was subsequently adopted by the media, US Christian organizations and the US government, who used the well-known moniker to garner sympathy for the young refugees and to justify the resettlement of thousands of 'orphan'[5] South Sudanese boys.

Many of the youngsters in refugee camps and settlements in Ethiopia, Kenya and Uganda were young male soldiers in the Sudan People's Liberation Army (SPLA) or other rebel groups who were sent there by their commanders to further their education. In spite of the brutal circumstances of war, military recruitment provided an opportunity for some to have access to education and autonomy. Both boys and girls were constrained by wartime imperatives and crushing conditions of widespread violence, disease and starvation, as well as community and household demands. It was, however, generally easier for boys and male youth than for their female counterparts to pursue their personal goals of mobility, education, and autonomy from the government and from their families. For these boys, war proved to be 'a double-edged sword, marked by great suffering, sacrifice, brutality and violence, but it also created an opportunity to access education and improve family livelihoods' (Grabska 2014: 41).

Only a limited number of girls managed to make their way to the refugee camps. Some younger girls had joined their brothers on their migration routes during cattle grazing periods. Migration for education and labour, on the other hand, was exclusively reserved for young males. Although there were also many older widowed women whose husbands had stayed in South Sudan to fight in the war, the official UNHCR (2006) statistics show a great imbalance in the percentage of girls and women to boys and men. This disparity was especially pronounced in the ratio of girls of marriageable age to boys or young men (Grabska 2014: 39).

The proportionally smaller group of unaccompanied and separated girls who managed to make their way to the refugee camps tended to be allocated to foster families rather than independent groups or homesteads. This option was considered more suitable as it allowed them to learn the South Sudanese way of life (Masumbuko Muhindi and Nyakato 2002), so they could transmit it to their children. While some foster families provided girls with a measure of support and protection, many others used girls as unpaid servants before marrying them off to whoever could afford to pay the requisite bride price (Harris 2009). Instances of rape and other forms of sexual violence, as well as 'survival sex' in exchange for food and other basic necessities, were frequent realities for girls in refugee camps (Stern 2011: 221).

The abduction of young women and children was also commonplace, both in South Sudan and abroad in refugee camps. As reported in a Sudan Human Security Baseline Assessment (HSBA 2012: 3),

[w]hereas sexual violence inside southern Sudan was often driven by ethnic or political motivations, in the camps it was largely a result of traditional cultural notions of early and forced marriage. Sudanese patriarchal norms

followed women into camps ... and they were often forced to adhere to practices set by male elders at home ... [Additionally] some women were abducted from the camps and forcibly 'remarried' back in southern Sudan if a higher dowry could be obtained.

This practice contributed to skew the gender and age imbalance in refugee camps and settlements even further. These demographic disparities, subsequently mirrored in the resettlement countries, were greatly influenced by the differentiated responsibilities of females and males in households and communities, with girls and women staying at home to look after homesteads while boys and men went to the battlefields. They were also determined by gendered access to mobility both as a life-improving option and a wartime survival strategy. For girls, gendered notions of femininity and their position in the household and community at large made them less mobile and more 'invisible' to humanitarian groups.

Another dimension of life in the camps that was clearly age- and gender-differentiated was the possibility of resettlement to a third country. The United States, Canada, Australia and a few other countries, sympathetic to the plight of the enormous numbers of refugees in camps such as Kakuma, agreed to the UNHCR's facilitated resettlement of a limited number of them. Children and youth, and particularly unaccompanied minors, were prioritized (Stern 2011: 223). Beginning in 2000, a total of 3,276 South Sudanese boys and 89 girls were accepted for resettlement into the United States (Harris 2009: 2).

A number of reasons have been offered as possible explanations for these glaring discrepancies. Candidates for resettlement were chosen mainly from lists of unaccompanied children living in the camp. Boys remained in large groups and were therefore more noticeable than girls (Harris 2009). Girls, who had often been integrated as members of their foster families, soon became 'invisible' on the official register of unaccompanied minors, or even deliberately concealed from the UNHCR by foster relatives reluctant to lose a girl's labour and potential bride price payment (Stern 2011: 223). It has also been suggested that when UNHCR consulted with Sudanese elders about resettlement priorities, the elders privileged boys assuming them more likely to benefit from the educational opportunities available abroad, thus becoming more valuable contributors in future to postwar reconstruction and nation-building efforts (DeLuca 2009, cited in Stern 2011: 223–24). A combination of these factors resulted in the Lost Boys' journey receiving wide international attention, while resettling the girls, whose plight was less publicized, came to be something of an afterthought.

On a positive side, Kakuma was one of the first camps where gender programming was implemented. As a key activity to facilitate girls' and women's empowerment, the UNHCR and a number of humanitarian and development NGOs sought to strengthen community-based organizations and promote women's leadership. Although most girls still referred to marriage and children as routes to womanhood, they also say contemplated other possibilities beyond being wives and mothers, reshaping concepts of femininity and planting seeds of change, even if limited and more in terms of consciousness than actual practice, for other women in South Sudan. In effect, many reported that 'despite the challenges, conditions [in refugee camps] were far safer than in war-torn Sudan' (Stern 2011: 221).

Girls and Boys in Wartime South Sudan

Living conditions for the boys and girls who stayed in South Sudan during the war were even more precarious, with structural violence and grossly inadequate humanitarian conditions compounding the pervasive conflict-related violence. The large numbers of small arms and light weapons that flooded into South Sudan replaced traditional spears, dehumanizing the act of killing or injuring others; '[t]his made it easier, psychologically as well as physically, for combatants to target women and children' (HSBA 2012: 1). It also made it possible for increasingly younger (male) children to become actively involved in the hostilities. As a result, male adolescents and youth started to be perceived less as victims of the generalized violence, and more as a potential force for social disruption, upheaval and even renewed conflict.

Research findings from South Sudan echo those from recent studies on youth and conflict from around the world, which suggest that factors such as poverty, unemployment, illiteracy, war- and displacement-related social disorganization, and a perception of local governments as weak and corrupt tend to encourage violent behaviour, particularly amongst male youth (Sommers and Schwartz 2011; Onouba 2014; Stites et al. 2014). Post-CPA gendered violence has been further compounded by what Sommers and Schwartz term 'the dowry economy' (2011: 4), in reference to increasingly high dowry (bride price)[6] demands that have prompted male youth to join cattle raids and enlist in militias, and have caused females to be routinely viewed as property that can generate family wealth (ibid.; Ensor 2014). It is worth noting that, while cattle raiding as well as inter- and intra-tribal fighting have been features of South Sudanese life for generations, the intensification of the scale and brutality of violence are more recent phenomena. Prior to the First Sudanese Civil War (pre-1955), community violence in South Sudan consisted of infrequent and short-lived skirmishes over resources such as grazing lands and fishing pools (Hutchinson and Jok 2002).

Jok Madut Jok draws attention to gender differentials in wartime human rights violations that went 'beyond the usual ways in which such state-sponsored violence affects women and children – through rape, abduction, sexual slavery, and labour exploitation' (Jok 2007: 206). This situation has been associated with the dictum issued by the late John Garang, founder of the SPLA, who, predicting the war would last a long time, urged the SPLA to 'keep back' and protect women so as not to sacrifice future generations (HSBA 2008). The SPLA went on to decree that females should not fight on the front line, but rather should 'actively procreate' in order to repopulate society and make up for the millions of lives that were being lost in the war (Jok 1999). This attitude towards females' role in society served as a justification for rape, forced pregnancy and other forms of sexual violence.

This situation persisted in the postwar environment of reduced economic opportunities; widespread economic dependence on dowry and the objectification of women often leave female youth with limited control over their lives. As Sommers and Schwartz report, quoting a high-ranking South Sudanese government official, 'once girls reach puberty, potential husbands come and apply [to marry them]. If the girl is found with a boyfriend, her family can kill her. If she is impregnated by a boyfriend, she can be beaten to death' (Sommers and Schwartz 2011: 5).

Studies of child marriage in societies across the world indicate that this widespread practice 'has a significant negative impact on women and girl's realization of key human rights, including their rights to health and education, physical integrity and the right to marry only when they are able and willing to give their free consent' (HRW 2013: 4). As is the norm in most other cases, child marriage in South Sudan takes places in a context of pronounced gender disparities and high poverty levels. Additionally, South Sudanese mothers suffer from the highest maternal mortality rate in the world, estimated at 2,054 deaths per 100,000 live births (ibid.).

Increasingly high dowry rates have devastated male youth, too. Some venture into Uganda or Kenya to marry local women, whose dowry prices are lower. Government officials explained that attempting elopement without paying dowry is a serious offence, often punishable by a long prison sentence, brutal beating, or even death. A young couple that attempts to elope must find a safe haven if they hope to elude such punishment. For male youth, one such haven is armed militia groups. Elopement is a common, albeit exceptionally dangerous, alternative to the dowry quandary. A recent Norwegian People's aid report supports indications in the authors' interview data that some young men join armed gangs, at least in part, because they believe it will help them to pay dowries (Richmond and Krause-Jackson 2011).

Life in the post-civil war period thus remained fraught with challenges for all, as females and males, children and adults strived to carve out meaningful lives in a context initially characterized by a tenuous 'negative peace' (Galtung 1964), followed by renewed active conflict since the end of 2013. In effect, many of the child protection concerns that dominated the wartime remained prevalent after peace was declared. Even before the recent resurgence of conflict, living conditions in post-independence South Sudan were only marginally more favourable than they had been during the Sudanese War period. Only 14 per cent of the population lived within five kilometres of a primary health-care centre. Among other issues, this led to the country having the highest prevalence of maternal mortality worldwide. Educational opportunities remained among the lowest in the world, especially for the young. South Sudan also had some of the lowest primary school enrolment rates, highest dropout rates and widest gender disparities. Less than half of the primary school-aged children were in school, and only 27 per cent of the population was literate (SSDDRC 2012: 6–8).

Children and the Resurgence of Violence and Displacement

In a replay of South Sudan's recent bloody history, thousands of women, children and men have been killed, and more than one million people have already been displaced. Preliminary information made available by several aid agencies working in the region report an unsurprising worsening of humanitarian conditions. An interim report on the conflict published by the South Sudan Government's Human Rights Commission documented 'gross violations of the right to life of not only combatants but also of innocent and defenceless civilians, including children, women and the vulnerable' (SSHRC 2014: 6). These violations have been confirmed by multiple additional sources (Amnesty International 2014a, 2014b; Human Rights Watch 2014; OCHA 2014; UNMISS 2014).

Furthermore, the prevalence of SGBV in the country affects at least four out of every ten women and girls, with many more cases going unreported. 'The current militarised environment, where armed men are ubiquitous and civilian law enforcement is virtually absent, places women and girls at a heightened risk of sexual violence. Persistent reports of sexual violence perpetrated by both government and opposition forces strongly indicate that conflict-related sexual violence is widespread' (Amnesty International 2014a: 27). A report issued by the United Nations Mission in South Sudan (UNMISS 2014) discusses the various forms of sexual violence committed by all parties to the conflict in connection with other violations of human rights and humanitarian law before, during and after heavy fighting, shelling, looting and house searches. 'The forms of sexual violence used during the conflict include rape, sometimes with an object (guns or bullets), gang-rape, abduction and sexual slavery, and forced abortion. In some instances, women's bodies were mutilated and, in at least one instance, women were forced to go outside of their homes naked' (UNMISS 2014: 49). Already ubiquitous prior to the current conflict, heightened levels of SGBV are likely to have far-reaching, long-term effects that will impact future generations – with children experiencing and/or witnessing sexual violence, children being born of rape, and children's mothers disappearing or being murdered.

The multiple manifestations of violence, both physical and structural, that are once again impacting South Sudanese children, are complex, multifaceted and interrelated. Since conflict erupted again, families in South Sudan have been unable to grow food themselves, as the fighting has driven them off the fields, preventing them from tilling the land. Consequently, the number of children, alone or accompanied by their mothers, queuing up for food handouts has been increasing dramatically. So has the violence committed against them during the long trips that are often required to reach the food distribution centres set up by the humanitarian agencies operating in the country.

Health problems such as malaria, typhoid and diarrhoea, common in the region at any time, have become even more widespread, with mortality rates much higher for smaller famine-weakened children. Furthermore, security threats remain a constant concern for those who have sought shelter in any of the overcrowded and grossly underfunded IDP camps where SGBV against girls and women, and to a lesser extent against boys and men, has become a common feature of life in exile. Relatedly, fieldwork in Nimule (Eastern Equatoria State), a town on the southern border that has been a gateway to nearby Uganda during all the conflicts, points to 'the combination of men with too little to do and girls with too little to eat as leading to sexual exploitation' (CARE 2014: 6).

Different forms of harassment, abuse and violence against youngsters of both sexes indeed constitute another ubiquitous aspect of the current conflict. Incidents of physical and sexual assault are most commonly happening in firewood collection places outside IDP and refugee camps, and sometimes at water points within the camp. Areas around water points are frequented by young men who hang around and often try to approach girls and young women going to fetch water. Victims will often refrain from speaking about an incident of rape for fear of being ostracized, blamed and 'given bad names' by the community, which might eventually prevent them from finding a suitable husband, or even result in them being obliged to marry the perpetrator. Indeed, incidents of SGBV are generally resolved through customary mechanisms that tend to prioritize patriarchal notions of 'social cohesion' over the individual welfare of the victims. As was the case in pre-current conflict refugee camps (Danish Refugee Council 2012), reporting of SGBV remains an uncommon occurrence despite its continued pervasiveness.

An additional concern is the arbitrary detention and killing of civilian children, the bodies of some of whom have been found with their hands tied behind their backs. These children and adolescents, the vast majority of whom are male, are receiving renewed attention on the part of the humanitarian community (Green 2012; UNMISS 2012, 2014), as is the military recruitment and use of minors in hostilities, often drafted from among those living in IDP and refugee camps, which has once again become commonplace. According to UNICEF, twelve thousand children, mostly boys, have been recruited and used as soldiers by armed forces and rebel groups in South Sudan in 2014 alone. In January 2015, the United Nations Children's Fund (UNICEF) announced the release of some three thousand South Sudanese child soldiers, almost all of them boys, in what was hailed as one of the largest ever demobilizations of children in a zone of conflict. South Sudan is one of seven countries highlighted in the UN's ongoing 'Children, Not Soldiers' campaign, which aims to end the recruitment and use of children by government armed forces in conflict by the end of 2016 (UN News Centre 2015). Indeed, the elimination of child soldiering has remained an international *cause célèbre* for the last fifteen years (Ensor 2012b, 2013b). Once again, war-affected boys are identified as 'lost' and in need of urgent assistance, while abused girls remain 'invisible', their suffering hidden under culturally prescribed layers of stigma and shame.

Concluding Thoughts: One Step Forward, Two Steps Back

As the previous discussion has illustrated, wartime violence and displacement entail deeply gendered and generational processes, both for those children forced to flee their hometowns – or making the (possibly constrained) choice to do so – and for those who stay behind. Physical displacement represents a clear indication of the human toll of conflict, and reflects larger geopolitical and demographic patterns. General trends during the first decade and a half of the new millennium suggest that countries with mass refugee situations will continue to be those in the Global South. These countries also have proportionately higher numbers of children and youth amongst their refugee populations. Dramatic changes brought about by war, renewed conflict, and uprootedness often have a profound effect on the traditional ideas and practices surrounding girlhood and boyhood, femininity and masculinity, and therefore influence the actual lives of girls and boys. A focus on gender and generational differences is also an indispensable dimension of conflict management at both institutional and societal levels. Gender-sensitive processes that include females and males of all ages are known to be more successful than those that do not (Bloomfield, Barnes and Huyse 2003).

In South Sudan, as in other war-torn countries where children and youth constitute the majority of the population, the experiences of young girls and boys must be factored into any efforts to develop strategies aimed at overcoming the many divides that characterize their scarred society. The renewed conflict in this beleaguered African country has been character-ized by extreme violence, leaving an as yet unknown number of people killed, maimed and injured, in addition to provoking an exacerbated hu-manitarian crisis. More than 2.3 million people – one in every five people in South Sudan – have been forced to flee their homes. Approximately 1.66 million people have been internally displaced, with 53.4 per cent of them estimated to be children. Nearly 644,900 had become refugees in neighbouring countries by the end of 2015 (OCHA 2016).

This massive scale of displacement over a relatively short period has been partly due to the extent of the atrocities committed against civilians – children and adults, females and males – and the considerable fear that has been generated as a result. A field report conducted by the International Refugee Rights Initiative on the refugees in the Adjumani District of northern Uganda in February 2014 concluded that '[m]ost of those who were interviewed had been displaced at least once before, and their (re) displacement points to the tragedy that is being played out for those who had returned to South Sudan leading up to and after independence' (Hovil 2014: 3). The fact that many new refugees are not strangers to displace-ment both emphasizes the pervasiveness of the hardships that people are once again being forced to endure, and reveals the instrumental deploy-ment of coping strategies acquired during previous waves of displacement, whether internally or in other countries.

After nearly two years of fighting, a power-sharing peace agreement was signed in August 2015, leading to the partial establishment of the Transitional Government of National Unity (TGONU). While many South Sudanese reportedly do not consider the TGONU a legitimate au-thority, there is a general acceptance that this agreement embodies the possibility of peace until more comprehensive and permanent solutions can be found. South Sudan is, nevertheless, currently still far from peace. The fifth anniversary of South Sudan's independence, marked on the 9 July 2016, was marred by a resurgence of violence. More than 250 people were killed after heavy gunfire broke out in Juba between soldiers loyal to President Salva Kiir and others backing Vice President Riek Machar (Vulliamy 2016).

This latest outbreak of violence raises concerns that the already fragile peace deal may be in jeopardy, and the country could once again return to full-blown civil war. Initially restricted to Juba, while also targeting a UN compound south-west of the city, the fighting has underscored the continued need for attention to the gender- and age-related dimensions of wartime violence. Evidencing prevalent cultural norms concerning who constitutes a legitimate target, fighters reportedly waited until women and children had entered the UN base before they opened fire on it (Worley 2016). Voicing a more positive outlook, South Sudanese anthropologist Jok Madut Jok reminds us that

> [i]f social norms on the protection of women and children can change for the worse, they can also improve ... With assistance, these women could capitalize on their strengths – in numbers and in solidarity as women – for positive, peaceful change ... Today, they have the potential to serve as more than mere symbols by becoming active as brokers of peace. (Jok 2012: 6)

It is impossible to predict how long this unabated violence will last, or how long it will be before those who sought safety across international borders can return home. The humanitarian crisis currently facing South Sudanese refugee women, children and their families must thus include provisions to make their stay in exile sustainable for as long as it might take for their country to become stable (Hovil 2014: 25). As the previous discussion has illustrated, age and gender dynamics in South Sudan continue to constitute powerful factors shaping the rapidly evolving and, at present, highly volatile and violent post-independence social landscape. Overall, the realities currently facing most young South Sudanese are fraught with seemingly insurmountable adversity. On the other hand, the noteworthy improvements made during the short-lived peace between 2005 and late 2013 hold the promise of positive social engagement and progress once peace is re-established again in the country. If the right opportunities are made available to them, the boys and girls of South Sudan need be neither 'lost' not 'invisible'.

Marisa O. Ensor, PhD in anthropology from the University of Florida, also holds a Masters of Law (LLM) in international human rights law from the University of Essex, UK, and a certificate in refugee studies from the University of Oxford. She is currently based at Georgetown University's Justice and Peace Program in Washington DC, and is also a research associate at the International Institute for Child Rights and Development. Her current research focuses on the link between child protection, social cohesion and non-violent forms of conflict resolution in Burundi and Chad. She recently completed a study of youth's role in processes of transitional justice, peacebuilding and reconciliation in Northern Uganda and South Sudan. Dr Ensor is the author of numerous publications on humanitarian crises, with a focus on the role of women and children/youth. They include the volumes *Children and Forced Migration: Durable Solutions during Transient Years* (Palgrave Macmillan, 2016, with Elżbieta M. Goździak); *African Childhoods: Education, Development and Peacebuilding in the Youngest*

Continent (Palgrave Macmillan, 2012); *Children and Migration: At the Crossroads of Resiliency and Vulnerability* (Palgrave Macmillan, 2010, with Elżbieta M. Goździak), and *The Legacy of Hurricane Mitch: Lessons from Post-Disaster Reconstruction in Honduras* (The University of Arizona Press, 2009).

Notes

1. It is important to recognize that South Sudan is a highly heterogeneous society, with ethnicity playing an important role in shaping gender and other power relations within the country. Although ethnic differences can be found in the ways in which these gender relations are manifested, female subordination remains a constant across South Sudanese society.
2. Recent studies have documented a trend among some families to marry off their daughters at an increasingly young age to obtain a 'bride price' as a survival strategy in the absence of other viable alternatives (HRW 2013).
3. South Sudan is one of eight countries involved in the campaign 'Children, not Soldiers', launched in March 2014 by the Special Representative and UNICEF. The campaign aims to end and prevent the recruitment and use of children by government security forces listed by the secretary-general in his annual report on children and armed conflict.
4. SGBV is rooted in discriminatory social norms and power inequalities between women and men in social, economic and political spheres of life. Rape and various forms of sexual assault have been used as a tactic to humiliate, intimidate, displace and traumatize communities in a number of contexts involving armed conflict globally. At the same time, the use of SGBV as a tactic of war has a deep, tacit link with the acceptability of these violent practices during times of peace (CARE 2014: 3).
5. The boys had been resettled as orphans, but some still had mothers, fathers and siblings in South Sudan, Ethiopia or Kakuma, and had often had direct contact with them, even before resettlement.
6. While the anthropological term for this practice would be 'bride price' or 'bride wealth', South Sudanese people commonly refer to it as 'dowry'. Cattle, and sometimes land, remain the preferred forms of dowry payment.

Bibliography

Abbink, J. 2005. 'Being Young in Africa: The Politics of Despair and Renewal', in J. Abbink and I. van Kessel (eds), *Vanguard or Vandals: Youth, Politics and Conflict in Africa*. Leiden: Koninklijke Brill Publishers, pp. 1–34.
Amnesty International. 2014a. 'Nowhere Safe: Civilians under Attack in South Sudan'. London.
___. 2014b. 'Breaking the Circle of Violence: US policy toward Sudan and South Sudan. Testimony by Adotei Akwei before the House Subcommittee on Africa,

Global Health, Global Human Rights, and International Organizations'. Washington DC.

Bloomfield, D., T. Barnes and L. Huyse. 2003. 'Reconciliation after Violent Conflict: A Handbook'. Stockholm: International Institute for Democracy and Electoral Assistance.

CARE International. 2014. '"The Girl Has No Rights": Gender-Based Violence in South Sudan'. Geneva.

Cornwall, A., E. Harrison and A. Whitehead (eds). 2007. *Feminisms in Development: Contradictions, Contestations and Challenges.* London: Zed Books.

Danish Refugee Council. 2012. 'A Sexual and Gender-Based Violence Rapid Assessment. Doro Refugee Camp, Upper Nile State, South Sudan'. Copenhagen.

DeLuca, L. 2009. 'Transnational Migration, the Lost Girls of Sudan and Global "Care Work": A Photo Essay', *Anthropology of Work Review* 30(1): 13–15.

Ensor, M. (ed.). 2012a. *African Childhoods: Education, Development, Peacebuilding and the Youngest Continent.* New York: Palgrave Macmillan Publishers.

——. 2012b. 'Child Soldiers and Youth Citizens in South Sudan's Armed Conflict', *Peace Review: A Journal of Social Justice* 24(3): 276–83.

——. 2013a. 'Youth Culture, Refugee (Re)integration, and Diasporic Identities in South Sudan', *Postcolonial Text* 8(3): 1–19.

——. 2013b. 'Participation under Fire: Dilemmas of Reintegration for Child Soldiers Involved in South Sudan's Armed Conflict', *Global Studies of Childhood Journal* 3(2): 153–62.

——. 2013c. 'Displaced Migrant Youth's Role in Sustainable Return', IOM Migration Research Series. Geneva: International Organization for Migration.

——. 2014. 'Displaced Girlhood: Gendered Dimensions of Coping and Social Change among Conflict-Affected South Sudanese Youth', *Refuge: Canada's Journal on Refugees* 30(2): 15–24.

Ensor, M., and Elżbieta M. Goździak (eds). 2010. *Children and Migration: At the Crossroads of Resiliency and Vulnerability.* Basingstoke: Palgrave Macmillan.

Galtung, J. 1964. 'An Editorial', *Journal of Peace Research* 1(1): 1–4.

Grabska, K. 2014. *Gender, Home & Identity: Nuer Repatriation to Southern Sudan.* Suffolk, UK: Currey.

Green, A. 2012. 'South Sudan: Returning Child Soldiers their Childhood', *All Africa*, 15 April 2012. Retrieved 13 July 2016 from http://allafrica.com/stories/201204160250.html.

Harris, A. 2009. 'Twice Forgotten: The "Lost Girls" of Sudan and Performative Integration into Australia'. Australian Association for Research in Education Conference, Canberra, 29 November – 3 December 2009.

Hoffman, D., and S.C. Lubkemann. 2005. 'Warscape Ethnography in West Africa and the Anthropology of "Events"', *Anthropological Quarterly* 78(2): 315–27.

Hovil, L. 2014. 'Conflict in South Sudan: Refugees Seek Protection in Uganda and a Way Home'. New York and Kampala: International Refugee Rights Initiative.

HRW (Human Rights Watch). 2013. '"This Old Man Can Feed Us, You Will Marry Him": Child and Forced Marriage in South Sudan'. New York.

____. 2014. 'South Sudan: War Crimes by Both Sides'. Human Rights Watch News, 26 February 2014. Retrieved 27 February 2014 from https://www.hrw.org/news/2014/02/26/south-sudan-war-crimes-both-sides.

HSBA (Human Security Baseline Assessment). 2008. 'No Standing, Few Prospects: How Peace Is Failing South Sudanese Female Combatants and WAAFG', Human Securiry Baseline Assessment. Sudan Issue Brief 13. Retrieved 20 June 2014 from http://www.reliefweb.int/rw/rwb.nsf/db900sid/lsgz-7jlsdd?OpenDocument.

____. 2012. 'Women and Armed Violence in South Sudan'. Geneva: Small Arms Survey. Retrieved 5 July 2014 from http://www.smallarmssurveysudan.org/fileadmin/docs/facts-figures/south-sudan/womens-security/HSBA-women-and-armed-conflict.pdf.

Hutchinson, S., and J.M. Jok. 2002. 'Gendered Violence and the Militarisation of Ethnicity: A Case Study from Southern Sudan.', in R. Werbner (ed.), *Postcolonial Subjectivities in Africa*. London: Zed Books, pp. 84–107.

Indra, D. (ed.). 1999. *Engendering Forced Migration: Theory and Practice*. New York and Oxford: Berghahn Books.

James, A., C. Jenks and A. Prout. 1998. *Theorising Childhood*. New York: Teachers College Press.

Jeffrey, C., P. Jeffery and R. Jeffery. 2008. *Degrees without Freedom: Education, Masculinities and Unemployment in North India*. Palo Alto, CA: Stanford University Press.

Johnson, D. 1989. 'The Structure of a Legacy: Military Slavery in Northeast Africa', *Ethnohistory* 36(1): 72–88.

____. 1992. 'Recruitment and Entrapment in Private Slave Armies: The Structure of the Zara'ib in the Southern Sudan', *Slavery & Abolition* 13(1): 162–73.

Jok, J.M. 1999. 'Militarization and Gender Violence in South Sudan', *Journal of Asian and African Studies* 34(4): 427–42.

____. 2005 'War, Changing Ethics and the Position of Youth in South Sudan', in J. Abbink and I. van Kessel (eds), *Vanguards or Vandals: Youth, Politics and Conflict in Africa*. Leiden: Brill, pp. 143–61.

____. 2007. *Sudan: Race, Religion, and Violence*. London: Oneworld.

____. 2012. 'Women and Armed Violence in South Sudan'. Sudan Human Security Baseline Assessment (HSBA). Geneva: Small Arms Survey.

Kibreab, G. 2003. 'Rethinking Household Headship among Eritrean Refugees and Returnees', *Development and Change* 34(3): 311–37.

Lindsay, L.A., and S.F. Miescher. 2003. *Men and Masculinities in Modern Africa*. Portsmouth, NH: Heineman.

Lubkemann, S.C. 2008. *Culture in Chaos: An Anthropology of the Social Condition in War*. Chicago and London: The University of Chicago Press.

Martin, S.F. 2004. *Refugee Women*. Lanham, MD: Lexington Books.

Masumbuko Muhindi, M., and K. Nyakato. 2002. 'Integration of the Sudanese "Lost Boys" in Boston, Massachusetts USA'. Research Report for the Mellon-MIT Program on NGO's and Forced Migration. Retrieved 27 February 2014 from http://web.mit.edu/cis/www/migration/pubs/Mahindi.pdf.

McSpadden, L.A. 1999. 'Negotiating Masculinity in the Reconstruction of Social Place: Eritrean and Ethiopian Refugees in the United States and Sweden', in

D. Indra (ed.), *Engendering Forced Migration: Theory and Practice*. New York and Oxford: Berghahn Books, pp. 242–60.

Newhouse, L. 2012. 'Urban Attractions: Returnee Youth, Mobility and the Search for a Future in South Sudan's Regional Towns', *New Issues in Refugee Research Paper* No. 232.

NSCSE/UNICEF (New Sudan Centre for Statistics and Evaluation in association with UNICEF). 2004. 'Towards a Baseline: Best Estimates of Social Indicators for Southern Sudan', *NSCSE Series Paper* No. 1.

Nordstrom, C. 1999. 'Girls and War Zones: Troubling Questions', in D. Indra (ed.), *Engendering Forced Migration: Theory and Practice*. New York and Oxford: Berghahn Books, pp. 63–82.

OCHA (United Nations Office for the Coordination of Humanitarian Affairs). 2014. 'South Sudan Crisis Situation Report No. 62 (as of 14 November 2014)'. Retrieved 10 December 2014 from http://reliefweb.int/report/south-sudan/ south-sudan-crisis-situation-report-no-62-14-november-2014.

——. 2016. '2016 Humanitarian Needs Overview: South Sudan'. Retrieved 23 May 2016 from http://reliefweb.int/sites/reliefweb.int/files/resources/2016_HNO_ South%20Sudan.pdf.

Onouba, F. 2014. 'Why Do Youth Join Boko Haram?' *United States Institute of Peace, Special Report* No. 348. Washington DC.

Richmond, M., and F. Krause-Jackson. 2011. 'Cows-for-Bride Inflation Spurs Cattle Theft in South Sudan', *Bloomberg News*, 26 July 2011. Retrieved 27 February 2014 from www.bloomberg.com/news/2011-07-26/cows-for-bride-inflation-spurs-cattletheft-among-mundari-in-south-sudan.html.

Rutter, J. 2006. *Refugee Children in the UK*. Maidenhead: Open University Press.

Save the Children. 2011. 'South Sudan: A Post-Independence Agenda for Action'. London.

Save the Children, Christian Aid, Oxfam, Care, IRC and Tearfund. 2002. 'The Key to Peace: Unlocking the Human Potential of Sudan'. Joint Agency.

Schrijvers, J. 1999. 'Fighters. Victims and Survivors: Constructions of Ethnicity, Gender and Refugeeness among Tamils in Sri Lanka', *Journal of Refugee Studies* 12(3): 307–33.

Sommers, M. 2012. *Stuck: Rwandan Youth and the Struggle for Adulthood*. Athens, GA and London: The University of Georgia Press.

Sommers, M., and S. Schwartz. 2011. 'Dowry and Division: Youth and State Building in South Sudan'. United States Institute of Peace, Special Report. Washington, DC.

SSDDRC (South Sudan Disarmament, Demobilization and Reintegration Commission). 2012. 'National DDR Strategic Plan 2012–2020'. Juba.

SSHRC (South Sudan Human Rights Commission). 2014. 'Interim Report on South Sudan Internal Conflict, December 15, 2013 – March 15, 2014'. Juba.

Stern, O. 2011. '"I Was Once Lost": South Sudanese Women in the Diaspora', in F. Bubenzer and O. Stern (eds), *Hope, Pain and Patience: The Lives of Women in South Sudan*. Johannesburg: Jacana Media, pp. 215–38.

Stites, E., et al. 2014. 'Engaging Male Youth in Karamoja, Uganda: An Examination of the Factors Driving the Perpetration of Violence and Crime by Young Men in Karamoja, and the Applicability of a Communications and

Relationships Program to Address Related Behaviour'. *LOGiCA Study Series* No. 3. Washington: The World Bank.

Tidey, C. 2014. 'With Conflict Raging in South Sudan, Recruitment of Children into Armed Groups is on the Rise', *UNICEF Newsline*, 5 May 2014. Retrieved 13 July 2016 from http://www.unicef.org/infobycountry/southsudan_73403.html.

UNICEF (United Nations Children's Fund). 2008. 'The State of African Children 2008: Child Survival'. Nairobi, Dakar and Amman.

―――. 2011. 'UNICEF Humanitarian Action Update: Republic of South Sudan (14 July 2011)'. Juba, Geneva and New York. Retrieved 10 June 2014 from www.unicef.org/hac2011/files/UNICEF_Humanitarian_Action_Update_The_Republic_of_South_Sudan_14_July_2011.pdf.

―――. 2014. 'Government of South Sudan Recommits to Action Plan to End Recruitment and Use of Children', *UNICEF News*, 24 June 2014. Retrieved 13 July 2016from http://www.unicef.org/media/media_73922.html.

UNMISS (United Nations Mission in South Sudan). 2012. 'SPLA Signs Agreement to Free Children', *UNMISS News*, 12–23 March 2012. Retrieved 22 June 2014 from http://unmiss.unmissions.org/LinkClick.aspx?link=Documents%2FUNMISS+News+Edition+7.pdf&tabid=3489&mid=7359&language=en-US.

―――. 2014. 'Conflict in South Sudan: A Human Rights Report'. Juba. Retrieved 10 May 2014 from http://unmiss.unmissions.org/Portals/unmiss/Human%20Rights%20Reports/UNMISS%20Conflict%20in%20South%20Sudan%20-%20A%20Human%20Rights%20Report.pdf.

United Nations News Centre. 2015. 'South Sudan: UN Welcomes Demobilization of Child Soldiers amid Signs of Peace', 27 January 2015. Retrieved 2 February 2015 from http://www.un.org/apps/news/story.asp?NewsID=49915#.VRrhe2xFDIU.

Vulliami, E. 2016. 'South Sudan: More than 250 dead as violence breaks out in capital of Juba', *The Independent*, 12 July 2016. Retrieved 13 July 2016 from http://www.independent.co.uk/news/world/africa/more-than-250-dead-as-violence-breaks-out-in-south-sudanese-capital-a7129726.html.

Watters, C. 2008. *Refugee Children: Towards the Next Horizon*. Abingdon: Routledge.

Wissing, M. 2014. 'South Sudan: Greater Humanitarian and Development Efforts Needed to Meet IDPs' Growing Needs', Internal Displacement Monitoring Centre. Retrieved 3 January 2015 from http://www.internal-displacement.org/sub-saharan-africa/south-sudan/2014/south-sudan-greater-humanitarian-and-development-effortsneeded-to-meet-idps-growing-needs.

Worley, W. 2016. 'South Sudan: At Least 115 Killed in Clashes on the Anniversary of Country's Fifth Independence Day', *Independent*, 9 July 2016. Retrieved 13 July 2016 http://www.independent.co.uk/news/world/africa/south-sudan-at-least-115-killed-in-clashes-on-the-anniversary-of-countrys-fifth-independence-day-a7128981.html.

10

Military Recruitment of Sudanese Refugee Men in Uganda

A Tale of National Patronage and International Failure

Maja Janmyr

Introduction

Refugee camps and settlements have throughout history become notorious for serious problems of insecurity, including armed attacks, arbitrary killings, torture, exploitation and sexual and gender-based violence (Janmyr 2014a: 136ff.; UNHCR 2000c: para. 1; 2006a: 18). Some fifteen years ago, the United Nations High Commissioner for Refugees even argued that militarized camps posed the single biggest threat to refugee security (UNHCR 2000c). This chapter seeks to explore one specific form of such militarization, namely that of military or forced recruitment of refugees. This practice constitutes one of the most problematic security issues within refugee camps worldwide (UNSC 2004; HRW 2006; CSUCS 2008: 91–95). It jeopardizes the civilian and humanitarian character of refugee camps, violates a number of core human rights norms, and may even be inconsistent with the refugees' right to seek and enjoy asylum.

More specifically, the forced recruitment of refugees is an often overlooked form of gender-based violence, that is, 'violence that is targeted at women or men because of their sex and/or their socially constructed gender roles' (Carpenter 2006: 83). As explained by Carpenter (ibid.: 92), forced recruitment may be gender-based in so far as it is sex-selective; adult men are generally targeted in ways that women and girls are, only to a lesser degree. It is moreover gender-based as it is 'justified and naturalised by collectively held assumptions about masculine identity, nationalism and militarism'. This also means that this form of recruitment not only deprives civilian men of their liberty and civilian families of their male kin, it also 'reproduces the sex-gender structures that naturalise gendered perceptions of threat and put other civilian males at risk of lethal violence' (ibid.: 93).

This chapter focuses on the military recruitment of (South) Sudanese refugees in northern Uganda in the 1990s and 2000s. Civil war ravaged this region for more than two decades, as rebel groups, some with considerable popular support, operated there ever since President Yoweri Museveni seized power in 1986.[1] In addition to roughly 1.6 million internally displaced persons (IDPs), northern Uganda hosted hundreds of thousands of (South) Sudanese refugees.[2] These refugees fled the civil war in Sudan in the 1990s only to end up in the midst of warfare in the northern Ugandan districts of Adjumani, Arua, Moyo, Kitgum (and later, Pader), and Masindi. In addition to severe armed attacks by the Ugandan rebel Lord's Resistance Army (LRA), these refugees were subject to torture, ill treatment and military recruitment by the Sudan People's Liberation Army (SPLA) (Payne 1998: 29; Lischer 2000; Hovil 2001: 6; 2002: 18). As this chapter will show, refugee militarization by the SPLA was intensified by the fact that both Sudan and Uganda supported each other's guerrilla movements, and the refugee 'issue' was a significant source of tension in the countries' historically frosty relations. Additionally, refugee military recruitment was aggravated by the largely negligible approach both to male victims of gender-based violence and to refugee camp militarization taken by UNHCR, the UN organ tasked with providing international protection and assistance to refugees.

In aiming to explore the circumstances of the SPLA's military recruitment of refugees in northern Uganda, this chapter first briefly lays out the methodology employed. It then explains the origins of the civilian and humanitarian character of asylum/refugee camps, which provides the most important legal basis for the prohibition of military recruitment of refugees. Third, it explores the historically tense relations between Uganda and Sudan when it comes to hosting each other's refugees. Fourth, and with a particular emphasis on the role of the Ugandan government, it describes SPLA's refugee camp militarization and thereafter the scope and form of military recruitment. Finally, it discusses the role of UNHCR in preventing military recruitment and mitigating SPLA militarization, arguing that UNHCR failed to pursue any meaningful intervention.

The chapter is primarily based on documentation analysis of UNHCR archives (e.g. Protection Reports, Global Reports, Global Appeals), as well as a legal analysis of international standards applicable to the military recruitment of refugees. It builds upon empirical material collected between 2009 and 2012, when I was a guest researcher on several occasions at Makerere University in Kampala, Uganda. My research included semi-structured interviews with NGO and UN workers, as well as with government representatives. Based on the snowball method, where interviewees were asked to nominate other individuals who could be asked to give information or opinions on this topic, twenty interviews were conducted, each lasting approximately ninety minutes. These interviews complement the findings from other secondary sources.

Asylum: Peaceful and Humanitarian

Ever since the very inception of the asylum regime, the international community has emphasized the provision of asylum as a peaceful and humanitarian act. In 1967, the UN General Assembly unanimously adopted the United Nations Declaration on Territorial Asylum (Res. 2312 (XXII)), which provided that '[s]tates granting asylum shall not permit persons who have received asylum to engage in activities contrary to the purposes and principles of the United Nations', and, more importantly, recognized that the grant of asylum is 'a peaceful and humanitarian act and … as such, cannot be regarded as unfriendly by another State' (Art. 4 and Preamble). This notion is also reflected in important legal instruments such as the 1951 Refugee Convention, the Preamble of which expresses the wish that 'all States, recognising the social and humanitarian nature of the problem of refugees, will do everything within their power to prevent this problem from becoming a cause of tension between States'. The regional 1969 Organisation of African Unity (OAU) Refugee Convention similarly recognizes that '[t]he grant of asylum to refugees is a peaceful and humanitarian act and shall not be regarded as an unfriendly act by any … State', and stresses the need to make a 'distinction between a refugee who seeks a peaceful and normal life and a person fleeing his country for the sole purpose of fomenting subversion from outside' (Art. 2 and Preamble). It specifically restricts participation of refugees in any subversive activities against an OAU member state, and further prohibits refugees from engaging in activities likely to cause tension between these states (Art. 3(2)). Indeed, by emphasizing that the granting of asylum by a host state should not be taken as an act of aggression by the country of origin, conventions such as these were concluded inter alia to tackle a difficult problem of inter-state relations (Alleweldt 2011: 238, para. 61).

The notion of asylum as a peaceful and humanitarian act was nevertheless considerably challenged by widespread ideologies of anti-colonialism during the 1950s, 1960s and 1970s, when many liberation movements were permitted by host states to pursue their armed struggles from bases in refugee camps on their territory (Crisp 2000; Milner 2004). In UNHCR's governing organ, the Executive Committee, a discussion raged about whether the primary onus was on the host states to ensure the civilian and humanitarian character of refugee camps, or on neighbouring states to abstain from attacking them (Janmyr 2014a: 136ff.). On the one hand were claims of a 'just war' waged by the encamped refugees based on the principle of self-determination and to secure a return home, and, on the other, the right of states – seeing the camps as legitimate military targets – to respond in self-defence to external aggression (see UNHCR 1982: para. 70(3)(c); 1983). Complicating the situation even more was the obligation of African states under the 1982 African Charter on Human and Peoples' Rights to support armed struggles conducted by national liberation movements (Art. 20(2) and (3); Mtango 1989: 88). Interestingly, the clauses of the 1969 OAU Refugee Convention prohibiting subversive activities were not intended to contradict this commitment.

It was only in 1987, after several strenuous years of discussion, that UNHCR's Executive Committee finally coined the specific 'principle of the civilian and humanitarian character of refugee camps' in its Conclusion No. 48 on military or armed attacks on refugee camps and settlements (UNHCR 1987: Preamble). Since then, its importance and relevance has been repeatedly emphasized, first by UNHCR and the UN General Assembly, but following the enormity of the militarization crisis taking place in Rwandan refugee camps in Zaïre during the mid-1990s, also by the UN Security Council (Janmyr 2014a: 136ff.). Most important among a considerable number of council resolutions concerning refugee camp security are those recognizing that a breach of the refugee camps' civilian and humanitarian character may develop into threats against international peace and security. In Resolution 1296, for example, the Security Council (UNSC 2000: para. 14) invites the Secretary-General to bring to its attention situations where refugee and IDP camps are vulnerable to infiltration by armed elements, and 'where such situations may constitute a threat to international peace and security'. Security Council Resolution 1208 on refugees in Africa (UNSC 1998: Preamble) furthermore recognizes that provision of security to refugees and the maintenance of the civilian and humanitarian character of refugee camps and settlements is an 'integral part of the national, regional and international response to refugee situations and can contribute to the maintenance of international peace and security'. Today, the principle is arguably part of customary international law, binding on all states of the world (Janmyr 2014a: 136ff.; 2014b). In addition, a number of other international law provisions also implicitly or expressly prohibit the military recruitment of refugees.[3] Notably, the practice can under certain circumstances amount to arbitrary deprivation of liberty or even torture, which means that it may be treated under one or more of the strongest protections that international law can offer.[4]

Uganda and Sudan: Frosty Relations and Refugee Flows

In addition to producing refugees, Uganda and Sudan both have a lengthy record of hosting refugees from each other's countries. Northern Uganda, in particular, has for decades provided for the majority of the country's Sudanese refugee population (Hovil 2001: 4–5). Due to historically frosty relations, in which Sudan and Uganda have been perceived as supporting the other's guerrilla movements, this refugee 'issue' has long been a considerable source of tension (Kaiser 2000: 43; Deng and Morrison 2001; Høigilt, Falch and Rolandsen 2010: 13ff.). This situation prevailed until at least 2005, when the Sudan People's Liberation Movement (SPLM) and the Sudanese authorities in Khartoum signed a peace agreement. The SPLM, of which the SPLA is the military wing, is now nominally the governing party of South Sudan, which seceded from Sudan in July 2011.

Uganda's support for armed groups opposing the Sudanese government, such as SPLA, dates far back. SPLA offered its support to Yoweri Museveni's National Resistance Army (NRA) – today the National Resistance Movement (NRM), currently in power and led by President Museveni – who sought to overthrow the then Ugandan president, Tito Okello, during Uganda's civil war in the 1980s. Back then, (South) Sudan hosted a significant number of Ugandan refugees, and SPLA allegedly gave many of these an ultimatum: either join the NRA that SPLA was supporting or be forcibly 'refouled' to Uganda (Rone et al. 1994: 192). Perhaps fearing that a concentration of half a million Ugandan refugees in Sudan could be used as a base for an anti-NRM insurgency, once Museveni and the NRM came into power in 1986, the SPLA assisted in attacking the Ugandan refugee camps in Sudan (Gersony 1997: 85). Indeed, some of the refugees who had sought refuge in Sudan prior to Museveni's rise to power were, after his instalment, recruited into rebel groups that challenged the NRM rule, such as the West Nile Bank Front and the LRA (Clark 2001: 266).

In 1989, if not earlier, the Ugandan government had permitted SPLA units to base themselves in northern Uganda, and SPLA had several branch offices both in Kampala and across the northern region (Gersony 1997: 85–86; Verdirame and Harrell-Bond 2005: 276). It was neither uncommon for SPLA soldiers to move 'freely with arms' in the northern region, nor for the Ugandan military to host SPLA soldiers in Ugandan army barracks. Indeed, SPLA soldiers are known to have received training on Ugandan soil, and SPLA officers allegedly have kept large weapons deposits in the northern part of the country (Confidential interview, NGO staff, Kampala, 15 April 2011; see also Mkutu 2006: 47–70; Matsiko 2007; Akalkal 2007; Komakech and Abonga 2010).

Sudanese refugees coming to Uganda from the 1980s onwards were thus, by virtue of their mere refugee presence in the country, generally assumed by Sudanese authorities in Khartoum to be supporters of the rebel SPLA. This was despite the fact that many actually fled the approach of the SPLA.[5] Despite a 1999 peace agreement between Uganda and Sudan, which committed the two governments to cease hostilities against each other and not to harbour, sponsor, or give military or logistical support to any rebel or hostile elements from each other's territory, there was a broad perception that the Ugandan government continued to be supportive of the SPLA.[6]

Statements made by representatives of the Ugandan government provide clear evidence of this – in 2000, for instance, Uganda's foreign minister, Eriya Kategaya, allegedly asserted that Uganda cannot abandon its 'moral support' for SPLA because its cause is 'genuine' (IRIN 2000a). Indeed, Sudanese refugees were consequently perceived by Khartoum as clients of the Ugandan government (ICG 2006: 14; Okudi and Okello 2009). This belief not only led the Sudanese government to pursue cross-border attacks, such as the aerial bombings of refugee-hosting Koboko and Adjumani in the 1990s, but also to send delegations directly to the Sudanese refugee camps (Neefjes 1999: 3; Hovil and Moorhead 2002: 15; Merkx 2002: 124). In fact, representatives of the Sudanese government visited Achol-pii camp on at least one occasion in 2002 to investigate claims that the settlement was being used as an SPLA training camp (Confidential interview, NGO staff, Gulu district, 8 December 2009). As I will show in this next section, the suspicion of the Sudanese government was not unwarranted.

SPLA and the Camps

While insecurity stemming from LRA violence was prevalent throughout the northern region of Uganda, a direct consequence of the proximity of the settlements for Sudanese refugees to the porous Sudan–Uganda border was also that it permitted SPLA soldiers easy access to the refugee population. This was particularly disconcerting considering that, in addition to fleeing atrocities committed in the context of the conflict between the Sudanese government and SPLA, many Sudanese refugees had specifically fled to Uganda in order to avoid abuse and military recruitment by the SPLA (Mugeere 2001; Merkx 2002: 113–46; Wawa 2008: 51–52). SPLA activities were not only limited to border regions such as Adjumani and Arua districts, but SPLA had also managed to infiltrate Achol-pii camp in Pader district, located farther away from the Sudanese border (Hovil and Moorhead 2002). In 1999, the late John Garang, leader of SPLA, even addressed the inhabitants of Kiryandongo refugee camp, situated in central Uganda, far from the Sudanese border, and where Sudanese refugees presumed they would be exempt from SPLA activity (Verdirame and Harrell-Bond 2005: 176).

The camps served as bases for the SPLA's rest and recuperation, and were also used to plan further military schemes in Sudan. Even though the SPLA did not maintain a large standing army in the refugee camps, its influence over the refugee population has been described as 'very strong' (HRW 2002: 140). By the mid-1990s, 'influential' SPLA representatives appear to have been present in the camps:

> It was alleged that some were armed; many others were simply acting as observers and informers for the Movement; some held administrative positions with the Sudanese People's Liberation Movement (SPLM), and were responsible for collecting dues, or for 'advising' refugee movement in and out of the settlement. (Payne 1998: 63)

In Arua district, for example, after the SPLA had 'liberated' several areas in southern Sudan in 1997, many refugees emptied the camps and returned, in some cases 'encouraged' by attacks on the camps (Leopold 2005: 24). It is widely believed that SPLA controlled this 'repatriation', by some commentators even considered a forced return, in an attempt to populate the liberated areas in Sudan (Confidential interview, NGO official, Gulu, 10 December 2009; see also Payne 1998; Kaiser 2000; Merkx 2002: 131).

Recruiting for 'The Cause'

While the SPLA is known to have used many refugee camps in East Africa for the purpose of military recruitment, the Sudanese camps in northern Uganda did not appear to be any exception in this regard (Crisp 1999: 5, 23; Hovil and Moorhead 2002: 14). On the contrary, refugee men seemed to be under persistent pressure to join the SPLA. The camps allegedly even had an SPLA recruiting officer in residence, in addition to a seemingly high prevalence of SPLA informers who were often engaged in recruiting new soldiers and searching for those who had deserted from military duty (Verdirame and Harrell-Bond 2005: 175). SPLA commanders visiting their families who resided in the settlements would also try and persuade the male youth to return and fight for 'the cause' (Confidential interview, NGO staff, Gulu, 10 December 2009), and claims were even made that

SPLA officials corresponded with individual refugees in the camps 'to remind them of their military duties' (Verdirame and Harrell-Bond 2005: 175; Lammers 2006: 22).

Young, male refugees were particularly insecure due to SPLA activity in the refugee camps. While there were female fighters within the SPLA, the prevailing culture in relation to conflict in (South) Sudan has been one of men as warriors and women as assets that should be kept away from combat duties (Beswick 2000). In fact, for the late John Garang, the decision to keep women away from the frontline was based on a long-term strategy for the war; as it was essential that the population levels of the South Sudanese be maintained, women had to keep up the 'reproductive front' (Stone 2011: 29). Anthropologists have similarly asserted that in Dinka and Nuer culture, women are regarded 'less fully as persons, or complete human beings', and this perception is allegedly magnified in 'the context of militarised glorifications of the raw masculine power of guns' (Hutchinson and Jok 2002: 105). The majority of women who were active in the war thus took on essential supportive roles: carrying supplies, cooking, and caring for children and the wounded (Stone 2011: 25).

Military recruitment in the camps generally varied in scope and over time (Rone et al. 1994: 189). The lack of coherent reporting by UNHCR and others makes it difficult, however, to ascertain the exact scale of this recruitment. Interviews in 2011 with UNHCR field safety advisors working in, or who had previously worked in, northern Uganda suggested that UNHCR was generally uninformed about the scope of this form of recruitment, primarily due to the fact that there had been no comprehensive reporting on SPLA activities in the refugee camps during the 1990s and 2000s (Confidential interviews, UNHCR staff, Kampala, 15–16 April 2011). Research conducted by Verdirame and Harrell-Bond (2005: 175) nevertheless describes the recruitment drives as 'recurrent', and UN reports suggest that forced recruitment practices continued well into 2005 (OCHA 2005). In many ways, the military recruitment in the Ugandan camps replicated the practice in Sudan, where SPLA's forced recruitment campaigns, labelled 'kashas', have been ongoing since at least the mid-1980s, and often took place prior to major battles. Notably, in Sudan, SPLA had previously pursued kashas both in the UNHCR-run Ugandan refugee camps and in the camps for IDPs. The kashas in the Ame, Aswa and Atempi camps during 1993 emerge as particularly blatant (see Rone et al. 1994: 189).

The kashas typically involved rounding up deserters, and camp leaders in the Sudanese camps in Uganda would often be instructed to recruit a certain number of refugees, often young male adults or children, in the same manner as village headmen in (South) Sudan would be. As one refugee in Koboko explained in another study:

There is mobilization going on. In Koboko it happened last year. They will just come; it will be during the night hours. You will be asleep; they will come and take you. There will not be meetings. There were some who were in school here. It was during the holidays they were taken ... they are there now but they don't write. They were not having identity cards saying they were students. That's why they were taken ... And sometimes [SPLA members] were conducting meetings with chiefs. They will mobilize the chiefs to get the persons they want for their activities. (Hovil and Werker 2001: 10)

Against the broad recognition of SPLA's general use of child soldiers (CSUCS 2008), it is hardly surprising that allegations of child soldier recruitment, for instance pressure to provide one child per family for military service, were rampant (Confidential interview, NGO staff, Gulu, 10 December 2009).

Upon the failure to voluntarily recruit the needed number of individuals, SPLA was known to use force. In Mirieyi reception centre, for example, '[t]he guerrillas march to and from the centre openly armed and intimidate and forcibly recruit refugee men and boys' (Smith 2004: 45–46), and in a 1999 recruitment drive the SPLA, with the assistance of the Ugandan army, rounded up Sudanese males from the camps in Keyo, Olua, Mirieyi and Adjumani town who ostensibly did not have adequate refugee documents (US Department of State 2002). Refugees in Achol-pii camp in Pader district also spoke of SPLA 'delegations' arriving in the camp and kidnapping refugees (Hovil and Moorhead 2002: 14).

Not only did the Ugandan government forcibly recruit a considerable number of Ugandan IDPs (Janmyr 2014c), it also played a substantial role in SPLA's military recruitment. Several large-scale recruitment drives were reportedly organized in cooperation between SPLA and the Ugandan army (Hovil 2001: 12; HRW 2002: 140). On at least one occasion, the government also assisted in rounding up and 'refouling' hundreds of what seemed to be SPLA deserters (IRIN 2000b).

While the Ugandan government has generally denied SPLA military recruitment of refugees altogether, it is noteworthy that, in 2003, local government authorities in Adjumani district requested UNHCR funding for 'recruitment awareness' campaigns in the settlements (Schmidt 2006: 310–11). A similar proposal – the 'Security Package for All Refugee Settlements in Uganda' (SPARE) – was also submitted by the Ugandan government to UNHCR in 2004. The proposal specifically sought funding to 'ensure and preserve the civilian characters of refugees' and to 'ensure there is no forced recruitment of children [or] abuses against *women* and *children*' (OPM 2004: 2, emphasis added). This wording is interesting in that it precludes an insurance against recruitment of adult Sudanese men (and perhaps even refugee adults in general), and can rather be read as a tacit support for the military recruitment of Sudanese refugee men.

Fleeing the Camps, Seeking Anonymity

Coupled with the lack of security caused chiefly by the LRA, the threat of forced recruitment by SPLA forced many refugees into a mode of recurrent flight to nearby towns or even to the capital, Kampala (Merkx 2002: 131). In Kampala, young men far outnumbered young women among the refugee population, and Lammers' research with urban refugees in Kampala found that the majority of young Sudanese men in Kampala mentioned 'insecurity in the camps' as 'the number one reason for coming to the capital and availing themselves of the city's anonymity' (Lammers 2006: 22, 65). Similarly, UNHCR's 1999 Country Report on Uganda recognized that '[f]orced recruitment of refugees, mainly by the SPLA ... remained a matter of concern to UNHCR and the refugees. The recruitment prompted an increasing number of refugees to quit the settlements for the capital in search of protection' (UNHCR 2000b: 166).

As such, some Sudanese refugees became displaced also within their country of asylum. Buscher (2003: 4) has asserted that male refugees are often among the most vulnerable amongst urban refugee caseloads, and in Uganda it was evident that this move from camp to city did not always lead to augmented protection. The families of high-ranking commanders frequently habituated Kampala, and SPLA intelligence were known to pursue widespread operations in the city. SPLA officers and intelligence agents would 'hang around' the refugee registration office in Kampala, causing many Sudanese refugees in Kampala to, out of fear, choose not to register since registration often entails waiting for hours, or sometimes days, outside the registration office. In 1999, SPLA also allegedly conducted house-to-house raids in areas where Sudanese were known to live in Kampala (Lorenzo and Harrell-Bond 1999; Macchiavello 2003; Verdirame and Harrell-Bond 2005: 176; Lammers 2006: 22, 65). Disturbingly, many Sudanese were also reluctant to report threats and attempted forced recruitment to the Ugandan police since many were reportedly accused by Ugandan authorities of fleeing a 'just cause' when they decided to leave the SPLA and the SPLA-controlled camps in northern Uganda (HRW 2002: 120). The Ugandan government's military and political interests in Sudan clearly exacerbated the protection concerns for many Sudanese refugees.

Fleeing Sudan, Seeking International Protection

As scholars such as Carpenter have noted, international efforts to address gender-based violence in conflict situations, and documents and reports advocating and evaluating such efforts, tend to focus primarily on the forms of gender-based violence to which *women* are exposed (Carpenter

2006: 84). This leads to a marginalization in humanitarian action of the harms men and older boys face during armed conflict and flight. In our case, the forced recruitment of Sudanese refugee men was clearly affected by the conduct of UNHCR. This organization has been granted a unique – almost supranational (Aga Khan 1976: 331) – mandate by the international community, in which the function of 'international protection' lies at the very heart. Not only does UNHCR appear to hold an affirmative duty to intervene to secure the basic rights of refugees and others of concern, it arguably also bears an obligation to ensure the basic rights of refugees, including physical protection (Janmyr 2014a). Considering the scope of this mandate, then, what played out in northern Uganda with regard to forced recruitment is indeed unsettling.

Even though refugees in northern Uganda lived with essentially chronic insecurity stemming from both LRA and SPLA activities, refugee security was largely overlooked in UNHCR programmes (Janmyr 2014a). Research into UNHCR's archives gives the impression that the organization focused disproportionately on material assistance. Its main task was the so-called Self-Reliance Strategy (SRS), launched with a view to make Sudanese refugees in Uganda self-sufficient through agriculture in refugee settlements (UNHCR and OPM 1998: 3). This almost exclusive attention to the SRS seemed to affect UNHCR's ability to provide adequate protection to the refugees. In order to cultivate the land designated for the SRS, and thus for the SRS to be successful, refugees were essentially required to live in the insecure northern region.[7] UNHCR's investment into the SRS appears to have been an efficient obstacle to any effort on the part of UNHCR to relocate the Sudanese refugees to safer regions of Uganda. Naturally, relocation would have undermined the implementation of the SRS, and it could therefore be argued that material security was bought at the cost of physical security (Schmidt 2006: 309).

UNHCR's donor-focused material, such as its Global Reports and Global Appeals, as well as its protection reports, persistently provide detailed accounts of technical aspects of the SRS, commenting at length on issues such as nutrition, crop cultivation, and water resources. In fact, the provision of material assistance has been put forward as the *main* objective of UNHCR's Uganda operations on a number of occasions (UNHCR 2000a, 2001, 2004a). The insecure environment and its consequences for refugee protection are only briefly addressed, as if they were tangential to the SRS in affecting the well-being of the Sudanese refugees (see, for instance, UNHCR 2004b). The volatile environment in which the camps were settled was commonly portrayed as a backdrop, or a factor that impeded UNHCR's own ability to perform, rather than as an issue that UNHCR had any opportunity to influence (Confidential interview, UNHCR staff, Kampala, 14 April 2011). In particular, UNHCR appears to have had a very limited protection monitoring system, which seldom captured the types of abuses related to refugee camp militarization or gender-based violence targeting refugee men. Most protection reports during the 1990s and 2000s simply gloss over protection concerns (Verdirame and Harrell-Bond 2005: 300; Janmyr 2014a). This may in part be explained by resource constraints and staff security concerns, which entailed that a continued presence of UNHCR in the Ugandan camps was rarely possible. The volatile camp locations contributed to many of the camps scoring high on the minimum operating security standards (MOSS), the UN's security ranking. Palorinya settlement, for example, was in 'Phase IV' in terms of danger throughout 1997, which allowed for the continuation of life-saving activities only, with minimal staff presence (see Payne 1998: 30–32; Verdirame and Harrell-Bond 2005: 157). UNHCR consequently had a large number of staff located at its main offices in Kampala who were engaged in 'distant' administrative and bureaucratic tasks.

The role of UNHCR in preventing SPLA activities in general, and the forced recruitment of refugee men in particular, appears to have been negligible, and especially so when compared to its more recent conduct in other countries. Following a raid in 2006 in which several hundred Sudanese refugees in Chad were recruited, for example, UNHCR strongly condemned the forced recruitment of refugees in a series of briefing notes (UNHCR 2006b, 2006c).[8] The Chadian case reportedly also prompted UNHCR to conduct an investigation into the forced recruitment (UNHCR 2006b) as well as to pursue several 'high-level meetings' with Chadian authorities to discuss the issue.[9] Later on, UNHCR also undertook awareness campaigns in the camps, including visits to schools to inform them of the danger of recruitment (UNHCR 2006d). In the Ugandan context, no serious intervention was made to prevent SPLA infiltration and military recruitment in the refugee camps (Schmidt 2006: 307–8; Verdirame and Harrell-Bond 2005: 179,). UNHCR staff working on security issues in Kampala and interviewed in the process of this research could not in fact recall *any* occasion when UNHCR had pursued any intervention – large or small – to prevent the forced recruitment of refugees in Uganda (Confidential interviews, UNHCR staff, Kampala, 18 April 2011). In stark contrast to the dozen or so UNHCR media reports on LRA attacks against the Sudanese camps, no corresponding media reports or briefings attend to the issue of SPLA activities within the camps. Also, UNHCR's protection reports pay little attention to SPLA's role in the camps.[10] In addition, it appears as if UNHCR largely disregarded the findings of several independent research reports which, to varying extents, addressed SPLA's militarization in the camps. UNHCR relations with the Refugee Law Project remained strained, and after the RLP published a report on SPLA activities in the camps, it was in fact banned from conducting research in the camps for a number of months (Schmidt 2006: 313, fn. 630; Sandvik 2011: 13).

While UNHCR generally failed comprehensively to acknowledge forced recruitment as one form of gender-based violence – the focus of UNHCR's gendered protection was rather combating the sexual and gender-based violence against women and girls – archival research suggests that only on a few occasions did UNHCR employ measures to prevent the military recruitment of Sudanese refugees. In 1999, it

> took appropriate measures to strengthen its relations with the military and security contingents within the various refugee-hosting areas in order to ensure continued protection for the refugees. UNHCR also established a chain of early-warning and reporting mechanisms at its field offices to alert local authorities promptly in the event of security problems. (UNHCR 1999)

The following year, UNHCR refers to the existence of 'incursions by armed rebel forces ... mainly to retrieve so-called deserters considered to be hiding among the refugee populations', and reports how it responded to the situation by providing 'advice on the issue to local military commanders as well as to the Government' (UNHCR 2000a). The problem with these types of interventions is not only that they appear exceptional in the Ugandan context and that they were completely delinked from UNHCR's gender-based violence programmes, but that they blatantly disregard the significant role of the Ugandan authorities in SPLA's militarization. For reasons explained earlier in this chapter, a UNHCR intervention that solely involved the 'informing' of local authorities and the strengthening of relations with security forces was limited at best, and entirely counterproductive at worst.

Conclusions

Asylum is a humanitarian institution, and, as such, military activities of any kind are incompatible with refugee status. This includes recruitment of, or volunteering by, refugees for participation in armed activities. As this chapter has highlighted, however, the Sudanese camps in northern Uganda experienced significant problems of military recruitment. The camps were situated in the midst of armed conflict between the Ugandan government and the LRA, generally perceived to be supported by the Sudanese authorities in Khartoum in response to Uganda's support for SPLA. The Ugandan government, having the primary responsibility to protect *all* individuals on its territory, seemed generally unwilling to secure the basic rights of the Sudanese refugees. Rather, and largely due to its support for the SPLA's cause, it contributed to the militarization of these camps, jeopardizing their civilian and humanitarian character.

This form of militarization had grave implications for the protection of refugee men and boys. The camps served as bases for the SPLA's rest and recuperation, and were also used to plan further military schemes in southern Sudan. More importantly, however, Sudanese refugee men seemed to be under persistent pressure to join the SPLA. While the military recruitment generally varied in scope and over time, the recruitment in the Ugandan camps in many ways replicated the practice in southern Sudan and focused almost exclusively on refugee men. The so-called *kashas* typically involved rounding up deserters, and camp leaders would often be instructed to recruit a certain number of refugees, often young adults or children. Upon the failure to recruit the needed number of individuals by persuasion alone, SPLA was known to use force. This general state of insecurity led many Sudanese male refugees to flee the camps in search for protection in larger towns or cities. As such, they became displaced also in their country of refuge.

To make matters worse, UNHCR – tasked by the international community to provide international protection to refugees – appeared to largely waive refugee security in favour of aspects of material assistance. It did not employ adequate or comprehensive measures to prevent the military recruitment of the Sudanese refugees, in contrast to its work in countries such as Chad. Indeed, promoting and administering material assistance was likely to be far less contentious for UNHCR than engaging in the thorny, and highly political, issue of protecting refugees from SPLA's militarization of the camps. Futhermore, cases such as this clearly highlight the fact that gender-based violence is not only a humanitarian concern, but has serious repercussions for international peace and security. Forced recruitment is indeed a form of gender-based violence that should be better understood and more forcefully addressed by protection agencies such as UNHCR.

Maja Janmyr (PhD) is a postdoctoral researcher at the Faculty of Law, University of Bergen. Her research focuses on human rights and refugee law, often from a socio-legal perspective. Previous work includes the monograph *Protecting Civilians in Refugee Camps: Unable and Unwilling States, UNHCR and International Responsibility* (Brill, 2013), and 'Recruiting Internally Displaced Persons into Civil Militias: The Case of Northern Uganda' in *Nordic Journal of Human Rights* 32(3): 2014.

Notes

1. For background on the war in northern Uganda, see Finnström (2008), Allen (2006) and Branch (2011).
2. Following the end of the civil war in Sudan in 2006, Uganda hosted an approximate 170,000 officially registered Sudanese refugees. By March 2010, however, only 20,301 registered Sudanese refugees remained in the camps. For more figures, see Kaiser (2000: 38–53), UNHCR (2005: 1), Okello et al. (2005), Bernstein (2005), and Wawa (2008: 52).
3. See, for instance, the 1907 Fifth Hague Convention (art. 4), and the 1949 Fourth Geneva Convention (art. 40). International law provides for several specific restrictions on the use of child soldiers, whether refugees or not: 1989 Convention on the Rights of the Child (arts. 19, 32–36); Optional Protocol to the Convention on the Rights of the Child on the involvement of children in armed conflict (art. 1); 1999 African Charter on the Rights and Welfare of the Child (art. 22). While international humanitarian law and refugee law expressly prohibit the recruitment of refugees, there are no analogous provisions as to IDPs.
4. Arbitrary deprivation of liberty is considered customary international humanitarian law, and the Working Group on Arbitrary Detention has made it clear that recruitment methods that do not have a legal basis constitute arbitrary deprivation of liberty. See art. 3 common to the four Geneva conventions. See also Henckaerts and Doswald-Beck (2005: 344ff.) and OHCHR (2009: para. 66–75).
5. SPLA has suffered deep internal divisions in the past decades; in 1991 it split into mutually hostile Dinka- and Nuer-based factions. The Dinka are the largest ethnic group in southern Sudan and have long had tense relations with the neighbouring Nuer. See Moro (2004: 420–36).
6. See Agreement between the Governments of Sudan and Uganda (1999).
7. It is interesting to note that the policy framework on SRS claims to integrate 'human security', and also recognizes that 'security is ... a prerequisite for development' (UNHCR and OPM 2004: 17).
8. These reports were also followed up by new denouncements several months later (see UNHCR 2006d).
9. 'Following our initial investigations in the camps, we had several high-level meetings over the past week with Chadian authorities and strongly stressed that the civilian character of the refugee camps must be maintained at all times, and respected in all circumstances. Forced recruitment of refugees, especially of minors, who came to Chad to seek asylum is totally unacceptable.' (UNHCR 2006b).
10. HCR 1996 protection report on Uganda notes that '[i]t was not possible to reduce the level of SPLA activity in the camp, and in fact this has increased' (UNHCR 1996).

Bibliography

Aga Khan, S. 1976. 'Legal Problems Relating to Refugees and Displaced Persons', *Le Recueil des cours* 149: 287–352.

Agreement between the Governments of Sudan and Uganda. 1999. Retrieved 4 June 2014 from http: //www.usip.org/sites/default/files/file/resources/collections/peace_agreements/sudan_uganda_12081999.pdf.

Akalkal, P. 2007. 'Impunity among Senior SPLA Commanders', *Sudan Tribune*, 25 March. Retrieved 4 June 2014 from http: //www.sudantribune.com/spip.php?article20955.

Allen, T. 2006. *Trial Justice: The International Criminal Court and the Lord's Resistance Army*. London and New York: Zed Books.

Alleweldt, R. 2011. 'Preamble 1951 Convention', in A. Zimmermann (ed.), *The 1951 Convention Relating to the Status of Refugees and its 1967 Protocol: A Commentary*. Oxford and New York: Oxford University Press, pp. 225–40.

Bernstein, J. 2005. 'A Drop in the Ocean: Assistance and Protection for Forced Migrants in Kampala', *RLP Working Paper* No. 16.

Beswick, S. 2000. 'Women, War and Leadership in South Sudan (1700–1994)', in J. Spaulding and S. Beswick (eds), *White Nile, Black Blood: War, Leadership, and Ethnicity from Khartoum to Kampala*. Asmara and London: Red Sea Press, pp. 93–111.

Branch, A. 2011. *Displacing Human Rights: War and Intervention in Northern Uganda*. Oxford and New York: Oxford University Press.

Buscher, D. 2003. 'Case Identification: Challenges Posed by Urban Refugees'. Annual Tripartite Consultations on Resettlement, Geneva, 18–19 June 2003.

Carpenter, C. 2006. 'Recognizing Gender-Based Violence against Civilian Men and Boys in Conflict Situations', *Security Dialogue* 37(1): 83–103.

Clark, J. 2001. 'Explaining Ugandan Intervention in Congo: Evidence and Interpretations', *Journal of Modern African Studies* 39(2): 261–87.

Crisp, J. 1999. 'A State of Insecurity: The Political Economy of Violence in Refugee-Populated Areas of Kenya', *New Issues in Refugee Research* No. 16.

———. 2000. 'Africa's Refugees: Patterns, Problems and Policy Challenges', *Journal of Contemporary African Studies* 18(2): 157–78.

CSUCS (Coalition to Stop the Use of Child Soldiers). 2008. 'Child Soldiers Global Report 2008'. London.

Deng, F.M., and J.S. Morrison. 2001. 'U.S. Policy to End Sudan's War: Report of the CSIS Task Force on U.S.–Sudan Policy'. Washington, DC: Center for Strategic and International Studies.

Finnström, S. 2008. *Living with Bad Surroundings: War, History, and Everyday Moments in Northern Uganda*. Durham, NC: Duke University Press.

Gersony, R. 1997. *The Anguish of Northern Uganda: Results of a Field-Based Assessment of the Civil Conflicts in Northern Uganda*. Kampala: USAID Mission.

Henckaerts, J.-M., and L. Doswald-Beck. 2005. *Customary International Humanitarian Law, Vol. 1: Rules*. Cambridge: Cambridge University Press and International Committee of the Red Cross.

Høigilt, J., Å. Falch and Ø.H. Rolandsen. 2010. 'The Sudan Referendum and Neighbouring Countries: Egypt and Uganda'. Oslo: Peace Research Institute.

Hovil, L. 2001. 'Refugees and the Security Situation in Adjumani District', *RLP Working Paper* No. 2.

———. 2002. 'Free to Stay, Free to Go? Movement, Seclusion and Integration of Refugees in Moyo District', *RLP Working Paper* No. 4.

Hovil, L., and A. Moorhead. 2002. 'War as Normal: The Impact of Violence on the Lives of Displaced Communities in Pader District, Northern Uganda', *RLP Working Paper* No. 5.

Hovil, L., and E. Werker. 2001. 'Refugees in Arua District: A Human Security Analysis', *RLP Working Paper* No. 3.

HRW (Human Rights Watch). 2002. 'Hidden in Plain View: Refugees Living without Protection in Nairobi and Kampala'.

———. 2006. 'Violence beyond Borders: The Human Rights Crisis in Eastern Chad'.

Hutchinson, S., and J.M. Jok. 2002. 'Gendered Violence and the Militarisation of Ethnicity: A Case Study from Southern Sudan', in R. Werbner (ed.), *Postcolonial Subjectivities in Africa*. London: Zed Books, pp. 84–108.

ICG (International Crisis Group). 2006. 'Sudan's Comprehensive Peace Agreement: The Long Road Ahead', *International Crisis Group Africa Report* No. 106.

IRIN. 2000a. 'Minister Vows Continued Support for SPLA'. *IRIN News*, 10 March. Retrieved 4 June 2014 from http://www.irinnews.org/report/12858/uganda-minister-vows-continued-support-for-spla.

———. 2000b. 'Uganda Set to Deport 200 Sudanese Rebels'. *IRIN News*, 6 September. Retrieved 4 June 2014 from http://www.irinnews.org/report/2034/uganda-uganda-set-to-deport-200-sudanese-rebels.

Janmyr, M. 2014a. *Protecting Civilians in Refugee Camps: Unable and Unwilling States, UNHCR and International Responsibility*. Leiden and Boston: Martinus Nijhoff.

———. 2014b. 'Revisiting the Civilian and Humanitarian Character of Refugee Camps', in J.F. Durieux and D. Cantor (eds), *Refuge from Inhumanity: War Refugees and International Humanitarian Law*. Leiden and Boston: Martinus Nijhoff.

———. 2014c. 'Recruiting Internally Displaced Persons into Civil Militias: The Case of Northern Uganda', *Nordic Journal of Human Rights* 32(3): 1–20.

Kaiser, T. 2000. 'The Experience and Consequence of Insecurity in a Refugee-Populated Area in Northern Uganda 1996–97', *Refugee Survey Quarterly* 19(1): 38–53.

Komakech, S., and C. Abonga. 2010. 'Two Injured in Kitgum Garage Bomb Blast', *Daily Monitor*, 5 April. Retrieved 6 June 2014 from http://allafrica.com/stories/201004050495.html.

Lammers, E. 2006. 'War, Refuge and Self Soldiers, Students and Artists in Kampala, Uganda'. PhD dissertation. Amsterdam: University of Amsterdam.

Leopold, M. 2005. *Inside West Nile: Violence, History and Representation on an African Frontier*. Kampala: Fountain Publishers.

Lischer, S.K. 2000. 'Refugee Involvement in Political Violence: Quantitative Evidence from 1987–1998', *New Issues in Refugee Research Paper* No. 26.

Lorenzo, M., and B. Harrell-Bond. 1999. 'The Need for Expanding Services for Refugees in Kampala: A Concept Paper'. Unpublished paper. Kampala.

Macchiavello, M. 2003. 'Forced Migrants as an Under-utilized Asset: Refugee Skills, Livelihoods, and Achievements in Kampala, Uganda', *New Issues in Refugee Research Paper* No. 95.

Matsiko, G. 2007. 'Uganda: General Arrested over Secret Troops', *The Monitor*, 1 April. Retrieved 4 June 2014 from http://allafrica.com/stories/200704021146. html.

Merkx, J. 2002. 'Refugee Identities and Relief in an African Borderland: A Study of Northern Uganda and Southern Sudan', *Refugee Survey Quarterly* 21(1–2): 113–46.

Milner, J. 2004. 'Golden Age? What Golden Age? A Critical History of African Asylum Policy'. Paper presented to the Centre for Refugee Studies, York University, 28 January.

Mkutu, K. 2006. 'Small Arms and Light Weapons among Pastoral Groups in the Kenya–Uganda Border Area', *African Affairs* 106(422): 47–70.

Moro, N. 2004. 'Interethnic Relations in Exile: The Politics of Ethnicity among Sudanese Refugees in Uganda and Egypt', *Journal of Refugee Studies* 17(4): 420–36.

Mtango, E.-E. 1989. 'Military and Armed Attacks on Refugee Camps', in G. Loescher and L. Monahan (eds), *Refugees and International Relations*. Oxford: Oxford University Press, pp. 87–121.

Mugeere, A. 2001. 'SPLA Recruits in Uganda Camps', *New Vision*, 16 August. Retrieved 4 June 2014 from http://allafrica.com/stories/200108160131.html.

Neefjes, K. 1999. 'Participatory Review in Chronic Instability: The Experience of Ikafe Refugee Settlement Programme, Uganda', *RRN Network Paper* No. 29.

OCHA (UN Office for the Coordination of Humanitarian Affairs). 2005. 'Humanitarian Update Uganda, 7(3)'. On file with author.

OHCHR (Office of the United Nations High Commissioner for Human Rights). 2009. 'Working Group on Arbitrary Detention, Opinion no. 8/2008 (Colombia)', A/HRC/10/21/Add.3.

Okello, M., et al. 2005. '"There Are No Refugees Living in This Area": Self-settled Refugees in Koboko', *RLP Working Paper* No. 18.

Okudi, M., and F.W. Okello. 2009. 'Uganda, Sudan Resolve Border Conflict', *Daily Monitor*, 25 November. Retrieved 6 June 2014 from http://www.monitor. co.ug/News/National/-/688334/805520/-/wevof4/-/index.html.

OPM (Office of the Prime Minister, Directorate of Refugees). 2004. 'Project Proposal for Security Package for All Refugee Settlements in Uganda (Spares-Uganda)', Kampala Action Plan.

Payne, L. 1998. *Rebuilding Communities in a Refugee Settlement: A Casebook from Uganda*. Oxford: Oxfam.

Rone, J., et al. 1994. *Civilian Devastation: Abuses by All Parties in the War in Southern Sudan*. New York: Human Rights Watch.

Sandvik, K.B. 2011. 'Blurring Boundaries: Refugee Resettlement in Kampala – between the Formal, the Informal, and the Illegal', *PoLAR: The Political and Legal Anthropology Review* 34(1): 11–32.

Schmidt, A. 2006. 'From Global Prescription to Local Treatment: The International Refugee Regime in Tanzania and Uganda'. PhD dissertation. Berkeley: University of California.

Smith, M. 2004. 'Warehousing Refugees: A Denial of Rights, a Waste of Humanity', *World Refugee Survey 2004*. Washington, DC: US Committee for Refugees and Immigrants.

Stone, L. 2011. '"We were all soldiers": Female Combatants in South Sudan's Civil War', in F. Bubenzer and O. Stern (eds), *Hope, Pain & Patience: The Lives of Women in South Sudan*. Auckland Park: Fanele/Jacana Media, pp. 25–52.

UNHCR (United Nations High Commissioner for Refugees). 1982. 'Addendum to the Report of the United Nations High Commissioner for Refugees'. EXCOM A/37/12/Add.1.

——. 1983. 'Report by Ambassador Felix Schnyder on Military Attacks on Refugee Camps and Settlements in Southern Africa and Elsewhere'. EXCOM report EC/SCP/26.

——. 1987. 'Military Attacks on Refugee Camps and Settlements in Southern Africa and Elsewhere'. EXCOM Conclusion No. 48 (XXXVIII).

——. 1996. 'Annual Protection Report'. Branch Office for Uganda.

——. 1999. 'Global Report, Uganda'. Geneva.

——. 2000a. 'Global Appeal, Uganda'. Geneva.

——. 2000b. 'Global Reports, Country Report Uganda 1999'. Geneva.

——. 2000c. 'The Security, Civilian and Humanitarian Character of Refugee Camps and Settlements: Operationalizing the "Ladder of Options"'. EC/50/SC/INF.4. Geneva.

——. 2001. 'Global Appeal, Uganda'. Geneva.

——. 2004a. 'Global Appeal, Uganda'. Geneva.

——. 2004b. 'Global Report, Uganda'. Geneva.

——. 2005. 'Country Operations Plan: Uganda, Planning Year 2006'. UNHCR COPS.

——. 2006a. 'Operational Guidelines on Maintaining the Civilian and Humanitarian Character of Asylum'. Geneva.

——. 2006b. 'UNHCR Strongly Condemns the Forced Recruitment of Sudanese Refugees'. *UNHCR Briefing Notes*, 31 March.

——. 2006c. 'UNHCR Condemns Forced Recruitment of Sudanese Refugees in Chad Camps'. *News Stories*, 31 March. Retrieved 4 June 2014 from http://www.unhcr.org/442d202b4.html.

——. 2006d. 'UNHCR Expresses Alarm over Continuing Reports of Forced Recruitment in Chad Refugee Camps'. *News Stories*, 16 May. Retrieved 4 June 2014 from http://www.unhcr.org/4469eba94.html.

UNHCR and OPM. 1998. 'From Local Settlement to Self-Sufficiency: A Long-Term Strategy for Assistance to Refugees in Uganda 1999–2002' (draft). Kampala.

——. 2004. 'Development Assistance for Refugee-Hosting Areas in Uganda – Programme Document 2004–2007'. Kampala.

UNSC (United Nations Security Council). 1998. 'Res 1208'. UN Doc S/RES/1208. 19 November.

——. 2000. 'Res 1296'. UN Doc S/RES/1296. 19 April.

——. 2004. 'Report of the Secretary-General on the Protection of Civilians in Armed Conflict'. UN Doc. S/2004/431.

US Department of State. 2002. 'Country Reports on Human Rights Practice: Uganda 2001'. 4 March.

Verdirame G., and B. Harrell-Bond. 2005. *Rights in Exile: Janus-faced Humanitarianism*. New York and Oxford: Berghahn Books.

Wawa, Y. 2008. *Refugee Aid and Development: A Case of Sudanese Refugees in West Nile, Uganda*. Kampala: Fountain Publishers.

11

Gender, Violence and Deportation

Angola's Forced Return of Congolese Migrant Workers

Alexander Betts

Introduction

Angola is estimated to have deported around half a million Congolese migrant workers back to the Democratic Republic of Congo (DRC) over a ten-year period between 2003 and 2013. While the use of forced return by states is not unusual (Schuster and Bloch 2005; Ellermann 2008; Gibney 2008; de Geneva and Peutz 2010; Vigneswaren and Sutton 2011; Anderson, Gibney and Paoletti 2012), the scale of the expulsions, the violent methods used to deport, and the vulnerabilities of many of those deported set this case apart from most state practices of deportation. Yet considering the scale of the human rights violations involved, the case of the Angolan deportations remains relatively undocumented, receiving little attention from the media, academics or international organizations.

The violence that took place in the process of forced return had particularly gendered effects. A significant proportion of those deported were women. Although both men and women were subjected to violence by the Angolan army and police, there were qualitative differences in the type of violence perpetrated against women. Violence against women included the systematic use of gang rape, sexual violence, beatings, unhygienic body cavity searches, mutilation, and extended periods of detention, as well as being forced to walk up to 200 km to the border, often without food or water (Betts 2013).

The response by the international community can also be interpreted as significantly gendered. There was relatively little concern by international organizations for the deportations and their consequences. The deportations were assumed not to be a human rights or humanitarian issue partly because they involved Angola engaging in an immigration control practice widely used by liberal states (Ellermann 2008; Gibney 2013). Among the staff of international organizations that failed to respond, the lack of action was justified in a range of ways, including highlighting that some of the women were prostitutes, and relativizing the number of rapes in comparison to the number in the Eastern DRC.

The case therefore offers an opportunity to examine violence in the context of deportation from a gender perspective. It enables an exploration of both the gendered nature of the violence and of the international response. In so far as the case involves violence perpetrated by the state, it draws attention to gendered violence as a human rights issue, and to the role and limitations of international organizations in responding to such violence. Indeed, while a significant amount of literature now exists on gender and forced migration (Pittaway and Bartolomei 1991; Crawley 2001; Fiddian-Qasmiyeh 2010, 2014a), little has been written about gender and deportation.

Furthermore, while this is in many ways a case about 'Women in Forced Migration', it can also be interpreted from a 'Gender and Forced Migration' (Fiddian-Qasmiyeh 2014b: 396–98) angle. On the one hand, this chapter therefore seeks to describe an untold story of violence against women. On the other hand, it also seeks to understand how and why this differentiated violence was rendered possible and to a significant extent legitimated within Angola and internationally. Indeed, its treatment as a 'humanitarian' issue and one of low priority, rather than a fundamental human rights issue, reveals underlying structures of hierarchy in the international community's engagement with relationship between gender, violence and security (Shepherd 2008).

This chapter therefore unpacks the history of these deportations and the forms of violence that they entailed. In order to do so, I draw upon the relatively few primary sources that are available to document the Angolan case. In particular, I draw upon the internal archives of Médecins Sans Frontières (MSF), as one of the few NGOs to engage seriously with this case. I triangulate this research by also drawing upon interviews with key stakeholders, conducted in Kinshasa, Brussels and Geneva. I argue that deportation needs to be understood in gendered terms, both in relation to its effects and the policy discourses of the deporting state and the international community.

This chapter divides into three main sections. First, it provides a background on who the Congolese migrants in Angola are and why they have been in Angola. Second, it examines the four main waves of deportations that took place between 2003 and 2013, documenting what happened in each one, and the response of the international community. Finally, the chapter assesses the account's implications for how we understand deportation and gender.

Congolese Migration to Angola

The majority of the deported Congolese originated from and were returned to two of the country's eleven provinces: Bandundu and Western Kasai. These provinces are in the south of the country and border Angola's Lunda Norte region. In contrast to those provinces in the DRC in which most violent conflict has taken place, such as North Kivu and South Kivu in the east, and wealthier areas of mineral extraction such as Katanga, the southern provinces generally receive little attention, and are largely neglected areas of the DRC. Even though these provinces are not afflicted by conflict in the same way as many other areas of the country, their border areas nevertheless exhibit the characteristics of state fragility, and have an infrastructure and environment that makes it almost impossible for the majority of people to sustain viable livelihood strategies in the absence of resorting to either external assistance or migration.

The border areas of Western Kasai are among the most impoverished of the DRC. Food security is a particular problem, and along with Eastern Kasai, government health statistics reveal that the Kasais form 'the most malnourished region of the DRC' (Butoke 2009), with up to fifty thousand deaths per year in Western Kasai as a result of malnutrition, and 44 per cent of under five-year-olds suffering from chronic malnutrition and 16 per cent from acute malnutrition. Low life expectancy means that 90 per cent of women over the age of fifty are widows (Betts 2013). Low levels of agricultural production are exacerbated by poorly functioning transportation, which means that there is no organized inter-province food market to supplement local food production.

The economy of the border area of Western Kasai is divided between the territory of Luiza and Tshikapa. The former is mainly agro-pastoralist but there is limited access to seeds, and crop productivity based on maize, beans, peanuts, soybeans and cassava is low. Tshikapa has almost no agricultural land and so the economy is based on diamond mining; however, it has no organized extraction and has virtually exhausted the sources of diamonds accessible to artisanal extractors (AIMC and Butoke 2008).

In both areas, is the population depends on external humanitarian assistance to maintain basic levels of food security, with FAO providing food support, UNICEF contributing to water and sanitation, and the local NGO, Butoke, offering a range of projects to facilitate increased food productivity. The border areas of Bandundu present similar challenges for inhabitants. As with Western Kasai, there is chronic food insecurity. The border area around the town of Kahemba is a mining zone in which artisanal diamond mining offers the main source of livelihood, albeit one that is gradually being exhausted. The area traditionally hosted large numbers of Angolan refugees. The agricultural land is of poor quality, with low levels of production due to a combination of poor techniques and poor nutritional training. Manioc is the only crop that can be grown indigenously without external intervention, and its production is far from self-sufficient, particularly since 80 per cent is exported from Kahemba. A UN interagency mission to the area highlighted a range of problems with a lack of medical facilities, poor sanitation, acute malnutrition among 21 per cent of the population, high levels of infant mortality, and the absence of functioning markets. It is traditionally an area from which parents are forced to leave their children with relatives in order to seek economic opportunity elsewhere, either by crossing into Angola or travelling within the DRC (UN 2007).

Unsurprisingly, many people cross the border to Angola in search of livelihood opportunities, and the economy of the southern provinces largely depends on trans-border mobility. In the words of one MSF doctor who has worked in the region: 'They have nothing; migration is a survival strategy; the average income in the area is less than US$10 a month. The motivation for moving is a combination of hope and despair' (Interview with Dr Lame Papys, MSF Belgium, Kinshasa, 9 November 2009). The overwhelming majority of the migrants are men who move, either individually or with their families, to Lunda Norte to work in the diamond mining sector as artisanal diggers (or 'garimpeiros'). A smaller number of the men who were deported from Angola were ex-military and had served as soldiers for the rebel group UNITA. Meanwhile, among the minority of women who travelled independently, many were traders, often travelling long distances from other parts of the DRC to sell fried fish, clothes or consumer products. With sex work being a significant activity in the border area, reinforced by the diamond activity, there are also a significant number of prostitutes working both in a professional capacity and on an occasional basis (MSF-B 2007b).

This type of cross-border movement is not new, as 'exchanges have always taken place between the two neighbouring countries' (OCHA

2007). The border area between Lunda Norte and the DRC was on the old trading routes in both the colonial and precolonial eras. The Imbangala in Angola and the Pende in the Congo would regularly interact in order to trade cloth, slaves and guns. It was only after Angolan independence in 1975, that the economic links became increasingly based on the development of a large-scale illicit diamond trade, connecting diggers, intermediaries and sellers across the border. Between 1975 and 1992 Angola had a socialist government, which enabled relatively open access to the diamond mining areas for artisanal diamond miners. However, civil war between the socialist Movimento Popular de Liberacao de Angola (MPLA), the National Liberation Front of Angola (FNLA) and the Western-backed Uniao Nacional para a Independencia Total de Angola (UNITA) hampered investment in developing the mining industry. In 1992, a ceasefire was brokered between UNITA and the MPLA, leading to Angola's first national elections. With an MPLA victory in the elections, UNITA reverted to civil war, seizing de facto control of the diamond mining areas in Lunda Norte and Lunda Sul, effectively partitioning the country and its natural resources.

During this period, up until UNITA leader Jonas Savimbi's death in 2002, UNITA dominated the diamond mining areas of the Lundas, often drawing upon Congolese labour to support its activities (de Boeck 2001: 554). The Congolese were able to buy a permit issued by UNITA to cross the border into Angola, and UNITA organized camps for Congolese workers. However, with UNITA's defeat and surrender in 2002, the MPLA government, in power since elections in 1992, asserted authority over the diamond mining areas of the Lundas. It recognized that as the world's third-largest producer of diamonds, Angola's diamond resources offered significant opportunity for national development and (allegedly) personal enrichment.[1] The territory of the Lundas became subject to increasingly strict rules governing freedom of movement, residency and economic activity on the territories. Even for nationals, conditions were difficult, and many people were displaced, deprived of their livelihoods or subjected to human rights violations (Marquez 2005).

The Waves of Deportations

The waves of deportations began on 23 December 2003. Units of the army, police and the Serviav de Migraigr Estrangeiro (SME) swept through the garimpeiro camps in the diamond provinces, rounded up illegal immigrants from other African nations and sent them back to their countries of origin. Over the next six years, the Government of Angola (GoA) launched a series of such operations, resulting in successive waves of deportations, each with their own patterns and underlying political dynamics. In total, it is possible to document at least 270,000 deportations, and OCHA suggests it is likely to have been around 400,000. However, compiling accurate figures is extremely problematic. The official figures recorded by Congolese border officials are significantly lower than estimates of other actors such as Caritas, United Nations Mission in the Democratic Republic of the Congo (MONUC) and local NGOs. One of the reasons for this is that there were allegations that the DRC border officials were demanding a fee of around US$100 to allow nationals back into the country (OCHA 2007). Furthermore, most deported migrants rapidly left the border zone to return to their own villages, making verification of numbers difficult (MSF-B 2008a). On the other hand, though, OCHA also warns that these underestimates may have been partly mitigated by the 'revolving door' nature of migration, with some Congolese returning to Angola after expulsion and being deported more than once (OCHA 2007).

There are different ways of dividing up the waves of expulsions, but four principal ones can be identified. First, the launch of 'Operacao Brilhante' signalled the first wave, entailing deportations in December 2003 and April 2004, which led to around 100,000 Congolese being forced back to Western Kasai and Bandundu. Second, some of the most serious human rights abuses were recorded by MSF and the 'Temoignages' (MSF-B 2007a) as a result of around 33,000 deportations between July 2007 and February 2008. Third, a 'Pre-Election Wave', took place in the run-up to the national legislative elections in September 2008, resulting in an estimated 120,000 Congolese being returned between May and August 2008. This was the highest number of deportations in a given period but entailed slightly reduced levels of rights violations, compared to the previous waves. Fourth, the 'Bas-Congo Episode' involved around 18,800 Congolese being deported between August and October 2009, mainly from the Cabinda province of Angola to Bas-Congo in the west of the DRC. This episode involved a different area of both Angola and the DRC, but is nevertheless an important part of the overall story because it was the first time that there had been a significant political response from the DRC, with the government reciprocally expelling Angolan refugees. Beyond these four episodes, however, the character of the deportations has shifted from acute waves to a chronic crisis based on ongoing expulsions that continue to the present day. The sections below discuss each wave in greater detail.

Wave 1: Operacao Brilhante

Considering many of the Congolese to be potential UNITA supporters, and estimating that the country loses US$375 m annually from diamond smuggling, it launched an anti-smuggling campaign known as 'Operacao Brilhante' (Operation Brilliant). It began on 23 December 2003 with a series of night-time and dawn raids in the Garimpeiro camps, and aimed to deport the thousands of foreign diamond miners and other workers in the Lunda areas, focusing particularly on the predominantly Congolese camps in the Lunda Norte mining towns (MSF-B 2007b). An NGO working on behalf of Congolese diaspora in Angola claimed that between 24 and 26 December FAA soldiers (Angolan army) entered villages/camps 'as if prepared for war', and forced the Congolese to leave the territory in Cafunfo (ACL 2004).

The patterns of the raids were characteristic of those that would define the deportations over the ensuing six years. Soldiers, police and immigration officials would descend on the makeshift camps and villages of Congolese artisanal miners, round them up, set their homes on fire, and take them to local prisons or military bases, where they would be detained, often alongside their children, and without food or water. They would then be marched or transported to the border and cross the River Tungila into the DRC. Along the way, however, many would be subjected to significant and degrading human rights abuses: men and women beaten in their homes, often in front of their children, some of the women raped, possessions stolen, and women subjected to degrading and unhygienic vaginal and anal searches for diamonds.

Although the first organized round-ups took place over Christmas 2003, it was not until April 2004 that the human consequences of Operacao Brilhante made the international media. From February, the GoA began a more systematic and larger-scale operation in the region of the major Lunda Norte mining towns around Cafunfo. MSF began to receive reports of people in distress crossing back into the DRC as early as February; and between 2 and 4 April, it received news that over 8,500 Congolese had crossed the River Tungila border at three different entry points in Bandundu in desperate conditions. At the same time, and based on announcements by the GOA, OCHA warned that between 80,000 and 100,000 Congolese would face expulsion. By 20 April, 67,000 Congolese had been registered as crossing five border posts in Bandundu and Western Kasai (MSF-B 2004a).

Inter-agency missions on the DRC side of the border, led by MSF-Belgium and OCHA during April, highlighted the immediate humanitarian challenge posed by the returns: most of the new arrivals had been robbed of possessions, there was no registration process for the new arrivals, there was water shortage, a lack of food, and people were arriving with health needs resulting from fatigue, shock and dehydration (MSF-B 2004b). International media coverage brought public attention to the 'brutal abuses against Congolese migrant workers' ('Congo miners "tortured" in

Angola' 2004) and the human consequences of the deportations. Based on the results of an OCHA-led inter-agency report, Reuters documented: 'The U.N. Office for the Coordination of Humanitarian Affairs continues to receive numerous reports of physical and psychological abuse of Congolese civilians reportedly perpetrated by Angolan security forces ... reports of rape, cruel, inhuman and degrading treatment, theft of personal belongings, arbitrary detention and killings'. OCHA claimed there to be 'an acute humanitarian crisis in the making ... These civilians, some of whom have never set foot in Congo, arrive traumatised from their ordeal and with little, if any, means to support themselves' ('Angolan Troops Reportedly Kill Congo Miners – U.N.' 2004). In response to the publicity, the GoA insisted on its sovereign right to control entry to and exit from its territory. On 30 April it published an editorial piece in the *Jornal de Angola* entitled 'Rights and Sovereignty', in which it stated that 'the Angolan government reasserts its sovereign right to expel illegal immigrants from its territory',[2] denouncing and dismissing criticism from NGOs such as MSF, and expressing its intention to continue with the operation. MSF responded to this with a press release, in which it argued that '[t]he question is not what is being done, it is how it is being done' (MSF-B 2004c). It has been suggested that, shortly afterwards, the DRC authorities made a formal request to the GoA to suspend deportations until better conditions of return had been assured (MSF-B 2004a). In late April, the GoA announced a 45-day moratorium on deportations, to be effective from mid-May, and from the first week in May there was a massive decrease in the number of new arrivals at the border (ibid.).

An OCHA-led inter-agency mission within Angola between 12 and 17 May, conducted in Lunda Norte and Lunda Sol to monitor Operacao Brilhante, showed that the main operation was over. However, it also demonstrated that by that stage, according to the GoA's own police records, a total of 127,788 people had been deported (124,289 to the DRC and 3,499 to West Africa) between 29 March and 27 April 2004 (OCHA 2004). By the time of the moratorium, the Angolan government had largely achieved its aim, with minimal intervention or criticism from the international community. In reflecting upon the international response, MSF highlighted the difficulty it had encountered in mobilizing partners: it described OCHA's engagement as 'timid', engaging in coordinating inter-agency missions but with few interventions on the ground; meanwhile UNHCR had participated in the inter-agency missions but had argued that the situation was 'outside its mandate' because the Congolese were in their country of origin and thus were not refugees. While the Red Cross had provided eight national staff, and UNICEF had loaned equipment to MSF, neither the humanitarian nor the diplomatic responses had been proportionate to the extent of the protection needs (MSF-B 2004b).

Wave 2: MSF and the 'Temoignages'

The second period of deportations, although involving fewer people, is arguably the most serious in terms of the extent of the human rights violations carried out by the GoA. It entailed the systematic use of rape as an instrument of deportation. The period also offers the closest documentation of those abuses, mainly as a result of MSF taking witness statements ('*temoignages*') from deported women. The first waves of expulsions were announced by the local NGO Butoke in February 2007 in Western Kasai, where five thousand returning Congolese registered with Caritas in the diocese of Luiza. Yet, despite these early indicators, the international community's response was slow, and it was not until the end of the year that there was any significant humanitarian response, and that was only as a result of unprecedented action – at the boundaries of its mandate – by MSF.

In response to successive calls from local NGOs, OCHA led an inter-agency mission from Kinshasa to Western Kasai between 12 and 14 April 2007, in which OCHA, UNHCR, MONUC and Caritas divided up their information gathering into the sectors in which they hold expertise (OCHA 2007). The report of the mission highlights that deportees were arriving in 'deplorable conditions' and documents thirty-four cases of rape and sexual violence by Angolan military and police. However, the report established that the situation was 'not a humanitarian crisis', stating that 'the mission judges that the situation, although worrying, is stable; it is not a catastrophe or humanitarian crisis' (ibid.). Instead, it highlighted the need to work through local partners to ensure better food security, the protection of the most vulnerable groups, and access to medical care, water and sanitation, citing malnutrition as the biggest problem. According to an internal document of one humanitarian organization, however, the OCHA-led mission had only stayed for four hours in Luiza and five hours in Tshikapa. The same organization would later argue that OCHA 'should have sent a plea to the authorities in Kinshasa concerning the situations', and questioned 'the lack of transparency, responsibility and professionalism of different humanitarian actors [involved in that mission]'.[3]

Deportation continued throughout the summer months, with virtually no intervention from the international humanitarian or diplomatic community. On 12 October 2007, Dr Cecile De Sweemer, a Butoke consultant based in Western Kasai, alerted MSF's Pool D'Urgence Congolais (PUC) – its emergency response team in Kinshasa – about a worrying situation. The NGO reported receiving a significant number of Congolese women who had suffered sexual violence during their expulsion from Angola (Interview with Brice de la Vigne – Head of PUC, MSF-B, 2007 – Brussels, 1 October 2009). In response, a PUC team of four or five people left Kinshasa on 23 October, arriving in Western Kasai for a fifteen-day mission to analyse the health situation of the women in consultation with other organizations, to begin to record testimonies of the women, and to offer care for the victims of sexual violence.

MSF staff were shocked by the accounts of sexual violence that they heard in the testimonies of women deported from the Lunda Norte towns. The patterns in the testimonies were almost identical. The Congolese settlements in Lunda Norte would be encircled at night by Angolan soldiers, arriving in several trucks. The men would often try to flee the site, leaving the women alone with their children. The soldiers would enter the houses in groups of at least five. They would make the women lie on ground at gun point, and then systematically gang rape them in front of their children, saying in French the same comments: 'Prostitute of Congo. Go home. Here is not your country. Pack up your things. We are raping you so that you will not come back'. The women and children would then be led away in handcuffs, and the villages pillaged and set on fire.

On average, the women spent three to seven days in detention, generally in military bases in Dundo or Nzaji, in overcrowded and unsanitary conditions, detained alongside their children and without access to food or water. In detention they were often escorted outside at night, where they were gang raped by their guards. They were then either forced to walk 200 km to the border – over a period of a few days to two weeks – or piled into overcrowded trucks and transported. During the journey, they passed through a number of checkpoints, often being raped at each. As they reached detention centres, about three hours walk from the border, they were subjected to unsanitary body searches of the anus and vagina. In the words of one woman: 'They performed anal and vaginal searches, one after the other without protection' (MSF 2007a). Men were also subjected to brutal violence, including mutilation and summary executions. Upon arrival at the border, most had had all of their possessions taken; yet they faced a lack of assistance in terms of water, food and access to medical care upon arrival (MSF 2007b).

The reports that MSF sent back to Kinshasa and Brussels reveal that staff who took the witness statements were themselves traumatized by the accounts they heard, with one staff member commenting that 'the most difficult thing was the heaviness of the testimonies' (Interview with MSF staff member). Given the gap in action by other international actors, MSF decided it had to act. It decided to send a team to the border town of Kamako in Western Kasai, where it was to set up a main clinic and four mobile clinics across the region. It arrived on 27 November 2007 with a mandate to care for the deported women who had suffered sexual violence. However, within two days of beginning consultations in a tent, it faced discontent from the local community who also wanted treatment and so it broadened treatment to the local population. Alongside its health-related work, MSF's press officer continued to record testimonies from the deported women.

MSF (2007a) published the witness statements of one hundred women interviewed in Kamako. On 5 December, it organized three simultaneous press conferences – in Kinshasa, Brussels and Johannesburg – to publicize the findings of the testimonies. The testimonies provide harrowing accounts of abuse, detention, rapes and beatings by Angolan military and police. One typical example is taken from a 31-year-old woman, married with four children, who having spent four years living and working in Maludi in Angola was expelled in May 2007:

> At 7 pm, the soldiers came with a truck. There was a whole battalion. My husband ran away. Husbands flee because they do not want to see their wives being raped. And in general, they get beaten up even harder in front of their wives. Four soldiers came into my house. They began to beat me with sticks. They ordered me to lie down and then raped me, in the anus and the vagina, one after the other. I was taken to prison with the children. I was in there for four days. We were given nothing to eat or to drink. In the prison, there were eight men, four women and children. We defecated in the room. On the first three days, I was beaten and raped every day by four soldiers, always the same men. The other women were subjected to the same treatment. They threw insults at us: 'Look at their breast, look at their buttocks. You're going to leave everything here'. We walked for twelve days and passed four checkpoints. At the first check point, the whole group was beaten up and then they let us go. At the second checkpoint, we were also beaten up. A soldier forced me into his hut and raped me. The other women were subjected to the same treatment. The same thing happened at the third checkpoint. At the fourth checkpoint, I was raped by two soldiers on the side of the road – and so were the other women. At the two borders, there were no incidents. I re-entered Congo at Kassa Mai. Shortly after Kassa Mai, my five-year-old child died of exhaustion. His body was thrown in the bush. I did not have any medical examination because I could not pay for one. I have no news from my husband. I do not know if he is still alive.

On a medical level, the MSF intervention had limited effectiveness. Most of the women had suffered sexual violence more than 72 hours earlier than they presented to MSF. This meant that there was nothing much that could be done medically in terms of HIV prevention. The only real support that MSF could offer was treatment of other STIs, and anti-tetanus or hepatitis B shots. Given MSF's primary role as a provider of medical assistance, this made its role questionable and highly contested. The now deputy director of MSF-B, Fabienne de Laval, who was the head of mission in the DRC at the time, claimed:

I didn't agree with the project we did. We were nine months too late. The big deportation was July and August 2007 ... Somebody had spoken to the women and heard about the horrors. But, most of the facts were from 6–9 months before ... as everywhere in DRC, we were in an area where access to healthcare is nearly zero, and we were coming with a very vertical project on just rape, which in a community is not accepted because you are only treating three people, when there are hundreds of people dying of anaemia, malaria... People were trickling in, but it is nearly impossible to access them on a however-long borderline. It is very difficult to pinpoint entry points. It is impossible to get access to post-exposure prophylaxis for HIV because it takes you 24 hours to get to the next village. The medical intervention was not viable unless we had been there at the peak of deportation. (Interview with Fabienne de Laval, deputy director MSF-B, Brussels, 10 October 2010)

The recognition that the main time period for viable intervention had elapsed led to a redefinition of the MSF mission to monitor the deportation situation after the 5 December press conference, to offer some medical support to women who had suffered sexual violence, and to try to co-ordinate a wider response by other NGOs to address malnutrition and malaria. These aims were met through establishing a clinic at Kamako for women suffering from the repercussions of sexual violence, and four mobile clinics in surrounding villages, all of which also opened their ser-vices to people from the local community. However, overall, MSF was able to contribute very little in medical terms and its mission closed on 1 February 2008.

It was in its less conventional role as the only organization that docu-mented and disseminated testimonies of the human rights violations, that MSF had a significant and important impact, filling a gap that other or-ganizations notably failed to address. Fabienne de Laval, in spite of her scepticism about the overall mission, confirmed: 'We did get *temoignage* of women who had really been violated in horrendous situations; the inter-vention of the Angolan military, the people on the protection side were the abusers. We had a press conference in Congo, Johannesburg and Brussels. For me that was a positive outcome' (Interview with de Laval). Indeed, there is evidence that the testimonies and subsequent press conference made a difference. The press conference coincided with the anniversary of the Universal Declaration of Human Rights (UDHR), and the MSF testi-monies were raised in Luanda by the Head of the OHCHR Angola Office at events to mark the anniversary (OHCHR 2007). On the very same day, the deputy chief of staff of the FAA, General Geraldo Sachipengo Nunda, publicly promised to investigate the allegations. General Nunda followed through on this commitment, calling for a change in the way in way in which deportations would be conducted in future. As Helene Lorinquer observed: 'One person took the lead for pushing change within the

Angolan government, and two to three people within the military were sanctioned' (Interview with Helene Lorinquer, coordinator of the Analysis and Advocacy Unit, MSF-B, in 2007). Indeed, after 11 December, there were changes in terms of expulsions: their frequency was reduced, the number of people declined, those deported did not generally suffer vaginal and anal body searches, most were not incarcerated, they were taken in trucks rather than being forced to walk to the border, and the levels of sexual violence reduced (MSF-B 2008a). MSF argued that this shift could be traced directly to its own role: 'One can reasonably believe that the reduction in the expulsions, and the end of mistreatment, are linked to the impact of the activities of MSF (the press conference and the presence on the border over several weeks)' (MSF-B 2008b). However, it also accurately foresaw that 'it should not be excluded that new waves may begin [again] following the cessation of our activities or the approach of the Angolan elections' (ibid.).

Wave 3: Pre-Election Deportations

Deportation resumed again on a larger scale on 25 May 2008 with what was described as 'Operation Broad Wings' (MSF-B 2007b). Angola's first legislative elections since 1992 had been postponed on a number of occasions since 2007, and were finally fixed for September 2008, with presidential elections intended to follow at a later date. In the build-up, the GoA launched a large-scale round-up and deportation operation, to last between forty-five and ninety days. Its intention was to remove people who might be UNITA supporters who could register to vote. By the end of June around 120,000 Congolese had been deported. However, compared to 2007, the pattern of the deportations had changed, with less brutality and fewer flagrant human rights violations (MSF-B 2007b). Details of the deportations were revealed in mid-2008 by two inter-agency missions – one was MSF in Bandundu and the other a UN mission in Western Kasai.

Upon receiving reports of new arrivals in Bandundu, MSF sent a mission from the PUC in Kinshasa to Bandundu in order to take testimonies in June. It arrived in Kahungulu, near the border, and spent time in the nearby towns of Tembo, Kikwit and Kahamba. It noted that even the official Direction Generale des Migrations (DGM) statistics of the government revealed that between 26 May and 11 June, 22,457 Congolese had been deported back to Bandundu in just seventeen days (MSF-B 2008b). However, based on the testimonies, it found that, compared to 2007, the pattern of deportations had changed. Although far from perfect from a human rights perspective, the shocking sexual violence recorded just six months earlier was no longer such a prominent feature.

The testimonies reveal a consistent story of the methods used in these deportations. The military would arrive at the garimpeiro settlements at night, encircling the camps, and assemble all Congolese in the middle of the camp. They would then explain that they must leave Angola immediately. The migrants would be given a few minutes to gather essential belongings. The camps would then be systematically set on fire, and helicopters used to check that no one had escaped. The Congolese would then be taken by truck or on foot to military bases, where they would be detained for between 24 hours and five days. In detention they would sometimes be given water and food – although not on a systematic basis. From there, they would be transported (women in trucks, men often on foot) in stages, towards the border post, stopping at checkpoints along the way. At the border, they would then cross the River Tingila by boat, and arrive at the border post of Kahungula, where the Congolese DGM, the Agence Nationale des Renseignements, the *le service de renseignments militaire*, and the police would all be present to undertake a count by age and sex. On arrival, nothing was organized or provided by the Congolese state. Most arrived exhausted and without possessions, resting in Kahungula before leaving again at 3 AM in the direction of the towns of Tembo or Kahemba with the aim of contacting families to arrange return to their place of origin by vehicle (ibid.).

While the human rights picture was still imperfect, and body cavity searches were still practised on a large scale, a number of positive changes can be identified in comparison to the earlier waves. This time, deportations were more organized, with the Angolan army rather than the police (which had played a part in the earlier waves and been complicit in some of the atrocities) carrying out all of the deportation process. There were reduced levels of sexual violence and rape. Although there were still isolated cases, these had become the exception rather than the rule: 'Rapes were not practised in a systematic fashion or on a large scale. Reported cases of sexual violence were isolated' (MSF-B 2008b). Unlike the earlier waves, some food and water was provided in detention. Women were less often subjected to the long walk to the border (MSF-B 2008c). This changing pattern of deportation meant that within Bandundu, the main needs of the returning population were in food assistance, rather than in the treatment of women suffering the consequences of sexual violence (MSF-B 2007c).

The picture within Western Kasai was similar to that in Bandundu. Between 5 and 10 July, OCHA led a UN inter-agency mission to the territory of Luiza to evaluate the deportations. Its report describes how people were arriving in waves of 100 to 150, in 'a deplorable humanitarian state, deprived of their possessions'.[4] Fewer than 50 per cent had access to drinkable water, they had lost all of their belongings, and had serious health needs. It further describes how 90 per cent of the women had been forced to undergo anal and vaginal searches for diamonds. However, despite highlighting these significant protection needs, resulting from obvious human rights violations, the inter-agency mission concurred with the MSF mission's assessment about the reduction in levels of sexual violence, reporting that only one of the twenty-four women interviewed had been raped in Angola. The UN report concluded that there were two basic interventions required: a strategic plan for inter-agency division of responsibility to address immediate needs along the border, and an OCHA appeal to the Congolese government to contact the Angolan government and ask for human rights and humanitarian law violations to cease (UN 2008). By the start of July, around 120,000 Congolese had been deported ruthlessly and efficiently by the Angolan army – but at least some of the worst excesses of the previous waves had been curbed.

Wave 4: The Bas-Congo Episode

The main waves of deportation in 2009 focused on a different part of the country, in what became referred to as 'Operation Crisis'. Between August and October, the GoA expelled around 18,800 Congolese from the far north-west of the country, with the overwhelming majority being deported from the isolated Cabinda Province to the immediate west of the DRC. Aside from the different geographical setting, two other significant differences stand out. First, the expelled population was different from the earlier waves. They were not recently arrived garimpeiros; there are no diamond mines in Cabinda. Rather they were professionals, artisans or traders who had been on Angolan territory for a long time. Second, even though the scale and seriousness of the human rights violations was arguably less serious, the episode received far greater international attention than the previous waves. The political response from the government of the DRC, and from international organizations on both sides of the border, was far greater than in 2004, 2007 or 2008. The episode, although different from the other cases, therefore serves to shed light on the relative neglect in the earlier more serious rights violations, in contrast to the wider engagement and political mobilization of 2009.

The province of Cabinda is separated from the rest of Angola by Congolese territory. Yet, it is territorially and economically important to the GoA because of its natural resources. However, the GoA has been concerned about the activity of the separatist group, Front for the Liberation of the Enclave of Cabinda (FLEC), which has become increasingly active, and in which a number of Congolese have been implicated. With growing concern about Congolese connections to FLEC, an increasing climate of xenophobia in Cabinda, and preparation for Angolan presidential elections on the horizon, the GoA began to expel the Congolese population from Cabinda (Interview with Mohamed Toure, assistant regional representative, UNHCR, Kinshasa, 11 November 2009). The Angolan army and police within Cabinda rounded-up single men, women and families, and ordered them to leave the territory, forcing them across the border into the Bas-Congo Province of the DRC. An OCHA-led inter-agency mission to Muanda and Tshela between 8 and 12 October revealed that while many of the deported migrants had quickly dispersed to their home communities, many had needed support. Churches, schools and host families offered shelter, while food, water and shelter were provided by an inter-agency response that worked mainly through Caritas and the Red Cross (OCHA 2009).

In contrast to the earlier waves, in which the government of the DRC had remained largely passive, Kinshasa this time responded strongly to the deportations. For the first time, it launched 'reciprocal' expulsions, engaging in the tit-for-tat deportation of Angolan refugees who had been residing in Bas-Congo since the Angolan civil war. Emboldened by the bilateral rapprochement between the DRC and Rwanda, Joseph Kabila felt able for the first time to respond in robust and unequivocal terms to Angola (Interview with Ebba Kalondo, deputy head, F24/RFI Africa Service, Kinshasa, 9 November 2009). The order to expel the Angolan refugees came right from the top, with the signature of the minister of the interior appearing on the expulsion order.[5] From September, some 39,000 Angolans were therefore expelled. The DGM, together with Congolese military and police, visited the most easily identifiable refugee settlements, giving refugees 24 hours' notice to leave the country, after which they would be driven back to the border in groups of thirty to fifty. On the other side of the border, the GoA's Ministry of Social Integration (MINARS) announced the arrival of the 39,000 expelled Angolans in Cabinda (2,000), Uige (7,800) and Zaire (28,000) provinces, where the Red Cross set up reception and transit facilities to provide basics such as shelter, clothing, water, health care, and sanitation (IFRC 2009).

Although there were no major human rights abuses in transit, the Angolan government condemned the response as 'disproportionate', and the diplomatic tussle led to the suspension of flights between Luanda and Kinshasa. Eventually, following bilateral talks, a moratorium on the tit-for-tat expulsions was agreed by the two countries in October 2009. While the rights violations involved – including arbitrary detention and the refoulement of refugees – cannot in any way be condoned, what is interesting about the case is the degree of attention it received in contrast to the earlier neglect of the much larger-scale and systematic violations of human rights during the earlier waves. This time, the DRC condemned the GoA's actions in ways that brought an end to deportation, UNHCR became involved on a diplomatic and practical level because the DRC's response implicated 'refugees' in the deportations (Interview with Toure), and, in contrast to 2004, 2007 and 2008, there was relatively widespread media coverage, perhaps reflecting the greater proximity to Kinshasa.

From Waves to Chronic Crisis

The expulsions did not end after 2009. However, their character changed. Rather than being based on a succession of waves connected to elections or political events within Angola, the expulsions became a more constant trickle of people back into the DRC. They became, in the words of one NGO worker returning from a mission in the region, 'every day and every day at a different door' (Interview with Aurelie Ponthieu, humanitarian adviser on displacement, MSF-Belgium, Brussels, 12 July 2012), reflecting the creation of a more systemic apparatus of immigration control within Angola.[6] By 2011 a more coherent monitoring system had been set up by the United Nations and implemented mainly through an Italian NGO called Comitato Internazionale Per lo Sviluppo dei Popoli (CISP), allowing data to be better recorded on the patterns of forced return and the experiences of those expelled. People were documented at the numerous borders posts of Western Kasai, Bandundu and Bas-Congo. However, the overwhelming majority of deportees, and especially those who were victims of violence, were in Western Kasai, and particularly the Kamako zone of Tshikapa.[7] In 2011, 55,590 deportees were registered by CISP in the three provinces, of whom 3,770 were victims of sexual violence by the Angolan authorities. Between January and May 2012, the number expelled was 13,000.[8] The patterns of expulsion, although more systematic and marginally less brutal than earlier episodes, remained consistently appalling. The Congolese would be arrested in Angola by men in uniform – described by victims as 'soldiers' in villages and at mines and markets. The many women remaining were subjected to violence and rape – although the patterns appear to have been less systematic than earlier – and taken to police stations or makeshift detention centres. One of the main detention facilities identified was a former prison near Dundu, and there have been strong and consistent rumours of people being held in a 'hole in the ground' near Dundu, where detention lasted an average of three days to a week. Conditions of detention have continued to be characterized by the absence of food and medical care, and by sexual abuse, poor sanitation, and a lack of separate facilities for women and children. One woman, aged 19, a mother of two, and expelled twice, explained her experience:

> This prison is near Dundu and is called Cundueji. It's a big hole in the ground where the Angolans put the Congolese. Everyone is mixed there, women, men, children ... We had to do our business altogether there on the ground. They gave us a handful of rice in the mornings and nothing more.

> There were no medicines and many people fell ill. People died. I saw three bodies. The Angolans threw them in the river. I stayed two weeks in this place and I was raped by six soldiers during my detention. (MSF-B 2012)

Following detention, deportees have been brought to the border in trucks and handed over to the Congolese border authorities. Compared to the start of the waves, levels of international organization and NGO presence at the border have increased. With money from UN-pooled funding, a short-term system of monitoring and assistance was implemented from 2011. However, despite greater monitoring, an exploratory mission by MSF-Belgium in May 2012 highlighted the absence of adequate medical care or assistance, with people dying at the border. It documented cases of torture, inhumane and degrading treatment – machete and bullet wounds, boiling water, bayonette injuries – and sexual and gender-based violence (SGBV), highlighting the ongoing inadequacy of response to these medical needs. Between January and May 2012 alone, the Red Cross buried ten people who had died as a result of the untreated effects suffered during deportation (Interview with Ponthieu).

Gender and the International Response

The patterns of violence used in the deportations are highly gendered. The violence perpetrated by the Angolan state was very different for men and women. Three broad types of violence can be identified: first, direct physical violence of a non-sexual nature (e.g. beatings); second, direct physical violence of a sexual nature (e.g. rape, sexual assault); and third, indirect physical violence (e.g. detention and food deprivation). Although men were subjected to beatings, mutilation and extra-judicial killing, sexual violence was almost exclusively used against women.

The patterns of violence perpetrated against women varied over time. One of the most significant features of the Angolan case was the use of rape as an instrument of deportation. At times, the patterns of rape and sexual violence imply its systematic use by the government. During the 2007–08 deportations, the scale of rape by state agents makes it almost unimaginable that it took place without the knowledge of senior officers within the military and the police. Reflecting this, it was also on the rare occasions when the GoA was overtly criticized by international NGOs and the media that patterns of violence changed such that, while still violent, the number of documented rapes declined.

In addition to the patterns of violence, the international community's response to the violence can also be read in gendered terms. Overall, the response was extremely limited. On the Angolan side, there was little engagement by human rights or humanitarian actors, due in part to lack of access to the relevant provinces of Angola, and also to very little diplomatic engagement by states and the UN country team to facilitate greater access to the Lundas by human rights and humanitarian actors. On the DRC side of the border, a humanitarian response to address the protection needs of expelled migrants was stymied by the affected group falling between the mandates and designated priorities of different humanitarian agencies.

Indeed, throughout the main waves of deportations, OCHA was criticized for its limited engagement (Interviews with a number of NGO and international organization staff). In interviews, OCHA staff provided a range of justifications for their limited involvement, but three in particular were repeatedly provided. First, events needed to be seen in African terms: 'You have to see it in African terms ... We haven't publicized it at the level that we are publicizing the situation in the Kivus. There are 20–30,000 rape cases reported in the DRC yearly ... You cannot expect the same degree of response as elsewhere in Africa. In the East, there are 500 rapes a week'. Secondly, many of the deported people are undeserving of assistance: one said 'They are economic migrants without the right papers. Even though OCHA does not talk publicly about it, many of the migrants were prostitutes'. Thirdly, European states are also abusive of irregular migrants: 'Is it that different from migration practices in Europe?' Consequently, 'the decision was made by humanitarians in general that this was not such a big thing' (Interviews with three members of OCHA staff in Kinshasa, November 2009).

Across the UN system, different actors mainly engaged with the four main waves of deportations through their participation with the humanitarian 'cluster' approach, participating in inter-agency missions to the border areas. However, across the UN system most agencies found ways to limit their commitment to an area that fell between the stools of different mandates. UNHCR repeatedly argued that it had limited responsibility in relation to the expelled Congolese in Bandundu and Western Kasai, highlighting that the area was 'outside the mandate', given that the deportees were (1) not refugees, (2) in their country of origin, and (3) the responsibility of the government of the DRC. However, in contrast, it did become actively involved during the Bas-Congo episode. The fact that Angolan refugees were expelled invoked its refugee protection mandate. Consequently, even though UNHCR acknowledged that it was preparing for repatriation of the Angolan refugees anyway, and that, in contrast to the other earlier episodes, there was no systematic violence perpetrated against the Angolan refugees, UNHCR became actively engaged on both sides of the border. Other UN agencies such as UNICEF and FAO played roles in contributing to basic sanitation, water needs, and equipment, mainly through local

NGO partners. Meanwhile, the International Organization for Migration (IOM) did not play a role, primarily because – despite expressing interest in becoming involved – it was not given funding by states to develop a project relating to the deportations. Its 'projectized' organizational structure meant that without specific earmarked funding from its core donors, it could not play a role.

In the absence of significant UN engagement, the response during the four main waves came from what might be referred to as 'networked protection actors': the ICRC working through the national Red Cross, Caritas working through its church network, and MSF responding to information from its network of doctors and local medical practices. These kinds of networked actors were especially important in a country like the DRC where it is difficult to get access or information relating to events in remote areas. The antenna structures of these networks allowed information and alerts, and rapid response. In this context, MSF was the most engaged international actor across the waves of deportation to Bandundu and Western Kasai. Despite its predominantly medical mandate, it found itself filling a significant part of the gap vacated by the international community. It chose to do so, largely on the basis of having a medical intervention but then recognizing that its presence, and what it witnessed, led it to have a wider moral responsibility to provide protection and assistance, and also to document what it observed. Its relative flexibility as an organization gave it organizational adaptability, in a way that was not possible for many of the other UN actors within the DRC.

It was only in 2011 that a slightly more coherent international response began to emerge, some seven years after the initial waves. This shift was triggered by Margot Wallstrom, the UN Special Rapporteur on Sexual Violence in Conflict, visiting the DRC and Angola in February and March 2011. Her visit to the region and subsequent comments led to a number of immediate outcomes. The UN and the GoA made a joint communication, committing to prevent or else punish sexual violence, and the GoA committed to facilitate UN-IOM monitoring of detentions and expulsions. A working group was also established in Kinshasa in order to better coordinate the activities of the UN system in responding to the issue. Perhaps most significantly though, a pot of US\$2.7 m from the UN pooled fund was disbursed to improve monitoring and assistance for those expelled (Interview Ponthieu).

The pooled funding was divided between the Italian NGO CISP, Caritas, WHO, and UNFPA to achieve a set of short-term objectives: WHO temporarily provided drugs to local clinics in the relevant provinces; UNFPA provided training to local medical services and NGOs until December 2011; and Caritas provided coordination of local church-based NGOs. Meanwhile, CISP used its US\$0.5 m share of the funding to establish assistance and monitoring at the border posts, through a number of local implementing partners, in a project initially funded to run between March 2011 and August 2012 (Interview Ponthieu). However, even this post-2011 response has been too inadequate to fully address either the underlying causes on the Angolan side or the humanitarian needs on the Congolese side. It has placed too much emphasis on recording numbers rather than providing assistance, its funding has been short-term, and it has continued to rely on local implementing partners with limited capacity (MSF-B 2012). Meanwhile, the main UN humanitarian organizations have continued to remain largely on the sidelines, with the exception of the working group set up in Kinshasa in 2011 and coordinated by OCHA (ibid.).

Overall, the international response can be considered as gendered in at least two ways. First, the absence of a response can be interpreted as the non-prioritization of issues relating to human rights and gender in contrast to Angola's position as a sovereign state and an important trade partner of Europe and the United States. Second, the nature of the response – in focusing on witness statements, health-related interventions, and limited humanitarian relief on the DRC side of the border – is inherently gendered. It reveals a pattern of intervention that contrasts within direct engagement with the underlying causes of the violence. It seeks to frame the crisis in purely humanitarian terms rather than as a fundamental human rights issue. In this sense, it reflects a highly gendered framing of the human consequences of the deportations as an accidental 'humanitarian' outcome rather than seeking to confront its underlying structural causes (Enloe 1992; Tickner 1993; Shepherd 2008).

Conclusion

Deportation has emerged as an important area of enquiry within forced migration studies. However, it has rarely been examined from a gender perspective. This chapter has provided a starting point for considering the relationship between gender, violence and deportation. Rather than examining the case of deportation by the liberal state, which remains the main focus of the deportation literature, the chapter has explored deportation by an archetypal illiberal state, Angola (Pearce 2005; de Oliviera 2011; Jones, de Oliviera and Verhoeven 2013). In that sense it represents an extreme case, but it is one that reveals aspects of both the gendered nature of deportation practices and of the international community's response to extreme forms of gendered violence relating to immigration control practices.

At its most superficial level, the case highlights the effects of deportation practices on women. It reveals a state that has engaged in the use of rape and sexual violence as a technique of immigration control. While some of the violence may have been opportunistic, the scale and patterns of sexual violence suggest a strategy, awareness by senior officials in the military and police, and the knowledge of the government. This is reflected in the ways in which the patterns of sexual violence fluctuated over time, depending on levels of international criticism.

Beyond that, the case also contributes to an interpretation of the inherently gendered nature of the relationship between violence and deportation. It highlights structures within the international system that enabled these patterns of sexual violence to occur, to be globally recognized, and yet to be largely ignored. Even when the response reached its peak, interventions were largely relegated to health-related 'humanitarian' relief along the DRC border. International organizations' staff justified their non-involvement by relativizing the numbers of rapes compared to other parts of the world, and openly engaged in judgement about the worthiness of 'prostitutes' as victims. States that import oil and diamonds from Angola prioritized these trade relations far beyond recognizing Angola's systematic use of rape as a human rights issue.

While the case is therefore an extreme example, it opens up avenues for future research. It highlights that deportation, as an example of immigration control practices more broadly, has gendered effects. While Angola may be an illiberal state, deportation practices are widely regarded as legitimate practice even within liberal states. This opens up the question of whether 'our' deportation practices entail gendered forms of violence, as well as whether a structural relationship exists between liberal state legitimation of deportation practices and the international tolerance towards those that emerged in Angola.

Alexander Betts is professor of Forced Migration and International Affairs, and director of the Refugee Studies Centre at the University of Oxford. His research focuses on the economics and politics of refugees. His books include *Survival Migration: Failed Governance and the Crisis of Displacement* (Cornell University Press, 2013), *Mobilising the Diaspora: How Refugees Challenge Authoritarianism* (Cambridge University Press, 2016), and *Refugee Economies: Forced Displacement and Development* (Oxford University Press, 2016). He has previously worked for UNHCR and as a consultant to a range of governments and international organizations, including UNICEF, OCHA and UNDP. He has written for the *New York Times*, the *Guardian*, and *Foreign Affairs*, and appears regularly on CNN, the BBC, and Al Jazeera. He is the founder of the Humanitarian Innovation Project, a TED speaker, and has been honoured as a World Economic Forum Young Global Leader. He was included in *Foreign Policy* magazine's list of top 100 global thinkers of 2016.

Notes

1. Production nearly doubled, from 5 million carats in 2002 to close to 9.5 million carats in 2006. Gross revenue from diamond sales has effectively doubled, from $638 m (US) in 2002 to $1.2 bn in 2006, while government income has more than tripled, from $45 m to $165 m over that same five-year period (Betts 2013: 110).
2. Copy of editorial piece on file with author.
3. Document on file with the author.
4. Inter-agency mission report, on file with the author.
5. On file with the author.
6. The GoA introduced new administrative and legislative reforms in 2011 to strengthen its control over immigration: (1) Presidential Decree No. 108/11 of 25 May on the Legal Framework Relating to Foreigners; and (2) Law No. 2/07 of 31 August on the Legal Framework Relating to Foreigners on the Territory of Angola.
7. The majority of the victims of violence have been returned to Western Kasai, of which two-third are in the Kamako zone of Tshikapa, most arriving at Kandjaji and Kamako (Interview with Ponthieu).
8. CISP database, as at 8 May 2012, on file with the author.

Bibliography

AIMC (Africa Inland Mission Canada) and Butoke. 2008. 'Narrative Project Report: Food Security and Nutrition Project in Western Kasai, March 2007 – February 2008'. Retrieved 26 August 2015 from http://www.butoke.org/AIM_Final_Report.pdf.

Anderson, B., M. Gibney and E. Paoletti (eds). 2012. *The Social, Political and Historical Contours of Deportation*. London: Springer.

'Angolan Troops Reportedly Kill Congo Miners – U.N.' 2004. *Reuters*, 22 April. Retrieved 26 August 2015 from http://reliefweb.int/report/angola/angolan-troops-reportedly-kill-congo-miners-un.

ACL (Association des Congolais de Lunda). 2004. 'Rapport Adresse aux Médecins Sans Frontières a Kahungula/RDC Pour Dénoncer les Traitements Inhumains et Dégradant Subis Par les Congolais Durant Leur Séjour en Angola et Pendant Leur Refoulement'.

Betts, A. 2013. *Survival Migration: Failed Governance and the Crisis of Displacement*. Ithaca, NY: Cornell University Press.

Butoke 2009. 'Butoke Update: April 30, 2009'. Retrieved 26 August 2015 from http://www.butoke.org/Update_2009-04-30.htm.

'Congo Miners "Tortured" in Angola'. 2004. *BBC News*, 22 April. Retrieved 26 August 2015 from http://news.bbc.co.uk/1/hi/3650655.stm.

Crawley, H. 2001. *Refugees and Gender: Law and Process*. Bristol: Jordan Publishing.

de Boeck, F. 2001. 'Garimperio Worlds: Digging, Dying and "Hunting" for Diamonds in Angola', *Review of African Political Economy* 28(90): 548–62.

de Geneva, N., and N. Peutz. 2010. *The Deportation Regime: Sovereignty, Space, and the Freedom of Movement.* Durham, NC: Duke University Press.

de Oliveira, R.S. 2011. 'Illiberal Peacebuilding in Angola', *Journal of Modern African Studies* 49(2): 287–314.

Ellermann, A. 2008. 'The Limits of Unilateral Migration Control: Deportation and Interstate Cooperation', *Government and Opposition* 43(2): 168–89.

Enloe, C. 1992. *Bananas, Beaches, and Bases: Making Feminist Sense of International Politics.* London: University of California Press.

Fiddian-Qasmiyeh, E. 2010. '"Ideal" Refugee Women and Gender Equality Mainstreaming: "Good Practice" for Whom?', *Refugee Survey Quarterly* 29(2): 64–84.

_____. 2014a. *The Ideal Refugees: Gender, Islam, and the Sahrawi Politics of Survival.* Syracuse, NY: Syracuse University Press.

_____. 2014b. 'Gender and Forced Migration', in E. Fiddian-Qasmiyeh et al. (eds), *The Oxford Handbook of Refugee and Forced Migration Studies.* Oxford: Oxford University Press, pp. 395–408.

Gibney, M. 2008. 'Asylum and the Expansion of Deportation in the United Kingdom', *Government and Opposition* 43(2): 146–67.

_____. 2013. 'Is Deportation a Form of Forced Migration?', *Refugee Survey Quarterly* 32(2): 116–29.

IFRC (International Federation for the Red Cross and Red Crescent Societies). 2009. 'Angola: Population Movement'. Geneva.

Jones, W., R.S. de Oliviera and H. Verhoeven. 2013. 'Africa's Illiberal State-Builders', *RSC Working Paper* No. 89.

Marquez, R. 2005. 'Lundas – The Stones of Death: Angola's Deadly Diamonds. Human Rights Abuses in the Lunda Provinces, 2004'. Retrieved from http://www.cabinda.net/ADDMarq.pdf.

MSF-B (Médecins Sans Frontières – Belgium). 2004a. 'Angola: MSF-Belgium Monthly Situation Report'. Brussels.

_____. 2004b. 'Refoulés d'Angola: Resume des Datas a Ce Jour'. Internal document. Brussels.

_____. 2004c. 'Response by MSF to editorial 30/4 comment'. Brussels.

_____. 2007a. 'Angola: Systematic Rapes and Violence against Expelled Congolese Migrants. The Women Testify'. Brussels.

_____. 2007b. 'PUC Memo, W.Kasai to Antenne Kinshasa'. Brussels.

_____. 2008a. 'RDC-Kasai Occidental: Violences Sexuelles a l'Egard des Femmes Congolaises Refoulées de l'Angola'. Brussels.

_____. 2008b. 'Refoulés Congolais: Informations Récoltée Par Le Pool D'Urgence Congo de MSF – Mission d'Evaluation et Prise en Charge des Refoulés entre le 02 et le 06 Juin 2008'. Brussels.

_____. 2008c. 'PUC: Draft Mission Explo Refoulés d'Angola a Kahungula'. Brussels.

_____. 2012. 'Rapport de Visite – Support AAU a la Mission Exploratoire Frontière RDC/Angola'. Internal document. Brussels.

OCHA (UN Office for the Coordination of Humanitarian Affairs). 2004. 'Luis Raya, OCHA Mexico to Paola Carosi, OCHA Angola 'Missao de Accompanhemento de 'Operacao Brilhante', nas provincias de Lunda Sul e Lunda Norte, 18/5/04'.

——. 2007. 'Rapport de la Mission d'Évaluation des Besoins Humanitaires des Refoulés de l'Angola a Luiza et Kamako en Province du Kasai Occidental'. Geneva.

——. 2009. 'Angola-DRC Expulsions: Regional Situation Report No. 1'. Geneva.

OHCHR (UN Office of the High Commissioner for Human Rights). 2007. 'Speech Delivered by the Head of the OHCHR Office in Angola, on 59th Anniversary of the UDHR'. Luanda.

Pearce, J. 2005. *An Outbreak of Peace: Angola's Situation of Confusion*. London: David Philip.

Pittaway, E., and L. Bartolomei. 1991. 'Refugees, Race and Gender: The Multiple Discrimination against Refugee Women', *Refuge* 19(6): 21–32.

Schuster, L., and A. Bloch. 2005. 'At the Extremes of Exclusion: Deportation, Detention and Dispersal', *Ethnic and Racial Studies* 28(3): 491–512.

Shepherd, L. 2008. *Gender, Violence, and Security*. Aldershot: Zed Books.

Tickner, J.A. 1993. *Gender in International Relations*. New York: Columbia University Press.

United Nations. 2007. 'Rapport de la Mission Inter-Agences d'Evaluation des Besoins Humanitaires des Populations des 2ZS du Territotoire de Kahemba'. Geneva.

——. 2008. 'Draft Rapport de Mission Inter-Agences d'Evaluation de la Situation des Congolais Expuses d'Angola dans le Territoire de Luiza Province du Kasai Occidental, 5–10 Juillet 2008'. Geneva.

Vigneswaren, D., and R. Sutton. 2011. 'A Kafkaesque State: Deportation and Detention in South Africa', *Citizenship Studies* 15(5): 627–42.

12

The Romance of Return
Post-exile Lives and Interpersonal Violence over Land in Burundi

Barbra Lukunka

Introduction

Refugee camps are created to provide safe havens and spaces away from violence. They are spaces that allow individuals to escape from the carnage and brutality of war. Many refugee camps have been home to multiple generations of refugees and are the only home some individuals know. This notwithstanding, camps can be sites where a significant amount of violence is perpetrated (Hyndman 2004: 193). Because refugee experiences are liminal, they are by definition unstable and prone to challenges, rendering refugee camps places where different acts of violence are easily committed. Even though refugees flee from violence and are settled in camps for safety, in many cases, rebels and other combatants follow and perpetrate violence against them. Camps are moreover frequently exploited as recruiting grounds to conscript zealous rebel fighters, child soldiers and the like. They are humanitarian-cared spaces that are often highly political and prone to manipulation. Refugee camps are also environments in which the occurrence of sexual and gender-based violence (SGBV) is often high. Escaping the prevalence of violence in camps is therefore inevitably a priority for many refugees.

Against this backdrop, in many cases refugees who repatriate to their countries of origin do so with zeal. Indeed, there are many refugees who, despite being informed that stability has returned in their home country, prefer to remain in refugee camps, or to be resettled to a third country. There are many, however, who look forward to reaching their homeland and to escaping the unsafe haven that is the refugee camps, to an extent that they even express a romanticized vision of their return while still in camp. But return does not always prove to be so pleasant, and the romance may quickly fade, as there appears to be a continuity of violence even after individuals return to their communities.[1]

Returnees can face violence for a number of reasons. Some are accused of having committed violent acts during the conflict and thus have to face revenge, while others return to unstable environments where post-conflict violence is rampant and weapons are numerous, exacerbating insecurity. Others return to find that their property and land has been occupied by those who did not flee, launching them into property and land disputes. The latter is the subject of this chapter, in which I discuss the violence faced – as well as perpetrated by – former Burundian refugees who return home and have their dreams of land ownership dashed.

The chapter advances a gendered perspective. One of the most prevalent forms of violence perpetrated among refugee populations is gender-based violence. Research on violence within refugee communities, particularly conducted by international organizations, has often portrayed a binary conception of women as victims and men as perpetrators. This chapter aims to move away from an approach that essentializes women by looking at the situation of both women and men after exile and during their reintegration in Burundi, highlighting the differences of their experiences. Upon return to Burundi, both women and men found themselves embroiled in battles over land. Women, however, were disadvantaged because Burundian law does not entitle them to inheritance of land, rather the patriarchal structure of the society rules that women are either dependants of their family or of their husbands. Land is therefore reserved for male family members. Many returnee women, in particular, were often starting from a disadvantaged point because they returned as widows and therefore could not rely on their husbands to have access to land. Many did not even know where their communities of origin were located, either because they had been in exile for so long that they have forgotten or because they were born in exile and had never set foot on their ancestral land. And yet, this structural, gender-based inequality did not prevent women from attempting to find ways to occupy land.

The chapter is based on anthropological field research conducted in Burundi from 2009 to 2011, in particular in four of Burundi's seven provinces, namely Bujumbura Rural, Bubanza, Makamba and Ruyigi. I interviewed returnees, individuals who had not fled, government officials and aid workers – in total, 163 research participants. A large part of the analysis in this chapter draws on the experiences of poor, rural return-ees who tended to have either spent over thirty years in exile because they fled in 1972, or between fifteen and twenty years because they fled in 1993. Some of the returnees lived in villages created by the government for people who could not remember, or did not know, where they were from. Other returnees lived in their communities of origin among family members and neighbours whom they had left behind prior to conflict. The vast majority of participants had limited education, with only very few having completed high school. Many worked the land to sustain their live-lihoods. Those who did not own land found ways to work the land either as labourers for landowners or by renting land with other individuals and sharing the harvest. Land was equally significant for women as for men. Women tended to be heads of households in many cases and therefore their reliance on land was also critical.

Refugee Return and Land Conflict

Between 2002 and 2011, over half a million Burundian refugees returned to their country of origin (UNHCR 2012), the vast majority being Hutu. For many, their return was not as romantic as they had hoped. The land conflict they faced was representative of the difficulties many refugee pop-ulations face after return. In Burundi, land conflict is ubiquitous; it affects all Burundians young and old, women and men, those who have never fled and those who are returning from refuge. Not all land disputes in this period were interpersonal in nature, and not all were violent. Some land conflicts were between families and communities, some were against the government, and many were resolved amicably. But even though land conflict was not uniquely a returnee problem, it was much more prolific in the returnee community. They were at the centre of the land conflict phenomenon because their re-entering the country subsequently required their (re-)instalment into the social, political and economic spheres, as well as into the physical space of the country. Return was therefore interlinked to the physical placement of individuals, which in essence conjured the land occupation and ownership battles.

In order to explain and understand the prevalence of violence over land affecting returnees, this chapter offers a close look at historical patterns of violence, the destabilizing nature of exile and return, and the pressures of economic survival, as well as structural issues such as inequality. I discuss the factors observed during this research that drove both men and women to engage in interpersonal violence over land, with a particular focus on the intersectionality of gender, class and ethnicity in addition to the returnee status that positioned returnee women at an additional socio-economic disadvantage upon return. I argue that, first, Burundi's long history of violence informed the way individuals interacted with each other. War and its consequences, particularly acts intended to break the link between peoples, such as forced displacement, had exacerbated social inequality and legitimized the need to fight for one's cause, position or property. Social norms that had prevented conflict prior to war had broken down and remained fragile, needing rebuilding in the post-conflict moment. Second, Burundi was overpopulated, which had and continues to have a profound impact on land conflicts, exacerbated by the en masse return of former refugees. Third, land had and continues to have significant economic value and also represents belonging, two factors that individuals are willing to fight for, especially returnees who have spent decades in exile longing to return home and to belong once again to their ancestral land. And fourth, social inequality, with the so-called rich hoarding a large proportion of the resources, had an effect, leading the poor to fight amongst themselves for the little they had, even if it meant fighting a member of one's own family.

These underlying factors that amplified land conflict in Burundi had a profound impact on former refugees, and particularly returnee women. Former refugees returned to Burundi to find that the land that they had owned prior to displacement was now occupied by others. Many, particularly those born in exile, could not even identify where their community of origin was located, let alone their land and property. Moreover, many returnees were poor and in dire need of assistance. Finally, through a gendered perspective, I discuss the differences in experiences between men and women, the impact of male dominance in the society, and how, in some ways, women's actions in their troubles have contributed to changes in gender dynamics.

Challenging Return Context in Burundi

In order to fully grasp the difficulties that former refugees faced when they returned to Burundi, one must delve into the social, economic and political context of the country. Burundi is in the Great Lakes Region and borders Rwanda to the north, Tanzania to the east, and the Democratic Republic of Congo (as well as Lake Tanganyika) to the west. It has a small surface area of 29,950 square kilometres, with a population of 8 million (Republic of Burundi 2012). It is home to three ethnic groups: the Hutu who are the majority, the Tutsi a minority, and the Twa who account for only 1 per cent of the population; 90 per cent of the total population live in rural areas (ibid.). Agriculture and livestock are a major source of income for the poor and there is a strong reliance on land in the country, especially among the poor (ibid.). While I was conducting research, Burundi socio-economically had very little to offer to its returning countrymen and women. It already had a large poor population that relied on land, fostering competition over this scarce resource and presenting additional pressures.

Initially, the country was welcoming and preparing for a large number of people. This was a national endeavour[2] that was not only the concern of the government but one that all citizens had to contend with. For returnees, it was a new beginning, yet they faced significant adjustments as they returned to a homeland from which they had been absent for many decades. Many had to learn/relearn their customs, their language and other cultural markers, as well as find ways to survive in this 'new' environment.

Violence, Gender and Life after Return

A central concern of this study is to understand violence in refugee communities and violence after refugees return, especially as it relates to land conflict. While conducting field research in Burundi, I noticed that violence was not only considered an inevitable aspect of the post-conflict moment but that understanding violence in refugee/returnee communities requires a look at the country's violent past, and at the circumstance in refuge as well as after return.

Many studies on violence among refugee populations focus on gender-based violence, particularly the rape of women and young girls. Women are at risk both inside refugee camps and when they go to their outskirts in order to collect firewood (Hyndman 2004; Martin 2004). As Ferris (2007) shows, the breakdown of social norms resulting from war often leads to domestic and community violence. Moreover, a high prevalence of domestic violence abounds (Carlson 2005; Horn 2010; Lukunka 2012). A considerable aspect is that gender roles often change in refugee camps, and men have to cope with their loss of breadwinner status (Turner 1999; Ferris 2007; Lukunka 2012). Refugees living in camps often lead irregular lives that are governed by NGOs, aid organizations and the host government. In protracted situations, refugees live for decades in these settings where they are unable to sustain their livelihoods without external assistance. This has a profound impact on the socio-psychological well-being of refugees to the extent that it fuels domestic violence. Men may feel emasculated in these situations and exert their masculinity through the use of violence against their wives, especially when their wives accuse them of not being good providers of the family (Lukunka 2012). The majority of violence is perpetrated by men against women; however, in some cases we find circumstances in which women are perpetrators and/or supporters of violence. Nevertheless, much of the literature portrays a binary of men as perpetrators of violence and women as victims. As noted by Hyndman (2004), a focus on women as victims of violence presents the risk of essentializing women and putting their gendered difference over differences such as ethnicity, clan or caste.

Refugee and returnee communities as groups of individuals who witnessed, fled, experienced and sometimes perpetrated violence are significantly shaped by the occurrence of violence. In this context, Ember and Ember's (1994) study examines the link between war and postwar violence, and concludes that war legitimizes violence because people witness violent acts, and this in turn increases the number of violent acts, including homicides, after war. This approach risks ignoring structural patterns that pre-exist war, and that account for deep-seated resentment and increased violence in the post-conflict moment. A war may thus exacerbate underlying antagonisms within a society, and prevail in the post-conflict period. Therefore, war itself should not be perceived as the sole driver of post-conflict violence; rather, it is often the catalyst for violent expression of already established structural problems.

A History of Violence and the Destruction of Social Norms

The land conflict affecting former refugees is informed by a history of violence that continues to live on within the memories of Burundians, influencing their social relationships. Historically, conflict in Burundi is linked to ethnic animosity between the majority Hutu and the minority Tutsi populations; the origins of ethnic stratification between the Tutsi, the Hutu and the Twa[3] predate colonialism, although they became even more conspicuous with the advent of colonialism. Colonialism deepened ethnic differences and created exclusion and grievances that led to decades of conflict. Burundians clung onto their ethnic identities and used them as tools around which to mobilize. This notwithstanding, there were a significant number of inter-marriages between ethnic groups, thereby creating an in-between group.

During the 1885 Berlin Conference, Burundi and Rwanda were designated as German territories. When Germany began losing the First World War, its colonies were put under the control of the League of Nations who gave the Belgians the mandate to govern Burundi and Rwanda from 1916. The area ended up being administered as Rwanda-Urundi until independence in 1962. Colonial rule re-enforced ethnic cleavages by putting the Tutsi in power and eliminating the Hutus' role in the administration, because they believed the Tutsis were born to be leaders and that the Hutus were born to be followers (Malkki 1995: 27).

Following independence, the Hutu challenged the supremacy of the Tutsi, resulting in Hutu uprisings in 1965, 1968 and 1969 in which thousands of Hutus were killed (Malkki 1995: 31). In 1972, the Hutus staged another uprising with the assistance of Congolese rebels, which led to systematic killings of educated Hutu (Uvin 2009: 10), and a total death toll of an estimated 250,000 (Malkki 1995: 33). Moreover, 150,000 refugees fled to neighbouring countries (Lemarchand 1996: 104) such as Tanzania, Rwanda and the Democratic Republic of Congo (then Zaire).

In 1988, the Hutus staged another uprising in which hundreds of Tutsis were killed (Uvin 2009: 11); it is estimated that the number of fatalities amounted to twenty thousand (Daley 2007: 334). This crisis, as well as the following one in 1991, led to the displacement of thousands into neighbouring countries (Lemarchand 1996: 172). Then, in 1993, Melchior Ndadaye, a Hutu, won the first democratic elections but was assassinated after only one hundred days in office, leading to attacks against Tutsi and an ensuing violent conflict causing the deaths of about two hundred thousand Burundians (Daley 2007: 334). In total, Burundi lost an estimated half million lives to civil war. Peace was brokered by the international community in 2000, which first created a transitional government and then opened the path to democratic elections and a lasting peace.

The ethnic animosity and political struggles had a profound impact on the day-to-day interactions between the Hutus and the Tutsis, including a strong gender component. On the one hand, Hutu women were rendered invisible and excluded from the social life of the country, and on the other, there was a strong hatred towards Tutsi women in particular by the Hutu. One Burundian refugee woman in Kanembwa refugee camp in Kibondo Tanzania noted:

> I am a Hutu. My father was killed by Tutsi in 1980. He was not in any political group. The man that killed my father is also dead. Life for us in Burundi was not very normal. People threatened to hurt me all the time because there were more Tutsi than Hutu in my community. It was rare to see Hutu women married to Tutsi men, and there were more Hutu men that married Tutsi women. My parents would tell me that there was a difference between Hutus and Tutsis. They told me that Tutsis had longer noses and that Hutus had flat noses. They told me that Tutsis are tall. They explained to me the ethnic differences. I learned that the Tutsi women were more beautiful. Many people believe this. Hutu women believed it but there are some Hutu women who are more beautiful. I believe it was the Tutsi men who said these things and tried to make everyone believe them. (Lukunka 2007: 95. Interview conducted in Kanembwa Refugee Camp, Kibondo Tanzania, 18 January 2007)

This quotation demonstrates the felt superiority that was ascribed to the Tutsi, especially Tutsi women who were considered to be more beautiful. The conflicts in Burundi were gendered, with women being both victims and perpetrators of violence.

The sense of superiority not only resided in perception, but also in material conditions since some Tutsi possessed and controlled more resources. As a consequence, some Hutus felt a sense of relative deprivation, resulting in grievances and eventually the expression of violence, including amongst people living side by side as neighbours, friends or even family. This popular participation in the violence led to lasting social frictions at the community level that prevail today. The history of violence creates memories of violence and informs the contemporary readiness to resort to violence. For instance, in my interviews, Burundians remembered violent acts and recounted their stories in detail. It is therefore not surprising that, as Burundian refugees returned home, they found themselves embroiled in interpersonal disputes, at times violent, particularly over land.

The history of violence between close family members and neighbours is clearly recurring today, albeit at a lower scale. To illustrate, I spoke with a 29-year-old Burundian returnee woman about her land conflict in the province of Ruyigi (Gisuru Commune, Ruyigi Province, 17 December 2009), who explained that her family owned land but when they returned from Tanzania they found it had been taken by their Tutsi neighbour. Although they took the case to court, they were unsuccessful in retrieving the land, resulting in resentment. She stated that every time she looks at her Tutsi neighbour she is angry, and she and her family fear that they will attempt to perpetrate violence against her family again. Her statement is significant because it points to the connection she and her family made between past and present. The fact that the vast majority of returnees were Hutu and they sometimes found that their Tutsi neighbours had occupied their land reignites feelings of ethnic distrust and animosity, potentially leading to new violence along ethnic lines.

Overpopulation, Significance of Land, and Social Inequality

Accounts of violence perpetrated by men and women over land – as expressed in the following quotations – were discussed on a daily basis, with the vast majority involving returnees.

> 'In Bururi province a man killed his sister ... Land conflict is behind the murder. The killer has been arrested by the police.' (Nouvelles Locales 2010)

> 'An elderly man was killed in Gitega Province. The murder occurred on Thursday night while he was sleeping in his bedroom. He was killed by his son. Land conflict is behind the killing.' (Nouvelles Locales 2013)

This was due to a number of factors, as outlined in the following.

Overpopulation and Resource Competition

The effects of overpopulation are a national concern, and the government as well as national and international organizations seek to address the challenges, particularly regarding the impact of refugee return on resources such as land. As a start, the government created a National Commission for Land and other Properties (CNTB), a body charged with addressing and mediating land disputes. The government also adopted a land policy in 2008 to organize certain aspects of access to land and natural resources. The need for the land policy and other mechanisms to address the land question was unprecedented because at least 70 per cent of conflicts brought before courts were related to land (Republic of Burundi 2008).

The national discourse surrounding land conflict was that it was linked to overpopulation and so-called hoarding because a wealthy few possessed large portions of land. It was also often explicitly stated by government officials that the return of refugees was exacerbating the land situation. Furthermore, the government deplored the fact that there was an over reliance on land for economic sustenance. While conducting my research and interviewing Burundian citizens, as well as the international organizations operating in Burundi such as UNHCR, I realized that these groups shared similar views. It was clear that the return of many Burundians from exile put a strain on the land, and resulted in competition over resources, particularly land. In an interview in Bujumbura, a government official working on returnee issues for the government agency called Projet d'Appui a la Réinsertion des Sinistrés (PARESI) stated that

> [t]hose who fled had land, the neighbours took their land. They feared that returnees would take back their land. This is when the CNTB comes in. Some will deny their own family to avoid giving up land. There are even crimes committed for land. You work your land for thirty years, and then have to give it up ... The main challenge is lack of land. (Lukunka 2013: 194; interview conducted in Bujumbura, 20 June 2011)

During an interview with a village leader in Ruyigi province in the east of the country, he explained to me that when it came to land conflict the problem was that the population was increasing, especially because returnees were coming back from exile. He stated that '[t]he land conflict was foreseen. When people returned, they came back in numbers because they got married and had children. There was an increase in people but the land remained the same size' (Lukunka 2013: 189–90; interview conducted in Ruyigi, 16 December 2009). For individuals at the local level, too, overpopulation and the return of refugees posed serious problems. Central to the question of overpopulation and insufficient resources was how this manifested itself in the lives of returnee women, because not only were they poor but they were also unable to inherit property due to the law, which discriminates women.[4]

In 2010, I interviewed an elderly returnee woman in the government-created village on the outskirts of the Burundian capital, Bujumbura (Buhomba Village, Bujumbura Rural, 13 February 2010). I asked the woman about her return journey and her experience in the village. She explained that she lived in the village because she did not have any land. When I asked her if this was because she could not remember where she was from, she indicated that she was aware of her community of origin but that her parents' land was occupied by her brother so that she could not claim it. When asked why she could not claim at least a portion of the land, she only replied that this was how things were. Most likely, the reason was due to the patriarchal inheritance law. However, some women were able to own land without being linked to men when, for instance, their husbands and fathers were killed and no one contested their use of the land. In Bubanza I met a 56-year-old woman who was a former internally displaced person and the head of the household of eight individuals who, as a widow, did not face any land conflicts (Rugazi Commune, Bubanza, 23 June 2011).

Nevertheless, many returnee women I interviewed did not have husbands or fathers to rely on and hence had become heads of households requiring land and other assets to feed their family. Some engaged in activities such as selling vegetables, working in associations with other women or rearing animals such as ducks or chickens, and some worked in construction as porters. Even though men and women worked in similar trades, men tended to receive higher wages because they were able to do more labour-intensive work and travel to urban centres where they could find higher paying work. Women also often found that they received lower wages because, being in a state of desperation, they had to accept the low wages offered to them. As a young returnee woman in Makamba Province in the south of Burundi explained: 'I am involved in weeding. The pay is decided beforehand. The pay can differ from one person to another. Because I am in need, I take whatever is given to me. Some of the challenges are that some employers don't pay; they don't respect the contract' (Lukunka 2013: 198; interview conducted in Musenyi Village, Makamba Province, 25 June 2011). In addition, women were often constrained by child-rearing duties that prevented them from travelling long distances or doing labour-intensive jobs due to carrying infants on their backs. Owning land was therefore not only important for returnee men, but it was pivotal for women returnees as well.

Significance of Land

While overpopulation and competition over resources due to the arrival of a large number of former refugees were the key causes for land-related violence in Burundi, the economic and social-cultural significance of land was also of importance. This was, for example, apparent in the media. For instance, the Kirundi television programme 'Ni Nde' has the objective to express salient themes in Burundian society, such as land conflict, betrayal, sexual violence, poverty and so on. One episode aired in December 2009 was particularly intriguing since it dealt with a married couple embroiled in a land conflict. They disagreed on how the land should be used, so the husband decided to have his wife killed. He tried to hire bandits and even went as far as going to the witch doctor to kill her, but none of his attempts were successful. The woman, in contrast, was prepared to fight him at any given moment for the land. I recount this fictitious TV story because it reflects very pressing concerns in Burundian society, recognized as such by Burundians, about the levels of desperation experienced by people, as well as the extent to which some will go to secure land.

When I spoke with Burundian informants who had never fled the country during the war, I asked for specific details about why individuals were perpetuating interpersonal violence over land, and why it involved all social categories such as men, women, husbands, children, neighbours and so on. It was explained that land ownership was linked to economic survival, and violence was often triggered by the decision of an individual to sell a piece of land. For example, if a husband wants to sell land against the wishes of his wife, she might resort to violence to the point of even attempting to kill her husband. Similarly, a son might kill his father and/or his mother in order to prevent them from selling land. While this was the case for many families and individuals who stayed, it was exacerbated in the context of return, for returnees often resorted to violence with family members or neighbours who had occupied their land while they were in exile. Many returnees felt that owning land was the only way to sufficiently sustain their livelihood.

Returnees without land title resorted to working as farm labourers, which the majority of my informants found to be somewhat demeaning. As a young returnee woman in Bujumbura Rural explained: 'We cultivate other people's land ... We have agreements with the land owners. We agree to work the land, and they give us [a] small [piece of] land for our personal use while still working their land. This is only done by returnees because we are the only ones without land' (Lukunka 2013: 199; interview conducted in Buhombe Village, Bujumbura Rural, 16 June 2011). Returnees often felt that they were the only ones who did not own land, which of course was not the case. Against this backdrop, in interviews returnee women in particular expressed their frustrations about not owning land and thus not being able to feed their families. Many had very limited formal education, so owning or working on land seemed to be their primary options to make a living, rather than working as manual labours in other income sectors.

Returnees discussed land in a variety of ways. As illustrated, land was often talked about as having significance for their livelihood. In order to survive and take care of the family, they felt they needed land. Yet land also had an important symbolic value; it was what linked them to Burundi. For instance, in 2010 and 2011 I spoke at length with returnee women in Buhombe village who lived in government-created villages in Bujumbura Rural because they did not know where their communities of origin were. The government villages provide returnees with housing, but without land to cultivate. The main concern for the returnees was to own land because they believed it was a key element that distinguished a citizen from a refugee. They felt like refugees in their own country if they did not own land, even leading them to consider returning to exile if they were unable to secure land. Owning land thus signified belonging. In a similar vein, a middle-aged refugee man living in the northern province of Bubanza said:

> I had a desire to see the land of my parents. I was born in Tanzania and had never visited Burundi. In Tanzania I spoke Kirundi. UNHCR, Burundi and Tanzania, met to find a solution for the 1972 refugees. They came up with the [option] of Tanzanian nationality or repatriation. I chose repatriation. The idea of staying never crossed my mind. I had wanted to return even before they made this decision. (Lukunka 2013: 124; interview conducted in Rugazi Commune, Bubanza Province, 20 February 2010)

In this explanation, the salient point is the reference to the informant's parent's land. Owning land after return symbolizes and effectuates the re-rooting of an individual who had considered him/herself uprooted while in exile. It is an act signifying the end of separation from one's homeland and the expression of belonging. After all, exile and refugee camps are not often places where individuals feel a sense of belonging. Their desire to own land was also motivated by their desire to realize their fantasies while in refuge. While in refuge, some explained, they were often told by the local community that they did not belong, that they could not own land while in refuge and that they should return to their home country. An elderly woman in Rugazi Commune explained her exile experience in Zaire. She stated: 'In Zaire we were told that there was no place for us. We arrived in 1974. Those we found in Zaire told us we had to leave' (Lukunka 2013: 124; interview conducted in Rugazi Commune, 20 February 2010). Therefore, owning land in Burundi meant belonging as a member of the community.

The two approaches to land, sustaining one's livelihood and providing a sense of belonging, made land very valuable and worth fighting for, even physically. Land was equally significant for women as for men, though, especially as women often became heads of households because they had lost their husbands during conflict.

Social Inequality

Another factor that contributed to the violence was social inequality. In Burundi, there is a paucity of land, and the so-called rich control much of it so that poorer sections of the population have to complete over even less land. The rich were often powerful individuals, including military officers and government officials, and some others were affiliated with the prominent political parties. For instance, during a press conference on 16 September 2011 the CNTB indicated that one of the main problems in Burundi was what is called 'hoarding land'. Moreover, while conducting research in Bujumbura Rural, I visited a large piece of land that was owned by a government official. But as he did not use it, he asked returnees to work on it for free to keep the soil in use – an opportunity many returnee women I spoke with had seized, harvesting cassava and other vegetables.

The rich were not always so generous. A female returnee explained that after her return to Burundi she went to her commune where she owned a house and a plot of land. She informed the local authorities of her return and was told to forget about it because 'rich people' had occupied her land and that if she pursued the case she risked being killed. As a result, the woman ended up in a government-created village (female informant, Buhomba village in Bujumbura Rural, 23 January 2010). This was not an isolated case; many returnees were warned about engaging in legal battles with the rich, forcing them to give up land that was rightfully theirs, and thus having to secure an income and find a home elsewhere. For returnees who were not fortunate enough to find a home in government-created villages, the inability to secure their land often meant sharing a house and land with relatives, creating more tensions as they risked becoming a burden to their family members in the longer run.

Gendered Perspective of Violence in Post-conflict Burundi

Here, a gendered perspective steers us to examine how returnee women and men experience post-conflict interpersonal violence differently, how they are involved and affected by it, and how gender roles change as a result. Employing a gendered analysis to the interpersonal violence over land in Burundi reveals three key aspects: (1) the vast differences in the experiences of men and women in the post-conflict moments; (2) the prevalence of male dominance in the society, and how it impacts on individual lives; and (3) perhaps most interesting, the changes in gender dynamics and roles in the post-conflict moment as returnees reintegrate in their homeland, revealing women's agency.

First and foremost, women and men had vastly different experiences in the post-conflict moment in Burundi. As Cynthia Cockburn notes, 'women can be understood only as part of a gender dyad, in which men and masculinity warrant as much attention as women and femininity ... we need to observe the functioning of gender as a relation, and a relation of power, that compounds power dynamics' (Cockburn 2004: 24). The differences in the experiences of both women and men returnees in Burundi was particularly conspicuous at the economic level. Relations between men and women were somewhat contentions as women found themselves at a disadvantage compared to men, and faced structural impediments that threatened their ability to sustain their livelihoods. Perceptions, for instance, that intensive labour conducted by only men was more valuable than the labour women conducted, point to much of this struggle.

Women and men faced considerable violence upon return due to land scarcity, but women's experience with violence differed from men in that women mainly experienced violence as targets. Women experienced violence as a continuum, starting from pre-conflict, to conflict and refuge, to post-conflict. I should clarify that men were targets of violence during conflict as well, but the conflict was fought by the military and militias – two highly masculine enterprises that often target women deliberately as part of their tactics of war. During the post-conflict moment, physical violence was sometimes perpetrated by women, and in the context of land conflict, violence was associated with socio-economic well-being.

Secondly, a gendered perspective reveals the pervasiveness of male dominance in the society. As noted by Erik Melander, '[t]raditional gender roles not only prescribe male violence as a means of establishing dominance and protecting honour but also legitimate the subordination of women' (Melander 2005: 698). Burundi experienced significant violence throughout its history, and much of that violence was directed towards women. Women faced violence in both the public and private realm. Violence in the public realm was not only in the form of physical violence during conflict, but also structural violence in which traditions dictated that women could not inherent land, thereby leaving them in a position of subordination. In the private realm, women faced domestic violence and were involved in interpersonal violence over land. Class and age are also significant differentiation factors whose effects on experience are compounded by gender. Returnee women who were poor and/or elderly suffered considerably more than others. They were on the fringes of society particularly because they were often widowed, some without their children because they had either died in conflict or remained in exile instead of returning. They had no rights to claim land, and although many worked on farms tilling land and cultivating, they were often much too elderly to work the long hours that would allow them to sustain their livelihoods.

Despite the challenges and the structures facing returnee women in post-conflict Burundi, women demonstrated a level of resilience and agency. They attempted to circumvent and resist barriers. Through new practices, some forced by circumstances, returnee women began to change the gendered roles and dynamics of Burundian culture. Women became bread-winners and took on more economic and financial responsibilities for their households. Melander (2005: 698) reminds us that since gender roles can be understood as constructed and prone to transformation, they are subject to change. This is precisely what was happening in Burundi. Women were not only reacting to violence but in some instances they were supporting and instigating violence in order to gain access to land. Violence over land was both a very private phenomenon that occurred in the intimate space of family households, but with time it became a very public phenomenon that generated significant media attention as well as the attention of aid workers in Burundi. It was known throughout the country that women and men were engaging in violence over land, thereby changing people's notions of women's passivity. Returnee women were playing an important role in changing the understanding of masculine and feminine identities, and in so doing were defying preconceived notions about gender roles and relations.

Conclusion

Returning to Burundi after decades in exile proved to be a significant challenge. The romance of return was often shattered by the difficult cir-cumstances returnees faced, with land being the biggest concern. In many cases, the disputes that resulted due to the desire and need for land led to interpersonal violence, perpetrated by both men and women, young and old.

This breakdown of the social fabric cannot be explained by one factor. What I witnessed in Burundi was influenced by a variety of factors. First, the memory of violence contributed to the recurrence of violence in post-conflict Burundi – individuals who had not fled, and those who were re-turnees, had experienced considerable violence over the years. Burundian returnees also had to contend with the fact that they were returning to a country with limited resources for a growing population, and thus to an in-secure economic situation. On a symbolic level, informants next expressed a strong attachment to land because it provided them with a sense of be-longing after having lived in exile for such a long time. Returning to the home country and feeling at home there meant a lot to my interviewees.

Finally, land conflict was driven by social inequality. Poor rural men and women had to compete for scarce land because much of it had been occupied by the so-called rich, even though it had initially belonged to returnees. This left a limited amount of land to be shared and competed over by the poor returnees as well as the poor Burundians who had never fled the country. For many refugees who had returned to Burundi, these factors contributed to a complex post-exile experience.

The post-conflict moment affected men and women differently. Women were at a greater disadvantage to men given the prevalence of male dominance in the culture. It was predominantly felt at the economic level where women were paid less for their labour and were prohibited from inheriting land. The post-conflict moment was contributing to changes in gender roles and relations as women engaged in unconventional practices such as becoming heads of households, and in some cases going as far as engaging in or supporting violence over land.

Barbra Lukunka is a social-cultural anthropologist with a PhD from American University, Washington, DC. Her dissertation, entitled 'Overcoming Invisibility: The Meaning and Process of Returnee Reintegration', examines the meaning and process of return and reintegration for Burundian refugees. Her research areas include forced migration, post-conflict reconstruction, gender and human security. She has conducted field research in Ethiopia, Tanzania and Burundi, and currently works for the United Nations Secretariat in New York City. She also has worked for the United Nations in Burundi and Haiti, and for the International Fund for Agricultural Development in Haiti. In 2014, she worked as an adjunct professor at Webster University's Institute for Human Rights and Humanitarian Studies.

Notes

1. The views expressed in this chapter are those of the author and do not necessarily reflect the views of the United Nations. See also Chapter 8 by Ulrike Krause in this volume.
2. The government adopted a national strategy for socio-economic reintegration of conflict-affected people, and embarked on a massive project with the assistance of international agencies and donor countries to assist the former refugees. The strategy takes into account geographic reintegration, which essentially is about where to place returnees after return, especially those who do not know or cannot remember where they are from. The government created villages for many former refugees. The strategy also takes into account reconciliation and mediation between individuals involved in land conflict.

The main component of the strategy is economic reintegration, which aims to come up with employment options for returnees.

3. For a scholarly discussion about the basis for ethnic differences, see Mamdani 2001. The three ethnic groups in Burundi not only share the same culture but more specifically share the same language. The fact that the groups have different points of origin is insignificant in contemporary Burundi, given the high level of intermixing.

4. Women in Burundi cannot inherit land, but they can possess land by buying it. In addition, the Family Code allows for joint management of property between men and women. The main issue, however, that concerns poor returnees is that they are unable to inherit land and they usually return from exile as widows. For an extended discussion on this subject, see Congelois and Pallas (2014).

Bibliography

Carlson, S. 2005. 'Contesting and Reinforcing Patriarchy: Domestic Violence in Dzaleka Refugee Camp', *RSC Working Paper Series* No. 23.

Cockburn, C. 2004 'The Continuum of Violence: A Gender Perspective on War and Peace', in W. Giles and J. Hyndman (eds), *Sites of Violence: Gender and Conflict Zones.* Berkeley: University of California Press, pp. 24–44.

Congelois, E., and S. Pallas. 2014. 'Securing Women's Land Rights: Learning from Successful Experiences in Rwanda and Burundi, *International Land Coalition.* Retrieved 1 March 2015 from http://www.rwandawomennetwork.org/IMG/pdf/r-wlr-securing-women-land-rights_web_en__0.pdf.

Daley, P. 2007. 'The Burundian Peace Negotiations: An African Experience of Peace-making', *Review of Africa Political Economy* 34 (112): 333–52.

Ember, C.R., and M. Ember. 1994. 'War, Socialization, and Interpersonal Violence: A Cross-Cultural Study', *The Journal of Conflict Resolution* 38(4): 620–46.

Ferris, E.G. 2007. 'Abuse of Power: Sexual Exploitation of Refugee Women and Girls', *Signs* 32(3): 584–91.

Horn, R. 2010. 'Exploring the Impact of Displacement and Encampment on Domestic Violence in Kakuma Refugee Camp', *Journal of Refugee Studies* 23: 356–76.

Hyndman, J. 2004. 'Refugee Camps as Conflict Zones: The Politics of Gender', in W. Giles and J. Hyndman (eds), *Sites of Violence: Gender and Conflict Zones.* Berkeley: University of California Press, pp. 192–212.

Lemarchand, R. 1996. *Burundi: Ethnic Conflict and Genocide.* Cambridge: University of Cambridge Press.

Lukunka, B. 2007. *UNHCR is My Husband: Interpreting the Nature of Militarized Refugee Women's Lives in Kanembwa Refugee Camp.* Washington, DC: School of International Service, American University.

____. 2012. 'New Big Men: Refugee Emasculation as a Human Security Issue', *International Migration* 50(2): 130–41.

——. 2013. 'Overcoming Invisibility: The Meaning and Process of Returnee Reintegration'. PhD dissertation. Washington, DC: Anthropology Department, American University.

Malkki, L.H. 1995. *Purity and Exile: Violence, Memory, and National Cosmology among Hutu Refugees in Tanzania*. Chicago: University of Chicago Press.

Mamdani, M. 2001. *When Victims Become Killers: Colonialism, Nativism, and the Genocide in Rwanda*. Princeton, NJ: Princeton University Press.

Martin, S.F. 2004. *Refugee Women*, 2nd edn. Oxford: Lexington Books.

Melander, E. 2005. 'Gender Equality and Intrastate Armed Conflict', *International Studies Quarterly* 49(4): 695–715.

'Nouvelles Locales'. 2010. *Arib News*, 20 January. Retrieved 1 July 2014 from http://www.arib.info/index.php?option=com_content&task=view&id=1584&Itemid=103.

——. 2013. *Arib News*, 8 February. Retrieved 1 July 2014 from http://www.arib.info/index.php?option=com_content&task=view&id=6681.

Republic of Burundi. 2008. 'Lettre de Politique Foncière'. Retrieved 20 May 2013 from http://pdf.usaid/pdf-docs/PNADN837.pdf.

——. 2012. 'Poverty Reduction Strategy Framework: PRSP II'. Washington, DC: International Monetary Fund.

Turner, S. 1999. 'Angry Young Men in Camps: Gender, Age and Class Relations among Burundian Refugees in Tanzania', *New Issues in Refugee Research* No. 9.

UNHCR. 2012. 'UNHCR Operations in Burundi Factsheet'. Bujumbura. Retrieved 20 May 2013 from http://reliefweb.int/sites/reliefweb.int/files/resources/Full%20Report_752.pdf.

Uvin, P. 2009. *Life after Violence: A People's Story of Burundi*. London: Zed Books.

Index

STUDIES IN FORCED MIGRATION

General Editors: Tom Scott-Smith and Kirsten McConnachie

This series, published in association with the Refugees Studies Centre, University of Oxford, reflects the multidisciplinary nature of the field and includes within its scope international law, anthropology, sociology, politics, international relations, geopolitics, social psychology and economics.